Preface

Those who must deal with scientific and technological issues—scientists, politicians, sociologists, business managers, and anyone who is concerned about a neighborhood dump or power plant, government intrusiveness, expensive space programs, or the morality of medical research, among many other issues—must be able to consider, evaluate, and choose among alternatives. Making choices is an essential aspect of the scientific method. It is also an inescapable feature of every public debate over a scientific or technological issue, for there can be no debate if there are no alternatives.

The ability to evaluate and to select among alternatives—as well as to know when the data do not permit selection—is called critical thinking. It is essential not only in science and technology but in every other aspect of life as well. *Taking Sides: Clashing Views on Controversial Issues in Science, Technology, and Society* is designed to stimulate and cultivate this ability by holding up for consideration 18 issues that have provoked substantial debate. Each of these issues has at least two sides, usually more. However, each issue is expressed in terms of a single question in order to draw the lines of debate more clearly. The ideas and answers that emerge from the clash of opposing points of view should be more complex than those offered by the students before the reading assignment.

The issues in this book were chosen because they are currently of particular concern to both science and society. They touch on the nature of science and research, the relationship between science and society, the uses of technology, and the potential threats that technological advances can pose to human survival. And they come from a variety of fields, including computer and space science, biology, environmentalism, law enforcement, and public health.

Organization of the book   For each issue, I have provided an *issue introduction,* which provides some historical background and discusses why the issue is important. I then present two selections, one pro and one con, in which the authors make their cases. Each issue concludes with a *postscript* that brings the issue up to date and adds other voices and viewpoints. I have also provided relevant Internet site addresses (URLs) on the *On the Internet* page that accompanies each part opener. At the back of the book is a listing of all the *contributors to this volume,* which gives information on the scientists, technicians, professors, and social critics whose views are debated here.

Which answer to the issue question—yes or no—is the correct answer? Perhaps neither. Perhaps both. Students should read, think about, and discuss the readings and then come to their own conclusions without letting my or their instructor's opinions (which perhaps show at least some of the time!) dictate theirs. The additional readings mentioned in both the introductions and the postscripts should prove helpful. It is worth stressing that the issues covered in this book are all *live* issues; that is, the debates they represent are active and ongoing.

Changes to this edition This fourth edition represents a considerable revision. There are 5 completely new issues: *Is Irradiated Food Safe to Eat?* (Issue 8); *Can Humans Go to Mars Now?* (Issue 9); *Should the Internet Be Censored?* (Issue 11); *Is Microsoft's Dominance of the Personal Computer Market About to End?* (Issue 12); and *Is It Ethical to Sell Human Tissue?* (Issue 17).

For the issues on decision making about science (Issue 1) and on the theory of evolution (Issue 3), the issue title has been changed and one selection has been replaced to bring a different focus to the issue. In addition, for 5 of the issues retained from the previous edition, one or both selections have been replaced to bring the debates up to date: *Does the Growing World Population Face Future Food Shortages?* (Issue 4); *Should Society Act Now to Halt Global Warming?* (Issue 5); *Are Environmental Regulations Too Restrictive?* (Issue 6); *Will It Be Possible to Build a Computer That Can Think?* (Issue 14); and *Is It Ethically Permissible to Clone Human Beings?* (Issue 18). In all, there are 18 new selections. The issue introductions and postscripts for the retained issues have been revised and updated where necessary.

A word to the instructor An *Instructor's Manual With Test Questions* (multiple-choice and essay) is available through the publisher for the instructor using *Taking Sides* in the classroom. It includes suggestions for stimulating in-class discussion for each issue. A general guidebook, *Using Taking Sides in the Classroom,* which discusses methods and techniques for integrating the pro-con approach into any classroom setting, is also available. An online version of *Using Taking Sides in the Classroom* and a correspondence service for *Taking Sides* adopters can be found at http://www.dushkin.com/usingts/.

Taking Sides: Clashing Views on Issues in Science, Technology, and Society is only one title in the Taking Sides series. If you are interested in seeing the table of contents for any of the other titles, please visit the Taking Sides Web site at http://www.dushkin.com/takingsides/.

Acknowledgments A special thanks goes to those professors who responded to the questionnaire with specific suggestions for the fourth edition: John Annexstad, Bemidji State University; John Bumpus, University of Northern Iowa; and Gerald Seibel, Central Florida Community College.

Thomas A. Easton
Thomas College

Contents In Brief

Contents

Philosopher Daniel C. Dennett argues that Charles Darwin had in his theory of evolution by means of natural selection the single best idea of all time. Far from being replaceable, he asserts, the theory has made its religious predecessors quite obsolete. Professor of the history of science Edward B. Davis reviews three books about evolution to support his assertion that the theory of evolution by means of natural selection does not adequately explain our existence. Davis maintains that religious views of evolution should be discussed in public schools.

Peter W. Huber, a senior fellow at the Manhattan Institute, argues that the environment is best protected by traditional conservation, which puts human concerns first. Environmental scientists Paul R. Ehrlich and Anne H. Ehrlich argue that many objections to environmental protections are self-serving and based in bad or misused science.

Writer Paul Brodeur argues that there is an increased risk of developing cancer from being exposed to electromagnetic fields (EMFs) given off by electric power lines and that the risk is significant enough to warrant immediate measures to reduce exposures to the fields. Physician Edward W. Campion counters that there is no credible evidence that there is any risk of developing cancer from EMF exposure and that it is time to stop wasting research resources on further studies.

P. J. Skerrett, a contributing writer for *Technology Review*, maintains that sterilizing food by means of ionizing radiation is an effective way to avoid disease and death due to food-borne bacteria and parasites. Furthermore, the opposition is guilty of "public fear mongering and scare tactics." Writer Hank Hoffman argues that the studies used to judge the safety of food irradiation are too flawed to trust, the process destroys nutrients, and the technology has the potential to cause widespread environmental contamination. In approving food irradiation, the government is "encouraging a policy that could lead to disaster," he concludes.

John Tierney, a columnist for *The New York Times*, argues that it is technically and economically possible to establish a human presence on Mars.

Author Sven Birkerts argues that electronically presented information (i.e., via computer screens) threatens traditional conceptions of literacy, the literary culture, and the sense of ourselves as individuals. Wen Stephenson, editor of the *Atlantic Monthly*'s online edition, argues that the essence of literature, literacy, and the literary culture will survive the impact of computers.

Research scientist Hans Moravec describes the necessary steps in what he considers to be the inevitable development of computers that match and even exceed human intelligence. Professor of philosophy John Searle argues that computers merely manipulate symbols, while biological brains have a consciousness that allows for the interpretation and understanding of symbols. Therefore, computers will not be able to achieve or exceed the level of consciousness of the human brain.

PART 6   ETHICS   279

Elizabeth Baldwin, research ethics officer of the American Psychological Association's Science Directorate, argues that animals do not have the same moral rights as humans do, that their use in scientific research is justified by the resulting benefits to both humans and animals, and that their welfare is protected by law. Research attorney Steven Zak maintains that current animal protection laws do not adequately protect animals used in medical and other research and that, for society to be virtuous, it must recognize the rights of animals not to be sacrificed for human needs.

Andrew Kimbrell, policy director of the Foundation on Economic Trends in Washington, D.C., argues that the development of genetic engineering is so marked by scandal, ambition, and moral blindness that society should be deeply suspicious of its purported benefits. James Hughes, assistant director of research at the MacLean Center for Clinical Medical Ethics in the Department of Medicine at the University of Chicago, contends that the potential benefits of genetic engineering greatly outweigh the potential risks.

Issue 17.   Is It Ethical to Sell Human Tissue?   324

Professor David B. Resnik argues that it is morally acceptable to sell body parts that do not have the potential to become human beings. Dorothy Nelkin and Lori Andrews contend that treating body parts as salable property endangers individual and cultural values, encourages exploitation, and threatens to turn people into marketable products.

Issue 18.   Is It Ethically Permissible to Clone Human Beings?   346

Computer scientist Steven Vere states that "human cloning has enormous potential benefits and few real negative consequences." He maintains that human cloning should be reasonably regulated but not banned. Biochemist Leon R. Kass argues that human cloning is "so repulsive to contemplate" that it should be prohibited entirely.

Introduction

Analyzing Issues in Science and Technology

Thomas A. Easton

Introduction

As civilization enters the twenty-first century, it cannot escape science and technology. Their fruits—the clothes we wear, the foods we eat, the tools we use—surround us. Science and technology evoke in people both hope and dread for the future, for although new discoveries can lead to cures for diseases and other problems, new insights into the wonders of nature, and new toys (among other things), the past has shown that technological developments can also have unforeseen and terrible consequences.

Those consequences do *not* belong to science, for science is nothing more than a systematic approach to gaining knowledge about the world. Technology is the application of knowledge to accomplish things that otherwise could not be accomplished. Technological developments do not lead just to such devices as hammers, computers, and jet aircraft, but also to management systems, institutions, and even political philosophies. And it is, of course, such *uses* of knowledge that affect people's lives for good and ill.

It cannot be said that the use of technology affects people "for good *or* ill." As Emmanuel Mesthene said in 1969, technology is neither an unalloyed blessing nor an unmitigated curse.[1] Every new technology offers both new benefits and new problems, and the two sorts of consequences cannot be separated from each other. Automobiles, for example, provide rapid, convenient personal transportation, but precisely because of that benefit they also cause suburban development, urban sprawl, crowded highways, and air pollution. *And many deaths*

Optimists vs. Pessimists

The inescapable pairing of good and bad consequences helps to account for why so many issues of science and technology stir debate in our society. Optimists tend to focus on the benefits of technology and to be confident that society will be able to cope with any problems that arise. Pessimists tend to fear the problems and to believe that the costs of technology will outweigh any possible benefits.

Sometimes the costs of new technologies are immediate and tangible. When new devices fail or new drugs prove to have unforeseen side effects, people can die. Sometimes the costs are less obvious. John McDermott, one of Mesthene's opponents, expressed confidence that technology led to the centralization of power in the hands of an educated elite; to his mind, technology was therefore antidemocratic.[2]

The proponents of technology answer that a machine's failure is a sign that it needs to be fixed, not banned. If a drug has side effects, it may need to be refined, or its list of permitted recipients may have to be better defined (the banned tranquilizer thalidomide, for example, is notorious for causing birth defects when taken early in pregnancy; it is apparently quite safe for men and nonpregnant women). And although several technologies that were developed in the 1960s seemed quite undemocratic at the time, one of them—computers— developed in a very different direction. Early on, computers were huge, expensive machines operated by an elite, but it was not long before they became so small, relatively inexpensive, and "user-friendly" that the general public gained access to them. Proponents lauded this as a true case of technological "power to the people."

Certainty vs. Uncertainty *important*

Another source of debate over science and technology is uncertainty. Science is, by its very nature, uncertain. Its truths are provisional, open to revision.

Unfortunately, people are often told by politicians, religious leaders, and newspaper columnists that truth is certain. By this view, if someone admits uncertainty, then their position can be considered weak and they need not be heeded. This is, of course, an open invitation for demagogues to prey upon people's fears of disaster or side effects (which are always a possibility with new technology) or upon the wish to be told that greenhouse warming and ozone depletion are mere figments of the scientific imagination (they have yet to be proven beyond a doubt).

Natural vs. Unnatural *Ask them*

Still another source of controversy is rooted in the tendency of new ideas— in science and technology as well as in politics, history, literary criticism, and so on—to clash with preexisting beliefs or values. These clashes become most public when they pit science against religion and "family values." The battle between evolution and creationism, for example, still stirs passions a century and a half after naturalist Charles Darwin first said that human beings had nonhuman predecessors. It is nearly as provocative to some to suggest that homosexuality is a natural variant of human behavior (rather than a conscious choice); or that there might be a genetic component to intelligence or aggressiveness; or that the traditional mode of human reproduction might be supplemented with in vitro fertilization, embryo cloning, surrogate mother arrangements, and even genetic engineering.

Many new developments are rejected as "unnatural." For many people, "natural" means any device or procedure to which they have become accustomed. Very few realize how "unnatural" such seemingly ordinary things as circumcision, horseshoes, and baseball are.

However, humans do embrace change and are forever creating variations on religions, languages, politics, and tools. Innovation is as natural to a person as building dams is to a beaver.

Public vs. Private: Who Pays, and Why?

Finally, conflict frequently arises over the function of science in society. Traditionally, scientists have seen themselves as engaged solely in the pursuit of knowledge, solving the puzzles set before them by nature with little concern for whether or not the solutions to those puzzles might prove helpful to human enterprises such as war, health care, and commerce. Yet again and again the solutions discovered by scientists have proved useful—they have even founded entire industries.

Not surprisingly, society has come to expect science to be useful. When asked to fund research, society feels that it has the right to target research on issues of social concern, to demand results of immediate value, and to forbid research it deems dangerous or disruptive. Private interests such as corporations often feel that they have similar rights with regard to research that they have funded. For instance, tobacco companies have displayed a strong tendency to fund research that shows tobacco to be safe and to cancel funding for studies that produce results that might interfere with profits. Another example is Boots Pharmaceuticals, which funded a university researcher to compare its version of synthetic thyroid hormone (Synthroid) with competing versions. When the researcher found that the versions were of comparable effectiveness, Boots tried to forbid publication of the report. See Dorothy S. Zinberg, "Editorial: A Cautionary Tale," *Science* (July 26, 1996).

One argument for public funding is that it avoids such conflict-of-interest issues. Yet politicians have their own interests, and their control of the purse strings—just like a corporation's—can give their demands a certain undeniable persuasiveness.

Public Policy Who should make the choices?

The question of how to target research is only one way in which science and technology intersect the realm of public policy. Here the question becomes, How should society allocate its resources in general? Toward education or prisons? Health care or welfare? Research or trade? Encouraging new technologies or cleaning up after old ones? The problem is that money is limited—there is not enough to finance every researcher who proposes to solve some social problem. Faced with competing worthy goals, society must make choices. Society must also run the risk that the choices made will turn out to be foolish.

The Purpose of This Book

Is there any prospect that the debates over the proper function of science, the acceptability of new technologies, or the truth of forecasts of disaster will soon fall quiet? Surely not, for some issues will likely never die, and there will always be new issues to debate afresh. (For example, think of the population debate, which has been argued ever since Thomas Malthus's 1798 "Essay on the Principle of Population," and then consider the debate over the manned exploration of space and whether or not it is worthwhile for society to spend resources in this way.)

Since almost all technological controversies will affect the conditions of our daily lives, learning about some of the current controversies and beginning to think critically about them is of great importance if we are to be informed and involved citizens.

Individuals may be able to affect the terms of the inevitable debates by first examining the nature of science and a few of the current controversies over issues of science and technology. After all, if one does not know what science, the scientific mode of thought, and their strengths and limitations are, one cannot think critically and constructively about any issue with a scientific or technological component. Nor can one hope to make informed choices among competing scientific or technological priorities.

Women and Minorities in Science

There are some issues in the area of science, technology, and society that, even though they are of vital importance, you will not find directly debated in this volume. An example of such an issue might be, "Should there be more women and minority members in science?" However, this is not a debate because no one seriously responds to this question in the negative. Although minorities compose 12 percent of college freshmen, they receive only 6 percent of the bachelor's degrees, 4 percent of the master's degrees, and 3.5 percent of the doctorates. The numbers have improved over recent decades, with one group—Asian Americans—gaining much more rapidly than African Americans, Hispanics, and American Indians. But whites still dominate science and engineering, holding 90 percent of the jobs, even more than they do the general workforce, where they hold 80 percent of the jobs.

Women earn more than half the bachelor's and master's degrees but only a third of the doctorates and 16 percent of the science and engineering jobs, mostly in biology, psychology, and health. Although income disparities between men and women have diminished, they still remain. Women computer scientists and analysts, registered nurses, laboratory technicians and technologists, and health aides all earn about 90 percent of what men in these occupations earn.

You should keep such considerations in mind as you read the issues in this book. And you should consider how the problems of discrimination and prejudice (based on race or class or gender) are played out in some of these debates.

Each year the American Association for the Advancement of Science (AAAS) publishes several issues of its journal *Science* that deal with careers in science and that pay frequent attention to women, minority, and foreign-born scientists. These issues contain a wealth of statistical information, interviews, and analyses invaluable to anyone who is considering a career in science. There are also vast amounts of other material available, such as *Women's Work: Choice, Chance or Socialization? Insights from Psychologists and Other Researchers* by Nancy Johnson Smith and Sylva K. Leduc (Detselig Enterprises, 1992).

People with Internet access can visit the AAAS and *Science* at http:// sci.aaas.org/. In particular, watch for this Web page's "Next Wave" section at http://nextwave.sciencemag.org.

The Soul of Science

The standard picture of science—a world of observations, hypotheses, experiments, theories, sterile white coats, laboratories, and cold, unfeeling logic—is a myth. This image has more to do with the way science is presented by scientists and the media than with the way scientists actually perform their work. In practice, scientists are often less orderly, less logical, and more prone to very human conflicts of personality than most people suspect.

The myth remains because it helps to organize science. It provides labels and a framework for what a scientist does; it may thus be especially valuable to student scientists who are still learning the ropes. In addition, the image embodies certain important ideals of scientific thought. These ideals make the scientific approach the most powerful and reliable guide to truth about the world that human beings have yet devised.

The Ideals of Science: Skepticism, Communication, and Reproducibility

How to teach in science hi school

The soul of science is a very simple idea: *Check it out.* Years ago, scholars believed that speaking the truth simply required prefacing a statement with "According to" and some ancient authority, such as Aristotle, or a holy text, such as the Bible. If someone with a suitably illustrious reputation had once said something was so, it was so.

This attitude is the opposite of everything that modern science stands for. As Carl Sagan says in *The Demon-Haunted World: Science as a Candle in the Dark* (Random House, 1995), "One of the great commandments of science is, 'Mistrust arguments from authority.' " Scientific knowledge is based not on authority but on reality. Scientists take nothing on faith; they are *skeptical*. When a scientist wants to know something, he or she does not look it up in the library or take another's word for it. Scientists go into the laboratory, or the forest, or the desert—wherever they can find the phenomena they wish to know about— and they "ask" those phenomena directly. They look for answers in nature. And if they think they know the answer already, it is not of books that they ask, "Are we right?" but of nature. This is the point of scientific experiments—they are how scientists ask nature whether or not their ideas check out.

The concept of "check it out," however, is an ideal. No one can possibly check everything out for himself or herself. Even scientists, in practice, look up information in books and rely on authorities. But the authorities they rely on are other scientists who have studied nature and reported what they learned. And, in principle, everything those authorities report can be checked. Experiments performed in the lab or in the field can be repeated. New theoretical or computer models can be designed. Information that is in the books can be confirmed.

In fact, a good part of the "scientific method" is designed to make it possible for any scientist's findings or conclusions to be confirmed. For example, scientists do not say, "Vitamin D is essential for strong bones. Believe me. I know." They say, "I know that vitamin D is essential for proper bone formation because I raised rats without vitamin D in their diet, and their bones became soft and crooked. When I gave them vitamin D, their bones hardened and straightened. Here is the kind of rat I used, the kind of food I fed them, the amount of vitamin D I gave them. Go and do likewise, and you will see what I saw."

Communication is therefore an essential part of modern science. That is, in order to function as a scientist, you must not keep secrets. You must tell others not just what you have learned but how you learned it. You must spell out your methods in enough detail to let others repeat your work.

Scientific knowledge is thus *reproducible* knowledge. Strictly speaking, if a person says, "I can see it, but you cannot," that person is not a scientist. Scientific knowledge exists for everyone. Anyone who takes the time to learn the proper techniques can confirm any scientific finding.

The Standard Model of the Scientific Method

As it is usually presented, the scientific method has five major components: *observation, generalization* (identifying a pattern), stating a *hypothesis* (a tentative extension of the pattern or explanation for why the pattern exists), *experimentation* (testing that explanation), and *communication* of the test results to other members of the scientific community, usually by publishing the findings. How each of these components contributes to the scientific method is discussed below.

Observation

The basic units of science—and the only real facts that the scientist knows— are the individual *observations*. Using them, scientists look for patterns, suggest explanations, and devise tests for their ideas. Observations can be casual or they may be more deliberate.

Generalization

After making observations, a scientist tries to discern a pattern among them. A statement of such a pattern is a *generalization*. Cautious experimenters do not jump to conclusions. When they think they see a pattern, they often make a few more observations just to be sure the pattern holds up. This practice of strengthening or confirming findings by replicating them is a very important part of the scientific process.

The Hypothesis

A tentative explanation suggesting why a particular pattern exists is called a *hypothesis*. The mark of a good hypothesis is that it is *testable*. But there is no way to test a guess about past events and patterns and to be sure of absolute truth in the results, so a simple, direct hypothesis is needed. The scientist says, in effect, "I have an idea that X is true. I cannot test X easily or reliably. But if X *is* true, then so is Y. And I can test Y." Unfortunately, tests can fail even when the hypothesis is perfectly correct.

Many philosophers of science insist on *falsification* as a crucial aspect of the scientific method. That is, when a test of a hypothesis shows the hypothesis to be false, the hypothesis must be rejected and replaced with another. This is not to be confused with the falsification, or misrepresentation, of research data and results, which is a form of scientific misconduct.

In terms of the X and Y hypothesis mentioned above, if it has been found that Y is not true, can we say that X is false too? Perhaps, but bear in mind that X was not tested. Y was tested, and Y is the hypothesis that the idea of falsification says must be replaced, perhaps with hypothesis Z.

The Experiment

The *experiment* is the most formal part of the scientific process. The concept, however, is very simple: an experiment is a test of a hypothesis. It is what a scientist does to check an idea out. It may involve giving a new drug to a sick patient or testing a new process to preserve apples, tomatoes, and lettuce.

If the experiment does not falsify the hypothesis, that does not mean that the hypothesis is true. It simply means that the scientist has not yet come up with a test that falsifies the hypothesis. As the number of times and the number of different tests that fail to falsify a hypothesis increase, the likelihood that the hypothesis is true also increases. However, because it is impossible to conceive of and perform all the possible tests of a hypothesis, the scientist can never *prove* that it is true.

Consider the hypothesis that all cats are black. If you see a black cat, you do not really know anything at all about the color of all cats. But if you see a white cat, you certainly know that not all cats are black. You would have to look at every cat on Earth to prove the hypothesis, but only one (of a color other than black) to disprove it. This is why philosophers of science often say that *science is the art of disproving*, not proving. If a hypothesis withstands many attempts to disprove it, then it may be a good explanation of the phenomenon in question. If it fails just one test, though, it is clearly wrong and must be replaced with a new hypothesis.

Researchers who study what scientists actually do point out that most scientists do not act in accord with this reasoning. Almost all scientists, when they come up with what strikes them as a good explanation of a phenomenon or pattern, do *not* try to disprove the hypothesis. Instead, they design experiments to *confirm* it. If an experiment fails to confirm the hypothesis, then the researchers try another experiment, not another hypothesis.

The logical weakness in this approach is obvious, but it does not keep researchers from holding onto their ideas for as long as possible. Sometimes they hold on so long, even without confirming the hypothesis, that they wind up looking ridiculous. Other times the confirmations add up over the years, and any attempts to disprove the hypothesis fail to do so. The hypothesis may then be elevated to the rank of a theory, principle, or law. *Theories* are explanations of how things work (the theory of evolution *by means of* natural selection, for example). *Principles* and *laws* tend to be statements of things that invariably happen, such as the law of gravity (masses attract each other, or what goes up must come down) or the gas law (if you increase the pressure on an enclosed gas, the volume will decrease and the temperature will increase).

Communication

Each scientist is obligated to share her or his hypotheses, methods, and findings with the rest of the scientific community. This sharing serves two purposes. First, it supports the basic ideal of skepticism by making it possible for others to say, "Oh, yeah? Let me check that." It tells the skeptics where to look to see what the scientist saw and what techniques and tools to use.

Second, communication allows others to use in their work what has already been discovered. This is essential because science is a cooperative endeavor. People who work thousands of miles apart build with and upon each other's discoveries—some of the most exciting discoveries have involved bringing together information from very different fields.

Scientific cooperation stretches across time as well. Every generation of scientists both uses and adds to what previous generations have discovered. As Sir Isaac Newton said in 1675, in a letter to fellow scientist Robert Hooke, "If I have seen further than [other men], it is by standing upon the shoulders of Giants."

The communication of science begins with a process called "peer review," which typically has three stages. The first stage occurs when a scientist seeks funding—from government agencies, foundations, or other sources—to carry out a research program. He or she must prepare a report describing the intended work, laying out the background, hypotheses, planned experiments, expected results, and even the broader impacts on other fields. Committees of other scientists then go over the report to determine whether or not the applicant knows his or her area, has the necessary abilities, and is realistic in his or her plans.

Once the scientist has acquired funding, has done the work, and has written a report of the results, that report will be submitted to a scientific journal, which begins the second stage. Before publishing the report, the journal's editors will show it to other workers in the same or related fields and ask them whether or not the work was done adequately, the conclusions are justified, and the report should be published.

The third stage of peer review happens after publication, when the broader scientific community can judge the work.

It is certainly possible for these standard peer review mechanisms to fail. By their nature, these mechanisms are more likely to approve ideas that do not contradict what the reviewers think they already know. Yet unconventional ideas are not necessarily wrong, as German geophysicist Alfred Wegener proved when he tried to gain acceptance for his idea of continental drift in the early twentieth century. At the time, geologists believed that the crust of the Earth—which is solid rock, after all—did not behave like liquid. Yet Wegener was proposing that the continents floated about like icebergs in the sea, bumping into each other, tearing apart (to produce matching profiles like those of South America and Africa), and bumping again. It was not until the 1960s that most geologists accepted his ideas as genuine insights instead of harebrained delusions.

Currently, the ideal of communication is failing in another way as well. Modern science—especially in biotechnology—is producing a wealth of results with immediate applications in business. Many scientists are keeping their discoveries private until they can file for patents, strike lucrative deals with major corporations, or form their own companies. See W. Wayt Gibbs, "The Price of Silence," *Scientific American* (November 1996).

The Need for Controls

Many years ago, I read a description of a "wish machine." It consisted of an ordinary stereo amplifier with two unusual attachments. The wires that would normally be connected to a microphone were connected instead to a pair of copper plates. The wires that would normally be connected to a speaker were connected instead to a whip antenna of the sort usually seen on cars.

To use this device, one put a picture of some desired item between the copper plates. It could be, for instance, a photo of a person with whom one wanted a date, a lottery ticket, or a college that one wished to attend. One test case used a photo of a pest-infested cornfield. The user then wished fervently for the date, the winning lottery ticket, a college acceptance, or whatever else one craved. In the test case, the testers wished that all the pests in the cornfield would drop dead.

Supposedly, the wish would be picked up by the copper plates, amplified by the stereo amplifier, and then sent via the whip antenna to wherever wish orders go. Whoever or whatever fills those orders would get the message and grant the wish. Well, in the test case, when the testers checked the cornfield after using the machine, there was no longer any sign of pests. What's more, the process seemed to work equally well whether the amplifier was plugged in or not.

You are probably now feeling very much like a scientist—skeptical. The true, dedicated scientist, however, does not stop with saying, "Oh, yeah? Tell me another one!" Instead, he or she says, "Let's check this out."[3]

Where must the scientist begin? The standard model of the scientific method says that the first step is observation. Here, our observations (as well as our necessary generalization) are simply the description of the wish machine and the claims for its effectiveness. Perhaps we even have the device itself.

What is our hypothesis? We have two choices, one consistent with the claims for the device and one denying those claims: the wish machine always works, or the wish machine never works. Both are equally testable and equally falsifiable.

How do we test the hypothesis? Set up the wish machine, and perform the experiment of making a wish. If the wish comes true, the device works. If the wish does not come true, the device does not work.

Can it really be that simple? In essence, yes. But in fact, no.

Even if you do not believe that wishing can make something happen, sometimes wishes do come true by sheer coincidence. Therefore, even if the wish machine is as nonsensical as most people think it is, sometimes it will *seem* to work. We therefore need a way to shield against the misleading effects of coincidence.

Coincidence is not, of course, the only source of error we need to watch out for. For instance, there is a very human tendency to interpret events in such a way as to agree with our preexisting beliefs, or our prejudices. If we believe in wishes, we therefore need a way to guard against our willingness to interpret near misses as not quite misses at all. There is also a human tendency not to look for mistakes when the results agree with our prejudices. The cornfield, for instance, might not have been as badly infested as the testers said it was, or a farmer might have sprayed it with pesticide between checks, or the testers may have accidentally checked the wrong field. The point is that correlation does not necessarily reflect cause. In other words, although an event seems to occur as the result of another, there may be other factors at work that negate the relationship.

We also need to check whether or not the wish machine does indeed work equally well when the amplifier is unplugged as when it is plugged in, and then we must guard against the tendency to wish harder when we know that it is plugged in. Furthermore, we would like to know whether or not placing a photo between the copper plates makes any difference, and then we must guard against the tendency to wish harder when we know that the wish matches the photo.

Coincidence is easy to protect against. All that is necessary is to repeat the experiment enough times to be sure that we are not seeing flukes. This is one major purpose of replication. Our willingness to shade the results in our favor can be defeated by having another scientist judge the results of our wishing experiments. And our eagerness to overlook errors that produce favorable results can be defeated by taking great care to avoid any errors at all; peer reviewers also help by pointing out such problems.

Other sources of error are harder to avoid, but scientists have developed a number of helpful *control* techniques. One technique is called "blinding." In essence, blinding requires setting up the experiment in such a way that the critical aspects are hidden from either the test subjects, the scientist who is physically performing the experiment, or both. This helps to prevent individuals' expectations from influencing the outcome of the experiment.

In the pharmaceutical industry, blinding is used whenever a new drug is tested. The basic process goes like this: A number of patients with the affliction that the drug is supposed to affect are selected. Half of them—chosen randomly to avoid any unconscious bias that might put sicker patients in one group[4]—are given the drug. The others are given a dummy pill, or a sugar pill, also known as a *placebo.* In all other respects, the two groups are treated exactly the same.

Although placebos are not supposed to have any effect on patients, they can sometimes have real medical effects, apparently because people tend to believe their doctors when they say that a pill will cure them. That is, when we put faith in our doctors, our minds do their best to bring our bodies into line with whatever the doctors tell us. This mind-over-body effect is called the "placebo effect." To guard against the placebo effect, experimenters employ either single-blind or double-blind techniques.

> *Single-Blind:*   With this approach, the researchers do not tell the patients what pill they are getting. The patients are therefore "blinded" to what is going on. Both placebo and drug then gain equal advantage from the placebo effect. If the drug seems to work better or worse than the placebo, then the researchers can be sure of a real difference between the two.

> *Double-Blind:*   If the researchers know what pill they are handing out, they can give subtle, unconscious cues that let the patients know whether they are receiving the drug or the placebo. The researchers may also interpret any changes in the symptoms of the patients who receive the drug as being caused by the drug. It is therefore best to keep the researchers in the dark too; and when both researchers and patients are blind to the truth, the experiment is said to be "double-blind." Drug trials often use pills that differ only in color or in the number on the bottle, and the code is not broken until all the test results are in. This way nobody knows who gets what until the knowledge can no longer make a difference.

Obviously, the double-blind approach can work only when there are human beings on both sides of the experiment, as experimenter and as experimental subject. When the object of the experiment is an inanimate object (such as the wish machine), only the single-blind approach is possible.

With suitable precautions against coincidence, self-delusion, wishful thinking, bias, and other sources of error, the wish machine could be convincingly tested. Yet it cannot be perfectly tested, for perhaps it only works sometimes, such as when the aurora glows green over Copenhagen, in months without an *r,* or when certain people use it. It is impossible to rule out all the possibilities, although we can rule out enough to be pretty confident that the gadget is pure nonsense.

Similar precautions are essential in every scientific field, for the same sources of error lie in wait wherever experiments are done, and they serve very much the same function. However, no controls and no peer review system, no matter how elaborate, can completely protect a scientist—or science—from error. Here, as well as in the logical impossibility of proof (remember, experiments only fail to disprove) and science's dependence on the progressive growth of knowledge, lies the uncertainty that is the hallmark of science. Yet it is also a hallmark of science that its methods guarantee that uncertainty will be reduced (not eliminated). Frauds and errors will be detected and corrected. Limited understandings of truth will be extended.

Those who bear this in mind will be better equipped to deal with issues of certainty and risk.

1. Mesthene's essay, "The Role of Technology in Society," *Technology and Culture* (vol. 10, no. 4, 1969), is reprinted in A. H. Teich, ed., *Technology and the Future*, 7th ed. (St. Martin's Press, 1997).
2. McDermott's essay, "Technology: The Opiate of the Intellectuals," *The New York Review of Books* (July 31, 1969), is reprinted in A. H. Teich, ed., *Technology and the Future*, 7th ed. (St. Martin's Press, 1997).
3. Must we, really? After all, we can be quite sure that the wish machine does not work because, if it did, it would likely be on the market. Casinos would then be unable to make a profit for their backers, deadly diseases would be eradicated, and so on.
4. Or patients that are taller, shorter, male, female, homosexual, heterosexual, black, white—there is no telling what differences might affect the test results. Drug (and other) researchers therefore take great pains to be sure groups of experimental subjects are alike in every way but the one way being tested.

On the Internet . . .

Science and Technology Policy

This page provides links to the United States of America's federal science and technology policy statements.

```
http://www.dtic.mil/lablink/areas_of_interest/
policy.html
```

The Institute for Creation Research

According to the developers of this site, the Institute for Creation Research (ICR) is a major center of scientific creationism.

```
http://www.icr.org
```

The Skeptical Inquirer

The Committee for the Scientific Investigation of Claims of the Paranormal encourages the critical investigation of paranormal and fringe-science claims from a responsible, scientific point of view and disseminates factual information about the results of such inquiries to the scientific community and the public. It promotes science and scientific inquiry, critical thinking, science education, and the use of reason in examining important issues, and it also publishes the *Skeptical Inquirer.*

```
http://www.csicop.org
```

The National Academy of Sciences

The National Academy of Sciences maintains this page of links and resources on science and creationism.

```
http://www4.nas.edu/opus/evolve.nsf
```

PART 1

The Place of Science and Technology in Society

*T**he partnership between human society and science and technology is an uneasy one. Science and technology offer undoubted benefits, in both the short term and the long, but they also challenge received wisdom and present us with new worries. The issues in this section deal with the best way to ensure that society benefits from science and technology, the best way to ensure that the citizenry understands the science and technology that pervade their lives, the conflict between science and traditional elements of society, and the debate over creationism versus evolution.*

- Should Peer Review Dominate Decision Making About Science?

- Is Science a Faith?

- Does the Theory of Evolution Explain the Origins of Humanity?

ISSUE 1

Should Peer Review Dominate Decision Making About Science?

YES: House Committee on Science, from *Unlocking Our Future: Toward a New National Science Policy* (September 24, 1998)

NO: David H. Guston and Kenneth Keniston, from "Updating the Social Contract for Science," *Technology Review* (November/ December 1994)

ISSUE SUMMARY

YES: The House Committee on Science contends that although the scientific enterprise must recognize society's needs and interests, decisions about priorities and funding must be made by scientists through the traditional peer review system.

NO: Assistant professor of public policy David H. Guston and professor of human development Kenneth Keniston argue that science can no longer set its own path. They conclude that public participation must be increased at all levels of decision making about science.

$\mathbf{W}$hat scientists do as they apply their methods is called research. Scientists who perform basic or fundamental research seek no specific result. Basic research is motivated essentially by curiosity. It is the study of some intriguing aspect of nature for its own sake. Basic researchers have revealed vast amounts of detail about the chemistry and function of genes, explored the behavior of electrons in semiconductors, revealed the structure of the atom, discovered radioactivity, and opened our minds to the immensity in both time and space of the universe in which we live.

Applied or strategic research is more mission oriented. Applied research scientists turn basic discoveries into devices and processes, such as transistors, computers, antibiotics, vaccines, nuclear weapons and power plants, and communications and weather satellites. There are thousands of such examples, all of which are answers to specific problems or needs, and many of which were quite surprising to the basic researchers who first gained the raw knowledge that led to these developments.

There was a time when both types of research were performed mostly by individual scientists and small teams, often working with very small budgets. But the payoffs have proved so useful that today research has become an enterprise for large teams and ample funding.

It is easy to see what drives the movement to put science to work. Society has a host of problems that cry out for immediate solutions. Yet there is also a need for research that is not tied to explicit need because such research undeniably supplies a great many of the ideas, facts, and techniques that problem-solving researchers then use in solving society's problems. Basic researchers, of course, use the same ideas, facts, and techniques as they continue their probings into the way nature works.

There is also an increasing pressure for public participation in deciding on what scientists work. Science, say some, must be removed from control by social, political, and intellectual elites, and scientists must be held accountable if they expect society to fund their work. Politicians expect a guarantee of results; the public craves guarantees of safety and of benefit to all society, not just the elite.

Yet scientists have long insisted that decisions about what research should be performed, funded, and published are properly made by scientists alone in the process known as "peer review." The National Research Council (NRC) believes that this should continue. Its 1995 report *Allocating Federal Funds for Science and Technology* urged that "panels of the nation's leading experts" should advise science policymakers. Working scientists—the "peers" in the peer review system—should decide what specific projects get funded. Except for unavoidable politicians and bureaucrats, nonexperts should stay out of the way, the report concluded.

In 1997 Representative Vern Ehlers (R-Michican), a nuclear physicist and vice chair of the House Science Committee, began a study aimed at devising a new government science policy justifying government support for research, linking basic and applied research more tightly, and speeding the movement of new discoveries into the marketplace to benefit society. The committee's report was presented to Congress in September 1998. The following excerpt from this report grants that in order to thrive, the scientific enterprise must recognize society's needs and interests, but just as the NRC said, decisions about priorities and funding must be made by the experts. Indeed, argues the committee, the peer review system should be expanded "to include the science and science-based decisions made in federal agencies [which] will help improve the credibility of the science conducted or supported by these agencies. Regulations should not be made on the basis of science that does not stand up to the rigors of the peer review process."

David H. Guston and Kenneth Keniston recognize that public attitudes toward scientific research are a product of the past successes of science and technology, the vast expense of the scientific enterprise, and a few spectacular technological failures. In the second selection, they say that in a democracy, the public should not be excluded from decision making about science. That is, decisions should not be left to the experts alone.

3

Unlocking Our Future: Toward a New National Science Policy

The notion of state support for scientific research has existed for centuries; Francis Bacon called for such funding as far back as the early 1600s, and some monarchs and nobles responded to his call. It was not until 1862, however, when the Land Grant Colleges were established, that the United States began to organize and provide federal support for its science and engineering enterprise. Even so, it took until the outbreak of World War II for the Nation to fully grasp the benefits of substantial federal support for scientific research. It was at the culmination of that war, fresh from its lessons, that Vannevar Bush wrote his seminal document *Science: The Endless Frontier.*

The political consensus necessary to build today's science and engineering enterprise was forged largely by the Nation's needs and priorities in the period following the second World War, when the threat of total destruction by nuclear weapons was frighteningly real. Under these circumstances, the exigencies of the Cold War made science politically unassailable.

Recent geopolitical changes will have tremendous ramifications for the scientific enterprise. We are now blessed to live in a time of relative peace. Today, threats from rogue nations or individuals wreaking terror have replaced the fear of utter annihilation by the former Soviet Union. While we must remain ever vigilant and militarily strong, the need to maintain economic strength has taken on primary importance today. We now recognize more clearly than ever that economic strength facilitates not only a strong defense, but promotes other societal needs, such as social and political stability, good health, and the preservation of freedom. The growth of economies throughout the world since the industrial revolution began has been driven by continual technological innovation through the pursuit of scientific understanding and application of engineering solutions. America has been particularly successful in capturing the benefits of the scientific and engineering enterprise, but it will take continued investment in this enterprise if we hope to stay ahead of our economic competitors in the rest of the world. Many of those challengers have learned well the lessons of our employment of the research and technology enterprise for economic gain.

From U. S. House of Representatives. House Committee on Science. *Unlocking Our Future: Toward a New National Science Policy.* Hearing, September 24, 1998. Washington, DC: Government Printing Office, 1998. Notes and references omitted.

A truly great nation requires more than simply economic power and the possession of military might, however. In a truly great nation, freedom triumphs. Diversity is not just tolerated, but celebrated. The arts flourish alongside the sciences. And strength is used not to conquer, but to assist. Economic stability brings more than a high standard of living in the purely material sense. It also promotes quality of life in the broadest sense.

Pursuing freedom requires confidence about our ability to manage the challenges raised by our increasing technological capabilities. Americans must remain optimistic about the ability of science and engineering to help solve their problems—and about their own ability to control the application of technological solutions. We must all possess the tools necessary to remain in control of our lives so that fear of the unknown does not slow down the pursuit of science. Science and engineering must be used to expand freedom, not to limit it.

As a nation, we have much to be proud of. But we ought always to be seeking to improve. Science and technology can play important roles in driving this improvement. These beliefs—that we can do better and that improvement can come, at least in part, through a strong science and technology program—are reflected in the vision that has guided the Committee on Science in formulating this policy study and in writing this report:

> The United States of America must maintain and improve its pre-eminent position in science and technology in order to advance human understanding of the universe and all it contains, and to improve the lives, health, and freedom of all peoples.

The continued health of the scientific enterprise is a central component in reaching this vision. In this report, therefore, we have laid out our recommendations for keeping the enterprise sound and strengthening it further. There is no singular, sweeping plan for doing so. The fact that keeping the enterprise healthy requires numerous actions and multiple steps is indicative of the complexity of the enterprise. The fact that we advocate not a major overhaul but rather a fine-tuning and rejuvenation is indicative of its present strength. It is also not something the Congress or even the federal government can do on its own—making these mid-course corrections will require the involvement of citizens and organizations from across the nation. . . .

The scientific enterprise in the United States represents one of our country's greatest strengths. It is an enterprise characterized by intricate interrelationships between governments, industry, and universities. It draws strength from the American eagerness to innovate, our entrepreneurial spirit, and a research and technology base of considerable depth and strength. However, this enterprise cannot be expected to remain strong without attention. We must ensure that its components are functioning well, and that the interactions between the various players in it are productive. Understanding the workings of the overall scientific and technology enterprise benefits from an awareness of the nature and practice of science itself. Science is fundamentally an inquiry-driven process; curiosity is at its core. It is a process of learning and discovery, not simply an accumulation of facts. Scientists seek to unlock the secrets that Nature holds, and since these secrets are closely held, only the clever and persistent questioner elicits answers. Thus pursuit of scientific understanding requires both intellectual dexterity [and] independence of thought. Although technology often finds its urging in necessity rather than curiosity, it requires no less resourcefulness and creativity in its pursuit.

These underpinnings in motive—curiosity versus need—have led to the designation of science as either "basic" or "applied." In the simplified versions of these descriptions, basic research is performed by academic researchers in search of knowledge, and applied research is carried out by inventors or industry researchers in pursuit of new and better products. These are artificial distinctions, as producing a new product, whether it is a microchip or a vaccine, often requires an understanding of underlying scientific principles. Similarly, insight into how or why something works often demands new tools. Thus the relationship between so-called basic and applied research is far from simple; it is instead complex, dynamic and interdependent.

Vannevar Bush's writings in *Science: The Endless Frontier,* which despite being more than 50 years old are still largely recognized as the basis for the Nation's existing science policy, reinforced the simplified demarcation between basic and applied research. Dr. Bush implied a linear relationship between them, with basic research directly giving rise to applied research and product development. Interestingly, Bush's own experiences as an inventor, engineer and researcher suggest that he understood the subtleties of the relationships between fundamental research and its development into applications far better than he allowed in his report. He was, in fact, a co-founder of technology-based companies while a researcher at MIT and, perhaps most importantly, directed the Office of Scientific Research and Development during WWII. In this latter position, he was responsible for bringing together scientists—mostly university researchers accustomed to pursuing their own curiosity—with engineers and technicians to develop the tools that helped win the war, such as radar, the proximity fuse and the atomic bomb. He was thus well aware of the synergy that can exist between basic and applied science.

The linear model describing the relationship between basic and applied research nevertheless made for an appealingly simple policy prescription, one that has become Dr. Bush's greatest legacy to science in the U.S. It was Bush who, recognizing the downstream benefits of science performed in the laboratory, suggested emphatically in *Science: The Endless Frontier* that the federal government facilitate this research by funding both researchers in the Nation's colleges, universities and National laboratories, and the costs of training the next generation of scientists. He indicated in his report that this research be done in support of three major goals: improving national security, health, and the economy.

The Bush Report and the subsequent influx of federal dollars into the Nation's research universities shaped the scientific enterprise dramatically. Before WWII, most scientific research pursued in American universities was funded by the universities themselves, by charitable foundations, or by private industry. Federal funding for university research was restricted largely to agricultural research, done primarily in the Nation's land grant colleges. Science performed in the United States in this first mega-era of science policy was of high quality, but it was done on a small scale, and often with scant funding. In the Bush-shaped, post-WWII era, the federal government funded an increasing share of research in the Nation's universities. These universities became centers of research excellence and the training grounds for future scientists and engineers unrivaled in the rest of the world.

Science—and science funding—during this second mega-era was affected greatly by the Cold War. Bush did not write his document with the intention of it being a Cold War manual; it was written in the brief window between assured victory in WWII and the onset of the Cold War. Nevertheless, the Cold War had an indelible effect on the scientific enterprise, as it provided a compelling rationale for research funding. Indeed, federal research dollars poured into science and technology during this period. The entire enterprise grew; greater numbers of research universities sprung up, more graduate students were trained to become scientists, and entire industries based on new technologies were founded. By 1961 the military-industrial complex had grown so powerful that President Eisenhower warned in his Farewell Address of the potential danger its dominance could have. He also expressed concern that either the scientists or the policymakers would become co-opted by the other.

The end of the Cold War had a profound impact on the Nation's research and development enterprise, and brought with it the end of the second mega-era of science policy. Without the backdrop of the Soviet military threat or the race to conquer outer space, convincing and often-used justifications for federal research funding became less compelling. Since then, the budgetary pressures exerted on research funding have grown. Today, while overall economic prospects appear favorable, growth of federal entitlements such as social security, health care and welfare threaten to overwhelm the federal budget and constrain discretionary spending—including funding for science—even further.

Our national experiment of federal funding for scientific research, however, has yielded enormous payoffs. In addition to fueling discoveries that save and improve lives, federally funded research represents an investment in the purest sense of the word, as it delivers a return greater than the initial outlay. Regardless of whether the relationship between basic and applied research is linear or more complex, the fact remains that the government's investment in fundamental research has yielded real dividends in every discipline—from astronomy to zoology. For example, research on the molecular mechanisms of DNA, the so-called "blueprint of life," led to recombinant DNA technology—gene splicing—which in turn spawned an entire industry. Experimental and theoretical studies of the interaction of light with atoms led to the prediction of stimulated emission of coherent radiation, which became the foundation of the laser, a now-ubiquitous device with uses ranging from the exotic (surgery, precise machining, nuclear fusion) to the everyday (sewer alignment, laser pointers).

We are currently in the third mega-era of science policy. In this time of global commerce and communication a strong economic foundation will be paramount in achieving the vision of improving the lives, health and freedoms of our Nation's citizens. A fragile national economy poses potentially grave ramifications. Without a strong economy, the national defense may be compromised. Basic health care may be limited, and biomedical research becomes a luxury. And without a strong economy, all citizens face far greater obstacles to partaking [of] the benefits of progress. Science, driven by the pursuit of knowledge, and technology, the outgrowth of ingenuity, will fuel our economy, foster advances in medical research, and ensure our ability to defend ourselves against ever more technologically-advanced foes. Science offers us an additional benefit. It can provide every citizen—not only the scientists who are engaged in it —with information necessary to make informed decisions as voters, consumers and policymakers. For the scientific enterprise to endure, however, stronger ties between this enterprise and the American people must be forged. Finally, our position as the world's most powerful nation brings opportunities as well as responsibilities that science and its pursuit can, and should, address. This report seeks to outline the steps needed to bring about these goals from a national, not simply a federal government, perspective. That is, the science policy described herein outlines not only possible roles for federal entities such as Congress and the Executive branch, but also implicit responsibilities of other important players in the research enterprise, such as States, universities and industry. We believe such a comprehensive approach is warranted given the highly interconnected relationships among the various players in the science and technology enterprise. In taking this broad view, our goal is to outline general principles and guidelines and to point out the importance of applying the discoveries from fundamental science to our daily lives and our needs. What our country needs now is not a complete re-structuring of our scientific enterprise, but instead an evaluation of our Nation's science and technology policies, and a determination of what changes are required to ensure the long-term health of this enterprise....

Summary of Recommendations

New ideas form the foundation of the research enterprise. It is in our interests for the Nation's scientists to continue pursuing fundamental, ground-breaking research. Our experience with 50 years of government investment in basic research has demonstrated the economic benefits of this investment. To maintain our Nation's economic strength and international competitiveness, Congress should make stable and substantial federal funding for fundamental scientific research a high priority.

Notwithstanding the short-term projections of budget surpluses, the resources of the federal government are limited. This reality requires setting priorities for spending on science and engineering. Because the federal government has an irreplaceable role in funding basic research, priority for federal funding should be placed on fundamental research. The primary channel by which the government stimulates knowledge-driven basic research is through research grants made to individual scientists and engineers. Direct funding of the individual researcher must continue to be a major component of the federal government's research investment. The federal government should continue to administer research grants that include funds for indirect costs and use a peer-reviewed selection process, to individual investigators....

The practice of science is becoming increasingly interdisciplinary, and scientific progress in one discipline is often propelled by advances in other, seemingly unrelated, fields. It is important that the federal government fund basic research in a broad spectrum of scientific disciplines, mathematics, and engineering, and resist concentrating funds in a particular area.

Much of the research funded by the federal government is related to the mission of the agency or department that sponsors it. Although this research is typically basic in nature, it is nevertheless performed with overriding agency goals in mind. In general, research and development in federal agencies, departments, and the national laboratories should be highly relevant to, and tightly focused on, agency or department missions....

We ... have the obligation to ensure that the money spent on basic research is invested well and that those who spend the taxpayers' money are accountable. The Government Performance and Results Act was designed to provide such accountability. Government agencies or laboratories pursuing mission-oriented research should employ the Results Act as a tool for setting priorities and getting the most out of their research programs. Moreover, in implementing the Results Act, grant-awarding agencies should define success in the aggregate, perhaps by using a research portfolio concept....

A private sector capable of translating scientific discoveries into products, advances and other developments must be an active participant in the overall science enterprise. However, there is concern that companies are focusing their research efforts on technologies that are closest to market instead of on mid-level research requiring a more substantial investment. Capitalization of new technology based companies, especially those that are focused on more long-term, basic research, should be encouraged. In addition, the R&D [research and development] tax credit should be extended permanently, and needlessly onerous regulations that inhibit corporate research should be eliminated.

Partnerships meant to bring about technology development also are important. Well-structured university-industry partnerships can create symbiotic relationships rewarding to both parties. These interactions and collaborations, which may or may not involve formal partnerships, are a critical element in the technology transfer process and should be encouraged. Partnerships that tie together the efforts of State governments, industries, and academia also show great promise in stimulating research and economic development. Indeed, States appear far better suited than the federal government to foster economic development through technology-based industry. As the principal beneficiaries, the States should be encouraged to play a greater role in promoting the development of high-tech industries, both through their support of colleges and research universities and through interactions between these institutions and the private sector.

The university community, too, has a role in improving research capabilities throughout its ranks, especially in states or regions trying to attract more federal R&D funding and high-tech industries. Major research universities should cultivate working relationships with less well-established research universities and technical colleges in research areas where there is mutual interest and expertise and consider submitting, where appropriate, joint grant proposals. Less research-intensive colleges and universities should consider developing scientific or technological expertise in niche areas that complement local expertise and contribute to local economic development strategies. To exploit the advances made in government laboratories and universities, companies must keep abreast of these developments. The RAND Corporation's RaDiUS database and the National Library of Medicine's PubMed database serve useful purposes in disseminating information. Consider expanding RaDiUS and PubMed databases to make them both comprehensive and as widely available as possible.

Intellectual property protections are critical to stimulating the private sector to develop scientific and engineering discoveries for the market. The Bayh-Dole Act of 1980, which granted the licensing rights of new technologies to the researchers who discover them, has served both the university and commercial sectors reasonably well. A review of intellectual property issues may be necessary to ensure that an acceptable balance is struck between stimulating the development of scientific research into marketable technologies and maintaining effective dissemination of research results.

While the federal government may, in certain circumstances, fund applied research, there is a risk that using federal funds to bridge the mid-level research gap could lead to unwarranted market interventions and less funding for basic research. It is important, therefore, for companies to realize the contribution investments in mid-level research can make to their competitiveness. The private sector must recognize and take responsibility for the performance of research. The federal government may consider supplementary funding for private-sector research projects when the research is in the national interest. Congress should develop clear criteria, including peer review, to be used in determining which projects warrant federal funding.

Science and engineering also provide the basis for making decisions as a society, as corporations and as individuals. Science can inform policy issues, but it cannot decide them. In many cases science simply does not have the answer, or provides answers with varying degrees of uncertainty. If science is to inform policy, we must commit sufficient resources to get the answers regulators need to make good decisions. At the earliest possible stages of the regulatory process, Congress and the Executive branch must work together to identify future issues that will require scientific analysis. Sufficient funding to carry out these research agendas must be provided and should not be overly concentrated in regulatory agencies.

For science to play any real role in legal and policy decisions, the scientists performing the research need to be seen as honest brokers. One simple but important step in facilitating an atmosphere of trust between the scientific and the legal and regulatory communities is for scientists and engineers to engage in open disclosure regarding their professional background, affiliations and their means of support. Scientists and engineers should be required to divulge their credentials, provide a resume, and indicate their funding sources and affiliations when formally offering expert advice to decision-makers. The scientific opinions these experts offer also should stand up to challenges from the scientific community. To ensure that decision-makers are getting sound analysis, all federal government agencies pursuing scientific research, particularly regulatory agencies, should develop and use standardized peer review procedures.

Peer review constitutes the beginning, not the end, of the scientific process, as disagreement over peer-reviewed conclusions and data stimulate debates that are an integral part of the process of science. Eventually, scientists generate enough new data to bring light to previously uncertain findings. Decision-makers must recognize that uncertainty is a fundamental aspect of the scientific process. Regulatory decisions made in the context of rapidly changing areas of inquiry should be re-evaluated at appropriate times.

Aside from being based on a sound scientific foundation, regulatory decisions must also make practical sense. The importance of risk assessment has too often been overlooked in making policy. We must accept that we cannot reduce every risk in our lives to zero and must learn to deploy limited resources to the greatest effect. Comprehensive risk analysis should be standard practice in regulatory agencies. Moreover, a greater effort should be made to communicate various risks to the public in understandable terms, perhaps by using comparisons that place risks in the context of other, more recognizable ones.

The judicial branch of government increasingly requires access to sound scientific advice. Scientific discourse in a trial is usually highly contentious, but federal judges have recently been given the authority to act as gatekeepers to exclude unreliable science from the courtroom. More and more judges will seek out qualified scientists to assist them in addressing complex scientific questions. How these experts are selected promises to be an important step in the judicial process. Efforts designed to identify highly qualified, impartial experts to provide advice to the courts for scientific and technical decisions must be encouraged. In Congress, science policy and funding remain scattered piecemeal over a broad range of committees and subcommittees. Similarly, in the Executive branch, science is spread out over numerous agencies and departments. These diffusive arrangements make effective oversight and timely decision making extremely difficult. Wherever possible, Congressional committees considering scientific issues should consider holding joint hearings and perhaps even writing joint authorization bills.

No factor is more important in maintaining a sound R&D enterprise than education. Yet, student performance on the recent Third International Math and Science Study highlights the shortcomings of current K–12 science and math education in the U.S. We must expect more from our Nation's educators and students if we are to build on the accomplishments of previous generations. New modes of teaching math and science are required. Curricula for all elementary and secondary years that are rigorous in content, emphasize the mastery of fundamental scientific and mathematical concepts as well as the modes of scientific inquiry, and encourage the natural curiosity of children must be developed.

Perhaps as important, it is necessary that a sufficient quantity of teachers well-versed in math and science be available. Programs that encourage recruitment of qualified math and science teachers, such as flexible credential programs, must be encouraged. In general, future math and science teachers should be expected to have had at least one college course in the type of science or math they teach, and, preferably, a minor. Ongoing professional development for existing teachers also is important. . . .

The revolution in information technology has brought with it exciting opportunities for innovative advances in education and learning. As promising as these new technologies are, however, their haphazard application has the potential to adversely affect learning. A greater fraction of the federal government's spending on education should be spent on research programs aimed at improving curricula and increasing the effectiveness of science and math teaching.

Graduate education in the sciences and engineering must strike a careful balance between continuing to produce the world's premier scientists and engineers and offering enough flexibility so that students with other ambitions are not discouraged from embarking on further education in math, science, or engineering. . . .

Educating the general public about the benefits and grandeur of science is also needed to promote an informed citizenry and maintain support for science. Both journalists and scientists have responsibilities in communicating the achievements of science. . . .

[T]here is no substitute for scientists speaking directly to people about their work. In part because science must compete for discretionary funding with disparate interests, engaging the public's interest in science through direct interaction is crucial. All too often, however, scientists or engineers who decide to spend time talking to the media or the public pay a high price professionally, as such activities take precious time away from their work, and may thus imperil their ability to compete for grants or tenure. Scientists and engineers should be encouraged to take time away from their research to educate the public about the nature and importance of their work. Those who do so, including tenure-track university researchers, should not be penalized by their employers or peers.

The results of research sponsored by the Federal government also needs to be more readily available to the general public, both to inform them and to demonstrate that they are getting value for the money the government spends on research. Government agencies have a responsibility to make the results of federally-funded research widely available. Plain English summaries of research describing its results and implications should be prepared and widely distributed, including posting on the Internet.

NO

David H. Guston and
Kenneth Keniston

Updating the Social Contract for Science

In the years following World War II, the United States established a scientific enterprise that became the envy of the world. This enterprise rested on a vision of science as an "endless frontier" that would replace the American West as the font of economic growth, rising standards of living, and social change. The institutions that supported this frontier were a distinctively American blend of public and private enterprises, eventually including an array of national laboratories, mission agencies, and even a National Science Foundation. The practices that supported it entailed what Harvard political scientist Don K. Price called a new type of federalism: the provision of financial support to scientists at public and private research universities without co-opting their independence.

Research universities were the intellectual centerpiece of this enterprise, since it was there that most of the basic research was performed. At the heart of federal support for universities was the practice of competitive, peer-reviewed grants. The bargain that was struck between the federal government and university science—what is often called the "social contract for science"—can be stated concisely. On one hand, government promised to fund the basic science that peer reviewers found most worthy of support. Scientists, on the other hand, promised to ensure that the research was performed well and honestly, and to provide a steady stream of scientific discoveries that would be translated into new products, medicines, or weapons.

After five decades, the social contract for science shows signs of extreme duress. Scientists and politicians have serious complaints about each other. The issues are, by now, familiar: scientific fraud and dishonesty, the adequacy of science funding, indirect costs of research, administrative burdens in science, scientific priorities, big science, pork-barrel science, and so on. Reports by the congressional Office of Technology Assessment, the National Academy of Sciences, and the Carnegie Commission on Science, Technology, and Government have analyzed what some perceive as a "crisis" in science policy.

Despite this scrutiny, the underlying causes of today's conflicts in science policy remain obscure. We do not believe that the antagonism between science and politics signals either a new or a terminal crisis. But today's struggles do indicate that the old contract between science and government needs updating;

From David H. Guston and Kenneth Keniston, "Updating the Social Contract for Science," *Technology Review,* vol. 97, no. 8 (November/December 1994). Copyright © 1994 by *Technology Review.* Reprinted by permission.

they also point to enduring and irreducible tensions between the principles of science and those of democratic government.

Changed Government

Although scientists sometimes lament the passing of a golden age of government support for science, the history of postwar science policy fails to reveal a truly privileged past. Throughout the last 50 years, controversies between the political and the scientific communities have always been present—over the loyalty of scientists and the merits of military research, over financial accounting for grants, over applied versus basic research, over payment for the indirect costs of research, and above all, over how much money Washington should dedicate to scientific research.

The pattern of federal funding for research and development [R&D] also belies any image of a lost golden age. Those who pine for the good old days usually recall the mid-1960s, when federal R&D spending reached an all-time high, whether measured as a percentage of the gross national product (in which case 1964 was the maximum) or as a share of total federal spending (in which case the peak came in 1965). But measured in constant dollars, the situation is less clear. By the Office of Management and Budget's method of discounting for inflation, the peak of real federal spending was 1966 or 1967. By the National Science Foundation's method, R&D spending in 1990 was about 30 percent *higher* than the supposed 1966 peak.

In any event, the mid-60s spending levels are a problematic reference point, because federal spending for science and technology in those years was inflated by competition with the Soviets and by the Apollo program. From 1963 to 1972, defense R&D accounted for almost 54 percent of federal expenditures in science and technology. The Reagan defense buildup raised average defense R&D spending between 1983 and 1992 to about 56 percent of total federal R&D. But the average defense share has since fallen to less than 53 percent, and President Clinton has promised to reduce the defense share to 50 percent. Furthermore, space-related R&D, which accounted for 27 percent of federal expenditures between 1963 and 1972, accounted for only 7 percent between 1983 and 1992.

Another way to look at R&D spending is to compare it with the rest of the federal budget. Over the last decade the share of R&D in the domestic discretionary budget has risen, while almost all other items have fallen. That is, through the 1980s, R&D consumed a growing share of the shrinking pie of nondefense, nonentitlement spending. For this reason, calls for greatly increased science budgets are ill-starred from the beginning. The sufferings of scientists may be real, but in the words of Rep. George Brown (D-Calif.), one of the strongest patrons of science, they are not unique.

It nevertheless remains true that irreversible changes have occurred in the last five decades. Indeed, perhaps the simplest explanation for the heightening of tensions between government and science is that the original contract was made between a kind of government that no longer exists and a kind of scientific community that has long since disappeared.

In the postwar years, both the executive and legislative branches have changed in ways that affect the support of science. At the executive level, the "imperial presidency" has extended the chief executive's prerogatives far beyond their prewar limits, and the "management presidency," centered in the Office of Management and Budget, has emphasized control of the sprawling bureaucracy. The White House has added analytical capabilities: the special assistant to the president for science and technology, and the president's Science Advisory Committee. More recently, scientific advisory committees have proliferated in other departments and agencies. The executive branch increasingly tries to coordinate federal R&D in the various agencies, the most recent mechanism being the National Science and Technology Council, composed of Cabinet chiefs and the heads of independent agencies and chaired by the president.

In Congress, the power of committee chairs has declined through the postwar years and has been replaced by a radically decentralized organization, with participation from subcommittees as well as action outside of committees. There has been a resurgence of congressional oversight directed at maintaining accountability over burgeoning programs and agencies. In the early 1970s, Congress augmented its analytical capabilities by creating the Office of Technology Assessment and the Congressional Budget Office, expanding the Congressional Research Service, and increasing control over the General Accounting Office. Committee and personal staffs have increased in size and professional competence. Congress has also created an Office of Inspector General in each major department and agency to monitor the implementation of policy.

Such changes—even if not intentionally related to science—have given both the executive and the legislative branch greater motivation and competence to evaluate and oversee the scientific community.

Changed Science

If government has been transformed in the last five decades, so has science. The scientific enterprise has grown vastly in workforce, complexity, and size of projects, and it has therefore grown more expensive to fund. For example, the scientific workforce nearly doubled between 1965 and 1988, from 495,000 to about 950,000. And the proportion of the nation's workforce who are scientists and engineers engaged in R&D rose from its previous high of 67.9 per 10,000 in 1968 to 75.9 per 10,000 in 1987.

Federal funding of research has always sought to turn out more PhDs so as to provide the nation with a highly trained scientific workforce. But however commendable this goal, it has a bizarre consequence: the more successful the program is, the greater will be the future demand for research financing. It is rather as if a welfare program created a half-dozen new welfare applicants for every one who is given federal assistance. This steady increase in the number of scientists means that despite real growth in R&D funding, a smaller percentage of applications for grants can be funded each year. The scarcity of research funds felt by the scientific community is quite genuine on a per capita basis.

The size and complexity of scientific projects have also increased greatly. The Manhattan Project and other wartime endeavors inaugurated a trend toward "megascience." Research projects today involve more people and require more expensive equipment than ever before. Science has become a vastly more complex aggregate of new technologies and advanced education. As a result, the price of research has gone up much faster than inflation. For this reason, too, scarcity is felt even in the midst of generous funding.

Meanwhile, popular support for science has waned. The almost unqualified public enthusiasm that characterized the immediate postwar period has given way to a far more nuanced view of science and technology. Attitudes have been negatively influenced by conspicuous technological failures—Chernobyl, Bhopal, *Challenger*—which raise concerns about science by the reverse application of the logic that predicts technological benefits from scientific triumphs. It was President Eisenhower who appointed the first special assistant to the president for science and technology. But it was also Eisenhower who warned the American public in his farewell address that "public policy could itself become the captive of a scientific-technological elite." The apprehension of such an elite found expression through many voices: social critics like Theodore Roszak, environmental activists like Rachel Carson, and antimilitary movements that blossomed on the campuses of research universities.

Of all the changes since the postwar negotiation of the social contract for science, the end of the Cold War is probably the most consequential. Ever since 1945, the promise of military applications and the specter of Soviet competition has driven federal R&D expenditures in both military and civilian agencies. The expected usefulness of science and technology to the conduct of the Cold War—both in material terms of building effective weapons and in symbolic terms of conquering the new frontiers of space, the atom, and the cell—meant that governments and publics (in the former Soviet Union and the United States alike) viewed science in a favorable light. But today, without an implacable communist foe, the instrumental value of science and technology has lost some of its urgency.

The result, especially for the physical sciences, is that a new rationale for public support is needed. Previously, the goal upon which almost everyone agreed was countering the Soviet threat. Today, other goals for science are alleged—or, more precisely, revived. For the founders of the American system of science funding, the military rationale was only one among many, including human betterment through fuller employment, a rising standard of living, and better health. The health claim has never lost its persuasiveness, but the rationales of employment and living standards are now being resurrected and redefined.

This redefinition sometimes involves a claim that science-based innovation is the elixir that will stimulate the nation's economy and improve its international economic competitiveness. According to this argument, such innovation has produced entire new industries—consider the transistor and genetic engineering—and will give the United States a technological advantage in competing with other nations for markets and high-wage jobs. In its simplest form, the argument posits a direct causal link between the advances of science, success in the international marketplace, and a rising standard of living.

In this simple version, the argument is open to an obvious criticism: the United States is unquestionably the world's leading scientific power, but it lags by international standards in health, has fallen behind in productivity gains, and is being overtaken in standard of living and international trade. More sophisticated versions of the theory therefore argue that good science is a necessary but not sufficient condition for productivity. A primary point of this more subtle formulation maintains that the postwar research system, even though highly successful so far, has become less effective in today's environment because it was geared toward a different set of military, political, technological, and economic challenges.

Even this cursory analysis of changes in the last five decades suggests that the current strains in government-science relations were inevitable and necessary. Government has increased in size, complexity, competence, and capacity both to support and to oversee science. Science, too, has grown and now faces the consequences of its maturity. The old military rationale for public support has lost much of its cogency, and science faces a more critical public than it did 50 years ago. The old contract was written in simpler days. It has become more fragile today partly because the two parties that agreed to it have changed.

The contract clearly must be updated. But it must also confront the basic tensions between science and democracy.

Science Versus Democracy

Imagine members of Congress commissioning a National Academy of Sciences report on the organization of science-funding agencies, then gathering testimony from scientists on priorities in science funding, the role of different sectors and institutions in the scientific enterprise, the tension between centralization and pluralism in research, the merits of large-scale versus small-scale projects, and the financial accountability of researchers. Is this Rep. Brown's recent Task Force on the Health of Research? Rep. John Dingell's Subcommittee on Oversight and Investigations? Rep. Don Fuqua's Science Policy Task Force of the mid-1980s? The Fountain Committee, the Elliot Committee, or the Daddario Subcommittee of the 1960s?

Actually, it is the Allison Commission of the 1880s, a select congressional committee that examined all these questions with regard to the federal scientific establishment. Like some dysfunctional family, the science policy community in the United States seems to confront the same problems, never finally resolving them even over many years. Why do the same problems constantly arise? Why is it that no institutional arrangements seem capable of eliminating the tensions between government and science?

One can find only a partial answer in the complaints that scientists and politicians make about each other. Politicians are charged with a lack of knowledge and appreciation of the scientific enterprise; scientists, with arrogance, elitism, and political naïveté. But the dysfunction exists not simply because politicians can be ignorant or scientists arrogant. The deeper reason lies in fundamental and ineradicable differences between the organizing principles of a democratic polity and the organizing principles of a democratic polity and the organizing principles of the scientific community.

There are three fundamental tensions that make for an uneasy relation between government and science. The first is simply that popular tastes and preferences are different from, and sometimes antagonistic toward, those of the scientific community. One might call this the populist tension, and it can result in popular pressure for a more equitable geographic distribution of research funds, for more applied research, for a particular focus of programmatic research such as women's health, or for a greater emphasis on teaching and patenting than on research itself.

Scientists rightly ask whether public opinion should matter in science, because popular pressures could seriously reduce the long-term viability of the scientific enterprise, and at times can reflect "antiscientific" attitudes. But in a democratic society, citizens must be allowed to choose between the viability of science and the viability of other valued enterprises. Even though science is the pursuit of the truth, it is still only one pursuit among many that citizens value. What the populist tension really does is force the advocates of scientific research to articulate a publicly compelling rationale for their activities and then, like any beneficiary of public funds, to be accountable for the outcomes.

The second tension derives from the fact that the economic organization necessary for science to flourish may be at odds with the economic organization necessary for democracy to flourish. One might call it the plutocratic tension, because of the importance of wealth in determining the distribution of scientific resources. This tension is obvious in political concerns about the concentration of R&D funding at a small number of major research universities, as well as worries about the real growth of the R&D budget when most other domestic programs are contracting. It is also evident in concern over the growing fuzziness between public and private interests, as public employees and private firms benefit financially from the fruits of publicly funded research. Another expression of this tension is the fear that the benefits of science-based technology—from the profits yielded by new drugs to the conveniences of consumer technologies—more often accrue to the haves of society than to the have-nots. The basic question behind the plutocratic tension is whether science, because it is relatively rich and privileged, will become richer and more privileged still, and will mostly benefit the non-scientists who are already rich and privileged.

The third tension between democratic politics and scientific practice arises from the fact that democratic processes and goals are largely incompatible with scientific processes and goals. One might call this the exclusionary tension, because the requirements for membership in decision making within science are more exclusive—that is, being a scientist or an expert—than for membership in democratic decision making in general. Democratic decision making constantly seeks to encourage and expand participation; scientific decision making limits it. There is a risk that science may oppose democratic decisions that deviate from or deny some scientifically defined truth. But as political theorist Robert Dahl has written about the idea of allowing experts to guard democracy against incorrect decisions, scientific guardianship, if carried to an extreme, is simply a prettier name for dictatorship.

The tensions between democracy and science boil down to conflicting values: democratic politics cherishes participation and the pursuit of justice; science cherishes inquiry and the pursuit of truth. Because the gap between participation and truth can never be closed, the tensions will always exist.

Any two parties with different goals and structures require a carefully wrought contractual relation if they are to collaborate productively. It therefore follows that something like a social contract for science continues to be necessary. It follows, too, that this contract should give explicit attention to the details of the interaction between government and science, or, more precisely, between the public and scientists. An attempt to run science on democratic principles would destroy science; but that does not mean that the existing institutions and processes of science are democratic enough. An attempt to run government on scientific principles would destroy democracy; but similarly, that does not mean that our current politics is sufficiently informed by scientific knowledge. Only by deliberately designing institutions and processes that confront the inevitable tensions between democratic government and scientific practice can these tensions be minimized.

The old contract between government and science was fragile because it denied these tensions, attempting to keep politics and science as separate as possible. Such a contract has indeed outlived its usefulness. The new contract as it evolves must take into account the blurred boundaries between politics and science, all the while recognizing that the differences between them are intrinsic.

The Future of the Contract

Scientists and politicians must be willing to concede to the other some role in each other's enterprise. The scientific community, in particular, must confront directly the fact that it is in competition for federal funding with other meritorious projects. Like it or not, if science expects public support, it moves into an arena where it must be political—in the best sense, and possibly the worst— in order to justify its claim to public support.

By being political, we do not simply mean joining the horde of lobbyists competing on behalf of clients for public boons—although in the United States, lobbying is a time-honored and appropriate activity. More than that, we mean recognizing and responding to the ways in which science and its support are embedded in public attitudes and public policy.

The scientific community and the research universities in which this community is rooted must undertake an educational role with a dual purpose: first, to make clear the nature and workings of science; and second, to bring to the greater community those scientific insights, findings, theories, outlooks, and facts that can indeed contribute to the public good.

In both regards, university science has only begun to explore its role. Academic scientists need to participate more actively in broadly educational activities such as training science and technology journalists, along with focused pedagogic activities like collaborating with educators in primary and secondary schools to improve scientific literacy.

Given that American science must compete with other good purposes and institutions for the favorable opinion and support of a democratic government, and given that the Cold War has ended, the future relationship between science and government depends heavily on the capacity of the scientific community to articulate a plausible rationale for public support and to demonstrate that rationale at every turn. As military preparedness yields to international economic competitiveness and domestic well-being on the list of national priorities, support for science will depend on the scientific community's willingness and capacity to help resolve economic and domestic problems.

What this requires is a program of vigorous outreach to the public, to public administrators, to leaders of the private sector, and to lawmakers. If academic science indeed has a contribution to make, it is no longer enough—if it ever was—for scientists to wait in their laboratories for the telephone to ring. More enterprising and collaborative projects are necessary. This change will be difficult for scientists whose talents lie in the laboratory rather than in public speaking. But there are others who are gifted teachers and interlocutors, and whose enthusiasm for science impels them to share its beauty and its relevance with others. The scientific community must treasure such individuals or risk undercutting public support for science.

At out own institution, we think of the Leaders in Manufacturing Program, an alliance of MIT [Massachusetts Institute of Technology] faculty with several major U.S. corporations, aimed at training a cohort of corporate leaders versed in the latest manufacturing technologies and management strategies. In the same vein is the creation of workshops for congressional staff members on science and technology. At a more general level, MIT's Knight Science Journalism Fellowship Program has expanded the knowledge of more than 100 leading science and technology journalists and media experts over the last 10 years.

The scientific community must initiate more activities like these: projects that move beyond lobbying to outreach and education, activities that constitute a series of "mini-contracts" between the needs of particular constituencies and the capacities of the scientific community to respond to those needs. It is not enough for the scientific community simply to claim that it is useful; the relevance of scientific knowledge and perspectives to the public interest must be demonstrated again and again in concrete projects.

Government, too, will require new strategies and perhaps new institutions if the contract with science is to be successfully renegotiated. One urgent and oft-noted need is for a more rational way to determine the level of overall federal spending for R&D and the priorities within those expenditures. Too often, public financing of science and technology is based on the political power of a particular disease lobby, the eagerness of members of Congress to earmark scientific and technological projects for their home districts, or intensive lobbying by a group of scientists for their own specialty. Needed instead is an orderly, open, and publicly accessible process. In this regard, the recently established White House National Science and Technology Council (NSTC) promises to be instrumental in drafting an overall R&D budget and in setting priorities within the budget. This body continues to rely on the tried-and-true process of peer review for evaluating individual projects.

What the NSTC needs is a reasonable and articulate strategy for choosing among projects and disciplines. Such a strategy might include giving priority to important disciplines in which the United States compares unfavorably with other nations (as a recent report of the National Academy of Sciences suggests) and inviting consumers of research in industry, education, health, and other fields to assess the output of federal research funding.

At the same time, however, the combination of political priority setting and scientific peer review must not shut out public input. Precisely because research is difficult and performing it can require many years of training, the temptation to confuse the performance of scientific research with the making of science policy is great. The making of science policy by the federal government, or for that matter by state and local governments, needs to be open and democratic. We have urged scientists to reach out to the public to explain what they do and to help ensure that their work is put to good use. This outreach goes for naught if the public is excluded from decision making about science. In this regard, public input, and not just expert advice, is essential at all levels of science policymaking. A "national forum" on science and technology priorities, such as that recently proposed by the Carnegie Commission on Science, Technology, and Government, could help provide such public input if properly constituted. Millions of Americans, not themselves scientists, have strong and legitimate opinions about the value to them and to the nation of space travel, local technology-development centers, and cancer research, among other scientific and technological projects. Their participation should be welcomed and respected.

A third major obligation of government is to preserve R&D as an example of the sturdy American principle of federalism—that decisions should be made and actions taken at the most local level possible. In science policy, this means resisting the temptation to micromanage scientific work, and the researchers and institutions that conduct it, from the distance of Washington. To be sure, government needs to establish standards: it may rightly impose exacting ethical and financial requirements upon researchers who receive public monies. But the only way to implement such requirements consistent with the federalism that inspired the social contract for science is to insist that universities and their researchers maintain primary responsibility. For example, an incentive system for dealing with indirect costs—in which the government sets the overall rate and universities can pocket the remainder if they come in under that rate— may be preferable on grounds of both principle and efficiency to either the preexisting system of making a separate agreement with each university, or any more invasive system in which government accountants would formulate budgets for overhead.

In science policy, as in other areas of governance, a primary responsibility of public officials is to preserve as many independent centers of initiative and locally governed activities as is consistent with the broad rules of accountability and fairness. In the long run, science and technology flourish when multiple independent centers of activity are encouraged; they fail to thrive under the heavy hand of centralized control and unified direction. This is just as it should be in a federal republic like the United States.

These amendments in the social contract for science will never resolve some of the tensions inherent between science and government. But in recognizing the tensions, the changes can make for a more robust and productive relationship. The American system of science and technology has been outstanding in the last half-century in good part because public policy was designed to foster a plurality of centers of scientific and technical excellence with the maximum possible autonomy and responsibility delegated to each local center. No better principle than federalism can be imagined for the new social contract for science.

POSTSCRIPT

Should Peer Review Dominate Decision Making About Science?

The debate reflected in these selections is not new. Before Vannevar Bush's 1945 report *Science, the Endless Frontier,* Senator Harley M. Kilgore (D-West Virginia) said that he wanted "federal research activities to be planned in accordance with liberal social purposes." See Daniel J. Kevles, "The Changed Partnership," *The Wilson Quarterly* (Summer 1995). Bush's report was in large part an effort to head off any attempt to put science under the explicit control of society, saying that it would surely pay off more handsomely if left to itself, though with generous public funding. On the record, Bush was quite right: science and technology helped to win World War II, antibiotics were the miracle drugs of the time, TV was just around the corner, and computers were just being built. Science and technology wore a definite shine.

Much of the shine wore off over the next few decades, however. Because so much of their funding came from the U.S. Defense Department and was aimed at winning wars, science and technology soon began to smell of death, not life. In the 1960s, when thousands of young people were rejecting established authority (particularly the government) for various reasons, government funding stripped science of legitimacy in many people's eyes. Technological disasters such as the Three Mile Island nuclear power plant failure did not help. And then science and technology proved helpless in the face of increasing poverty (psychiatric medications were even held responsible, in part, for the rise in numbers of the homeless) and new diseases such as AIDS.

J. Michael Bishop, in "Enemies of Promise," *The Wilson Quarterly* (Summer 1995), states that a good part of the dilemma lies in the public's sense of betrayal when science fails to solve problems, due largely to the public's failure to understand just what science can and cannot do. He also notes that ignorance is surprisingly widespread in academia, where specialization can mean that a physicist does not know what a gene is and " 'post-modernists' [believe that] the supposedly objective truths of science are in reality all 'socially constructed fictions,' no more than 'useful myths,' and science itself is 'politics by other means.' " Meanwhile, crystal power, astrology, alien abductions, and other aberrations of pseudoscience are astonishingly popular among the general public. See Carl Sagan, *The Demon-Haunted World: Science as a Candle in the Dark* (Random House, 1995).

ISSUE 2

Is Science a Faith?

YES: Daniel Callahan, from "Calling Scientific Ideology to Account," *Society* (May/June 1996)

NO: Richard Dawkins, from "Is Science a Religion?" *The Humanist* (January/February 1997)

ISSUE SUMMARY

YES: Bioethicist Daniel Callahan argues that science's domination of the cultural landscape unreasonably excludes other ways of understanding nature and the world and sets it above any need to accept moral, social, and intellectual judgment from political, religious, and even traditional values.

NO: Biologist Richard Dawkins maintains that science "is free of the main vice of religion, which is faith" because it relies on evidence and logic instead of tradition, authority, and revelation.

Science and technology have come to play a huge role in human culture, largely because they have led to vast improvements in nutrition, health care, comfort, communication, transportation, and mankind's ability to affect the world. However, science has also enhanced understanding of human behavior and of how the universe works, and in this it frequently contradicts what people have long thought they knew. Furthermore, it actively rejects any role of God in scientific explanation.

Many people therefore reject what science tells us. They see science as just another way of explaining how the world and humanity came to be; in this view, science is no truer than religious accounts. Indeed, some say science is just another religion, with less claim on followers' allegiance than other religions that have been divinely sanctioned and hallowed by longer traditions. Certainly, they see little significant difference between the scientist's faith in reason, evidence, and skepticism as the best way to achieve truth about the world and the religious believer's faith in revelation and scripture.

The antipathy between science and religion has a long history. In 1616 the Catholic Church attacked the Italian physicist Galileo Galilei (1564–1642) for teaching Copernican astronomy and, thus, contradicting the teachings of

*-discuss

the Church; when invited to look through the telescope and see the moons of Jupiter for themselves, the Church's representatives reportedly refused (Pope John Paul II finally pardoned Galileo in 1983). On the other side of the conflict, the French Revolution featured the destruction of religion in the name of rationality and science, and the worship of God was officially abolished on November 10, 1793.

To many people, the conflict between science and religion is really a conflict between religions, or faiths, much like those between Muslims and Hindus or between conservative and liberal Christians. This view often becomes explicit in the debates between creationists and evolutionists.

The rejection of science is also evident among those who see science as denying both the existence of God and the importance of "human values" (meaning behaviors that are affirmed by traditional religion). This leads to a basic antipathy between science and religion, especially conservative religion, and especially in areas—such as human origins—where science and scripture seem to be talking about the same things but are contradicting each other. This has been true ever since evolutionary theorist Charles Darwin first published *On the Origin of Species by Means of Natural Selection* in 1859.

Religious people are not the only ones who see in science a threat to "human values." Science also contradicts people's preferences, which are often based less on religion than on tradition and prejudice. For instance, science insists that no race or gender is superior to another; that homosexuality is natural, not wicked; that different ways of living deserve respect; and that it is possible to have too many children and to cut down too many trees. It also argues that religious proscriptions that may have once made sense are no longer relevant (the Jewish practice of not eating pork, for example, is a good way to avoid trichinosis; however, says science, so are cooking the meat at higher temperatures and not feeding pigs potentially contaminated feed).

Many people feel that there is a baby in the bathwater that science pitches out the window. Science, they say, neglects a very important side of human existence embodied in that "human values" phrase. Daniel Callahan sees this side as the source of moral, political, and intellectual judgment, which science by its dominance of society tends to evade. Science, he argues in the following selection, has become an ideology in its own right, as intolerant as any other, and it sorely needs judgment or criticism to keep it from steamrollering the more human side of life.

In the second selection, Richard Dawkins maintains that science differs profoundly from religion in its reliance on evidence and logic—not on tradition, authority, and revelation—and is therefore to be trusted much more.

25

Don't agree that his arguments are re: science as faith

Faith is something not based on evidence — he isn't arguing about evidence — is arguing about science not being accountable + arrogant

Daniel Callahan

➡ **YES**

Calling Scientific Ideology to Account

Icome to the subject of science and religion with some complex emotions and a personal history not irrelevant to my own efforts to think about this matter. It seems appropriate for me to lay this history out a bit to set the stage for the argument I want to make. For the first half of my life, from my teens through my mid-thirties, I was a serious religious believer, a church member (Roman Catholic), and someone whose identity as both a person and as an intellectual had a belief in God at its center. During that time I had little contact with the sciences; literature and philosophy caught my imagination. I was a fine example, for that matter, of the gap between the two cultures that C. P. Snow described, caught up as I was in the humanities and generally ignorant about science. I spent most of my time among humanists and religious believers (though believers of a generally liberal kind).

All of that changed in my late thirties. Two events happened simultaneously. The first was a loss of my religious faith, utterly and totally. I ceased to be a theist, became an atheist, and so I remain today. I did not, however, have any revolt against organized religion (as it is sometimes pejoratively called) or the churches; nor did I lose respect for religious believers. They just seem to me wrong in their faith and mistaken in their hope. The second event was my discovery of the field of biomedical ethics, seemingly a fertile area for my philosophical training and an important window into the power of the biomedical sciences to change the way we think about and live our lives. With this new interest I began spending much of my time with physicians and bench scientists and worked hard to understand the universe of science that I was now entering (through the side door of biomedical ethics).

Meanwhile, as I was undergoing my own personal changes, the relationship between science and religion was shifting in the country as well. When I was growing up, there was still considerable debate about religion and science, with some believers arguing that there was a fundamental incompatibility between them and others holding that they were perfectly congenial. Some scientists, for their part, wrote books about religion, saying that they had found God in their science. Others, of a more positivistic bent, thought that science had forever expunged the notion of a God and that science would eventually offer an explanation of everything.

From Daniel Callahan, "Calling Scientific Ideology to Account," *Society,* vol. 33, no. 4 (May/June 1996). Copyright © 1996 by Transaction Publishers. Reprinted by permission. All rights reserved.

This debate seemed to subside significantly in the 1970s and 1980s. Science came almost totally to win the minds and emotions of educated Americans, and technological innovation was endlessly promoted as the key to both human progress and economic prosperity, a most attractive combination of doing good and doing well. While public opinion polls and church attendance figures, not to mention the gestures of politicians, showed the continuing popularity of religion, it was science that had captured the academy, the corridors of economic power, and high-brow prestige in the media. There remained, to be sure, skirmishes here and there over such issues as the teaching of creationism in the schools, particularly in the Bible Belt, and mutterings about the "religious Right" and its opposition to abortion, embryo and fetal research, and the like. Although there had been some bursts of anti-technology sentiments as part of the fallout of the 1960s culture wars, they had little staying power. The "greening of America" soon ran into a drought.

Science, in short, finally gained the ascendancy, coming to dominate the cultural landscape as much as the economic marketplace. This was the world of science I entered and in which I still remain enmeshed. My reaction to the news in May 1995 that a religious group, with the help of Jeremy Rifkin, was entering a challenge to the patenting of life was one of rueful bemusement: what a quixotic gesture, almost certainly doomed to failure but not, perhaps, before a round of media attention. Such battles make good copy, but that's about it.

The specific issue of the patenting of life deserves discussion, and someone or other would have raised it. Yet it hardly signals a new struggle between science and religion. It is neither that central an issue, nor did it appear even to galvanize a serious follow-up response among most religious groups. Congress, moreover, has given no indication that it will take up the issue in any serious way. In other words, it appears to have sunk as an issue as quickly as it arose.

Yet I confess to a considerable degree of uneasiness here. Science should not have such easy victories. It needs to have a David against its Goliath. This is only to say that scientific modernism—that is, the cultural dominance of science—desperately needs to have a serious and ongoing challenger. By that I mean the challenge of a different way of looking at nature and the world, one capable of shaking scientific self-satisfaction and complacency and resisting its at-present overpowering social force. Science needs, so to speak, a kind of loyal opposition.

This kind of opposition need not and should not entail hostility to the scientific method, to the investment of money in scientific research, or to the hope that scientific knowledge can make life better for us. Not at all. What it does entail is a relentless skepticism toward the view that science is the single and greatest key to human progress, that scientific knowledge is the only valid form of knowledge, and that some combination of science and the market is the way to increased prosperity and well-being for all. When religion can only fight science with the pea-shooters of creationism and antipatenting threats, it has little going for it. That response surely does not represent a thoughtful, developed, and articulate counterbalance to the hold of science on modern societies.

Do you agree that science needs a counterbalance? What is his concern? Can religion be the answer?

I say all of this because what I discovered upon entering the culture of science—that is, scientism—was something more than a simple commitment to the value and pursuit of scientific knowledge. That is surely present, but it is also accompanied socially by two other ingredients, science as ideology and science as faith.

Science as Ideology

By science as ideology I mean that constellation of values that, for many, constitutes a more or less integrated way of interpreting life and nature, not only providing a sense of meaning but also laying out a path to follow in the living of a life. At the core of that ideology is a commitment to science as the most reliable source of knowledge about the nature of things and to technological innovation as the most promising way to improve human life. Closely related features of that ideology are an openness to untrammeled inquiry, limited by neither church nor state, skepticism toward all but scientifically verifiable claims, and a steady revision of all knowledge. While religion should be tolerated in the name of toleration rather than on grounds of credibility, it should be kept in the private sphere, out of the public space, public institutions, and public education. The ideology of scientism is all-encompassing, a way of knowing, and, culturally embodied, a way of living.

By science as faith I mean the ideology of science when it includes also a kind of non-falsifiable faith in the capacity of science not simply to provide reliable knowledge but also to solve all or most human problems, social, political, and economic. It is non-falsifiable in the sense that it holds that any failure to date of science to find solutions to human problems says nothing at all about its future capacity to do so; such solutions are only a matter of time and more refined knowledge. As for the fact that some of the changes science and technology have wrought are not all good, or have both good and bad features, science as faith holds that there is no reason in principle that better science and new knowledge cannot undo earlier harm and avoid future damage. In a word, no matter what science does, better science can do even better. No religious believer, trying to reconcile the evil in the world with the idea of a good and loving God, can be any more full of hope that greater knowledge will explain all than the scientific believer. And there is no evidence that is allowed to count against such a belief, and surely not religious arguments.

It is at just this point that I, the former religious believer, find it hard to confidently swallow the ideology of science, much less the serene faith of many of its worshippers. I left one church but I was not looking to join another. Nonetheless, when I stepped into the territory of science that appeared to be exactly the demand: If you want to be one of us, have faith. Yet a perspective that aims to supply the kind of certain metaphysical and ethical knowledge once thought limited to religion and to provide the foundations for ways of life seems to me worthy of the same kind of wariness that, ironically, science first taught me to have about religion. If science warns us to be skeptical of traditionalism, of settled but unexamined views, of knowledge claims poorly based on hard evidence, on acts of faith that admit of no falsifiability, why should I

Is he upset about colleagues in science, or about science itself?

not bring that same set of attitudes to science itself? That interesting magazine, *The Skeptical Inquirer*, dedicated to getting the hard facts to debunk superstition, quackery, and weird claims by strange groups, does not run many articles devoted to debunking science or claims made in behalf of the enlightenment it can bring us. (I believe it has yet to publish even one such article, but I may be wrong about that.)

Maybe that is not so surprising. Such rebelliousness seems utterly unacceptable to scientism, utterly at odds with its solemn pieties and liturgical practices. To question the idea of scientific progress, to suggest that there are valid forms of nonscientific knowledge, to think that societies need something more than good science and high technology to flourish is to risk charges of heresy in enlightened educated circles every bit as intimidating as anything that can be encountered in even the most conservative religious groups. The condescension exhibited toward the "religious Right" surely matches that once displayed by Christianity toward "pagans." Even a Republican-dominated, conservative Congress knows it can far better afford politically to drastically cut or eliminate funding for the National Endowments for the Humanities and the Arts than for the National Science Foundation or the National Institutes of Health.

Now I come to the heart of my problem with the ideology and faith of scientism. Like any other human institution and set of practices, science needs to be subject to moral, social, and intellectual judgment; it needs to be called to task from time to time. Ideally that ought to be done by institutions that have the cultural clout to be taken seriously and by means of criteria for judgment that cannot themselves easily be called into question. Religion itself has always had this notion as part of its own self-understanding: It believes that it —churches, theologies, creeds—stands under the higher judgment of God and recognizes that it can itself fall into idolatry, the worship of false gods. One might well complain that the churches have seemed, in fact, exceedingly slow in rendering negative judgment upon themselves. Even so, they have the idea of such judgment and on occasion it has indeed been exercised.

Isn't this against what he's complaining about?

Unfortunately—and a profound misfortune it is—science no longer has seriously competitive ways of thinking or institutions that have a comparable prestige and power. Science no longer has a counterweight with which it must contend, no institution or generally persuasive perspective that can credibly pass judgment on scientific practices and pretensions. No secular force or outlook or ideology exists to provide it. Religion once played that role: Popes, prelates, and preachers could once rain some effective fire and brimstone down on science, often enough mistakenly yet sometimes helpfully. But religion, too, concerned to protect its own turf, too unwilling to open its eyes to new possibilities and forms of knowledge, offered mainly condemnation along with, now and then, some lukewarm support. Moreover, the gradual secularizing of the cultures of the developed countries of the world, relegating religion to the domestic sphere, took away religion's platform to speak authoritatively to public life. Scientific modernism was there to fill the gap, and it has been happy to do so. It is not possible to utter prayers in public schools, but there are no limits to the homage that can be lavished upon science and its good works.

isn't science progress?

Do you agree that science is always praised?   *this is whining*

Can there be a limit (imposed) on science?

The absence of a counterweight to the ideology of science has a number of doleful effects. It helps to substantiate the impression that there is no alternative, much less higher, perspective from which to judge science and its works. If you are the king of the hill, all things go your way and those below you are fearful or hesitant to speak out. It helps as well to legitimate the mistaken belief that all other forms of knowledge are not only inferior but that they are themselves always subject to the superior judgment of science. Accordingly, claims of religious knowledge of a credible kind were long ago dismissed by science. *because of intent* At its best, science is benignly tolerant of religion, patting it on the head like a kindly but wiser grandparent. At its worst, it can be mocking and dismissive. The kinds of knowledge generated by the humanities fare a little better, but not all that much.

From the perspective of my own field, bioethics, it is distressing to see the way that claims for the value or necessity of scientific research are treated with an extraordinary deference, usually going unquestioned. A recent federal panel on embryo research, for instance, set the issue up as a struggle between the moral status of the embryo, on the one hand, and that of the "need" (not just *what does the want* desire on the part of researchers) for embryo research, on the other. In a fine display of nuanced, critical thinking, the panel took apart excessive claims for the rights of embryos, urging "respect" but allowing research. As for the claims of research, they were accepted without any doubts or hesitations at all; they seemed self-evident to the panel, not in need of justification. Even Henry VIII, the king of his hill, hardly got that kind of deference, even from those luckless wives he had beheaded. In a culture saturated with the ideology of science, there seems hardly any forceful voice to call it to account.

If there was a loyal opposition, it would not let the claims and triumphalism of the scientific establishment go unchallenged. It would treat that establishment with respect, but it would fully understand that it is an *establishment*, intent on promoting its own cause and blowing its own horn, critical of its opponents and naysayers, and of course never satisfied with the funds available to it (funds that, if forthcoming in greater quantity, will someday find a cure for cancer, discover the molecular basis for disease, give us cheap energy generated by cold fusion, etc., etc.). A loyal opposition would bring to science exactly the same cool and self-critical eye that science itself urges in the testing of scientific ideas and hypotheses. One of the great intellectual contributions of science has been its methodological commitment to self-criticism and self-revision; and that is one reason it came to triumph over religion, which has not always shown much enthusiasm for skepticism about its key doctrines.

But if self-criticism and self-revision are at the heart of the scientific method, then a good place to begin employing them is at home, on the scientific ideology that culturally sustains the whole apparatus. A loyal opposition would do this not only to temper exaggerated self-congratulations on the part of science but also to keep science itself scientific.

The insuperable limitation of the scientific method is that it cannot be used to criticize the ideology of science or its methods. To try to do so only begs the question of its validity. In the end, we judge that method more by its fruits and consequences than by its a priori validity. The problem here is

[handwritten margin note top: distrust/fear of x's from technology from luddite revolt of 1811: against English textile factories that sed from craftsmen to machine]

that science cannot tell us what consequences we ought to want, what kind *[margin: very true]* of knowledge we need, or what uses are best for the knowledge that science demonstrates. Science, that is, is far more helpful with our means than our *[margin: true]* ends. Good science cannot tell us how to organize good societies or develop good people (or even tell us how to define "good") or tell us what is worth knowing. There is no scientific calculus to tell us how much a society should invest in scientific research; that is a matter of prudence.

[margin: hys solution?] It is here that the other forms of knowledge ought and must come into play: the knowledge developed by the humanities or the "soft" social sciences; the political values and structures created by democratic societies, built upon argument, some consensus, and some compromise. My own domain, that of the humanities, was long ago intimidated by science. It does not complain about the grievous disparity between research resources lavished upon it in comparison with science. Those humanists who dare enter the church of science and mutter to its high priests are given the back of the scientific hand, quickly labeled as cranks or, black mark of black marks, Luddites. The scientific establishment should help to encourage and support other forms of knowing and should be *[margin: how?]* willing to learn from them; that would be to display the openness and creativity it touts as its strength. It does not, however, take the fingers of even one hand to count the number of Nobel laureates in science who have petitioned Congress for stronger support for the humanities.

What is a proper role for religion in a society captured by the ideology of science? Its most important role, the one it has played from time to time with other principalities and powers, would be simply to urge some humility *[margin: hot religion]* on science and to call it to task for pretentiousness and power grabbing. Science ought to stand under constant moral judgment, and there is an important role for religion to play in formulating some of the criteria for such judgment. It is thus proper for religion to remind science of something religion should always be reminding itself of as well: Neither science nor religion are whole and entire unto themselves. Religion stands under the judgment of God (it tells us), and science stands under the judgment of the collective conscience of humankind (which religion does *not* tell us). Religion can remind the world, and those in science, that the world can be viewed from different perspectives. And it can remind that world, including science, what it means to attempt, as does religion, to make sense of everything in some overall coherent way. There is no need to agree with the way in which religion comprehends reality in order to be reminded of the human thirst for some sense of coherence and meaning in the world.

There has always been an aspect of science that overlaps with supernatural religion. That is the kind of natural piety and awe that many scientists feel in the face of the mysteries and beauty of the natural world. This can be called a kind of natural religion, and some scientists easily make the move from the natural to the supernatural, even if many of their more skeptical colleagues— who also share the sense of natural awe—do not follow them in taking that step. This natural awe frequently expresses itself in a hesitation to manipulate nature for purely self-interested ends, whether economic or medical. The concern of ecologists for the preservation of biodiversity, the hesitations of population geneticists about germ-line therapy, the worry of environmentalists about the protection of tropical forests or of biologists for the preservation of even rare species, all testify to that kind of natural piety. It is here that there is room for an alliance between science and religion, between that science that sees the mystery and unprobed depths of the natural world and that religion that sees nature as the creation and manifestation of a beneficent god.

It is important, for that matter, that science find allies in its desire to keep its natural piety alive and well. The primary enemies of that piety are the casual indifference of many human beings to nature and the more systematic despoiling of nature carried out in the name of the market, human betterment, or the satisfying of private fantasies and desires. Environmentalism has long been torn by a struggle that pits conservationists against preservationists. Conservationists believe that the natural world can be cultivated for human use and its natural resources protected if care is taken. Preservationists, and particularly the "deep ecologists," are hostile to that kind of optimism, holding that nature as it is needs to be protected, not manipulated or exploited. Conservationism has a serious and sober history and has been by no means oriented toward a crude exploitation of nature. But it is a movement that has often been allowed to shade off into that kind of technological optimism that argues that whatever harm scientific progress and technological innovation cause, it can just as readily be undone and corrected by science.

This is the ideology of science taken to extremes, but a common enough viewpoint among those who see too much awe of nature, too much protectionism, as a threat to economic progress. Religion could well throw its weight behind responsible conservation, and it would not hurt a bit if some theologians and church groups took up the cause of deep ecology. That is an unlikely cause to gain great support in an overcrowded world, and particularly in the poverty-stricken parts of that world. But it is a strong countercurrent worth introducing into the larger stream of efforts to preserve and respect nature. A little roughage in the bowels helps keep things moving.

Perhaps the cultural dominance of science is nowhere so evident as in a feature of our society frequently overlooked: the powerful proclivity to look to numbers and data as the key to good public policy. Charts, tables, and graphs are the standard props of the policy analyst and the legislator. This is partly understandable and justifiable. With issues of debate and contention, hard data is valuable. It can help to determine if there is a real problem, the dimensions of that problem, and the possible consequences of different solutions. But the soft underside of the deification of data is the too frequent failure to recognize that data never tells its own story, that it is always subject to, and requires, interpretation.

There is no data that can carry out that work. On the contrary, at that point we are thrown back upon our values, our way of looking at the world and society, and our different social hopes and commitments. The illusion of the inherent persuasiveness of data is fostered by scientism, which likes to think that there can be a neutral standpoint from which to assess those matters that concern us, that scientific information plays that role, and that the answer to any moral and social battles is simply more and better information.

i don't agree The dominance of the field of economics in social policy itself tells an interesting story: the need to find a policy discipline that has all the trapping of science in its methods and that can capture its prestige. It is a field that aspires to be a science and that speaks the culturally correct language of modeling, hypothesis testing, and information worship. And it has been amply rewarded for its troubles, recently gaining the blessing of a Nobel prize for its practitioners to signal its status as a science, and for many years capturing the reins of public power and office in a way unmatched by any other academic discipline.

There is a prestigious government Council of Economic Advisors. There is not now, and probably never will be, a Council of Philosophical Advisors, or Historical Advisors, or Humanistic Advisors. But then, that is likely to be the fate of any field that cannot attach itself to the prestige of science. It will lack social standing, just as religion now lacks serious intellectual standing. Note that I say "intellectual standing." There is no doubt that religion can still have a potent political status or that religion can from time to time make trouble for science (or, more accurately, make trouble for the agendas of some scientists, for example, for those who would like to do embryo research). But in the larger and more enduring world of dominant ideas and ideologies, science sits with some serenity, and much public adulation, in an enviable position. It is interesting to note what no one seems to have noticed. In the demise of communism as a political philosophy and a set of political regimes, one of its features has endured nicely: its faith in science. That is the one feature it shared with the Western capitalist democracies that triumphed over it. It is also, let it be noted, a key feature of a market ideology, the engine of innovation, a major source of new products, and—in its purported value neutrality—a congenial companion for a market ideology that just wants to give people the morally neutral gift of freedom of economic choice, not moralisms about human nature and the good society of a kind to be found in the now-dead command economies of the world.

Allow me to end as I began. There was a time when I hoped my own field, bioethics, might serve as the loyal opposition to scientific ideology, at least its biomedical division. In its early days, in the 1960s and 1970s, many of those first drawn to it were alarmed by the apparently unthinking way in which biomedical knowledge and technologies were being taken up and disseminated. It seemed important to examine not only the ethical dilemmas generated by a considerable portion of the scientific advances but also to ask some basic questions about the moral premises of the entire enterprise of unrelenting biomedical progress. That latter aspiration has yet to be fulfilled. Most of those who have come into the field have accepted scientific ideology as much as most scientists, and they have no less been the cultural children of their times, prone to look to medical progress and its expansion of choice as a perfect complement to a set of moral values that puts autonomy at the very top of the moral hierarchy. Nothing seems to so well serve the value of autonomy as the expanded range of human options that science promises to deliver, whether for the control of procreation or the improvement of health or the use of medical means to improve our lives. Not many people in bioethics, moreover, care to be thought of as cranks, and there is no faster way to gain that label than to raise questions about the scientific enterprise as a whole. Bioethicists have, on the whole, become good team players, useful to help out with moral puzzles now and then and trustworthy not to probe basic premises too deeply. Unless one is willing to persistently carry out such probes, the idea of a loyal opposition carries no weight.

Can religion, or bioethics, or some other social group or force in our society call science to account when necessary? Can it do so with credibility and serious credentials? Can it do so in a way that helps science to do its own work better, and not simply to throw sand in the eyes of scientists? I am not sure, but I surely hope so. I can only say, for my part, that I left one church and ended in the pews of another one, this one the Church of Science. In more ways than one—in its self-confidence, its serene faith in its own value, and its ability to intimidate dissenters—it seems uncomfortably like the one I left. How can it be made to see that about itself?

NO

Richard Dawkins

Is Science a Religion?

It is fashionable to wax apocalyptic about the threat to humanity posed by the AIDS virus, "mad cow" disease, and many others, but I think a case can be made that *faith* is one of the world's great evils, comparable to the smallpox virus but harder to eradicate.

Faith, being belief that isn't based on evidence, is the principal vice of any religion. And who, looking at Northern Ireland or the Middle East, can be confident that the brain virus of faith is not exceedingly dangerous? One of the stories told to young Muslim suicide bombers is that martyrdom is the quickest way to heaven—and not just heaven but a special part of heaven where they will receive their special reward of 72 virgin brides. It occurs to me that our best hope may be to provide a kind of "spiritual arms control": send in specially trained theologians to deescalate the going rate in virgins.

Given the dangers of faith—and considering the accomplishments of reason and observation in the activity called science—I find it ironic that, whenever I lecture publicly, there always seems to be someone who comes forward and says, "Of course, your science is just a religion like ours. Fundamentally, science just comes down to faith, doesn't it?"

Well, science is not religion and it doesn't just come down to faith. Although it has many of religion's virtues, it has none of its vices. Science is based upon verifiable evidence. Religious faith not only lacks evidence, its independence from evidence is its pride and joy, shouted from the rooftops. Why else would Christians wax critical of doubting Thomas? The other apostles are held up to us as exemplars of virtue because faith was enough for them. Doubting Thomas, on the other hand, required evidence. Perhaps he should be the patron saint of scientists.

One reason I receive the comment about science being a religion is because I believe in the fact of evolution. I even believe in it with passionate conviction. To some, this may superficially look like faith. But the evidence that makes me believe in evolution is not only overwhelmingly strong; it is freely available to anyone who takes the trouble to read up on it. Anyone can study the same evidence that I have and presumably come to the same conclusion. But if you have a belief that is based solely on faith, I can't examine your reasons. You can retreat behind the private wall of faith where I can't reach you.

Now in practice, of course, individual scientists do sometimes slip back into the vice of faith, and a few may believe so single-mindedly in a favorite theory that they occasionally falsify evidence. However, the fact that this sometimes happens doesn't alter the principle that, when they do so, they do it with shame and not with pride. The method of science is so designed that it usually finds them out in the end.

true

Science is actually one of the most moral, one of the most honest disciplines around—because science would completely collapse if it weren't for a scrupulous adherence to honesty in the reporting of evidence. (As [famous magician] James Randi has pointed out, this is one reason why scientists are so often fooled by paranormal tricksters and why the debunking role is better played by professional conjurors; scientists just don't anticipate deliberate dishonesty as well.) There are other professions (no need to mention lawyers specifically) in which falsifying evidence or at least twisting it is precisely what people are paid for and get brownie points for doing.

Science, then, is free of the main vice of religion, which is faith. But, as I pointed out, science does have some of religion's virtues. Religion may aspire to provide its followers with various benefits—among them explanation, consolation, and uplift. Science, too, has something to offer in these areas.

Humans have a great hunger for explanation. It may be one of the main reasons why humanity so universally has religion, since religions do aspire to provide explanations. We come to our individual consciousness in a mysterious universe and long to understand it. Most religions offer a cosmology and a biology, a theory of life, a theory of origins, and reasons for existence. In doing so, they demonstrate that religion is, in a sense, science; it's just bad science. Don't fall for the argument that religion and science operate on separate dimensions and are concerned with quite separate sorts of questions. Religions have historically always attempted to answer the questions that properly belong to science. Thus religions should not be allowed now to retreat from the ground upon which they have traditionally attempted to fight. They do offer both a cosmology and a biology; however, in both cases it is false.

I disagree — all people

Consolation is harder for science to provide. Unlike Religion, science cannot offer the bereaved a glorious reunion with their loved ones in the hereafter. Those wronged on this earth cannot, on a scientific view, anticipate a sweet comeuppance for their tormentors in a life to come. It could be argued that, if the idea of an afterlife is an illusion (as I believe it is), the consolation it offers is hollow. But that's not necessarily so; a false belief can be just as comforting as a true one, provided the believer never discovers its falsity. But if consolation comes that cheap, science can weigh in with other cheap palliatives, such as pain-killing drugs, whose comfort may or may not be illusory, but they do work.

Uplift, however, is where science really comes into its own. All the great religions have a place for awe, for ecstatic transport at the wonder and beauty of creation. And it's exactly this feeling of spine-shivering, breath-catching awe —almost worship—this flooding of the chest with ecstatic wonder, that modern science can provide. And it does so beyond the wildest dreams of saints and mystics. The fact that the supernatural has no place in our explanations, in our

I agree

understanding of so much about the universe and life, doesn't diminish the awe. Quite the contrary. The merest glance through a microscope at the brain of an ant or through a telescope at a long-ago galaxy of a billion worlds is enough to render poky and parochial the very psalms of praise.

Now, as I say, when it is put to me that science or some particular part of science, like evolutionary theory, is just a religion like any other, I usually deny it with indignation. But I've begun to wonder whether perhaps that's the wrong tactic. Perhaps the right tactic is to accept the charge gratefully and demand equal time for science in religious education classes. And the more I think about it, the more I realize that an excellent case could be made for this. So I want to talk a little bit about religious education and the place that science might play in it.

I do feel very strongly about the way children are brought up. I'm not entirely familiar with the way things are in the United States, and what I say may have more relevance to the United Kingdom, where there is state-obliged, legally enforced religious instruction for all children. That's unconstitutional in the United States, but I presume that children are nevertheless given religious instruction in whatever particular religion their parents deem suitable.

Which brings me to my point about mental child abuse. In a 1995 issue of the *Independent,* one of London's leading newspapers, there was a photograph of a rather sweet and touching scene. It was Christmas time, and the picture showed three children dressed up as the three wise men for a nativity play. The accompanying story described one child as a Muslim, one as a Hindu, and one as a Christian. The supposedly sweet and touching point of the story was that they were all taking part in this nativity play.

What is not sweet and touching is that these children were all four years old. How can you possibly describe a child of four as a Muslim or a Christian or a Hindu or a Jew? Would you talk about a four-year-old economic monetarist? Would you talk about a four-year-old neo-isolationist or a four-year-old liberal Republican? There are opinions about the cosmos and the world that children, once grown, will presumably be in a position to evaluate for themselves. Religion is the one field in our culture about which it is absolutely accepted, without question—without even noticing how bizarre it is—that parents have a total and absolute say in what their children are going to be, how their children are going to be raised, what opinions their children are going to have about the cosmos, about life, about existence. Do you see what I mean about mental child abuse?

Looking now at the various things that religious education might be expected to accomplish, one of its aims could be to encourage children to reflect upon the deep questions of existence, to invite them to rise above the humdrum preoccupations of ordinary life and think *sub specie alternitatis.*

Science can offer a vision of life and the universe which, as I've already remarked, for humbling poetic inspiration far outclasses any of the mutually contradictory faiths and disappointingly recent traditions of the world's religions.

For example, how could any child in a religious education class fail to be inspired if we could get across to them some inkling of the age of the universe? Suppose that, at the moment of Christ's death, the news of it had started traveling at the maximum possible speed around the universe outwards from the earth? How far would the terrible tidings have traveled by now? Following the theory of special relativity, the answer is that the news could not, under any circumstances whatever, have reached more than one-fiftieth of the way across one galaxy—not one-thousandth of the way to our nearest neighboring galaxy in the 100-million-galaxy-strong universe. The universe at large couldn't possibly by anything other than indifferent to Christ, his birth, his passion, and his death. Even such momentous news as the origin of life on Earth could have traveled only across our little local cluster of galaxies. Yet so ancient was that event on our earthy time-scale that, if you span its age with your open arms, the whole of human history, the whole of human culture, would fall in the dust from your fingertip at a single stroke of a nail file.

The argument from design, an important part of the history of religion, wouldn't be ignored in my religious education classes, needless to say. The children would look at the spell-binding wonders of the living kingdoms and would consider Darwinism alongside the creationist alternatives and make up their own minds. I think the children would have no difficulty in making up their minds the right way if presented with the evidence. What worries me is not the question of equal time but that, as far as I can see, children in the United Kingdom and the United States are essentially given *no* time with evolution yet are taught creationism (whether at school, in church, or at home).

It would also be interesting to teach more than one theory of creation. The dominant one in this culture happens to be the Jewish creation myth, which is taken over from the Babylonian creation myth. There are, of course, lots and lots of others, and perhaps they should all be given equal time (except that wouldn't leave much time for studying anything else). I understand that there are Hindus who believe that the world was created in a cosmic butter churn and Nigerian peoples who believe that the world was created by God from the excrement of ants. Surely these stories have as much right to equal time as the Judeo-Christian myth of Adam and Eve. . . .

When the religious education class turns to ethics, I don't think science actually has a lot to say, and I would replace it with rational moral philosophy. Do the children think there are absolute standards of right and wrong? And if so, where do they come from? Can you make up good working principles of right and wrong, like "do as you would be done by" and "the greatest good for the greatest number" (whatever that is supposed to mean)? It's a rewarding question, whatever your personal morality, to ask as an evolutionist where morals come from; by what route has the human brain gained its tendency to have ethics and morals, a feeling of right and wrong?

Should we value human life above all other life? Is there a rigid wall to be built around the species *Homo sapiens,* or should we talk about whether there are other species which are entitled to our humanistic sympathies? Should we, for example, follow the right-to-life lobby, which is wholly preoccupied with *human* life, and value the life of a human fetus with the faculties of a worm over the life of a thinking and feeling chimpanzee? What is the basis of this fence we erect around *Homo sapiens*—even around a small piece of fetal tissue? (Not a very sound evolutionary idea when you think about it.) When, in our evolutionary descent from our common ancestor with chimpanzees, did the fence suddenly rear itself up?

... [S]cience could give a good account of itself in religious education. But it wouldn't be enough. I believe that some familiarity with the King James version of the Bible is important for anyone wanting to understand the allusions that appear in English literature. Together with Book of Common Prayer, the Bible gets 58 pages in the *Oxford Dictionary of Quotations.* Only Shakespeare has more. I do think that not having any kind of biblical education is unfortunate if children want to read English literature and understand the provenance of phrases like "through a glass darkly," "all flesh is as grass," "the race is not to the swift," "crying in the wilderness," "reaping the whirlwind," "amid the alien corn," "Eyeless in Gaza," "Job's comforters," and "the widow's mite."

I want to return now to the charge that science is just a faith. The more extreme version of this charge—and one that I often encounter as both a scientist and a rationalist—is an accusation of zealotry and bigotry in scientists themselves as great as that found in religious people. Sometimes there may be a little bit of justice in this accusation; but as zealous bigots, we scientists are mere amateurs at the game. We're content to *argue* with those who disagree with us. We don't kill them.

But I would want to deny even the lesser charge of purely verbal zealotry. There is a very, very important difference between feeling strongly, even passionately, about something because we have thought about and examined the evidence for it on the one hand, and feeling strongly about something because it has been internally revealed to us, or internally revealed to somebody else in history and subsequently hallowed by tradition. There's all the difference in the world between a belief that one is prepared to defend by quoting evidence and logic and a belief that is supported by nothing more than tradition, authority, or revelation.

POSTSCRIPT

Is Science a Faith?

Nicely done

The conflict between science and religion is deep and broad. The root reason may be simply that science says, "Check it out—don't take anyone's word for the truth," while religion says, "Take the word of your preacher or your scripture. Believe—but don't even *think* about checking." Scientific skepticism is always a threat to established authority. It challenges old truths. It revises and replaces beliefs, traditions, and power structures.

Does this mean that science is a threat to society? Those who share the beliefs under attack often think so. They may believe that the Bible or the Koran is a much better guide to the nature of the world than science is. They may believe in crystal power and magic spells. They may tie knots in their electric cords to trim the size of their electric bills. They may even be postmodernist university professors who say that science is just a "useful myth," no different from any other fiction. Or they may, like Callahan, wish that there were some segment of society with sufficient stature to sit in judgment over science, to criticize it, and perhaps to rein it in, certainly to keep it from arrogantly quashing other views, such as those of religion. And although most Americans welcome the benefits of science and technology, they are often very leery of the unrestricted inquiry that characterizes science and challenges tradition. See, for example, Janet Raloff, "When Science and Beliefs Collide," *Science News* (June 8, 1996); Gerald Holton, *Einstein, History, and Other Passions: The Rebellion Against Science at the End of the Twentieth Century* (Addison-Wesley, 1996); and "Science Versus Antiscience?" *Scientific American* (January 1997). Even some scientists feel threatened by the conflict between their professional and private beliefs. Some have therefore spent a great deal of effort searching for ways to reconcile science and religion. For instance, Leon Lederman and Dick Teresi write about the quest for the most fundamental fragment of the atom in *The God Particle* (Dell, 1994). Stephen Hawking, in *A Brief History of Time* (Bantam Books, 1988), expresses the thought that science might lead humanity to "know the mind of God."

Can these scientists be speaking in more than metaphorical terms? Perhaps not, for science deals in observable reality, which can provide at best only hints of a designer, creator, or God. Science cannot provide *direct* access to God, at least as people currently understand the nature of God. Still, it is not only creationists who see signs of design. Some scientists find the impression of design quite overwhelming, and many feel that science and religion actually have a great deal in common. Harvard University astronomer and evangelical Christian Owen Gingerich says that both are driven by human beings' "basic wonder and desire to know where we stand in the universe." It is therefore not terribly surprising to find the two realms of human thought intersecting very frequently or to find many people in both realms concerned with reconciling differences. See Gregg Easterbrook, "Science and God: A Warming Trend?" *Science* (August 15, 1997).

On the other hand, some scientists find attempts to reconcile science and religion strange at best. Eugenie Scott, of the National Center for Science Education, insists that "science is just a method" and that people who see God in the complexity of biology or astronomy are "going beyond their data" and misusing science "to validate their positions." Paul Gross, former director of the Woods Hole Marine Biological Laboratory and coauthor of *Higher Superstition: The Academic Left and Its Quarrels With Science* (Johns Hopkins University Press, 1994), even finds those who see God in science frightening. More recently, Gross, Norman Levitt, and Martin W. Lewis coedited *The Flight from Science and Reason* (New York Academy of Sciences, 1997) to consider the opposition to the scientific, rational approach to the world that now finds wide expression in many nonscientific academic areas.

Are such views no more than an illustration of Callahan's claim that science—or "scientism"—has become an ideology and a faith as intolerant of others as any religion? Certainly some feel that science can provide many of the same rewards as religion. See Chet Raymo's *Skeptics and True Believers* (Walker & Company, 1998), in which he seeks a kind of spirituality without belief, finding all the awe, wonder, and mystery anyone could wish in the universe revealed by science.

ISSUE 3

Does the Theory of Evolution Explain the Origins of Humanity?

YES: Daniel C. Dennett, from *Darwin's Dangerous Idea: Evolution and the Meanings of Life* (Simon & Schuster, 1995)

NO: Edward B. Davis, from "Debating Darwin: The 'Intelligent Design' Movement," *The Christian Century* (July 15, 1998)

ISSUE SUMMARY

YES: Philosopher Daniel C. Dennett argues that Charles Darwin had in his theory of evolution by means of natural selection the single best idea of all time. Far from being replaceable, he asserts, the theory has made its religious predecessors quite obsolete.

NO: Professor of the history of science Edward B. Davis reviews three books about evolution to support his assertion that the theory of evolution by means of natural selection does not adequately explain our existence. Davis maintains that religious views of evolution should be discussed in public schools.

Before science came along, the usual answer to questions such as "Why do elephants have trunks?" or "Why is the sky blue?" was "Because God made it that way." No one could add any more. Today children still hear such answers in Sunday School, but the rest of us generally believe that more complete and satisfying answers have come from scientists who were not satisfied with "God's will" as an answer. It has long been a dogma of scientific faith that "why" questions are unreasonable to ask. They are teleological; that is, they presume that there is an intent or design behind the phenomena we wish to explain. As an answer, "God's will" is out of bounds largely because accepting it means accepting that it is a waste of time to look for other answers. Outside science, on the other hand, "God's will" is very much *in* bounds. This leads to a continuing struggle between the forces of faith and the forces of reason. Conservative Christians in the southern United States, Texas, and California have mounted vigorous campaigns to require public school biology classes to give equal time to both biblical creationism and Darwinian evolution. For many years, this meant that evolution was hardly mentioned in high school biology textbooks.

42

Prove their view by disproving Darwinian theory + evidences

For a time, it looked like evolution had scored a decisive victory. In 1982 federal judge William K. Overton struck down an Arkansas law that would have required the teaching of straight biblical creationism, with its explicit talk of God the Creator, as an unconstitutional intrusion of religion into a government activity: education. But the creationists have not given up. They have returned to the fray with something they call "scientific creationism," and they have shifted their campaigns from state legislatures and school boards to local school boards, where it is harder for lawyers and biologists to mount effective counter-attacks. See Gary Stix, "Postdiluvian Science," in "Science Versus Antiscience?" *Scientific American* (January 1997). "Scientific creationism" tries to show that the evolutionary approach is incapable of providing satisfactory explanations. For one thing, it says that natural selection relies on random chance to produce structures whose delicate intricacy really could only be the product of deliberate design. Therefore, there must have been a designer. There is no mention of God—but, of course, that is the only possible meaning of "designer" (unless one believes in ancient extraterrestrial visitors). Scientific creationists reinforce their claim that evolution is inadequate by seeking weaknesses in the evidence —fossils, anatomy, embryology, DNA, and more—that more conventional biologists cite in their own discussions of evolution and natural selection. They hope to thereby weaken the credibility of evolutionists. At the same time, scientific creationists can present the quest for weaknesses in the evolutionists' argument as perfectly appropriate scientific skepticism—after all, they are *scientific* creationists.

William Johnson, associate dean of academic affairs at Ambassador University in Big Sandy, Texas, offered another argument for replacing the theory of evolution in a 1994 speech reprinted in "Evolution: The Past, Present, and Future Implications," *Vital Speeches of the Day* (February 15, 1995). He argued that the triumph of Darwin's theory "meant the end of the traditional belief in the world as a purposeful created order ... and the consequent elimination of God from nature has played a decisive role in the secularization of Western society. Darwinian theory broke man's link with God and set him adrift in a cosmos without purpose or end." Johnson suggested that evolution—and perhaps the entire scientific approach to nature—should be abandoned in favor of a return to religion because of the untold damage it has done to the human values that underpin society. Matt Cartmill, in "Oppressed by Evolution," *Discover* (March 1998), is less extreme as he argues that scientists need to exercise more humility and refrain from assertions about the presence or absence of "divine plans or purposes."

In the following selections, Daniel C. Dennett argues that Charles Darwin's theory of evolution by means of natural selection is more accurate than the religion-based alternatives. Dennett asserts that in Darwin's idea lies our hope of finding the truest meaning of life. Edward B. Davis discusses three books espousing the "intelligent design" (ID) view. He is critical because he feels that ID proponents fail to recognize that "the philosophical landscape has changed" since Darwin's day. However, he also states that religious views should not be completely rejected.

Daniel C. Dennett

Darwin's Dangerous Idea:
Evolution and the Meanings of Life

We used to sing a lot when I was a child, around the campfire at summer camp, at school and Sunday school, or gathered around the piano at home. One of my favorite songs was "Tell Me Why." ...

> Tell me why the stars do shine,
> Tell me why the ivy twines,
> Tell me why the sky's so blue.
> Then I will tell you just why I love you.
> Because God made the stars to shine,
> Because God made the ivy twine,
> Because God made the sky so blue.
> Because God made you, that's why I love you.

This straightforward, sentimental declaration still brings a lump to my throat—so sweet, so innocent, so reassuring a vision of life!

And then along comes Darwin and spoils the picnic. Or does he? ... From the moment of the publication of *Origin of Species* in 1859, Charles Darwin's fundamental idea has inspired intense reactions ranging from ferocious condemnation to ecstatic allegiance, sometimes tantamount to religious zeal. Darwin's theory has been abused and misrepresented by friend and foe alike. It has been misappropriated to lend scientific respectability to appalling political and social doctrines. It has been pilloried in caricature by opponents, some of whom would have it compete in our children's schools with "creation science," a pathetic hodgepodge of pious pseudo-science.[1]

Almost no one is indifferent to Darwin, and no one should be. The Darwinian theory is a scientific theory, and a great one, but that is not all it is. The creationists who oppose it so bitterly are right about one thing: Darwin's dangerous idea cuts much deeper into the fabric of our most fundamental beliefs than many of its sophisticated apologists have yet admitted, even to themselves.

The sweet, simple vision of the song, taken literally, is one that most of us have outgrown, however fondly we may recall it. The kindly God who lovingly fashioned each and every one of us (all creatures great and small) and sprinkled the sky with shining stars for our delight—*that* God is, like Santa Claus, a myth of childhood, not anything a sane, undeluded adult could literally believe in. *That* God must either be turned into a symbol for something less concrete or abandoned altogether.

Not all scientists and philosophers are atheists, and many who are believers declare that their idea of God can live in peaceful coexistence with, or even find support from, the Darwinian framework of ideas. Theirs is not an anthropomorphic Handicrafter God, but still a God worthy of worship in their eyes, capable of giving consolation and meaning to their lives. Others ground their highest concerns in entirely secular philosophies, views of the meaning of life that stave off despair without the aid of any concept of a Supreme Being—other than the Universe itself. Something *is* sacred to these thinkers, but they do not call it God; they call it, perhaps, Life, or Love, or Goodness, or Intelligence, or Beauty, or Humanity. What both groups share, in spite of the differences in their deepest creeds, is a conviction that life does have meaning, that goodness matters.

But can *any* version of this attitude of wonder and purpose be sustained in the face of Darwinism? From the outset, there have been those who thought they saw Darwin letting the worst possible cat out of the bag: nihilism. They thought that if Darwin was right, the implication would be that nothing could be sacred. To put it bluntly, nothing could have any point. Is this just an over-reaction? What exactly are the implications of Darwin's idea—and, in any case, has it been scientifically proven or is it still "just a theory"?

Perhaps, you may think, we could make a useful division: there are the parts of Darwin's idea that really are established beyond any reasonable doubt, and then there are the speculative extensions of the scientifically irresistible parts. Then—if we were lucky—perhaps the rock-solid scientific facts would have no stunning implications about religion, or human nature, or the meaning of life, while the parts of Darwin's idea that get people all upset could be put into quarantine as highly controversial extensions of, or mere interpretations of, the scientifically irresistible parts. That would be reassuring.

But alas, that is just about backwards. There are vigorous controversies swirling around in evolutionary theory, but those who feel threatened by Darwinism should not take heart from this fact. Most—if not quite all—of the controversies concern issues that are "just science"; no matter which side wins, the outcome will not undo the basic Darwinian idea. That idea, which is about as secure as any in science, really does have far-reaching implications for our vision of what the meaning of life is or could be.

In 1543, Copernicus proposed that the Earth was not the center of the universe but in fact revolved around the Sun. It took over a century for the idea to sink in, a gradual and actually rather painless transformation. (The religious reformer Philipp Melanchthon, a collaborator of Martin Luther, opined that "some Christian prince" should suppress this madman, but aside from a few such salvos, the world was not particularly shaken by Copernicus himself.) The Copernican Revolution did eventually have its own "shot heard round the world": Galileo's *Dialogue Concerning the Two Chief World Systems*, but it was not published until 1632, when the issue was no longer controversial among scientists. Galileo's projectile provoked an infamous response by the Roman Catholic Church, setting up a shock wave whose reverberations are only now dying out. But in spite of the drama of that epic confrontation, the idea that our planet is not the center of creation has sat rather lightly in people's minds. Every schoolchild today accepts this as the matter of fact it is, without tears or terror.

In due course, the Darwinian Revolution will come to occupy a similarly secure and untroubled place in the minds—and hearts—of every educated person on the globe, but today, more than a century after Darwin's death, we still have not come to terms with its mind-boggling implications. Unlike the Copernican Revolution, which did not engage widespread public attention until the scientific details had been largely sorted out, the Darwinian Revolution has had anxious lay spectators and cheerleaders taking sides from the outset, tugging at the sleeves of the participants and encouraging grandstanding. The scientists themselves have been moved by the same hopes and fears, so it is not surprising that the relatively narrow conflicts among theorists have often been not just blown up out of proportion by their adherents, but seriously distorted in the process. Everybody has seen, dimly, that a lot is at stake.

Moreover, although Darwin's own articulation of his theory was monumental, and its powers were immediately recognized by many of the scientists and other thinkers of his day, there really were large gaps in his theory that have only recently begun to be properly filled in. The biggest gap looks almost comical in retrospect. In all his brilliant musings, Darwin never hit upon the central concept, without which the theory of evolution is hopeless: the concept of a *gene*. Darwin had no proper *unit* of heredity, and so his account of the process of natural selection was plagued with entirely reasonable doubts about whether it would work. Darwin supposed that offspring would always exhibit a sort of blend or average of their parents' features. Wouldn't such "blending inheritance" always simply average out all differences, turning everything into uniform gray? How could diversity survive such relentless averaging? Darwin recognized the seriousness of this challenge, and neither he nor his many ardent supporters succeeded in responding with a description of a convincing and well-documented mechanism of heredity that could combine traits of parents while maintaining an underlying and unchanged identity. The idea they needed was right at hand, uncovered ("formulated" would be too strong) by the monk Gregor Mendel and published in a relatively obscure Austrian journal in 1865, but, in the best-savored irony in the history of science, it lay there unnoticed until its importance was appreciated (at first dimly) around 1900. Its triumphant establishment at the heart of the "Modern Synthesis" (in effect, the synthesis of Mendel and Darwin) was eventually made secure in the 1940s, thanks to the work of Theodosius Dobzhansky, Julian Huxley, Ernst Mayr, and others. It has taken another half-century to iron out most of the wrinkles of that new fabric.

The fundamental core of contemporary Darwinism, the theory of DNA-based reproduction and evolution, is now beyond dispute among scientists. It demonstrates its power every day, contributing crucially to the explanation of planet-sized facts of geology and meteorology, through middle-sized facts of ecology and agronomy, down to the latest microscopic facts of genetic engineering. It unifies all of biology and the history of our planet into a single grand story. Like Gulliver tied down in Lilliput, it is unbudgeable, not because of some one or two huge chains of argument that might—hope against hope—have weak links in them, but because it is securely tied by hundreds of thousands of threads of evidence anchoring it to virtually every other area of human knowledge. New discoveries may conceivably lead to dramatic, even "revolutionary" *shifts* in the Darwinian theory, but the hope that it will be "refuted" by some shattering breakthrough is about as reasonable as the hope that we will return to a geocentric vision and discard Copernicus.

Still, the theory is embroiled in remarkably hot-tempered controversy, and one of the reasons for this incandescence is that these debates about scientific matters are usually distorted by fears that the "wrong" answer would have intolerable moral implications. So great are these fears that they are carefully left unarticulated, displaced from attention by several layers of distracting rebuttal and counter-rebuttal. The disputants are forever changing the subject slightly, conveniently keeping the bogeys in the shadows. It is this misdirection that is mainly responsible for postponing the day when we can all live as comfortably with our new biological perspective as we do with the astronomical perspective Copernicus gave us.

Whenever Darwinism is the topic, the temperature rises, because more is at stake than just the empirical facts about how life on Earth evolved, or the correct logic of the theory that accounts for those facts. One of the precious things that is at stake is a vision of what it means to ask, and answer, the question "Why?" Darwin's new perspective turns several traditional assumptions upside down, undermining our standard ideas about what ought to count as satisfying answers to this ancient and inescapable question. Here science and philosophy get completely intertwined. Scientists sometimes deceive themselves into thinking that philosophical ideas are only, at best, decorations or parasitic commentaries on the hard, objective triumphs of science, and that they themselves are immune to the confusions that philosophers devote their lives to dissolving. But there is no such thing as philosophy-free science; there is only science whose philosophical baggage is taken on board without examination.

The Darwinian Revolution is both a scientific and a philosophical revolution, and neither revolution could have occurred without the other. As we shall see, it was the philosophical prejudices of the scientists, more than their lack of scientific evidence, that prevented them from seeing how the theory could actually work, but those philosophical prejudices that had to be overthrown were too deeply entrenched to be dislodged by mere philosophical brilliance. It took an irresistible parade of hard-won scientific facts to force thinkers to take seriously the weird new outlook that Darwin proposed. Those who are still ill-acquainted with that beautiful procession can be forgiven their continued allegiance to the pre-Darwinian ideas. And the battle is not yet over; even among the scientists, there are pockets of resistance.

Let me lay my cards on the table. If I were to give an award for the single best idea anyone has ever had, I'd give it to Darwin, ahead of Newton and

Einstein and everyone else. In a single stroke, the idea of evolution by natural selection unifies the realm of life, meaning, and purpose with the realm of space and time, cause and effect, mechanism and physical law. But it is not just a wonderful scientific idea. It is a dangerous idea. My admiration for Darwin's magnificent idea is unbounded, but I, too, cherish many of the ideas and ideals that it *seems* to challenge, and want to protect them. For instance, I want to protect the campfire song, and what is beautiful and true in it, for my little grandson and his friends, and for their children when they grow up. There are many more magnificent ideas that are also jeopardized, it seems, by Darwin's idea, and they, too, may need protection. The only good way to do this—the only way that has a chance in the long run—is to cut through the smokescreens and look at the idea as unflinchingly, as dispassionately, as possible.

On this occasion, we are not going to settle for "There, there, it will all come out all right." Our examination will take a certain amount of nerve. Feelings may get hurt. Writers on evolution usually steer clear of this apparent clash between science and religion. Fools rush in, Alexander Pope said, where angels fear to tread. Do you want to follow me? Don't you really want to know what survives this confrontation? What if it turns out that the sweet vision—or a better one—survives intact, strengthened and deepened by the encounter? Wouldn't it be a shame to forgo the opportunity for a strengthened, renewed creed, settling instead for a fragile, sickbed faith that you mistakenly supposed must not be disturbed?

There is no future in a sacred myth. Why not? Because of our curiosity. Because, as the song reminds us, *we want to know why.* We may have outgrown the song's answer, but we will never outgrow the question. Whatever we hold precious, we cannot protect it from our curiosity, because being who we are, one of the things we deem precious is the truth. Our love of truth is surely a central element in the meaning we find in our lives. In any case, the idea that we might preserve meaning by kidding ourselves is a more pessimistic, more nihilistic idea than I for one can stomach. If that were the best that could be done, I would conclude that nothing mattered after all....

At what "point" does a human life begin or end? The Darwinian perspective lets us see with unmistakable clarity why there is no hope at all of *discovering* a telltale mark, a saltation in life's processes, that "counts." We need to draw lines; we need definitions of life and death for many important moral purposes. The layers of pearly dogma that build up in defense around these fundamentally arbitrary attempts are familiar, and in never-ending need of repair. We should abandon the fantasy that either science or religion can uncover some well-hidden fact that tells us exactly where to draw these lines. There is no "natural" way to mark the birth of a human "soul," any more than there is a "natural" way to mark the birth of a species. And, contrary to what many traditions insist, I think we all do share the intuition that there are gradations of value in the ending of human lives. Most human embryos end in spontaneous abortion—fortunately, since these are mostly *terata,* hopeless monsters whose lives are all but impossible. Is this a terrible evil? Are the mothers whose bodies abort these embryos guilty of involuntary manslaughter? Of course not. Which is worse, taking "heroic" measures to keep alive a severely deformed infant, or taking the equally "heroic" (if unsung) step of seeing to it that such an infant dies as quickly and painlessly as possible? I do not suggest that Darwinian thinking gives us answers to such questions; I do suggest that Darwinian thinking helps us see why the traditional hope of solving these problems (finding a moral algorithm) is forlorn. We must cast off the myths that make these old-fashioned solutions seem inevitable. We need to grow up, in other words.

Among the precious artifacts worth preserving are whole cultures themselves. There are still several thousand distinct languages spoken daily on our planet, but the number is dropping fast (Diamond 1992, Hale et al. 1992). When a language goes extinct, this is the same kind of loss as the extinction of a species, and when the culture that was carried by that language dies, this is an even greater loss. But here, once again, we face incommensurabilities and no easy answers.

I began . . . with a song which I myself cherish, and hope will survive "forever." I hope my grandson learns it and passes it on to his grandson, but at the same time I do not myself believe, and do not really want my grandson to believe, the doctrines that are so movingly expressed in that song. They are too simple. They are, in a word, wrong—just as wrong as the ancient Greeks' doctrines about the gods and goddesses on Mount Olympus. Do you believe, literally, in an anthropomorphic God? If not, then you must agree with me that the song is a beautiful, comforting falsehood. Is that simple song nevertheless a valuable meme? I certainly think it is. It is a modest but beautiful part of our heritage, a treasure to be preserved. But we must face the fact that, just as there were times when tigers would not have been viable, times are coming when they will no longer be viable, except in zoos and other preserves, and the same is true of many of the treasures in our cultural heritage.

The Welsh language is kept alive by artificial means, just the way condors are. We cannot preserve *all* the features of the cultural world in which these treasures flourished. We wouldn't want to. It took oppressive political and social systems, rife with many evils, to create the rich soil in which many of our greatest works of art could grow: slavery and despotism ("enlightened" though these sometimes may have been), obscene differences in living standards between the rich and the poor—and a huge amount of ignorance. Ignorance is a necessary condition for many excellent things. The childish joy of seeing what Santa Claus has brought for Christmas is a species of joy that must soon be extinguished in each child by the loss of ignorance. When that child grows up, she can transmit that joy to her own children, but she must also recognize a time when it has outlived its value.

The view I am expressing has clear ancestors. The philosopher George Santayana was a Catholic atheist, if you can imagine such a thing. According to Bertrand Russell (1945, p. 811), William James once denounced Santayana's ideas as "the perfection of rottenness," and one can see why some people would be offended by his brand of aestheticism: a deep appreciation for all the formulae, ceremonies, and trappings of his religious heritage, but lacking the faith.

Santayana's position was aptly caricatured: "There is no God and Mary is His Mother." But how many of us are caught in that very dilemma, loving the heritage, firmly convinced of its value, yet unable to sustain any conviction at all in its truth? We are faced with a difficult choice. Because we value it, we are eager to preserve it in a rather precarious and "denatured" state—in churches and cathedrals and synagogues, built to house huge congregations of the devout, and now on the way to being cultural museums. There is really not that much difference between the roles of the Beefeaters who stand picturesque guard at the Tower of London, and the Cardinals who march in their magnificent costumes and meet to elect the next Pope. Both are keeping alive traditions, rituals, liturgies, symbols, that otherwise would fade.

But hasn't there been a tremendous rebirth of fundamentalist faith in all these creeds? Yes, unfortunately, there has been, and I think that there are no forces on this planet more dangerous to us all than the fanaticisms of fundamentalism, of all the species: Protestantism, Catholicism, Judaism, Islam, Hinduism, and Buddhism, as well as countless smaller infections. Is there a conflict between science and religion here? There most certainly is.

Darwin's dangerous idea helps to create a condition in the memosphere that in the long run threatens to be just as toxic to these memes as civilization in general has been toxic to the large wild mammals. Save the Elephants! Yes, of course, but not *by all means*. Not by forcing the people of Africa to live nineteenth-century lives, for instance. This is not an idle comparison. The creation of the great wildlife preserves in Africa has often been accompanied by the dislocation—and ultimate destruction—of human populations. (For a chilling vision of this side effect, see Colin Turnbull 1972 on the fate of the Ik.) Those who think that we should preserve the elephants' pristine environment *at all costs* should contemplate the costs of returning the United States to the pristine conditions in which the buffaloes roam and the deer and the antelope play. We must find an accommodation.

I love the King James Version of the Bible. My own spirit recoils from a God Who is He or She in the same way my heart sinks when I see a lion pacing neurotically back and forth in a small zoo cage. I know, I know, the lion is beautiful but dangerous; if you let the lion roam free, it would kill me; safety demands that it be put in a cage. Safety demands that religions be put in cages, too—when absolutely necessary. We just can't have forced female circumcision, and the second-class status of women in Roman Catholicism and Mormonism, to say nothing of their status in Islam. The recent Supreme Court ruling declaring unconstitutional the Florida law prohibiting the sacrificing of animals in the rituals of the Santeria sect (an Afro-Caribbean religion incorporating elements of Yoruba traditions and Roman Catholicism) is a borderline case, at least for many of us. Such rituals are offensive to many, but the protective mantle of religious tradition secures our tolerance. We are wise to respect these traditions. It is, after all, just part of respect for the biosphere.

Save the Baptists! Yes, of course, but not *by all means*. Not if it means tolerating the deliberate misinforming of children about the natural world. According to a recent poll, 48 percent of the people in the United States today believe that the book of Genesis is literally true. And 70 percent believe that "creation science" should be taught in school alongside evolution. Some recent writers recommend a policy in which parents would be able to "opt out" of materials they didn't want their children taught. Should evolution be taught in the schools? Should arithmetic be taught? Should history? Misinforming a child is a terrible offense.

A faith, like a species, must evolve or go extinct when the environment changes. It is not a gentle process in either case. We see in every Christian sub-species the battle of memes—should women be ordained? should we go back to the Latin liturgy?—and the same can also be observed in the varieties of Judaism and Islam. We must have a similar mixture of respect and self-protective caution about memes. This is already accepted practice, but we tend to avert our attention from its implications. We preach freedom of religion, but only so far. If your religion advocates slavery, or mutilation of women, or infanticide, or puts a price on Salman Rushdie's head because he has insulted it, then your religion has a feature that cannot be respected. It endangers us all.

It is nice to have grizzly bears and wolves living in the wild. They are no longer a menace; we can peacefully coexist, with a little wisdom. The same policy can be discerned in our political tolerance, in religious freedom. You are free to preserve or create any religious creed you wish, so long as it does not become a public menace. We're all on the Earth together, and we have to learn some accommodation. The Hutterite memes are "clever" not to include any memes about the virtue of destroying outsiders. If they did, we would have to combat them. We tolerate the Hutterites because they harm only themselves —though we may well insist that we have the right to impose some further openness on their schooling of their own children. Other religious membes are not so benign. The message is clear: those who will not accommodate, who will not temper, who insist on keeping only the purest and wildest strain of their heritage alive, we will be obliged, reluctantly, to cage or disarm, and we will do our best to disable the memes they fight for. Slavery is beyond the pale. Child abuse is beyond the pale. Discrimination is beyond the pale. The pronouncing of death sentences on those who blaspheme against a religion (complete with bounties or rewards for those who carry them out) is beyond the pale. It is not civilized, and is owed no more respect in the name of religious freedom than any other incitement to cold-blooded murder.[2] ...   *Terrorism ?*

Long before there was science, or even philosophy, there were religions. They have served many purposes (it would be a mistake of greedy reductionism to look for a single purpose, a single *summum bonum* which they have all directly or indirectly served). They have inspired many people to lead lives that have added immeasurably to the wonders of our world, and they have inspired many more people to lead lives that were, given their circumstances, more meaningful, less painful, than they otherwise could have been. ...

Religions have brought the comfort of belonging and companionship to many who would otherwise have passed through this life all alone, without glory or adventure. At their best, religions have drawn attention to love, and made it real for people who could not otherwise see it, and ennobled the attitudes and refreshed the spirits of the world-beset. Another thing religions have accomplished, without this being thereby their *raison d'être*, is that they have kept *Homo sapiens* civilized enough, for long enough, for us to have learned how to reflect more systematically and accurately on our position in the universe. There is much more to learn. There is certainly a treasury of ill-appreciated truths embedded in the endangered cultures of the modern world, designs that have accumulated details over eons of idiosyncratic history, and we should take steps to record it, and study it, before it disappears, for, like dinosaur genomes, once it is gone, it will be virtually impossible to recover.

We should not expect this variety of respect to be satisfactory to those who wholeheartedly embody the memes we honor with our attentive—but not worshipful—scholarship. On the contrary, many of them will view anything other than enthusiastic conversion to their own views as a threat, even an intolerable threat. We must not underestimate the suffering such confrontations cause. To watch, to have to participate in, the contraction or evaporation of beloved features of one's heritage is a pain only our species can experience, and surely few pains could be more terrible. But we have no reasonable alternative, and those whose visions dictate that they cannot peacefully coexist with the rest of us will have to quarantine as best we can, minimizing the pain and damage, trying always to leave open a path or two that may come to seem acceptable.

If you want to teach your children that they are the tools of God, you had better not teach them that they are God's rifles, or we will have to stand firmly opposed to you: your doctrine has no glory, no special rights, no intrinsic and inalienable merit. If you insist on teaching your children falsehoods—that the Earth is flat, that "Man" is not a product of evolution by natural selection—then you must expect, at the very least, that those of us who have freedom of speech will feel free to describe your teachings as the spreading of falsehoods, and will attempt to demonstrate this to your children at our earliest opportunity. Our future well-being—the well-being of all of us on the planet—depends on the education of our descendants.

What, then, of all the glories of our religious traditions? They should certainly be preserved, as should the languages, the art, the costumes, the rituals, the monuments. Zoos are now more and more being seen as second-class havens for endangered species, but at least they are havens, and what they preserve is irreplaceable. The same is true of complex memes and their phenotypic expressions. Many a fine New England church, costly to maintain, is in danger of destruction. Shall we deconsecrate these churches and turn them into museums, or retrofit them for some other use? The latter fate is at least to be preferred to their destruction. Many congregations face a cruel choice: their house of worship costs so much to maintain in all its splendor that little of their tithing is left over for the poor. The Catholic Church has faced this problem for centuries, and has maintained a position that is, I think, defensible, but not obviously so: when it spends its treasure to put gold plating on the candlesticks, instead of providing more food and better shelter for the poor of the parish, it has a different vision of what makes life worth living. Our people, it says, benefit more from having a place of splendor in which to worship than from a little more food. Any atheist or agnostic who finds this cost-benefit analysis ludicrous might pause to consider whether to support diverting all charitable and governmental support for museums, symphony orchestras, libraries, and scientific laboratories to efforts to provide more food and better living conditions for the least well off. A human life worth living is not something that can be uncontroversially measured, and that is its glory.

And there's the rub. What will happen, one may well wonder, if religion is preserved in cultural zoos, in libraries, in concerts and demonstrations? It is happening; the tourists flock to watch the Native American tribal dances, and for the onlookers it is folklore, a religious ceremony, certainly, to be treated with respect, but also an example of a meme complex on the verge of extinction, at least in its strong, ambulatory phase; it has become an invalid, barely kept alive by its custodians. Does Darwin's dangerous idea give us anything in exchange for the ideas it calls into question?

. . . [T]he physicist Paul Davies proclaim[ed] that the reflective power of human minds can be "no trivial detail, no minor by-product of mindless purposeless forces," and [I] suggested that being a by-product of mindless purposeless forces was no disqualification for importance. And I have argued that Darwin has shown us how, in fact, *everything* of importance is just such a product. Spinoza called his highest being God or Nature *(Deus sive Natura),* expressing a sort of pantheism. There have been many varieties of pantheism, but they usually lack a convincing *explanation* about just how God is distributed in the whole of nature.... Darwin offers us one: it is in the distribution of Design throughout nature, creating, in the Tree of Life, an utterly unique and irreplaceable creation, an actual pattern in the immeasurable reaches of Design Space that could never be exactly duplicated in its many details. What is design work? It is that wonderful wedding of chance and necessity, happening in a trillion places at once, at a trillion different levels. And what miracle caused it? None. It just happened to happen, in the fullness of time. You could even say, in a way, that the Tree of Life created itself. Not in a miraculous, instantaneous whoosh, but slowly, slowly, over billions of years.

Is this Tree of Life a God one could worship? Pray to? Fear? Probably not. But it *did* make the ivy twine and the sky so blue, so perhaps the song I love tells a truth after all. The Tree of Life is neither perfect nor infinite in space or time, but it is actual, and if it is not Anselm's "Being greater than which nothing can be conceived," it is surely a being that is greater than anything any of us will ever conceive of in detail worthy of its detail. Is something sacred? Yes, say I with Nietzsche. I could not pray to it, but I can stand in affirmation of its magnificence. This world is sacred.

Notes

1. I will not devote any space [here to] cataloguing the deep flaws in creationism, or supporting my peremptory condemnation of it. I take that job to have been admirably done by others.
2. Many, many Muslims agree, and we must not only listen to them, but do what we can to protect and support them, for they are bravely trying, from the inside, to reshape the tradition they cherish into something better, something ethically defensible. *That* is—or, rather, ought to be—the message of multiculturalism, not the patronizing and subtly racist hypertolerance that "respects" vicious and ignorant

doctrines when they are propounded by officials of non-European states and religions. One might start by spreading the word about *For Rushdie* (Braziller, 1994), a collection of essays by Arab and Muslim writers, many critical of Rushdie, but all denouncing the unspeakably immoral "fatwa" death sentence proclaimed by the Ayatollah. Rushdie (1994) has drawn our attention to the 162 Iranian intellectuals who, with great courage, have signed a declaration in support of freedom of expression. Let us all distribute the danger by joining hands with them.

NO

Edward B. Davis

Debating Darwin:
The 'Intelligent Design' Movement

> "The time has come," the lawyer said,
> "To talk of many things,
> Of Gods, and gaps, and miracles,
> Of lots of missing links,
> And why we can't be Darwinists,
> And whether matter thinks."
>
> — with apologies to Lewis Carroll

In 1874, 15 years after Charles Darwin published *On the Origin of Species,* the great Princeton theologian Charles Hodge replied with his own book, *What Is Darwinism?* Darwin had proposed that natural selection, a blind, purposeless process operating through random variations, had produced the myriad forms of life that inhabit our planet. Hodge contended that this denial of design in nature "is virtually the denial of God." Hodge noted that although Darwin might personally believe in a creator who had in the distant past "called matter and a living germ into existence," Darwinism implied that God had "then abandoned the universe to itself to be controlled by chance and necessity, without any purpose on his part as to the result, or any intervention or guidance." Such a God was "virtually consigned, so far as we are concerned, to nonexistence." Thus Darwinism was "virtually atheistical."

The authors of the three books reviewed here [*Darwin's Black Box: The Biochemical Challenge to Evolution,* Michael J. Behe; *Defeating Darwinism by Opening Minds,* Phillip E. Johnson and *The Creation Hypothesis: Scientific Evidence for an Intelligent Designer,* Edited by J. P. Moreland] understand Darwinism as Hodge did, and like Hodge they believe that a God who is not involved in creation and with human beings in obvious, highly visible, scientifically detectable ways is no God at all. They seek to marshal evidence for the truth of Christian theism, based partly on the perceived deficiencies of Darwinian evolution. Although certain elements of their position may warrant further consideration, it is neither very convincing nor particularly original.

From Edward B. Davis, "Debating Darwin: The 'Intelligent Design' Movement," *The Christian Century* (July 15-22, 1998). Copyright © 1998 by The Christian Century Foundation. Reprinted by permission of *The Christian Century.*

In the century and a quarter since Hodge leveled his pen at the offending theory, many Christians have come to terms with evolution. They have done this in different ways, however. Some evolutionists who maintain belief in God, especially those who are theologically moderate or conservative such as Richard Buhe and Howard Van Till, regard science and theology as separate (though ultimately complementary) modes of knowledge. In this view, science deals with mechanism and material reality ("how"), while theology deals with meaning and spiritual reality ("why"), which are in another domain or on another level. This approach is best summed up in the famous phrase that Galileo borrowed from Cardinal Baronio: "The Bible tells how to go to heaven, not how the heavens go."

Other thinkers, including liberal Protestants such as Ian Barbour and Arthur Peacocke, employ more integrative models. They decry the intellectual schizophrenia and theological insulation of the separation model, proclaiming instead the need for a genuine conversation between theology and modern science that shapes both enterprises. But much of this conversation is dominated by one side: many leading advocates of integration are process theologians or panentheists (believing that God includes the world as a part of God's being) who call for doctrinal reformulation in light of modern scientific knowledge but do not intend to ask scientists to reformulate their theories in light of theology.

Indeed, none of these Christian evolutionists proposes what might be called a Christian *science,* one in which Christian beliefs influence the actual content of scientific theories so that the rules of science might be different for Christians than for non-Christians. Instead they represent various Christian *views of science* in which the rules of science are assumed to be the same for all scientists in a particular discipline, without regard to their religious beliefs, and with differences arising only at the level of personal worldview.

In other words, adherents of all of these views accept methodological naturalism, which claims that scientific explanations of phenomena always ought to involve natural causes—which are usually understood as mechanistic causes operating without any intelligence or purpose apparent *within the phenomena themselves.* Whether or not any intelligence or purpose has been imposed upon natural processes from the outside is a separate question that science alone is not competent to answer, although scientific knowledge may have some influence on the kinds of answers one might offer. Science is seen as religiously neutral; evidence for or against theism has to be found elsewhere.

The books under review reject the notion that methodological naturalism is religiously neutral. They also reject the idea that evolution is compatible with theism. All three books offer a highly sophisticated form of antievolutionism known as intelligent design theory (ID).

The essence of ID and the motivation behind it are clearly explained by Phillip Johnson. Theistic evolution, he argues, is a "much-too-easy solution" that "rests on a misunderstanding of what contemporary scientists mean by the word evolution." Like Cornell biologist William Provine and Cambridge biologist Richard Dawkins, Johnson defines evolution as "an unguided and mindless process" that admits no possibility of being a divine work. It implies that "our existence is therefore a fluke rather than a planned outcome."

To prevent students from being indoctrinated with this type of irreligion, Johnson offers them a primer on thinking critically about evolution and a brief account of ID. The latter is essentially the opposite of the strong biological reductionism associated with Dawkins, according to which (in Johnson's accurate description) "everything, including our minds, can be 'reduced' to its material base." For Johnson, matter is preceded both ontologically and chronologically by intelligence, in the form of the information necessary to organize it into living things, and this is "an entirely different kind of stuff from the physical medium [e.g., DNA] in which it may temporarily be recorded."

A principal goal of the ID movement is to convince scientists that information cannot and does not spring from matter, which they understand as brute and inert. This is essentially the same dualistic conception of matter that was shared by 17th-century founders of mechanistic science such as René Descartes, Robert Boyle and Isaac Newton. Although the mind-matter distinction remains philosophically problematic, and although some types of dualism may be possible to defend, most contemporary scientists (including most Christian scientists) no longer hold to this type of dualism, even if they retain the mechanistic science with which it was once linked. The same is true of many contemporary theologians, especially those committed to panentheism or process theology. They generally hold a more active view of matter and its capabilities, believing either that matter itself can think or that cognition arises out of it in some naturalistic manner yet to be determined. An important flaw in the program of the ID adherents is that they don't really confront the fact that the philosophical landscape has changed, and they fail to engage those Christian thinkers who recognize this.

Johnson bases his case substantially on Michael Behe's notion of *"irreducible* complexity"—the idea that because certain parts of living organisms are so complex, and are composed of many separate parts that cannot function properly on their own, we cannot account for them (in reductionistic fashion) as merely the products of blind selection. Rather, we are forced to invoke a deus ex machina who assembled the parts supernaturally according to a preconceived design. Johnson uses this strong form of the teleological argument to challenge both materialism and naturalism. He calls his strategy "the wedge" and sees himself opening up a crack in scientific materialism.

Behe attempts to widen that crack. A biochemist at Lehigh University, he is not a creationist in the sense in which that word is most often used. For example, he believes that the earth is billions of years old, something self-styled scientific creationists deny, and he thinks that natural selection can account for much of life's diversity, which an old-earth creationist like Johnson probably does not accept (if so, he is awfully quiet about it). What natural selection cannot explain, in Behe's opinion, is how the original building blocks of living things were formed.

Darwin's Black Box, a detailed study of certain biochemical machines in humans and other organisms, is aimed at realizing one of Darwin's worst nightmares. Darwin worried that the origin of complex organs such as the eye would

Black boxes – weaken science? Darwin's theory?
weaken

be difficult to explain in terms of the gradual, stepwise evolutionary process outlined by his theory. The best he could do was to speculate that the complex eye might have developed from simple light-sensitive cells that could give a competitive advantage to an organism that possessed them. But the molecular biology of vision, as Behe notes, was a "black box" to Darwin. Darwin and his contemporaries took the simplicity of cells for granted, treating them as black boxes that needed no further explanation.

Now that we know how complex even the simplest cells are, Behe argues, we can no longer ignore the question of how they originated, nor can we deny the lack of progress in answering that question within a Darwinian paradigm. Behe examined every issue of the *Journal of Molecular Evolution* (a top journal in the field) since it began in 1971. He could not find even one article that *"has ever proposed a detailed model by which a complex biochemical system might have been produced in a gradual, step-by-step Darwinian fashion." This lack of an explanation, Behe says, is "a very strong indication that Darwinism is an inadequate framework for understanding the origin of complex biochemical systems."

Reviewers in scientific journals are generally highly critical of Behe. But some of the critics, including biochemist James Shapiro of the University of Chicago, think that Behe has pinpointed a real problem in evolutionary theory, a problem that invites novel approaches—though not the invocation of an intelligent designer, which would mean giving up hope of a scientific (or naturalistic) solution.

Notre Dame philosopher of science Ernan McMullin argues perceptively that Behe's proposed solution is itself just another "black box," for his appeal to ID slams the door on further inquiry at the level of secondary causes, denying in principle our ability to learn how irreducibly complex structures were assembled. Van Till takes this point further, arguing that we must distinguish between the claim that the world is a product of creative intelligence (a belief he shares with the ID camp) and the additional claim, implicit in the ID position, that certain products of that intelligence could not have been assembled naturalistically.

Behe realizes that it will be difficult for most scientists to give ID fair consideration, mainly for philosophical rather than purely scientific reasons. The scientific community, he notes, is committed to methodological naturalism, which rules out a priori any appeal to design. Furthermore, "many important and well-respected scientists just don't *want* there to be anything beyond nature." It's true that many scientists regard methodological naturalism as intimately linked to the worldview of philosophical materialism. A challenge to one is a challenge to the other. But there is no necessary connection between the two positions. Many scientists (including most Christian scientists) accept methodological naturalism without extrapolating from it to philosophical materialism.

agree

Since the ID proponents reject the middle-ground position of a theist who practices methodological naturalism, their challenge will probably produce more heat than light. This likelihood is increased by the highly apologetic thrust of certain essays in *The Creation Hypothesis*, edited by Biola University philosopher J. P. Moreland. Consider, for example, the title of the essay by Canadian astrophysicist Hugh Ross, head of Reasons to Believe, a Pasadena-based ministry specializing in apologetics: "Astronomical Evidences for a Personal, Transcendent God." Or consider Moreland's own essay, "Theistic Science and Methodological Naturalism," which presents the two as competing alternatives. The latter distinction is drawn even more starkly by Johnson, who refers elsewhere to methodological naturalism as "methodological atheism" and to those Christian scientists who defend it as "mushy accommodationists."

As Moreland defines it, theistic science claims that God "has through direct, primary agent causation and indirect, secondary causation created and designed the world for a purpose and has directly intervened in the course of its development at various times," including "history prior to the arrival of human beings." Primary causes are "God's unusual way of operating; they involve his direct, discontinuous, miraculous actions," whereas "secondary causes are God's normal way of operating." Either way, Moreland stresses, "God is constantly active in the world, but his activity takes on different forms."

In spite of this clear affirmation that God is never absent or inactive in the creation (and similar statements by others), the ID program is widely viewed as being committed to a "God-of-the-gaps" theology. In such a theology (as Dietrich Bonhoeffer noted with objections) God is invoked only when natural explanations fail.

It is not accurate to say that Behe and Johnson's God is merely a God of the gaps, if by that we mean a God who has nothing else to do but occasionally fine-tune the clock-like workings of the universe. Nevertheless, their argument does rely on a God-of-the-gaps strategy. That is, they argue from the existence of gaps in our knowledge of nature to the existence of gaps in the actual processes of nature, and on the basis of these gaps they infer that there is an agent outside of nature. What makes this a sophisticated God-of-the-gaps theory, and distinguishes their project from garden variety creationism, is that they justify their appeal to divine causation by pointing not simply to the absence of plausible naturalistic explanations but to the presence of an *irreducible* complexity which suggests to them that no naturalistic explanation for the phenomenon in question *can* be found.   *Is not testable*

Pointing out the inadequacies of any received theory, including Darwinian theory, is important work. But to my mind, the most important part of the ID program is not what it denies but what it affirms, namely, that some real causes might not be purely mechanistic, and that this line of inquiry might prove productive. Some interesting and fruitful science has been done by scientists who hold such a view. Newton, for example, offered no mechanical explanation for gravitation (prompting Leibniz to call it a "perpetual miracle"). Kepler based his hypothesis about the orbital radii of the planets on the assumption that God, in laying out the solar system, used the five Platonic solids as "archetypal causes."

For ID to fit into this category of fruitful science, however, its advocates will have to spell out much more closely what an account of the origin of biological diversity based on ID would look like and show how this perspective would further scientific inquiry rather than hinder it. I remain skeptical that this will happen, but the movement is still in its infancy, and it has some very bright people associated with it. They may prove me wrong.

Thus far ID is only a highly sophisticated form of special creationism, usually accompanied by strong apologetic overtones that tend to keep the debate at the ideological level. All too frequently science becomes a weapon in culture wars, denying in practice the clean theoretical distinction between science and religion that is otherwise widely proclaimed. Provine has said that "evolution is the greatest engine of atheism ever invented." Johnson would agree, though of course he thinks the engine is faulty while Provine thinks it's true. Johnson's audience would be much smaller if scientists like Provine and Dawkins did not make it so easy for him to equate evolution and methodological naturalism with atheism, but in fact that pair does speak for a good number of scientists and other academics. Because their approach flies in the face of the beliefs of many religious Americans, antievolutionism is not likely to go away any time soon, whether or not Johnson and his associates convince many scientists to adopt their program.

⚜

We could move a long way toward correcting the excesses of both the Johnsons and the Provines if public education were more genuinely pluralistic. As long as public education essentially ignores the religious values of many families and pretends to remain neutral toward religion while actually promoting secularism, many religious people will feel disenfranchised. Johnson is at his best when he decries what he elsewhere calls "scientific fundamentalism," the tendency of scientific materialists to monopolize the conversation about science in public schools.

Johnson effectively analyzes the film version of *Inherit the Wind,* the play that depicts the Scopes trial [1925 trial of Tennessee high school teacher for teaching evolution] as the triumph of academic freedom over an ignorant, intolerant fundamentalism. Henry Drummond, whose character is loosely based on Clarence Darrow, warns Matthew Harrison Brady, the character drawn from William Jennings Bryan, not to deny others freedom of thought, and asks him to consider that there could come a time when a law would be passed "that only *Darwin* should be taught in the schools!" This, Johnson tells us, is exactly what happened:

> The real story of the Scopes trial is that the stereotype it promoted helped the Darwinists capture the power of the law, and they have since used the law to prevent other people from thinking independently. By labeling any fundamental dissent from Darwinism as "religion," they are able to ban criticism of the official evolution story from public education far more effectively than the teaching of evolution was banned from Tennessee schools in the 1920s.

Johnson wants Americans to think more critically about evolution and about tough religious questions related to it; so do I. In my opinion, the teaching of evolution should be coupled with serious discussions both of its perceived religious implications and of the various ways religious thinkers have responded to it. Public schools seem unable to undertake such highly inclusive, controversial conversations, given the prevailing interpretation of the antiestablishment clause of the First Amendment. An accomplished legal theorist, Johnson might better direct his efforts toward persuading his colleagues to reconsider their interpretation of the Constitution rather than toward criticizing the basic tenets of what remains scientifically a well-supported theory of the origin of biological diversity.

good point

I disagree
Teach all religious values? How?

what is wrong with science monopolizing conversations/classes in science?

To do otherwise means we accept that there is no distinction between what science and religion can and can not do.

science does not label all dissent from Darwinism as religion —

POSTSCRIPT

Does the Theory of Evolution Explain the Origins of Humanity?

In October 1996 Pope John Paul II announced that "new knowledge leads us to recognize that the theory of evolution is more than a hypothesis." This endorsement had little noticeable impact on the creationism-evolution debate because creationism is a thing of fundamentalist Protestant sects. The debate between creationists and evolutionists will thus go on for the foreseeable future. Nor do the creationists seem likely to grow more moderate in their demands; at the extreme, they crave to replace all of human knowledge with something more consistent with their scriptures. See Jack Hitt, "On Earth as It Is in Heaven: Field Trips With the Apostles of Creation Science," *Harper's* (November 1996).

The debate has at times turned abusive, as it did in May 1996, when biologists attempting to inform the Ohio House Education Committee of how thoroughly the evidence supports the theory of evolution were heckled, jeered, and shouted down. See Karen Schmidt, "Creationists Evolve New Strategy," *Science* (July 26, 1996). As Janet Raloff notes, in "When Science and Beliefs Collide," *Science News* (June 8, 1996), harsh reactions to scientists are not surprising, considering that nearly half the U.S. population misunderstands or rejects "many of the basic precepts and findings of science." And these reactions are not seen only in churches and before legislative committees but also at academic meetings. As Barbara Ehrenreich and Janet McIntosh note, in "The New Creationism: Biology Under Attack," *The Nation* (June 9, 1997), there is a movement among feminists, cultural anthropologists, social psychologists, and other academics, amounting to a kind of "secular creationism" that insists human beings are not shaped by their biology, unlike all other living things, and shouts down all mention of Darwin, DNA, and even science. This "new creationism . . . represents a grave misunderstanding of biology and science generally," say Ehrenreich and McIntosh, but it is not about to go away, because secular creationists do not brook contradiction of their cherished beliefs.

Stephen Jay Gould, in "The Persistently Flat Earth," *Natural History* (March 1994), makes the point that irrationality and dogmatism serve the adherents of neither science nor religion well: "The myth of a war between science and religion remains all too current and continues to impede a proper bonding and conciliation between these two utterly different and powerfully important institutions of human life."

The argument from design is well critiqued by Kenneth R. Miller in "Life's Grand Design," *Technology Review* (March 1994). Also invaluable is Ronald L. Numbers, *The Creationists: The Evolution of Scientific Creationism* (Alfred A. Knopf, 1992).

On the Internet . . .

The Worldwatch Institute

The Worldwatch Institute is dedicated to fostering the evolution of an environmentally sustainable society, one in which human needs are met in ways that
do not threaten the health of the natural environment or the prospects of future
generations.

http://www.worldwatch.org

National Oceanic and Atmospheric Administration

The mission of the National Oceanic and Atmospheric Administration (NOAA)
is to describe and predict changes in Earth's environment and to conserve
and manage wisely U.S. coastal and marine resources to ensure sustainable
economic opportunities.

http://www.noaa.gov

Global Warming

The Environmental Protection Agency maintains this site to summarize the
current state of knowledge about global warming.

http://www.epa.gov/globalwarming/

National Renewable Energy Laboratory

The National Renewable Energy Laboratory (NREL) is the leading center for
renewable energy research in the United States.

http://www.nrel.gov

The Heritage Foundation

The Heritage Foundation is a think tank whose mission is to formulate and
promote conservative public policies based on the principles of free enterprise, limited government, individual freedom, traditional American values, and
a strong national defense.

http://www.heritage.org

PART 2

The Environment

*A*s the damage that human beings do to their environment in the course of obtaining food, wood, ore, fuel, and other resources has become clear, many people have grown concerned. Some of that concern is for the environment—the landscapes and living things with which humanity shares its world. Some of that concern is more for human welfare; it focuses on the ways in which environmental damage threatens human health or even human survival.

Some environmental issues are well known. These include over-population and the prospect for an adequate future food supply, global warming, and the impact of environmentalism on individual freedoms and property rights. All have provoked extensive debate over details and degrees of certainty, over what can or should be done to prevent future difficulties, and even over whether or not the issues are real.

- Does the Growing World Population Face Future Food Shortages?

- Should Society Act Now to Halt Global Warming?

- Are Environmental Regulations Too Restrictive?

ISSUE 4

Does the Growing World Population Face Future Food Shortages?

YES: Lester R. Brown, from "Can We Raise Grain Yields Fast Enough?" *World Watch* (July/August 1997)

NO: D. Gale Johnson, from "Food Security and World Trade Prospects," *American Journal of Agricultural Economics* (December 1998)

ISSUE SUMMARY

YES: Lester R. Brown, president of the Worldwatch Institute, argues that the physical and biological barriers to continued growth in food productivity are so significant that there is a strong chance that the food supply will fall behind population growth unless the population is stabilized and soil is protected.

NO: D. Gale Johnson, the Eliakim Hastings Moore Distinguished Service Professor of Economics Emeritus at the University of Chicago, counters that world food productivity will continue to improve, the supply will continue to exceed demand, and the growing world population will not suffer from food shortages.

I n 1798 the British economist Thomas Malthus published his *Essay on the Principle of Population.* In it, he pointed with alarm at the way the human population grew geometrically (a hockey-stick curve of increase) and at how agricultural productivity grew only arithmetically (a straight-line increase). It was obvious, he said, that the population must inevitably outstrip its food supply and experience famine. Contrary to the conventional wisdom of the time, population growth was not necessarily a good thing. Indeed, it led inexorably to catastrophe. For many years, Malthus was something of a laughingstock. The doom he forecast kept receding into the future as new lands were opened to agriculture, new agricultural technologies appeared, new ways of preserving food limited the waste of spoilage, and the birth rate dropped in the industrialized nations (the "demographic transition"). The food supply kept ahead of population growth and seemed likely—to most observers—to continue to do so. Malthus's ideas were dismissed as irrelevant fantasies.

Yet overall population kept growing. In Malthus's time, there were about 1 billion human beings on Earth. By 1950—when Warren S. Thompson worried that civilization would be endangered by the rapid growth of Asian and Latin American populations during the next five decades (see "Population," *Scientific American* [February 1950])—there were a little over 2.5 billion. In 1999 the tally passed 6 billion. By 2025 it will be over 8 billion. Statistics like these presented in *World Resources 1998-99*, a report of the World Resources Institute in collaboration with the United Nations Environment and Development Programmes (Oxford University Press, 1998), are positively frightening. The Worldwatch Institute's yearly reports *State of the World* (W. W. Norton) are no less so. By 2050 the UN expects world population to be between 9 and 10 billion and to be still rising; some estimates peg the 2050 population as high as 12 billion. While global agricultural production has also increased, it has not kept up with rising demand, and—because of the loss of topsoil to erosion, the exhaustion of aquifers for irrigation water, and the high price of energy for making fertilizer (among other things)—the prospect of improvement seems to many observers exceedingly slim.

Some people are still laughing at Malthus and his forecasts of doom, which two centuries never saw come to pass. Among the scoffers are Julian Simon, a "cornucopian" economist who believes that the more people we have on Earth, the more talent we have available for solving problems, and that humans can indeed find ways around all possible resource shortages. See his essay "Life on Earth Is Getting Better, Not Worse," *The Futurist* (August 1983).

But more and more people—including some economists—are coming to realize that Malthus's error lay not in his prediction but in his timing. He was quite correct to say that a growing population must inevitably outrun its food supply. The only question is how long human ingenuity can stave off the day of reckoning.

Can population really go as high as many predict? If it does, can the world possibly feed that many people? There are famines in the world today. Won't they grow far, far worse long before we approach the 10 billion mark in 2050? Paul R. Ehrlich and Anne H. Ehrlich, in "Ehrlich's Fables," *Technology Review* (January 1997), write that "a new kit of tools to expand food production is required to carry us into the future, yet no such kit appears to be on the horizon."

In the following selections, Lester R. Brown shares the Ehrlichs' concern. He sees physical and biological barriers to ensuring an adequate food supply in population growth, loss of cropland to other uses, loss of irrigation water, and limits to how much crop yields can be increased even with fertilizer and selective breeding. D. Gale Johnson argues that for the next quarter century, "all the broad trends point to an improvement in world food security and a reduction in the number of persons adversely affected by both long-term or short-term inadequate access to food."

 **YES**

Can We Raise Grain Yields Fast Enough?

After a half-century of global surpluses of wheat, rice, corn, and other grains, it is easy to be complacent about the food prospect for the twenty-first century. We have come to take for granted the supply of grain that provides half of humanity's food energy when consumed directly and a good portion of the remainder when consumed indirectly in the form of livestock products.

But this complacency can be dangerous. Each year, as population continues to expand, the world's farmers must stretch their production capacity to feed an additional 80 million people. Beyond that, they must now satisfy the needs generated by record rises in affluence. As people make more money, they consume more beef, pork, poultry, milk, eggs, beer, and other grain-intensive products. A kilogram of pork, for example, may require four kilograms of grain to produce, so as people are able to afford more pork their demand for grain increases. And Third World incomes are now rising at record rates. In Asia, where more than half the world's people live, incomes are rising faster than they have on any continent at any time in history. This combination of more people and more consumption per person is putting heavy pressure on the land.

The world's farmers responded heroically to past increases in demand, nearly tripling the grain harvest from 630 million tons in 1950 to 1.8 billion tons in 1990. Most of this expansion came not from plowing a lot more land, but from more than doubling the amount of grain produced on existing farmland. Between 1950 and 1990, the yield per hectare grew at 2.1 percent per year. Augmented by whatever new land could be added to grain production, including that from expanded irrigation in arid regions, this boosted total grain production by an average of nearly 3 percent a year throughout that four-decade run—well ahead of population growth.

Although there were disastrous shortages from time to time during this period—in China, Ethiopia, and Somalia, for example—and although some 800 million people are still hungry and malnourished, *overall* supply has not been a major issue. In the United States, the government paid farmers not to plant part of their land. The steady growth in the harvest, and resultant decline in grain prices, created a psychology of surpluses—a psychology that has made it easy for policymakers both to put off the difficult task of stabilizing human population and to take their farmers' capacities to meet future challenges for granted.

The world's total demand for food is likely to nearly double its present level by 2030, and there is little new land available to plow. The key to food security in the years ahead, then, is whether farmers can continue to rapidly raise the productivity of their land, as they have done in the past. However, assessments of the potential for raising land productivity vary widely. In a recent World Bank report, researchers indicated that they expect grain yields to increase at 1.5 to 1.7 percent per year, or "at rates comparable to those in recent years...." With this rosy outlook, the Bank projects a surplus capacity in world agriculture as a whole, accompanied by declining food prices. This Worldwatch Institute analysis comes to a very different conclusion.

The World Bank economists base their projections on simple extrapolation, arguing that "historically, yields have grown along a linear path from 1960 to 1990, and they are projected to continue along the path of past growth." Although extrapolating past yield trends worked well enough in previous decades, it won't work in a world where the yields simply are not continuing to climb rapidly. In contrast to the robust increases of 2.1 percent per year between 1950 and 1990, the rise between 1990 and 1995 averaged only 1 percent a year. Although this period is too short to establish a clear trend, it may offer a strong indication of what the future holds.

Reliance on the World Bank projections by governments is leading to underinvestment in both agriculture and family planning. Funding for agricultural research is being cut by many governments, including that of the United States. At the international level, a striking example is the fate of the Philippines-based International Rice Research Institute (IRRI), which gave Asia the high-yielding rices. In 1996, several donor governments, facing cutbacks in their aid budgets, cut their general support funding of IRRI, the world's premier rice research institute, forcing a heavy cutback in core staff. Similarly, in 1996 the U.S. Congress voted to cut fiscal year 1997 funding of international family planning assistance by 60 percent from 1995 levels, with little consideration of how this would affect the increasingly precarious balance between population and food supply. Fortunately, the new congress voted in early 1997 to restore part of the funding.

The Bank projections breed complacency, not urgency. They permit governments to treat prime cropland like a surplus commodity—one that can be paved over, built on, or otherwise frittered away with impunity. One result can be seen in California's Central Valley, where housing projects are marching up the valley unimpeded, consuming some of the world's finest farmland. In China, this process is taking place on an even larger scale, as the government paves over millions of hectares of cropland so the bicycle can be replaced with the automobile. And in Indonesia, fertile riceland is being converted to golf courses.

The central question now is whether farmers can restore the rapid rise in land productivity. Moreover, that question needs to be addressed in terms that point to realistic possibilities for farmers working under the natural constraints of their own environments—the availability of sunlight, water, and good soil.

Rather than analyzing yields on experimental plots or those achieved by the best farmers, this analysis will assess the long-term yield potential under field conditions by individual countries.

The Century of Soaring Productivity

The first recorded case in which a country's farmers achieved a sharp increase in output per unit of land—a "yield takeoff"—began more than a century ago in Japan. In 1878, Japanese rice farmers got an average of 1.4 tons of grain per hectare. By 1984, the average yield had more than tripled, to 4.7 tons. Since then, it has plateaued—fluctuating between 4.3 and 4.6 tons in all but three years.... Despite the fact that Japan supports the price paid to its farmers for rice at four times the world level, thereby offering a powerful financial incentive to raise yields higher—and despite its ability to provide the best technology available—it has been unable to improve average yields for more than a decade.

In the United States, the first yield takeoff came more than a half century later, with wheat. During the nearly 80 years between the Civil War and World War II, U.S. wheat yields had fluctuated around 0.9 tons per hectare. As World War II got underway, and demand for U.S. grain rose as production was disrupted abroad, farmers began investing in higher-yielding seeds and in fertilizer. By 1983, yields had climbed to 2.65 tons per hectare, nearly tripling the traditional level. Since then, however, there has been no further rise. Although the wheat yield takeoff in the United States began decades after that of rice in Japan, farmers in the two countries appear to have "hit the wall" at about the same time. Two questions arise: Can scientists restore the historical growth in yields, or does this plateauing in two of the most agriculturally advanced countries signal a future leveling off in other countries, as farmers exhaust the principal means of increasing yields?

The Factors That Increase Yields

The 2.5-fold increase in world grain land productivity since 1950 has come from three sources: genetic advances, agronomic improvements, and some synergies between the two.

On the genetic front, most growth has come from redistributing the share of the plant's photosynthetic product (photosynthate) going to the various plant parts (leaves, stems, roots, and seeds) so that a much larger share goes to the seed—the part we use for food. On the agronomic front (where farmers' practices weigh heavily), advances that help plants realize their full genetic potential include the use of fertilizer, irrigation, the control of plant diseases and predatory insects, and the eradication of weeds.

Scientists estimate that the originally domesticated wheats devoted roughly 20 percent of their photosynthate to the development of seeds; they were stalk-heavy, harvest-light. Through plant breeding, it has been possible to raise the share of photosynthate going into seed—the "harvest index"—in today's high-yielding grain to some 50 to 55 percent. Given the plant's basic requirements of an adequate root system, a strong stem, and sufficient leaves for photosynthesis, scientists believe the physiological limit is around 60 percent.

One of the earliest gains in this area came in the late nineteenth century, when Japanese scientists incorporated a dwarf gene into both rice and wheat plants. Traditional varieties of these grasses were tall and thin, because their ancestors growing in the wild needed to compete with other plants for sunlight. But once farmers began controlling weeds among the domesticated plants, there was no longer a need for tall varieties. As plant breeders shortened both wheat and rice plants, reducing the length of their straw, they also lowered the share of photosynthate going into the straw and increased that going into seed. I. T. Evans, a prominent Australian soil scientist and plant physiologist who has long studied cereal yield gains and potentials, notes that in the high-yielding dwarf wheats, "the gain in grain yield approximately equals the loss in straw weight."

With corn, similarly, varieties grown in the tropics were reduced in height from an average of nearly three meters to less than two. But Don Duvick, for many years the director of research at the Pioneer Hybrid seed company, observes that with the hybrids used in the U.S. corn belt, the key to higher yields is the ability of varieties to "withstand the stress of higher plant densities while still making the same amount of grain per plant." One of the keys to growing more plants per hectare is to replace the horizontally inclined leaves of traditional strains that droop somewhat with more upright leaves, thereby reducing the amount of self-shading.

But while breeders can manipulate the distribution of photosynthate within the plant, the amount produced by a given leaf area remains unchanged from that of the plant's wild ancestors. Although plant breeders have greatly increased the share of the photosynthate going to the seed of the various grains, they have not been able to alter the basic process of photosynthesis itself.

On the agronomic front, the principal means of increasing land productivity have been to expand irrigation, use more fertilizer, and to more effectively control diseases, insects, and weeds. All of these tactics help plants reach more of their full genetic yield potential. Between 1950 and 1990, the amount of irrigated land in the world increased from 94 million to 240 million hectares, or 2.4 percent per year. Between 1990 and 1994, however, the official data show irrigated area increasing by only another 9 million hectares, or 0.9 percent per year. And because governments do not always report the land taken out of irrigation, some analysts doubt that there has been any net growth in irrigated area at all since 1990.

In the United States and China, the world's two largest grain producers, losses are all too visible—and in some instances perhaps irreversible. Texas, a major farming state that has historically relied heavily on irrigation, has lost 14 percent of its irrigated area since 1980 as a result of aquifer depletion. California, Kansas, and Oklahoma, too, are losing irrigation water. In China's Hebei Province, irrigation water is being diverted to cities to satisfy mushrooming urban and industrial demands for water. In the agricultural region around Beijing, farmers have not been allowed to draw water from the reservoirs since 1994, because all the region's water is now needed to satisfy the capital city's growing thirst.

David Seckler, head of the International Irrigation Management Institute in Sri Lanka, believes that world irrigated area actually may have started to shrink. If the future brings little or no growth in irrigated area, the world will have lost a major source of rising land productivity, since the expansion of irrigation also greatly expands the potential for using fertilizer.

Fertilizer helps to ensure that plant growth won't be inhibited by any lack of nutrients. With a ten-fold rise in fertilizer use, from 14 million tons in 1950 to some 140 million in 1990, this has been by far the most important agronomic source of higher land productivity since mid-century. But in the 1990s, use of fertilizer—like that of irrigation—has leveled off in many countries. U.S. farmers, after discovering that there are optimal levels beyond which further applications aren't cost-effective, are using less fertilizer in the mid-1990s than they were in the early 1980s. The leveling off in the United States has been followed by a similar trend in Western Europe and Japan. In the former Soviet Union, fertilizer use fell precipitously after subsidies were removed in 1988 and fertilizer prices climbed to world market levels.

Other agronomic contributions to higher cropland productivity include the more timely planting of crops made possible by mechanization and higher plant populations per hectare, the latter applying particularly to corn. More timely planting boosts yields because in the temperate zones there is typically a brief window of time for seeding, usually measured in days, when optimum yields can be obtained. If planting is delayed, then yields decline with each day of delay.

Advances in plant breeding and agronomy often reinforce each other. The dwarfing of wheat and rice plants not only reduced the amount of photosynthate that went for straw, for instance, but increased the benefit of adding more fertilizer. For example, the traditional tall, thin-strawed wheat varieties grown in India could effectively use only about 40 kilograms of nitrogen per hectare. Applications above that made the plants grow heavier heads of grain, but these would often "lodge," or fall over (especially in storms), leading to crop losses. With the dwarf varieties, however, farmers could boost nitrogen applications up to 120 kilograms per hectare or more, thus greatly increasing the yield, but with little fear of lodging. This synergy between genetics and agronomics helps to explain the doubling or tripling of yields achieved with the first generation of high-yielding wheats and rices that were at the heart of the Green Revolution.

With corn, the greater tolerance for crowding enabled growers to greatly increase the plant population—and hence the number of ears harvested—per hectare. At the same time, herbicides were being developed that would control weeds, eliminating the traditional need to plant corn rows far enough apart to permit mechanical cultivators to pass through the field during the earlier part of the growing season. As a result of these two advances, plant populations have climbed. In Iowa, for example, corn plant densities have nearly tripled since 1930.

For each of the three major grains—wheat, rice, and corn—the major worldwide gains in productivity took place between 1950 and 1990. Since 1990, gains have been much smaller, and the question now facing planners is just how much more can be expected. . . .

Facing Biological Reality

For individual grains in individual countries, the historic trends show a sobering pattern. In every farming environment, where yields are increased substantially, there comes a time when the increase slows and either levels off or shows signs of doing so. It is equally revealing to look at the global trends. In doing so, we use three-year averages for the decennial or mid-decennial years in order to minimize the effects of weather variations. For example, the yield shown for 1990 is an average of the yield from 1989–91 and that for 1995 is the average for 1994–96.

During the four decades from 1950 to 1990, the world's grain farmers raised the productivity of their land by an unprecedented 2.1 percent per year, but since 1990, there has been a dramatic loss of momentum in this rise. If the former Soviet Union is excluded from the global data for 1990 to 1995, because of the uncharacteristic drop in yields associated with economic reforms and the breakup of the country into its constituent republics, then the rate of yield gain is not . . . 0.7 percent per year . . . but 1.1 percent—roughly half that of the preceding 40 years. And while the first half of the 1990s is too short a period to determine a new trend, it does provide a reason for concern. In addition to the plateauing of wheat yields in the United States and Mexico, . . . those in Canada and Egypt have shown no improvement so far in the 1990s.

Global trends for the three major individual grains, moreover, follow the pattern seen for grain as a whole. Rice production, which was modernized later than wheat and corn, achieved an annual increase in productivity of 2.1 percent per year between 1960 and 1990, but has dropped to 1.0 percent per year since 1990. Wheat yields grew between 1960 and 1990 at an average of 2.6 percent per year, then slowed to 0.1 percent during the 1990s. (If the former Soviet Union is excluded from the global trend after 1990, wheat yields increase by 1.0 percent.) Corn averaged 2.6 percent from 1950 to 1980, then fell to 1.3 percent in the 1980s. The rise in corn yields accelerated slightly during the first half of the 1990s, reaching 1.7 percent, largely because of a belated surge in yields in both China and Brazil.

With this slower rise in grainland productivity thus far during the 1990s, the obvious next question is whether the momentum can be regained through biotechnology. Yet, on that front too, progress is not promising. After two decades of research, biotechnologists have not yet produced a single, high-yielding variety of wheat, rice, or corn. Why haven't some of the leading seed companies put their biotechnologists to work to develop a second generation of varieties that would again double or triple yields, enabling farmers to sustain a rapid rise?

The answer, say plant scientists, is that plant breeders using traditional techniques have largely exploited the genetic potential for increasing the share of photosynthate that goes into seed. Once this share is pushed to its limit, the remaining options tend to be relatively small, clustering around efforts to raise the plant's tolerance of various stresses, such as drought or soil salinity. The one major option left to scientists is to increase the efficiency of the process of photosynthesis itself—something that has thus far remained beyond their reach.

Once plant breeders have pushed genetic yield potential close to the physiological limit, then further advances rely on the expanded use of basic inputs such as the fertilizer and irrigation needed to realize the plant's full genetic potential, or on the fine-tuning of other agronomic practices such as the use of optimum planting densities or more effective pest controls. Beyond this, there will eventually come a point in each country, with each grain, when farmers will not be able to raise yields any further.

U.S. Department of Agriculture plant scientist Thomas R. Sinclair observes that advances in plant physiology now enable scientists to quantify crop yield potentials quite precisely. He notes that "except for a few options, which allow small increases in the yield ceiling, the physiological limit to crop yields may well have been reached under experimental conditions." This means that in those situations where farmers are using the highest yielding varieties that plant breeders can provide, and the agronomic inputs and practices needed to realize their genetic potential, there may be few options left for raising land productivity.

Viewed broadly, one can begin to see an S-shaped growth curve emerging for the historical rise in world grainland productivity. Throughout most of human history, land productivity was static. Then, beginning around 1880, Japan began to raise its rice yield per hectare in a steady, sustained fashion. By the mid-1950s, nearly all the industrial countries were expanding their grain harvest by raising grainland productivity. And by 1970, they had been joined by nearly all the leading grain producers in the developing world.

For the 15 years from 1970 to 1985, yields rose in a steady, sustained fashion in virtually all the grain-producing countries of any size. Then this unique period came to an end, as wheat yields in the United States and Mexico and rice yields in Japan leveled off. If these countries cannot restore the rise in yields and if, as now seems likely, more countries "hit the wall" in the years immediately ahead, it will further slow the rise in world grainland productivity, dropping it well below growth in the world demand for grain.

Eight Observations

Except for the general warning by biologists that grain yields would eventually plateau, there does not seem to be any record of specific warnings in the early 1980s that the long rise of rice yields in Japan, or the shorter term rise of wheat yields in the United States or Mexico, were about to level off. Nor is anyone likely to anticipate precisely when, for example, wheat yields will level off in France or China, though this could occur at any time. A review of the last half-century's experience in raising yields does, however, offer certain generalizations.

One, the slower rise in grain yields since 1990 is not the result of something peculiar to individual grains or to individual countries, but rather reflects a systemic difficulty in sustaining the gains that characterized the preceding four decades.

Two, every country that initiated a yield takeoff was able to sustain it for at least a few decades.

Three, most countries that have achieved a yield takeoff have managed at least to double, if not triple or even quadruple, their traditional grain yields. Among those that have quadrupled traditional levels are the United States and China with corn; France, the United Kingdom, and Mexico with wheat; and China with rice.

Four, once plant breeders have essentially exhausted the possibilities for raising the genetic yield potential and farmers are using the most advanced agronomic practices, including irrigation, the yield potential for any particular grain in a given country is determined largely by the physical environment of the country—most importantly by soil moisture, but also by temperature, day length, and solar intensity. These factors are fundamentally unalterable.

Five, all countries are drawing on a common backlog of unused agricultural technology that is gradually diminishing and, for some crops in some countries—such as wheat in the United States and rice in Japan—that has largely disappeared.

Six, as a general matter, the more recently a country has launched a yield takeoff, the faster its yields rise and the shorter the time between yield takeoff and level-off.

Seven, despite the slower rise in yields worldwide in recent years and the plateauing of yields in a few countries, there are still many opportunities for raising grainland productivity in most countries. These are most promising in those countries where there is room for improvement in economic policies affecting agriculture. Although most governments subsidize agriculture, some still have economic policies that discourage investment in agriculture. In these countries, the key to realizing the full genetic yield potential of crops is the restructuring of economic policies to encourage investment in agriculture, such as that now underway in Argentina.

Eight, even with a concerted worldwide effort to increase grain yields, the rise during the last half of this decade could slow still further, dropping below 1 percent per year—far below the 2.1 percent that sustained the world from 1950 to 1990.

Responding to the Challenge

This slowdown comes at a time when population growth and rising affluence are combining to drive up the demand for grain at a near-record pace. Even as the rate of world population growth edges down, the absolute number of people on the planet is projected to climb by some 80 million people per year well into the next century. Meanwhile, record numbers of people are shifting to diets rich in grain-intensive livestock products, which means that in some countries per-capita grain consumption is growing even faster than population is.

The resulting disparity between projected growth in demand and supply cannot, of course, exist in the real world. Prices will rise. That won't greatly hurt the affluent, who spend only a small portion of their income for food. But for the world's poor, particularly the 1.3 billion people who live on $1 per day or less, higher grain prices could quickly become life-threatening. Heads of households who cannot afford enough food to keep their families alive may well hold their governments responsible and take to the streets. The result could be unprecedented political instability in Third World cities.

If widespread political instability does materialize, it could affect the earnings of transnational corporations, the performance of stock markets, the earnings of pension funds, and even the stability of the international monetary system. As rising food prices threaten political stability and economic progress in a world economy more integrated than ever before, the problem of the world's poor becomes everyone's problem.

Among other things, the slower rise in world grainland productivity calls for an urgent assessment of the carrying capacity of land and water resources in countries everywhere, but particularly in the low-income countries where they are using all their available land and where the demand for water already exceeds the sustainable yield of aquifers.

In a world where land productivity is rising more slowly, the food security of the next generation depends on quickly slowing population growth. This begins with public education programs on the consequences of continuing rapid increases in population. It means filling the family planning gap by getting family planning services to those women who need them. And it means investing heavily in the education of young females in the Third World to accelerate the shift to smaller families.

Future food security also depends on a sharp increase in investment in agricultural research and in better grain storage facilities. It means boosting the efficiency of water use, largely by moving to water markets. And it means taking strong steps to protect cropland from conversion to nonfarm uses.

To mobilize on all these fronts, political leaders need to know that the rise in cropland productivity is slowing and that the growth in the grain harvest is falling behind the growth of demand. If the foregoing analysis is at all close to the mark, it would be irresponsible for the World Bank not to revise its outmoded supply and demand projections. Otherwise, its projection of surplus capacity and falling grain prices will only reinforce the prevailing complacency, and lead to potentially tragic underinvestment in both food production and population stabilization.

NO

D. Gale Johnson

Food Security and World Trade Prospects

Food security depends on available world supplies of food, the income of the designated population, and the population's access to the available supplies. Consequently, though seldom recognized in national food security policies, there is a direct relationship between food security, world trade in food, and the domestic policies that govern access to international markets for food. On all three scores, I believe we can be optimistic about improvements in world food security over the next quarter century.

Over the next quarter century, the world's supply of food will grow somewhat more rapidly than will the demand for it, leading to lower real prices of food. Thus, the trend of food prices, as measured by grain prices, is likely to continue the trend of the current century, though at a slower rate of decline.[1] The remarkable reduction in the international price of grain that has occurred in [the twentieth] century is given all too little emphasis in discussions of the world food situation, certainly so in the discussions of the food pessimists.

I am confident that the real per capita incomes of the majority of the population in the developing countries will continue to increase, contributing to an improvement in food security. Finally, I believe that, with the changes in agricultural policies in the major industrial countries, world trade in farm products, especially grains, will be further liberalized in the future. In addition, more and more developing countries are reducing barriers to trade, thus increasing access to world food supplies. Thus, all the broad trends point to an improvement in world food security and a reduction in the number of persons adversely affected by both long-term or short-term inadequate access to food.

This does not mean that in every country food security will improve. Some governments may continue to follow national and trade policies related to food that restrict domestic food production, limit the growth of per capita incomes, and restrict access to the available world food supplies. When this happens, food security and adequacy will not be improved or not improved as much as they potentially could be. At this time, there can be little doubt that the poor performance of agriculture and the insecurity of food supplies in sub-Saharan Africa over the past quarter century have been due primarily to inappropriate policies—to policies that discriminated against agriculture and

From D. Gale Johnson, "Food Security and World Trade Prospects," *American Journal of Agricultural Economics*, vol. 80, no. 5 (1998). Copyright © 1998 by The American Agricultural Economics Association. Reprinted by permission of The American Agricultural Economics Association; permission conveyed through Copyright Clearance Center, Inc. Some notes omitted.

resulted in large-scale governmental interventions in international trade. Mis-government plus civil and ethnic wars have exacted and continue to exact a heavy toll on the people of Africa.

There are those who argue that Africa's agricultural problems stem from the low and declining real prices of their major exportable products. But even a casual analysis indicates that the prices of agricultural exports from the region declined no more, in real terms, than did the prices of wheat, corn, and rice. Until policies are changed—and they are changing in a number of countries —and peace prevails, there will be little improvement in food security in this region of the world. When policies are inappropriate, farmers find themselves at an enormous disadvantage in making effective use of their natural and human resources.

A Brief Look at the Past

Before looking to the future, let us briefly look at the developments in world food supplies during the last half of the twentieth century. During these years, there has been more improvement in the available supplies of food for the world and in the developing countries than in all of previous human history. Much of the improvement occurred after 1960. Between 1960 and 1990, the per capita caloric supplies in the developing countries increased by 27%, reaching an average of 2,473 in 1988–90 (FAO). The improvement in per capita caloric supplies occurred while population growth was at the highest rate ever recorded and while the real prices of grains in international markets declined by approximately 40% from their levels in the late 1950s. Was it not quite remarkable that per capita food supplies in the developing countries reached their historic peak while grain prices fell to their lowest level in the twentieth century and while population was growing rapidly? This certainly does not support the view that supply lagged behind demand.

What brought about this remarkable development? Basically, it was the application of modern biological and chemical sciences to agriculture, first in the developed countries and, with a lag, in the developing countries. I doubt if there are many who know that, during the last half of the 1930s, the grain yields per hectare were the same in developing and developed countries at 1.15 tons per hectare—world yields are now nearly 2.5 times that amount (FAO). A yield differential soon emerged between the developed and developing countries, reaching 59% in 1961–65 but declining to 29% in 1990–92. I believe that it is reasonable to assume that the differential will narrow even further in the future.

Success Goes Unrecognized

It is perhaps useful to pause at this time to ask why it was that, during a period with such positive developments, there were repeated claims that the growth of demand for food was outpacing the growth of supply. True, since 1960 there have been three price spikes—in 1972–74, 1979–81, and 1995–96. The spikes lasted no more than two or three years and did not interrupt the long-term decline in real grain prices. Yet throughout this period, doom and gloom made the headlines—Lester Brown's repeated and erroneous predictions, Paul Ehrlich's claim that there would be mass starvation in the world in the 1970s, and the Club of Rome's prophecies of doom—to name a few of the doomsayers.

It is quite remarkable that, in 1994, researchers at three international agencies—the Food and Agriculture Organization, the International Food Policy Research Institute (Islam), and the World Bank (Bos et al.)—independently published studies of prospective trends in food demand and supply and came to the same conclusion. This conclusion was that the world food situation would continue to improve over the next two or so decades and that world grain prices would continue to decline (Islam). Yet these three competent studies received hardly any notice in the world's press while claims by Lester Brown that the world faced food shortages were widely reported, and even greater attention was given to his fanciful paper "Will China Starve the World?" What does this prove? A promising view of the future is not news, but a pessimistic view or prediction of a calamity is news. Bad news sells; good news doesn't.

Prospective Growth of Food Supply and Demand

It is difficult to believe that, given the record of the last four or five decades, there should be significant doubt about the world's ability to expand the supply of food more rapidly than the growth of demand over the next quarter century. Some argue that the rate of growth of food supply in the future will be slower than in the recent past—and they will be right. The rate of demand growth over the next three decades will be substantially less than between 1960 and 1990. True, real per capita incomes are anticipated to increase, and this will increase the per capita demand for food, especially through the shift toward livestock products. However, the big shifter of total demand for food is population growth. While you wouldn't believe it from what you read in the press, the rate of growth of population has slowed down, not by a little but by a lot. No country in Europe except Albania is now reproducing its population, and a considerable number of developing countries now have fertility rates below the replacement level as well—South Korea, Taiwan, Singapore, Hong Kong—and Turkey, Sri Lanka, and China have reached or are approaching that level.

The consensus estimate of the three major studies referred to above is that the annual growth in grain use (as a proxy for total food use) for 1990 to 2010 is projected at 1.5%–1.7% (Islam, p. 86). This compares with a growth of 2.46% for 1960–90 and represents a 30%–40% decrease in the rate of growth of world grain use. This is a very large decline.

The projections for 1990 to 2010 of an annual increase in grain production and use can be moved ahead for a further decade. The 1.5%–1.7% projected annual increase in grain production and consumption was based on a projected population growth rate of 1.5% annually. The population projections that Islam used have already been reduced from an annual rate of 1.5% to 1.385%. For 2010 to 2020, the projected annual rate of population growth is now about 1.1%. If the population projections hold true, the growth of per capita consumption in developing countries would be greater than projected in these studies or, more likely, the growth in world demand will be lower than projected.

Nonetheless, let us return to the original studies, accepting their data as then known. Their projections imply no increase in world per capita production and consumption of grain. How can this be? Does this bear out the predictions of the food pessimists? How can world per capita use or production of grain remain constant if the developing countries have income growth and increase their demand for grain both for direct consumption and indirect consumption through livestock products? Hopefully, this is exactly what will occur, and per capita grain use in developing countries will increase over the next quarter century as has been the case over the last half century. Assuming that per capita grain production and use in the developed countries remains constant or increases slightly, why was there not a projected increase in world per capita production or consumption? The reason is that the world per capita figures are almost meaningless in interpreting the changes in production, consumption, or income. The statement that the world's per capita production of grain is declining contains almost no useful information concerning consumption levels in either developing or developed countries.

The world per capita figure holds little meaning because, over time, it is based on shifting weights—the relative importance of the developing countries in world population has increased and is increasing. Since the developing countries have much lower per capita consumption than the developed countries, when they increase their per capita consumption, the world average may be unchanged or actually decline. For example, in the FAO grain production projections for 1990–92 to 2010, world per capita production is constant at 326 kilograms (Islam, p. 27). However, per capita production in both developed and developing countries was projected to increase—by 7% and 4%, respectively. This seeming anomaly resulted from the projected increase in the percentage of the world's population in the developing countries—from 77% in 1990 to 80.7% in 2010. Since per capita grain production in the developing countries in 1990–92 was 214 kilograms versus 692 kilograms in the developed countries, an increase in the relative weight of the developing countries had to have an adverse effect on the world average. The world average, by itself, tells little or nothing about what has occurred in individual regions or income groups when the relative importance of the units is included in the average change.

Much has been made of the decline in the rate of growth of world grain production and yields since 1990. This concern is largely misplaced. Much of the slowdown has been concentrated in Central and Eastern Europe and has occurred without the slightest negative impact on the supply of grain in the rest of the world. In fact, the demand for grain in that region has fallen by more than supply and the import of grain by the countries in the region has declined substantially—by approximately 30 million tons annually since the late 1980s. If the region had maintained grain production at the 1985–89 level, world grain production in 1996 would have been more than 100 million tons greater than it was. It would have increased by 11% compared to 1990 and at a compound annual rate of 1.8%. This is roughly the same as the annual rate of grain output growth during the 1980s, though at a slower rate than for 1960–90, but still faster than the less than 1.5% rate of world population growth for the 1990s (FAO).

Thus, it is not obvious that there has been a significant decline in the rate of growth of world grain production during the 1990s if we account for the drastic adjustments taking place in Central and Eastern Europe resulting from the difficulties of moving from a planned to a market economy. I believe that the territory of the former Soviet Union will emerge as a major grain exporter, though admittedly at a later date than I earlier believed (Johnson 1993). This possibility should be factored into long term projections of the world's supply potential as well as into the trade picture.

Why is it that many believe some reduction in the growth of food output would represent disaster? Given the demand conditions that are likely to prevail, it would be a disaster for the world's farmers if world output grew at the 1960–90 rate. Why is it that the literature on world food supply and demand seldom, if ever, mentions the effects of various outcomes on the welfare of farmers? If I were an agricultural policy maker in a developing country, I would give as much emphasis to the problems associated with low food prices as to food scarcity and high prices over the next quarter century. I believe that grain prices in the early 1990s were at such low levels that they discouraged expansion of grain production during the first half of the decade. Grain inventories declined, but this was a reasonable economic response to low and possibly falling prices. The 1995 and 1996 increases in grain prices were very short lived, with U.S. export prices of wheat and corn returning to the early 1990 prices by the end of 1997.

Price Variability May Increase

Policy developments now underway in the world have both positive and negative effects on price stability in world markets. The governments that have held large stocks of grain have discovered that holding grain stocks is very expensive, and they now have little or no interest in having stocks large enough to play a stabilizing role for world prices. Of course, in the past, the large stocks that had been held did not always restrain the price rises, as was true in 1972–74 because of policy errors made in pricing the grain sold to the USSR by the United States and Canada. On the other hand, there has been the liberalization of international trade in grain that will add a degree of stability to world grain prices. As I argued at the time, the steep increases in world grain prices in 1972–74 did not arise because of any serious shortfall in world grain production but was due to the policies followed by nearly all major exporters to protect their domestic consumers from the large increase in world grain prices (Johnson 1975). The European Community (EC), for example, taxed wheat exports in order to stabilize domestic prices. Both Canada and Australia restricted grain exports and held domestic prices significantly below world prices. Of the major exporters, only the United States permitted its domestic prices to reflect the world market prices and actually sharply increased its grain exports, at the expense of domestic use. This kind of intervention in grain markets is now much less likely than in the 1970s or 1980s, though one may note that, in 1995, the EU once again introduced an export tax on wheat and held domestic prices below world prices. The United States eliminated its export subsidies but at least let its prices equal the world market prices.

If there were (relatively) free trade in grains, world grain prices would be more stable than they are with current policies. Most governmental interventions that affect imports and exports add to price instability in world markets. The exception was when Canada and the United States held very large stocks and were willing to add to or release stocks when world prices moved outside a narrow range. All other policies that result in a difference between domestic and world prices act to destabilize international market prices. In spite of the liberalization of trade that has occurred, there is still some distance to go before the total world supply of a product is available to all at essentially the same price, after adjustment for quality and location.

Prospects for Trade

I find it difficult to say anything about the future of international trade in agricultural products, especially grain. Trade is a residual—for each country, it is the difference between production and consumption. Trade in grain has varied relatively little from an annual average of about 200 to 240 million tons since 1980. Researchers at IFPRI (Pinstrup-Andersen, Pandya-Lorch, and Rosegrant) project an increase in grain imports in the developing countries from approximately 95 million tons in 1993 to about 225 million tons in 2020. This conclusion rests on the expectation that grain imports will increase significantly in developing countries, especially in sub-Saharan Africa, South Asia, Latin America, and China.

Will world grain trade break out of its doldrums and increase by 50% over the next quarter century? I am not so sure. Except for sub-Saharan Africa, there is a significant possibility that the other developing areas will not markedly increase grain imports. Agricultural production growth in much of Latin America has been held back in recent years by overvalued currencies, which have taxed exports and encouraged imports, and high interest rates. The overvalued currencies will not go on forever, and when they are more realistically valued—due in part to a decline in the inflow of foreign capital—then agriculture will face a more encouraging economic environment and output may once again grow at rates that are at least as great as the growth in demand. While there are responsible researchers who believe that China may import 30 to 40 million tons of grain by 2020, I have my doubts. There is considerable potential for further increases in grain yields in China. The current official estimates of grain yields are too high by at least a third. The reason for this is that the grain-sown area is seriously underestimated—the total area of cropland is a third or more greater than is now officially recognized. If the output figure is approximately correct and it is divided by an underestimate of the grain-sown area, yields are significantly overestimated. The Chinese government knows of the underestimate of cropland and presumably will correct its data in the not too distant future, perhaps even in this century!

It needs to be recognized that the growth rate of China's population over the period from 1995 to 2025 is projected to be 23% (Bos et al.), only a little more than a third of the 66% increase in population between 1965 and 1995. It should be remembered that China was a substantial net importer of grain in 1979–84 and a net exporter from 1992–94. While it imported almost 19 million tons of grain in 1995, that year turned out to have a bumper crop and the importation was probably unnecessary and ended up as an addition to stocks and not to consumption. In 1997, China once again became a small net exporter of grain. Consequently, if China met the large increase in demand that occurred between 1979 and 1995, it is highly likely it will be able to meet the much smaller increase in demand over the next thirty years.[2]

I have recently returned from China, where, in May, the government introduced a price support policy designed to increase the real price of grain. The government of China is now concerned about the effects of having too much grain rather than too little. It fears that, if market prices are permitted to go too low, farmers will reduce future grain output, resulting in higher prices at some future date. The plan for grain output for 2000 was 500 million tons; this level was exceeded in 1996. China has huge grain stocks and, if it is successful in increasing the market prices of grain by 20%–30%, it will have even larger stocks. Thus, instead of China being an important importer of grain as the 20th Century ends, it is likely that it will be a net exporter.

During a period of rapid population growth—greater than 2% annually —India has achieved self-sufficiency in grain production over the past three decades. India's population growth rate is projected to decline to 1% annually by 2020. Even with rising incomes due to economic reforms, if realized, for cultural reasons, India is not likely to greatly expand its consumption of meat. The increase in demand for grain will come primarily from direct human consumption. The rate of increase in grain use will only slightly exceed the rate of population growth.

There exists a degree of pessimism about the ability to increase yields, especially of rice, in South Asia. There is evidence that there has been little or no increase in the yields of the high-yielding rice varieties for the past two decades or more. True, the rice yields have increased in South Asia, but this has been due, it is argued, to the replacement of the traditional varieties by the high-yield varieties and not because the yields of the latter have increased very much, if at all. One difficulty with such yield comparisons is that, presumably, the high-yield varieties were first introduced where their yield advantage was the greatest—under relatively favorable growing conditions—and as time went on, replaced the traditional varieties where both the relative advantage was less and the absolute yields were lower. Nonetheless, it probably is true that much of the observed yield increases have been due to the replacement of the traditional varieties and not from significant increases in the yield potential of the existing high-yield varieties.

Is this yield pessimism appropriate? Has IRRI exhausted its capacity to innovate? An announcement, apparently somewhat premature, that IRRI had developed a new high-yield variety that outyielded the current high-yield varieties by at least 20% was made some time ago. If this development is realized, it would go some considerable distance toward meeting the increased demand for rice in South Asia over the next quarter century. Obviously, my crystal ball may be as clouded as that of others. My purpose here is simply to raise questions concerning the prospects for a major increase in world grain trade. It could happen, but if I were a farmer in a country that exports grain, I would not now or in the near future make investments dependent on it actually occurring. I would wait and see.

A major factor of uncertainty with respect to world trade in grain is the prospective development of grain production in the former Soviet Union. The difficulties of the transition process have been much greater than anyone envisaged. Yet I believe that it will be only a matter of time before the combination of human and natural resources are utilized in efficient combinations and the area becomes a net grain exporter once again. . . .

Concluding Comments

I am an optimist about the future trends in food supply and demand. By that, I mean that there will be continued improvements in productivity, the rate of growth of supply will exceed that of demand, and real international prices of food will decline. Farmers will increase their real incomes only as they adjust to the changing conditions. The percentage of the world's resources used to produce food will continue to decline, and farmers must adjust to this fact.

This is not a new conclusion for me. I have been an optimist for the last three decades and I have been right. I have long been confident that farmers could expand food production at least as rapidly as demand. However, I must admit that I did not anticipate the large decline in the real prices of grain that has occurred since 1960. The decline in the real price and cost of grain was little short of a miracle, unprecedented in its magnitude. The gain in welfare for hundreds of millions—no, billions—of people was enormous, and the number that could have benefitted would have been even greater if more governments had followed appropriate policies with respect to agricultural production, prices, and trade.

I do not foresee such a large decline in costs and prices over the next three decades. But I do anticipate, along with some other researchers, that real grain and food prices will continue to decline in the years ahead. Farmers will continue to contribute to the wealth of nations.

Notes

1. Not everyone agrees that real grain or food prices will decline. Two recent studies conclude that real grain or food prices will increase. The studies are the OECD's *The Agricultural Outlook 1998-2003* and Luther Tweeten's recent study of global food supply and demand balance. The OECD study projects international price increases between 1997 and 2003 of 17% for wheat and 7% for corn. Tweeten is quite bullish for food prices, projecting an annual rate of price increase of more than 1.2% for the next two decades.

2. With rising real consumer incomes, there will be a significant increase in the demand for and consumption of livestock products. Will this increase in demand be large enough to offset the decline in growth due to the slowdown in population growth? It is difficult to say. There are currently quite different estimates of the amount of meat consumed in China. The estimates derived from the annual household surveys indicate a per capita consumption of meat and poultry of about 15 kilograms. This presumably refers to consumption in the home and may not count the meat eaten outside the home, which might be another 20%. The data on production of meat and poultry imply per capita availability of 37 kilograms. There may be some difference in what is counted as meat—carcass weight versus retail or home weight. However, the difference is very great and leaves one uncertain about how much meat consumption is likely to increase with increased incomes.

References

Bos, E., M. T. Yu, E. Massiah, and R. A. Bulatao. *World Population Projections: Estimates and Projections with Related Demographic Statistics.* Baltimore MD: The Johns Hopkins Press (for the World Bank), 1994.

Brown, L. R. "Who Will Feed China?" *World Watch* 7 (September/October 1994):10–19.

Ehrlich, P. R. *The Population Bomb,* Revised Ed. New York: Sierra Club/Ballantine Books, year.

Food and Agricultural Organization (FAO). *Production Yearbook.* Rome: FAO. Selected issues.

Islam, N., ed. *Population and Food in the Early Twenty-First Century: Meeting Future Food Demand of an Increasing Population.* Washington DC: International Food Policy Research Institute, 1994.

Johnson, D. G. *World Agriculture in Disarray.* London: Macmillan, 1973.

——. "World Agriculture, Commodity Policy, and Price Variability." *Amer. J. Agr. Econ.* 5 (December 1975):823–28.

——. "Trade Effects of Dismantling the Socialized Agriculture of the Former Soviet Union." *Comparative Econ. Stud.* 35 (Winter 1993):421–34.

Pinstrup-Andersen, P., R. Pandya-Lorch, and M.W. Rosegrant. *The World Food Situation: Recent Developments, Emerging Issues, and Long-Term Prospects.* Washington DC: International Food Policy Research Institute. year.

POSTSCRIPT

Does the Growing World Population Face Future Food Shortages?

Janet Raloff, in "Can Grain Yields Keep Pace?" *Science News* (August 16, 1997), notes that many experts believe that although there are genuine difficulties in continuing to produce a food supply that is adequate to feed a growing world population, it can be done. She quotes Gurdev S. Khush, the chief rice breeder at the International Rice Research Institute in Manila, Republic of the Philippines, as saying, "If we manage our resources properly and continue to put money into research, we should be able to meet world food needs for at least the next 30 years." For other optimistic voices, see William H. Bender, "How Much Food Will We Need in the Twenty-First Century?" *Environment* (March 1997) and Dennis T. Avery, "The Myth of Global Hunger," *The World & I* (January 1997).

Roy L. Prosterman, Tim Hanstad, and Li Ping, in "Can China Feed Itself?" *Scientific American* (November 1996), discuss how China is reforming its agricultural system. Its eventual success in feeding its populace, however, will also depend on its parallel attempts to rein in population growth.

Food and population come together in the concept of "carrying capacity," defined very simply as the size of the population that the environment can support, or "carry," indefinitely, through both good years and bad. It is not the size of the population that can prosper in good times alone, for such a large population must suffer catastrophically when droughts, floods, or blights arrive or the climate warms or cools. It is a long-term concept, where "long term" means not decades or generations, nor even centuries, but millennia or more.

What is Earth's carrying capacity for human beings? It is surely impossible to set a precise figure on the number of human beings the world can support for the long run. As Joel E. Cohen discusses in *How Many People Can the Earth Support?* (W. W. Norton, 1996), estimates of Earth's carrying capacity range from under a billion to over a trillion. The precise number depends on our choices of diet, standard of living, level of technology, willingness to share with others at home and abroad, and desire for an intact physical, chemical, and biological environment, as well as on whether or not our morality permits restraint in reproduction and our political or religious ideology permits educating and empowering women. The key, Cohen stresses, is human choice, and the choices are ones we must make within the next 50 years. To support this point, Cohen judiciously analyzes a great many population studies and resource estimates. Again and again, he says that there is no one neat answer. But there are clearly limits, and they seem to be in the neighborhood of population sizes that we may see well before the year 2100.

Others are more willing to be definite. Sandra Postel, in the Worldwatch Institute's *State of the World 1994* (W. W. Norton, 1994), says, "As a result of our population size, consumption patterns, and technology choices, we have surpassed the planet's carrying capacity. This is plainly evident by the extent to which we are damaging and depleting natural capital" (including land and water).

In *State of the World 1999* (W. W. Norton, 1999), Brown says, "Adequately feeding the projected increases in population poses one of the most difficult challenges that modern civilization faces." See also Brown, *Tough Choices: Facing the Challenge of Food Scarcity* (W. W. Norton, 1996). In "Facing Food Scarcity," *World Watch* (November/December 1995) and in "Averting a Global Food Crisis," *Technology Review* (November/December 1995), Brown argues that the most obvious things that we can do to increase food availability are only stopgaps or temporary measures. For instance, putting back into use cropland the United States and Europe have set aside to keep prices high could produce 34 million tons of grain per year and feed 15 months' worth of additional population growth. Land now used to grow tobacco could feed 6 months' worth of new mouths. If food could be grown on half of the land now used to grow cotton, 11 months' population growth could be covered. And feeding 10 percent of the grain now used as animal feed to people instead would take care of population growth for 28 months.

Can we avert catastrophe? Courtland L. Smith, in "Assessing the Limits to Growth," *BioScience* (July/August 1995), asserts the following:

> Culture, institutions and technology can mitigate the growth of population and affluence. When culture, institutions, and technology do not change to reduce environmental impact, then population and affluence do create a greater environmental impact.
>
> Biologists with a strict limits-to-growth view of the future and economists who emphasize human capabilities to moderate their impacts can both be right. The question to be resolved in the limits-to-growth debate is how large and how fast must be the change in culture, institutions, and technology.

ISSUE 5

Should Society Act Now to Halt Global Warming?

YES: Robert Kunzig and Carl Zimmer, from "Carbon Cuts and Techno-Fixes: Ten Things to Do About the Greenhouse Effect (Some of Which Aren't Crazy)," *Discover* (June 1998)

NO: Malcolm Wallop, from "Unless Stopped, the Global Warming Movement Could Cause Economic Disaster," *World Oil* (September 1998)

ISSUE SUMMARY

YES: Robert Kunzig and Carl Zimmer, editors of *Discover* magazine, argue that the debate over whether or not global warming is happening is essentially over; the issue now is what to do about it.

NO: Malcolm Wallop, founder and chairman of the Frontiers of Freedom Institute, maintains that global warming is a myth based not on science but on propaganda "put forward by a crowd that hates modern industrial society."

Scientists have known for more than a century that carbon doxide and other "greenhouse gases" (including water vapor, methane, and chlorofluorocarbons) help prevent heat from escaping the Earth's atmosphere. In fact, it is this "greenhouse effect" that keeps the Earth warm enough to support life. Yet there can be too much of a good thing. Ever since the dawn of the industrial age, humans have been burning vast quantities of fossil fuels, releasing the carbon they contain as carbon dioxide. Because of this, some estimate that by the year 2050, the amount of carbon dioxide in the air will be double what it was in 1850. By 1982 an increase was apparent. Less than a decade later, many researchers were saying that the climate had already begun to warm. Now there is a strong consensus that the global climate is warming and will continue to warm. There is less agreement on just how much it will warm or what the impact of the warming will be on human (and other) life. See Spencer R. Weart, "The Discovery of the Risk of Global Warming," *Physics Today* (January 1997).

The debate has been heated. The June 1992 issue of *The Bulletin of the Atomic Scientists* carries two articles on the possible consequences of the greenhouse effect. In "Global Warming: The Worst Case," Jeremy Leggett says that although there are enormous uncertainties, a warmer climate will release more carbon dioxide, which will warm the climate even further. As a result, soil will grow drier, forest fires will occur more frequently, plant pests will thrive, and methane trapped in the world's seabeds will be released and will increase global warming much further—in effect, there will be a "runaway greenhouse effect." Leggett also hints at the possibility that polar ice caps will melt and raise sea levels by hundreds of feet.

Taking the opposing view, in "Warming Theories Need Warning Label," S. Fred Singer emphasizes the uncertainties in the projections of global warming and their dependence on the accuracy of the computer models that generate them, and he argues that improvements in the models have consistently shrunk the size of the predicted change. There will be no catastrophe, he argues, and money spent to ward off the climate warming would be better spent on "so many pressing—and real—problems in need of resources."

In 1991 many scientists testified on "Global Climate Change and Greenhouse Emissions" before the Subcommittee on Health and the Environment of the House Committee on Energy and Commerce. Some scientists maintain that the problem is real and potentially serious. Others assert that they are not impressed by the data and computer models assembled to date. For instance, Sallie Baliunas, deputy director of the Mt. Wilson Observatory and the chairwoman of the Science Advisory Board at the George C. Marshall Institute in Washington, D.C., contends that global warming in the next century will amount to no more than a few tenths of a degree, "indistinguishable from natural fluctuations in temperature." Richard Lindzen, in "Absence of Scientific Basis," *Research & Exploration* (Spring 1993), even argues there is no real evidence at all for global warming.

Yet 1998 was the warmest year of the past millennium, announced the American Geophysical Union in *Geophysical Research Letters* (March 15, 1999). In May 1999 the Worldwatch Institute said that the warmth is leading "to more evaporation and rainfall and powering more destructive storms... weather-related damage worldwide totaled $92 billion in 1998, up a staggering 53 percent from the previous record of $60 billion in 1996 [and] drove an astounding 300 million or more people from their homes."

Ross Gelbspan, in *The Heat Is On: The Climate Crisis, the Cover-Up, the Prescription* (Perseus, 1997), asserts that the problem of global warming is real and that the scientific consensus is stronger today than it was just a few years ago. Those who still question global warming, says Gelbspan, are serving a fossil-fuels industry campaign of disinformation. (His book includes a "scientific critique of the greenhouse skeptics.") Action is essential, as outlined by Robert Kunzig and Carl Zimmer in the following selection.

Malcolm Wallop speaks for the greenhouse skeptics when he argues that global warming is a myth based on faulty science, propaganda, and hatred of modern industrial society.

Robert Kunzig and Carl Zimmer  **YES**

Carbon Cuts and Techno-Fixes

There are two basic points of view on global warming: it's a problem or it's not. In most of the world that argument is over and the pessimists have won, but not in the United States. And yet politically, if not scientifically, the argument seemed to be settled long ago—on October 15, 1992, to be precise, when the United States became the fourth country, after Mauritius, the Seychelles, and the Marshall Islands, to ratify the United Nations Framework Convention on Climate Change. George Bush had signed the treaty at Rio de Janeiro four months earlier. It committed us to an objective: "Stabilization of greenhouse gas concentrations in the atmosphere at a level that would prevent dangerous anthropogenic interference with the climate system." All the important details were missing; that's what the meeting in Kyoto last December was all about. But as a nation we formally accepted the basic principle—global warming is a problem and something has to be done about it—back in 1992.

Assuming we have a problem, then, what should we do about it? Again there are two basic answers: stop doing things that warm the planet—burning fossil fuels, mostly—or go on polluting and fix the planet so it won't warm. The Kyoto Protocol adopts the first answer, requiring the United States to emit 7 percent less of six greenhouse gases by the year 2012 than it did in 1990. Those cuts are much less than environmentalists would have liked—but since 1990 our emissions have surged. Fossil fuel prices have fallen, and so we are using more of them. The voluntary restraint that George Bush promised at Rio never happened. The Department of Energy [DOE] predicts that by 2010, if nothing has changed, U.S. greenhouse emissions will be a third higher than they were in 1990.

So complying with the Kyoto Protocol would require a big effort. To reduce carbon emissions we would have to either tax or regulate them—which is why industry and union lobbyists have promised to see that the protocol isn't ratified. They predict it would put a million Americans out of jobs and cut the gross national product by several percent. Whole industries would flee to developing countries, which did not commit to any emissions cuts at Kyoto. "Unilateral economic disarmament," the head of the American Petroleum Institute called the agreement. "An error of staggering dimensions."

Of course, industries that are about to be regulated often predict that the costs will be staggering. When the Environmental Protection Agency instituted tradable sulfur-dioxide-emissions permits in 1990—the system that may be a model for how to reduce carbon emissions—the permits were priced at $1,500 per ton, because that was the industry estimate of how much it would cost to stop emitting SO_2. By 1996 those permits were trading for a tenth their initial price; apparently the industry estimate had been wrong. In the case of the Kyoto Protocol, some economists do predict disaster if it is adhered to, but others do not. A study completed last fall by the DOE concluded that something close to the Kyoto cuts could be made at no net cost to the U.S. economy—because the money spent on controlling carbon would also save energy. The study assumed that carbon permits would sell for $50 a ton, or about 12.5 cents on a gallon of gas.

One industry criticism of the Kyoto agreement is certainly true, though: it alone will not prevent an environmental disaster, if indeed one looms in our future. Steep as they may seem, the Kyoto emissions cuts are nowhere near enough to stabilize greenhouse gas concentrations. They'll just slow the rise a bit. Which brings us to the second response to global warming—the planet fixers.

For as long as there have been environmentalists worrying about global warming, there have been "geoengineers" designing simple solutions—on the backs of envelopes, as it were—that could spare us the pain of cutting our consumption of coal, oil, and gas. In 1992 a National Academy of Sciences panel, one that included environmental types alongside men from General Motors and DuPont, reviewed a number of these schemes. The panel found some of them plausible and worth investigating—including, for instance, the idea that we might point battleship guns straight up and fire 10 million one-ton shells full of sun-blocking dust into the stratosphere every year. Since that report, however, most of those ideas have not been pursued much. Geoengineers have a bit of an image problem: environmentalists are apt to see them as irresponsible tinkerers who haven't grasped that tinkering with the planet is what got us into this mess—and whose fix-it schemes could distract the public from the real task of cutting carbon. Geoengineers, on the other hand, tend to see environmentalists as puritanical killjoys who find our control of nature sinful and like telling people what to do. The chasm is almost religious.

And yet sometime during the next century we may all have to get along. Today we can argue about whether the "fingerprint" of man-made global warming is evident yet in the results of climate models. Then it may be so evident—in the form of shifting climate zones and rising seas—that no model is needed to detect it. If we start now, and if the Kyoto agreement is followed by more stringent ones, we may be able to reduce carbon emissions enough to forestall a dramatic change. The first five items below describe some of the ways we might do this. But if there is one thing that the debate about Kyoto makes clear—not to mention our casual indifference to the promise we made at Rio—it is that we may not do enough soon enough to avoid changing the climate. Someday we may find ourselves needing a quick fix. And so the last five items describe a few geoengineering ideas, arranged along a scale of increasing wackiness. Read them and weep, or rejoice, as your faith dictates.

1. Begin at Home

The average American household sends 6,376 pounds of carbon in the form of carbon dioxide into the atmosphere every year. With 99 million households, that adds up to 287 million metric tons of carbon, or a fifth of U.S. emissions. (CO_2 emissions are usually expressed in terms of the mass of the carbon; the total mass, including the oxygen, is about four times greater.) Some of the easiest and least futuristic savings are to be found on the home front. The operative metaphor here is not *The Jetsons*—it's *This Old House*. Individuals can slash their carbon emissions merely by trying to cut their utility bills.

Simply wrapping a water heater in a $20 insulating jacket, for example, can save a homeowner $45 a year and eliminate 169 pounds of carbon. Efficient showerheads use half the hot water of conventional heads, cutting 379 pounds of carbon. And caulking can reduce heating bills by 25 percent and save 464 pounds a year. If every American house was spruced up in such ways, the United States could take care of a third of its obligation under the Kyoto agreement, according to Christopher Moser of the Safe Energy Communication Council.

Even more drastic cuts can be made when new houses are built. South-facing windows save heating costs, and trees can provide cooling shade in the summer. Double- or triple-pane windows with insulating pockets of gas let far less heat escape than the old single-pane kind, and many don't cost much more. If home builders are feeling particularly ambitious, they can put solar panels on the roof or make the walls of rammed earth or adobe, which soak up heat during the day and release it into the house at night.

"Instead of the typical home emitting 6,300 pounds of carbon per year, I can envision homes being just as comfortable emitting less than 2,700 pounds," says Richard Heede, of the Rocky Mountain Institute, an energy think tank. (Heede practices what he preaches: the house he recently built himself in Old Snowmass, Colorado, at a quarter the cost of a conventional house, uses one-eighth as much propane.) "We know everything we need to know already. We just don't pay enough attention to it."

2. Teach a Cow Some Manners

Compared with a car or a factory, a farm might not seem like a notable source of air pollution. But agriculture is responsible for a fifth of man-made greenhouse emissions. When farmers till fields, they break up the clumps of soil into fine particles, creating a football field's worth of surface area on a square yard of field. Bacteria can attack the organic carbon on these surfaces—carbon that in previous years had been sucked out of the atmosphere by photosynthesizing plants—and digest it using the oxygen that flows freely through the plowed soil. In the process the bugs return carbon dioxide to the air.

Soil conservation experts have been designing new tilling machines that stir up less soil, leave behind larger clumps, and thus keep carbon from escaping. Researchers estimate that an acre in a typical U.S. cornfield has lost 33,000 pounds of carbon in the past century and will lose 357 more pounds in the coming 100 years. (Farmland loses carbon fastest during the first two decades of plowing.) With careful tillage and other methods, the trend could be reversed and the acre could store 6,500 pounds of carbon over the next century. Even larger carbon vaults could be built up elsewhere, says ecologist Emilio Laca of the University of California at Davis, by letting farmland revert to rangeland —which sucks in carbon and stores it in soil, roots, and peat. The steppes of central Asia are good candidates, according to Laca, because they were recently converted to agriculture and have been abandoned since the fall of the Soviet Union.

Unfortunately, carbon dioxide isn't the only greenhouse gas that agriculture can kick up; there's also methane. Humans emit only 360 million metric tons of it, but molecule for molecule, it traps 21 times more heat than carbon dioxide, and 30 to 40 percent of it come from agriculture. The chief sources are rice paddies, lagoons of livestock manure, and grazing cattle. Methane-producing bacteria in a ruminant's rumen—a chamber of its stomach—help it digest tough plant tissue, and as the animal regurgitates its cud, it belches out the methane. When cows are fed high-quality food, such as corn and alfalfa, the bacteria don't have to work so hard and produce less methane. But that is only sometimes economical.

3. Don't Commute in a Truck

When automobiles replaced horses at the turn of the century, they were an environmental boon: the horse manure that carpeted American cities disappeared, and with it a lot of tuberculosis-causing bacteria. But since then the number of cars has doubled every 25 years. In the United States alone, transportation produces 469 million metric tons of carbon a year, about a third of that from cars.

Lately the trend has not been great. Between 1973, the year of the OPEC oil embargo, and 1988 the average fuel economy of new American cars doubled, from 14 miles per gallon to more than 28. Since then it has stayed about the same. It's not hard to see why: the federal government has not required further increases in efficiency, and gasoline is selling at pre-1973 prices (after inflation). The big three automakers now say they plan to achieve the prototype of an 80-miles-per-gallon car by 2004, by making engines more efficient and using lighter materials. Meanwhile, sales of sport-utility vehicles, which average below 20 miles a gallon, are booming. If people were to drive efficient cars around the suburbs instead, it would make a big difference—but without a hike in gas costs, it's unlikely.

What will people drive when the gas era ends? Research is now moving chiefly in two directions. One is toward a battery-powered electric car. Some manufacturers are starting with hybrid designs: Toyota, for example, now sells a car in Japan that uses a small internal combustion engine to drive a generator that charges a battery. Below 18 miles an hour, the battery alone powers the car; at faster speeds, the engine takes over. In city traffic, the car gets 66 miles per gallon, and even at 75 miles per hour it gets more than 50.

Here in the United States the focus has been on developing an all-electric car—thanks in large part to California's environmental regulations, which require that by 2003, 10 percent of the cars on the road produce zero emissions. General Motors has come out with a car that can travel 75 miles on one hour's charge. Better performance may come from lithium batteries, which now power cameras and other small devices. "Right now lithium looks very expensive, but it's our belief that research can bring those costs way down," says Richard Moorer of the DOE's Office of Transportation Technologies. "We want to see if lithium batteries can triple the range we're getting out of lead-acid batteries."

Batteries are not the only way to power an electric car. There is also the so-called fuel cell, which strips the electrons off hydrogen found in a fuel such as gasoline and uses them to create an electric current. Car manufacturers are talking about a prototype being ready by 2004; such a vehicle would produce half the carbon emissions from a tank of gasoline as a conventional car. What's particularly attractive about the latest fuel cells is that they are able to use a number of different fuels, such as gasoline mixed with ethanol from corn. In the more distant future, they might use compressed hydrogen and release no carbon at all.

But big savings are possible already. "Frankly, having even a third of cars be very fuel efficient would have a large impact on our carbon-dioxide emissions," says Joseph Romm of the DOE. "We don't have to replace every car on the road."

4. Create Industrial Ecosystems

In many countries, industry could cut a quarter of its carbon emissions just by refitting factories with the most efficient technology now available. Such improvements would shave only a few percent, however, from the 482 million metric tons that U.S. factories emit. To cut even more, we may have to rethink the way industry works.

Every factory needs both heat and electricity, which it typically gets from separate sources. But it's possible to create both kinds of energy at the same time—an idea known as "co-generation." "Instead of having to purchase all of its electricity from a power grid and using coal plants for heat, a pulp and paper mill can burn the wastes it has, creating electricity that it might use for pump motors and steam that it could use in drying," says Marilyn Brown of the Oak Ridge National Laboratory. Turbines are now being developed that burn natural gas or biomass fuel to generate both electricity and steam.

Cogeneration emerges out of a relatively new way of thinking about factories, known as industrial ecology. Natural ecosystems, unlike factories, recycle most of their waste—animal droppings and dead organic matter are scavenged by insects and bacteria, which build up the soil and become prey for other organisms. Industrial ecologists use that thrift as an inspiration for industrial design.

Their shining example is the town of Kalundborg, in Denmark. A coal-burning plant there generates electricity, and the excess steam is captured and pumped into Kalundborg's 5,000 houses and many of its factories. An oil refinery gets 40 percent of the heat it needs; a pharmaceutical factory gets all it needs to make its drugs and warm its building. The steam also runs a fish farm, where 57 warmed ponds produce 250 tons of fish each year. The power plant's sulfur-dioxide scrubber produces gypsum as a by-product, which is used by a nearby wallboard manufacturer. Cinders once shipped from the coal plant to a landfill are now used to make cement. The other factories, in turn, make profits from their own wastes. Fertilizers are made out of both the sludge from the fish ponds and the waste from the microbes used for producing the pharmaceuticals. The oil refinery supplies the wallboard company with petroleum by-products to fire its ovens. The power plant burns some of those, too, saving 30,000 tons of coal a year. All told, Kalundborg saves 130,000 tons of CO_2 emissions a year.

At least 14 "eco-industrial parks" are being designed in the United States. But according to John Ehrenfeld, a chemical engineer at MIT, the Danish success can't be immediately reproduced. "Kalundborg took about 35 years to develop," says Ehrenfeld. "It was never planned. This was an evolution, a series of independent transactions. The eco-parks are trying to do it all at once, but my guess is that this first round will not be full-blown symbioses. I hope folks don't get frustrated if it's not happening instantly. Kalundborg is very seductive—because it's a good idea."

5. Switch to the Sun (Or at Least to Gas)

The industrial revolution was built on electricity generated from coal, and two centuries later little has changed. In the United States the production of electricity accounts for 36 percent of carbon emissions—about 530 million metric tons. As the rest of the world industrializes, the global contribution of electricity to carbon emissions may well soar. India and China, with their booming populations and vast coal reserves, are expected to become leading polluters —which is why the lack of any commitment from them at Kyoto was a disappointment. By 2020, if business proceeds as usual, electricity generation will produce 2,300 to 4,100 million tons of carbon every year.

Business will indeed proceed as usual unless other cheap, powerful sources of electricity turn up soon. Nuclear power is expensive and unpopular, and no one has figured out how to dispose of the radioactive waste. Fusion power—the kind generated by the sun—will probably remain a pipe dream for decades. Hydropower is carbon-free and widely available—but dams are expensive blots on the landscape that drown whole ecosystems.

In the long run, solar energy may become the best option. Although photovoltaic cells have been touted for decades, they've always been too expensive. But in the past few years the way they are made has changed. They used to be crafted from silicon crystals, which were sawed into wafers. Now engineers can vaporize semiconductors such as cadmium and tellurium and then have them settle, atom by atom, onto a piece of plain glass. The result is an ultrathin solar cell that doesn't squander raw materials and provides abundant electricity. Even now solar cells are so cheap that sales went up worldwide by 38 percent in 1997.

The cheaper solar cells become, the better chance they'll have of supplanting some of those coal-fired power plants that will otherwise spring up in India and China. Solar energy researchers hope that the same laws of rapidly rising efficiency and plummeting cost that characterize the computer industry will apply to their own field. "Once the money is there, I'm pretty sure we'll see photovoltaic cells that will cost just one-fifth of what they cost now," predicts Ken Zweibel of the DOE's National Renewable Energy Laboratory. A company called Solar Cells in Toledo is now automating the entire process and predicts that the cost of building a solar power panel will drop to a dollar per watt—the same as coal and natural gas in many parts of the United States—in three to five years.

Even if that happens, solar power will not be how we meet the Kyoto targets. A more important way to reduce emissions in the next decade would be simply to convert some U.S. coal plants to natural gas, which burns a lot cleaner. Coal-fired boilers would have to be replaced with turbines powered by natural gas. According to researchers at the Oak Ridge National Laboratory, the government would have to require carbon-emissions permits at $25 to $50 per ton in order to make such a conversion financially attractive to coal-plant operators. But because gas-burning technology is so efficient, the researchers don't think the tax would lead to a big price hike for consumers. If every coal plant located near a gas pipeline was converted, the U.S. would reduce its carbon emissions by 40 million tons a year.

6. Dump It Somewhere Else

In the middle of the North Sea, about halfway between Scotland and southern Norway, Statoil, the Norwegian oil company, has to get rid of 1 million tons of carbon dioxide a year. (That's a quarter million tons of carbon.) The CO_2 does not come from the burning of fossil fuels; it's an impurity that must be removed from the natural gas that Statoil is extracting from its Sleipner West field. A decade ago, Statoil would just have pumped it into the air. But in 1991 Norway began taxing emissions at the rate of about $50 per ton of CO_2 (or $200 per ton of carbon). A tax bill of $50 million didn't make developing the field unprofitable. But it made other options for disposing of the CO_2 worth considering.

This is the one Statoil chose. The natural gas at Sleipner West is pumped into the bottom of a 115-foot-tall tower filled with steel pellets. As it percolates up, it meets a fluid solution of amine coming down. The amine strips the CO_2 from the natural gas, and as the fluid exits the bottom of the tower, the pressure on it is released, allowing the CO_2 to bubble out of solution—and to get channeled back to the seafloor through a steel pipe. Half a mile below the seafloor, the pipe penetrates a cap of impermeable shale and enters a 700-foot-thick layer of extremely porous sandstone. At the bottom of that mushy layer, high-pressure CO_2 squirts from small holes in the pipe.

"The whole of this porous formation is filled with salt water," explains Olav Kaarstad, the researcher in charge of Statoil's climate program. "The CO_2 will displace the salt water. Part of it will be dissolved in the water, and part of it will react with minerals, but most of it will form a big bubble. It will slowly rise and spread out under the shale roof. But that will take hundreds and hundreds of years." Statoil has been injecting carbon dioxide just since August 1996.

There is no reason the CO_2 has to come from gas fields: it could come from power plants. "We think of Sleipner as a demonstration project," says Kaarstad. "This could be a technology for handling CO_2 on a much larger scale." The shale-capped sandstone under Sleipner, he points out, extends under most of the North Sea. In theory, it could soak up more than a hundred times the annual CO_2 output of all the countries of the European Union.

Seafloor sandstones are not the only possible reservoirs. For the past decade researchers in Japan have explored the idea of pumping CO_2 directly into seawater, which contains 60 times as much CO_2 as the atmosphere and presumably can take a little more. At one time they considered simply dumping cubes of dry ice over the side of a ship. But the current idea, explains Takashi Ohsumi of the Central Research Institute of the Electric Power Industry in Abiko, is to load liquid CO_2 onto a tanker directly at a power plant—most Japanese power plants are on the coast. In the open Pacific 500 miles east of Japan, the CO_2 would be transferred to a second ship, which would steam slowly back and forth and pump it down a 6,500-foot vertical pipe. The CO_2 would emerge in a fine mist at the bottom and—it is hoped—spread around the world at depth instead of bubbling back up to the atmosphere. Three ships working full-time, Ohsumi estimates, could meet the needs of a single large (1 gigawatt) coal-fired power plant. "Around 2010," he says, "I hope a small CO_2 disposal business will be started in Japan."

Researchers at MIT are pursuing the same hope for the United States, albeit with much less government support. Their idea is to run pipelines directly out to sea from coastal power plants. The main danger is that the CO_2 would make the water around the pipe more acidic. But if dispersed in fine droplets, says Eric Adams of MIT—as it would be in either the Japanese or the MIT scenario—the concentration might never be greater than what marine animals could tolerate. "We believe you can reach zero impact," says Adams. So far, that conclusion is based only on a review of the rather limited biological literature on what acidity levels are lethal to plankton. But Adams and Howard Herzog of MIT, in collaboration with Ohsumi and other Japanese and Norwegian researchers, are now organizing an actual experiment that will take place in 2000 on the coast of Hawaii. They will pump as much as a hundred tons of liquid CO_2 out to sea, to a depth of several thousand feet, and monitor the acidity.

The MIT researchers hate being called geoengineers—the CO_2 they propose to put in the ocean, they point out, would otherwise go into the atmosphere, and after a long and potentially damaging stay there, it would be absorbed by the ocean anyway. If they can get CO_2 to go directly into the ocean and stay there—still a big *if*, given the uncertainties about how seawater moves around—they would just be shortening the circuit to eliminate the damage. "It's really a carbon-management issue," says Herzog. "If we don't want to put the carbon in the atmosphere, where do we put it? The only other choice is to leave it in the ground. And that just doesn't seem like it's going to happen."

7. Fertilize the Ocean

The Marshall Islands in the western Pacific are a nation of 58,000 people living on 70 square miles of coral atolls whose average elevation is seven feet. A sea level rise caused by global warming would have a big effect on this country, which helps explain why it was one of the first to ratify the Rio treaty. Last year the government of the Marshalls also signed another document—a contract with a Springfield, Virginia, entrepreneur named Michael Markels. The contract gives Markels an option on the country's entire Exclusive Economic Zone [EEZ], an area of some 800,000 square miles—"almost the size of the Louisiana Purchase," says Markels. Beginning in 2000, he and his new company, Ocean Farming, hope to start fertilizing those waters with iron. The idea is to create a fishery where now there is none, and also to draw carbon dioxide out of the atmosphere.

The underlying theory was first put forward a decade ago by the late John Martin of the Moss Landing Marine Laboratories on Monterey Bay, in California. Martin proposed that in vast regions of the sea that are mysteriously infertile—regions where the single-celled plants, or phytoplankton, don't flourish even though they have all the nitrogen and phosphorus they need—there is a dearth of iron. The amount the plankton need is minute, but the main source is dust blowing off the land, and in the infertile regions, said Martin, there just isn't enough. In 1995 his successors at Moss Landing, Kenneth Coale and Kenneth Johnson, proved him right. When they sprayed a five-mile-wide square of ocean near the Galapagos Islands with half a ton of iron sulfate, the water turned green with phytoplankton.

Martin himself had suggested that iron fertilization could be a last resort to help protect ourselves from global warming—the blooming plants would suck up CO_2. The biggest infertile region is the Southern Ocean around Antarctica, which also happens to be a region of vigorous sinking currents. If that whole vast region were fertilized regularly with iron, Martin said—which was technically conceivable because the amount needed was so small—then much of the resulting boom in biomass would end up sinking to the ocean floor, taking carbon with it. In 1999 or 2000, Coale and Johnson hope to repeat their fertilization experiment in the Antarctic. . . .

After some inconclusive tests in the Gulf of Mexico last January, Markels is planning more tests there. . . . But by 2000 he hopes to be fertilizing the Marshalls EEZ. It's not the ideal place, because the water there needs phosphate too—but in exchange for royalties, the Marshalls have given Markels property rights. "We're in this to make money," he emphasizes. By fertilizing 100,000 square miles of ocean continually and seeding the barren waters with anchovetas—tunas would swim in on their own to eat the anchovetas—Markels claims he can produce more fish in a year, about 100 million tons, than are currently harvested worldwide. By fertilizing 300,000 square miles, he thinks he can dispatch as much CO_2 to the seafloor as the United States produces. He's hoping polluters will pay him to do that one day.

Though his optimistic calculations probably shouldn't be taken too seriously, in principle his scheme could work—it's just that no one knows whether it will actually work off the Marshall Islands. Even if the plankton there did bloom with an iron supplement, no one knows how much of that carbon would really sink to the seafloor instead of getting belched back into the atmosphere. And no one, least of all Markels, knows what impact fertilization will have on the environment. Decaying plankton will draw oxygen out of the water, and that clearly could be dangerous to coral—the stuff the Marshalls are made of. Markels says he'll do the fertilization well offshore. He sees no reason to think of farming the ocean any differently than we think of farming the land—as a boon to mankind. "The main environmental impact," he predicts, "is going to be happy fish."

8. Block That Sun

Before S. S. Penner retired from the University of California at San Diego, he was for two decades the director of its Energy Center. A chemist and an aeronautical engineer, he was also a prolific chairman of government committees, many of them having to do with how best to burn fossil fuels. In 1983, when Penner was invited to give a paper at an astronautical conference on some socially useful application of aircraft or satellites, global warming was beginning to be talked about a lot. A solution to that, Penner decided, would certainly be useful.

He considered first the possibility of putting 9 million 2,000-foot-wide Mylar balloons into orbit to block some sunlight. But a back-of-the-envelope calculation told him that the launch cost alone would run to $315 trillion. So Penner started to think smaller. Another quick calculation told him that if you used half-micron particles as reflectors, it would take surprisingly few of them to offset the greenhouse effect caused by a doubling of CO_2—only about 15 million tons spread over the whole planet. If you put particles that small in the stratosphere, between 40,000 and 100,000 feet, they would stay up there for decades, Penner figured. His idea for how to get them there was downright elegant (at least compared with firing dust salvos at the stratosphere with battleships): if you just adjusted all the jet engines in the world so they burned a little richer and emitted 1 percent of their fuel as tiny particles of soot, you'd get your 15 million tons' worth. The cost would be derisory, "And you'd hardly know that the particles were there," says Penner.

Unfortunately, commercial jets don't spend much time above 40,000 feet; Penner now says he has in mind a twenty-first-century world crisscrossed by high-flying ssts. And particles don't stay in the stratosphere as long as Penner assumed, so canceling all of global warming wouldn't be quite as cheap or easy as he figured. The eruption of Mount Pinatubo in 1991 shot a sulfurous plume up to 70,000 feet—but within three years even the smallest sulfate particles had fallen to Earth.

On the other hand, Pinatubo did cool the planet—by nearly a degree Fahrenheit, at least in the tropics. "If you had a volcano like Pinatubo going off every two years, you would be completely offsetting CO_2 warming," says V. Ramaswamy, a climate modeler at the Geophysical Fluid Dynamics Laboratory in Princeton. But that doesn't mean we know yet how to do what the volcano did. The problem is not just the potential side effects of a stratospheric parasol—the particles might help destroy ozone—it's that even the effects on climate are uncertain. Putting jet soot into the stratosphere would block sunlight, but what would happen as the particles settled into the zone of clouds? A recent NASA study showed that jet contrails evolve into cirrus clouds as water droplets freeze around the sulfate and soot particles. Cirrus clouds, however, actually warm the planet—they bounce more heat back to Earth than sunlight to space. So sootier jet exhaust would not necessarily be a good thing.

Still, the basic idea—that it might be possible to cool the planet by scattering particles in the atmosphere—"is not entirely wacky," as Ramaswamy puts it. A particle screen would certainly be cheap, and it could be dismantled quickly —by letting the particles fall to Earth—if things went awry. Many of the unanswered questions about it are ones climatologists are trying to answer anyway. But a focused look into the geoengineering possibilities would seem prudent. "There has been no research program on this activity," says Penner. "People are very reluctant to do this—and I think rightly. But I wasn't saying go out and do this. I was saying go out and study this."

9. Dam That Sea

To Robert Johnson, a prudent hedge against climate disaster would be to start work on a dam across the Strait of Gibraltar, right now. Even before retiring from the Honeywell Corporation, where he spent a career working on physics problems related to heating and cooling buildings, Johnson had an interest in global climate control too. An adjunct professor at the University of Minnesota —a state that was once submerged under a thick sheet of ice—Johnson thinks an ice age could start again soon, as a result of global warming and the construction of the Aswan High Dam in Egypt. The Gibraltar dam is his idea for preventing that.

The idea that global warming could lead to a surge of northern ice sheets, if not a full-blown ice age, is counterintuitive but not crazy. The warming will cause more water to evaporate from the oceans, so globally it should increase precipitation. In places like northern Canada and Greenland it will still be cold enough for that precipitation to fall as snow. More snow could lead to more ice. "And once you've given the ice sheets a kick in the butt, they don't stop," says Johnson.

Johnson believes the last big kick came from the Mediterranean. Based on some 20-year-old oceanographic data, he proposes that dense, salty Mediterranean water, flowing due north after it leaves the Med at a depth of half a mile or more, slams into shoals and wells up to the surface off Ireland. There it also runs into the much larger North Atlantic Drift, the warm extension of the Gulf Stream. Today, says Johnson, that water mass flows on into the Norwegian Sea, where it helps warm northern Europe. But at the start of the last ice age, he claims, some thing different happened. The flow of freshwater into the

Mediterranean from the Nile diminished, the Med got saltier, and so the outflow at Gibraltar increased. The upwelling off Ireland became powerful enough to push the North Atlantic Drift into the Labrador Sea. All that warm water increased evaporation there and rerouted snowstorms over eastern Canada. The ice sheets surged south.

Thanks to us, says Johnson, the next glacial kick may already be under way: Egyptian dams are already diverting 90 percent of the Nile. Global warming will make matters much worse by increasing evaporation from the Med. . . .

What do people who actually study ocean currents think of Johnson's fluidic switch hypothesis, let alone the idea of a Gibraltar dam? On the whole, not a whole lot. "There is no evidence at all that Med water upwells and diverts the North Atlantic current," says Jim Price of the Woods Hole Oceanographic Institution, who is an expert on the Mediterranean outflow. But Johnson sees no wackiness in his suggestion that we should start designing the dam now. "These things have to be researched," he says. "You've got to feel your way, engineering-wise, because nothing like this has been done before. If you wait until the climate has changed, you'll have a lot of hardship."

10. Do Nothing

Of course, we could just stick with the geoengineering scheme we've got—the one that consists of putting 7 billion tons a year of carbon in the form of carbon dioxide into the atmosphere, along with generous dollops of other greenhouse gases. Some people, mostly in the United States, do advocate that policy. Last fall, for instance, the *Wall Street Journal* published an opinion column by two chemists at the Oregon Institute of Science and Medicine, whose title should one day give historians a chuckle: "Science Has Spoken: Global Warming Is a Myth." If science has said one thing clearly, it is that the planet will almost certainly get warmer. It's just not clear whether the warming has begun already.

Or what the effects will be. They will probably be significant, and some may be nice: Manitoba (and Minnesota) may become more pleasant, and farms there more productive. On the other hand, Africa may be hit by severe droughts, coastlines everywhere could be threatened by rising seas, and the Gulf Stream could be shut down, bringing an abrupt chill to northern Europe. All of this is very uncertain—and so to some people, given the costs of doing something about global warming, doing nothing and hoping for the best seems rational. To others, that would be the wackiest scheme of all.

 **NO**

Unless Stopped, the Global Warming Movement Could Cause Economic Disaster

Mainstream America must debunk the myths behind the Kyoto Protocol, says former U.S. Senator Malcolm Wallop, otherwise the Clinton Administration will commit us to crippling restrictions imposed by international "green police."

Q. Mr. Wallop, would you explain why you have been so critical of the Kyoto Protocol?

A. The Kyoto Protocol is a colossal fraud, based not on real science, but real propaganda. It is not an environmental program, but a political effort put forward by a crowd that hates modern industrial society and preaches "small is beautiful." Twenty-five years ago, these prophets of catastrophe were led by Jerry Brown (Governor Moonbeam) and the alarmist Club of Rome. They predicted that the world was running out of food and oil and that a new Ice Age was just around the corner. These political elitists are always in search of an impending disaster to justify bigger government, greater control and the redistribution of wealth. Now that the world finds itself with an abundance of food and oil, they advance the threat of global warming. The new prophet of doom is Vice President Gore, who says American society is dysfunctional because of its addiction to fossil fuels and the automobile. His answer is more intrusive government regulation—and on a global level, ceding U.S. sovereignty to world government.

Q. What would be the effect of the Kyoto Protocol on the U.S., and the oil industry in particular?

A. Implementing Kyoto would precipitate an economic disaster. Carbon energy (oil, gas and coal) is the basis of our industrial civilization and sustains our standard of living. Energy is the foundation stone of national wealth. The worldwide industry that has been created since Edwin Drake brought in his

Titusville well in 1859 has produced an unimaginable boon for Americans and mankind. Implementing the Kyoto Protocol would mean millions of lost jobs and a substantial fall in the average standard of living.

For those who worship a pristine Planet Earth, wind and solar power are the only politically correct renewable sources of electric energy. These cost 2 to 3 times as much to produce as conventional sources. The environmentalists have ruled out nuclear power and hydroelectric power as alternatives. Furthermore, by prescribing Third World poverty as a permanent circumstance, it would compound the environmental disasters caused by poverty. *ask* *see wnot guide*

Q. How would compliance with the Kyoto Protocol be monitored and enforced?

A. It will require a new United Nations "green police" empowered to enforce compliance and monitor each nation's adherence to agreed limits. The details of this new UN "green police" bureaucracy are supposed to be settled at the next round of negotiations in Buenos Aires this November. Somebody at the UN will track the satellites, interpret their data and mete out fines and punishments.

However they disguise it, Americans will be facing a UN-based global environmental regime with the power to allocate energy consumption between nations. If the global environmental power seekers have their way, the U.S. will no longer control its own economic destiny. American citizens will not have the freedom to make everyday decisions about their way of life, including such things as what kinds of cars they drive and how warm or cool they keep their homes.

Q. Would you explain why the science behind the predictions of global warming is flawed?

A. Despite the endless claims by Vice President Gore and his doomsaying allies, there is no scientific consensus that we face catastrophic global warming. There is no consensus nor anything approaching consensus that whatever minimum changes in the climate that have been observed from time to time are man-caused.

The documents that everybody points to as evidence of this alleged scientific consensus are the successive reports of what became known as the Intergovernmental Panel on Climate Change or IPCC. The original predictions in the Toronto Statement of 1988 were indeed scary—temperature increases of 0.8 [degrees] C per decade, totaling over 3 [degrees] C by 2030 and rises in ocean levels between twenty and one hundred fifty centimeters. Global warming of that magnitude in such a short period could indeed pose serious problems for mankind and for much of the earth, but it cannot be demonstrated by any known climate patterns.

Then along came the 1992 IPCC report, which revised these predictions from 0.8 [degrees] C down to 0.3 [degrees] C per decade, or a total of 1.2 [degrees] C by 2030, and a sea level rise of only fifteen to forty centimeters. The latest IPCC report in 1995 further lowered the predicted temperature rise to 0.2

[degrees] per decade, or 0.8 [degrees] C total by 2030, and a sea level rise of five to thirty-five centimeters. This temperature range over this time frame reduces the problems potentially posed by global warming to an obviously manageable level if they occur at all. A majority of climate scientists now believes they will not reach even that reduced level.

The political debate has proceeded as though this 75% reduction in predicted temperature increases didn't exist. Obviously, it is essential for the prophets of global catastrophe that the public never notices these more recent figures.

Indeed, on current trends, the next IPCC report may predict insignificant warming into the foreseeable future as the result of burning fossil fuels. Recognizing this threat to their carefully orchestrated scenario of impending apocalypse, the Clinton Administration has moved to place its own agent, Dr. Robert Watson, in charge of producing the next IPCC report. In that way, they plan to fully politicize the scientific conclusions, or at least make sure they don't get in the way of the political message.

Global warming skeptics, such as Dr. Patrick Michaels, Professor and Director of the State Office of Climatology, University of Virginia, and Dr. Fred Singer, former Director, U.S. Weather Satellite Service, have a good point when they criticize even the IPCC's ever-more-modest predictions. More than one hundred qualified scientists and meteorologists have joined them as signatories to the Leipzig Declaration. The problem with all the predictions is that they are not based on observation. Surface temperature readings over the last century show a very small warming before 1940. More accurate NASA satellite readings show a slight cooling trend over the last two decades.

Instead of actual data, the doomsday predictions are based on computer models. Supercomputers perform billions of calculations for weeks to come up with results. The funny thing is that while the environmental zealots express total confidence in temperature predictions for 50 or 100 years into the future, they conceal the fact that these computer models are so imperfect that they can't account for the actual temperature record for the last 50 or 100 years. The reasons for this are that the climate is enormously complex, that climate science is in its infancy and that many possible factors are not included or are not given the correct weight in the models.

It is only wise, therefore, to doubt that the computer models are more reliable than the observed data. Moreover, there is an assumption in all the talk about global warming that is seldom examined or even mentioned. The prophets of darkness never look on the bright side of global warming. All is gloom and doom—as the oceans rise and Florida disappears, tropical diseases will spread to the Maine coast. Catastrophic floods and catastrophic droughts will alternate over the Great Plains. Palm trees will invade the great Northwest Forests. Denver will be as hot as Houston, and Houston will be hotter than Calcutta.

Despite the assumption that any man-made change must be bad, there are strong reasons to think that the negative aspects of global warming, in the unlikely event that they will occur, will be far outweighed by the positive effects. Twenty or thirty years ago, prophets of an impending ice age, including

Dr. Stephen Schneider, now one of the chief prophets of global warming, made the point that the next ice age is overdue. Perhaps taking fossil fuels out of the earth and returning them to the carbon cycle is actually forestalling the next ice age. *read*

Thomas Gale Moore of the Hoover Institution has just published a book, *Climate of Fear: Why We Shouldn't Worry About Global Warming*, which summarizes much useful information about the effects of temperature variations over the last several thousand years. For instance, less than 1,000 years ago, Greenland really was green, and the Vikings could grow crops there. This ended with the onset of the Little Ice Age, which is not yet fully over. Moore's analysis concludes the potential economic benefits of global warming outweigh the potential costs by tens of billions of dollars. This is especially true of agricultural activity, which should rise dramatically as a result of higher CO_2 levels, more rainfall and longer growing seasons. *ask*

This point is also made in the petition of scientists now being circulated by Dr. Arthur Robinson of the Oregon Institute of Science and Medicine, and others. In addition to urging rejection of the Kyoto Protocol on the grounds "that there is no convincing scientific evidence that human release of... greenhouse gases is causing... catastrophic heating of the Earth's atmosphere...," the petition goes on to state that "... there is substantial scientific evidence that increases in carbon dioxide may produce many beneficial effects upon the natural plant and animal environments of the Earth." Over 16,400 American scientists, two thirds with advanced degrees, have signed this petition in the past few months. *does not mean anything*

There is a third aspect worth noting. If human activities are causing the climate to warm, the Kyoto Protocol will do next to nothing to slow the warming trend. This obvious fact was confirmed by the Energy Information Administration on April 22nd. It estimated that without the Kyoto Protocol, human induced global CO_2 emissions would grow by 79% from 1995 to 2020, but still would represent less than one-tenth of total CO_2 from all sources. Even if the Protocol could be strictly enforced, EIA forecasts CO_2 levels will still go up by 67%. That is because China, India, Brazil and all other developing countries are exempt from the Protocol's limits. *good point*

Q. Why are the Clinton Administration, in particular Vice President Al Gore, and some environmental groups pushing so hard for implementation of Kyoto when it would harm the country?

A. Most, but not all, alarmists mean no harm. A profound misperception of reality convinces them that they are staving off evil. That is why I challenge their fundamental premises, their contention that whatever global warming may be taking place is attributable to human activity and that it is leading to a catastrophe. Unsound genetic science led to bad racial and public *true* health policies earlier this century. On the basis of unsound economic science, good men like Prime Minister Clement Atlee did their countrymen enormous disservice by adopting the disastrous economic formula called socialism. On the other hand, to some power seekers, scientific truth is whatever conforms to or enhances their ideology. Remember Marxism was first called "scientific socialism."

Q. It appears that the U.S. Senate will not ratify the Protocol, so why worry about it?

A. Today the Senate would not ratify the Protocol, but unless its flawed underlying scientific premise is rebutted, the drumbeat of propaganda about an impending, yet preventable, catastrophe will have a pernicious long-term effect. Kyoto's proponents have embarked on a strategy of piecemeal implementation, justifying each step they take as a sort of minimum insurance policy.

Q. What can be done to stop implementation through presidential executive order and regulatory "hanky panky" by EPA, DOE, DOI, etc.?

A. Covert implementation of the Protocol has to be addressed immediately as a case of regulatory over-reaching being perpetrated on the basis of unsound science by big government enthusiasts. Both the Congress and state legislatures should explicitly prohibit bureaucratic implementation of the unratified Protocol. Congressional appropriations committees should remove every one of the President's budget requests that aim for Executive Branch implementation without Senate ratification.

Q. What can be done to resolve these different interpretations of the science? Is there an independent arbitrator?

A. There should be great concern in Congress that the Clinton Administration is skewing the design and award of research grants to buttress Mr. Gore's preconceptions, and doing that in a way that is having a chilling effect on scientists inclined to contrary conclusions. Grants are the lifeblood of research universities, especially in the field of hard science. Grant seeking is a profession, and professional grant seekers craft their proposals to appeal to the prejudices of funding providers.

Your mention of an impartial arbitrator is fascinating because there is a precedent for such an approach. In the 1970s, there was great debate over the accuracy of military versus CIA estimates of Soviet military power. A group of non-government experts who became known as the "B Team" was asked to independently review the same data the National Security Council and CIA had used in making its estimates. The B Team's conclusions differed substantially from the CIA's and buttressed the position of the opponents of the SALT II treaty. Congress might want to replicate that approach and mandate that the National Research Laboratories at Los Alamos, New Mexico, and Livermore, California, form an independent B Team of analysts to review all of the raw data concerning global warming on which the U.S. government and the IPCC based its controversial findings.

Q. British Petroleum and Shell have changed course on global warming, saying that they will work to comply with Kyoto requirements. Can you speculate about their change of heart and intention?

A. The fact that these are not American companies is elemental to their posture on Kyoto. British Petroleum should be expected to give British interests priority. A large chunk of BP's stock used to be owned by the British Government. Kyoto gives Britain an advantage because the UK has already begun switching its electric generation from coal to natural gas, of which it has an abundant supply. And of course burning gas produces much less CO_2 per BTU.

The Royal Dutch Shell group is a joint venture dominated by British and Dutch interests. Operating across the European continent, Shell has to placate left-wing green parties and extremist groups that make Vice President Gore sound moderate. In Germany, extremist groups like Greenpeace actually firebombed Shell service stations in the case of one environmental dispute. Equally important, Kyoto will be a boon for the Europeans and a burden for Americans.

The European Union is already more Kyoto-compliant than the U.S. because of the British changeover and because of the shutdown of heavy industry in East Germany after 1990, which is the base year for measuring emissions reductions. The Kyoto Protocol turns these differences into an advantage for the Europeans. BP and Shell ought to be expected to do what is in the national interest of their homeland. Let's hope American companies will defend our national interest.

I don't agree

Q. The media presents and our schools teach global warming as accomplished fact. Against this overwhelmingly successful propaganda onslaught, how can the opposing view be put before the public?

A. He who bears news of impending catastrophe always gets attention. Many of today's hysterical, global warming doomsayers, made the front pages 25 years ago when they told us the world was about to run out of oil and that a new ice age was on the horizon. Global warming just provides a different rationale for the proponents of big government. Elitists are always searching for an excuse to manage people's lives.

The problem is that their message is resonating in our schools and in the media because it is funded by the bureaucratic-educational complex. Huge grants from government and many of our major charitable foundations, such as the Pew Charitable Trust, are involved. It's ironic and sad that the left-wing Pew Trust was funded by one of the great oilmen.

A number of good organizations are working to debunk the myths behind Kyoto. The Frontiers of Freedom Institute is implementing a sound science education project, but we must count on the support of mainstream, productive Americans like the readers of *World Oil.* *

Global warming is one of the key public policy issues that the Frontiers of Freedom Institute (FFI) hopes to influence. The organization believes the Kyoto agreement is based on partial and faulty science, and would be catastrophic to the U.S economy and sovereignty.

---

* [Editor's note: In December 1997, the nations of the world met in Kyoto, Japan, to negotiate a treaty that sets mandatory limits on greenhouse gas (CO_2) emissions. The outgrowth of the conference was the Kyoto Protocol, a treaty that mandates the amount each country must reduce these emissions. In the case of the U.S., these emissions must be reduced by more than one-third from levels occurring in the arbitrary base year of 1990.]

POSTSCRIPT

Should Society Act Now to Halt Global Warming?

The United Nations Conference on Environment and Development in Rio de Janeiro, Brazil, took place in 1992. High on the agenda was the problem of global warming, but despite widespread concern and calls for reductions in carbon dioxide releases, the United States refused to consider rigid deadlines or set quotas. The uncertainties seemed too great, and some thought the economic costs of cutting back on carbon dioxide might be greater than the costs of letting the climate warm.

However, James Kasting of Pennsylvania State University and James Walker of the University of Michigan warn that if one looks a little further into the future than the next century, the prospects look much more frightening. They predict that by 2100 the amount of carbon dioxide in the atmosphere will reach double its preindustrial level. By the 2200s it could be 7.6 times the preindustrial level. With draconian restrictions, it could be held to only 4 times the preindustrial level. Correspondingly, global warming will turn out to be much worse than anyone is now predicting for the next century.

By 1994 the world's insurance industry was already very concerned, for its losses due to storm and flood damage had been increasing rapidly. In September 1995 the Intergovernmental Panel on Climate Change (IPCC) reported the consensus view that global warming is real, and Thomas Karl of the National Climatic Data Center in Asheville, North Carolina, said, "There's a 90 to 95% chance that we're not being fooled." As of May 1997, despite broad agreement that global warming is a real and significant threat, the prospect for agreement on what to do about it did not look good. See Richard Monastersky, "Beyond Hot Air," *Science News* (May 24, 1997). In December 1997, the nations that signed the UN Framework Convention on Climate Change in Rio de Janeiro in 1992 met again in Kyoto, Japan, to set carbon emissions limits for the industrial nations. See Bill McKibben, "Warming up to Kyoto," *Audubon* (March/April 1998). The United States agreed to reduce its annual greenhouse gas emissions 7 percent below the 1990 level between 2008 and 2012. In November 1998 they met in Buenos Aires, Argentina (see Christopher Flavin, "Last Tango in Buenos Aires," *World Watch* [November/December 1998]) to work out practical details. Unfortunately, developing countries, where carbon emissions are growing most rapidly, face few restrictions, and political opposition in developed nations —especially in the United States—remains strong. Some of that opposition is visible in Jonathan H. Adler, "Hot Air," *National Review* (August 17, 1998).

ISSUE 6

Are Environmental Regulations Too Restrictive?

YES: Peter W. Huber, from "Saving the Environment from the Environmentalists," *Commentary* (April 1998)

NO: Paul R. Ehrlich and Anne H. Ehrlich, from "Brownlash: The New Environmental Anti-Science," *The Humanist* (November/December 1996)

ISSUE SUMMARY

YES: Peter W. Huber, a senior fellow at the Manhattan Institute, argues that the environment is best protected by traditional conservation, which puts human concerns first.

NO: Environmental scientists Paul R. Ehrlich and Anne H. Ehrlich argue that many objections to environmental protections are self-serving and based in bad or misused science.

Concern for the environment in America is not much more than a century old. In 1785 Thomas Jefferson invented the idea (if not the wording) of NIMBY ("Not In My Back Yard") when he wrote, "Let our workshops remain in Europe." He thought that an American factory system would have undesirable social, moral, and aesthetic effects. Clearly, he was alone in that thought, for America developed its industrial base very quickly. The workshop builders flourished, and the effects that concerned Jefferson did indeed come to pass. The first national park, Yosemite, resulted from legislation signed by President Abraham Lincoln in 1864. Yellowstone was approved in 1872. Both were responses to an awareness that if the areas' unique features were not protected, they would be destroyed by ranchers, miners, loggers, and market hunters, as had already happened elsewhere.

By the 1960s people were beginning to realize that other activities, such as the use of pesticides, also threatened treasured features of the environment, such as songbirds (see Rachel Carson, *Silent Spring* [Houghton Mifflin, 1962]), as well as human health. The result was government regulation of pesticides, air pollution, water pollution, and much, much more. Lead has been removed from gasoline and paint, chlorofluorocarbons from aerosol deodorants and refrigerants, and phosphates from laundry detergents. Developers have been told they cannot fill in swamps and other wetlands. Loggers have been forbidden to log in many areas. And commercial fishing seasons have been limited or eliminated entirely.

The economic impact of environmental regulation has not been as great as it might have been if Jefferson had had his way in 1785, but in each case someone's economic benefit has been interfered with. In other cases—such as when users of off-road vehicles have been barred from driving on the nesting grounds of rare shorebirds—the freedom to do as one wishes has been interfered with. In nations such as China, which instituted a "one child per couple" population control policy in 1979, the freedom in question is the freedom to have as many children as one wishes. As the environmental regulations have proliferated, so has the interference with freedoms that people once took for granted. And so have the objections. Conservative politicians and lobbyists for industry, recreation, and home-owner groups struggle to block or weaken every new environmental regulation and to repeal old regulations, often in the name of individual freedom and property rights. Environmentalists counter that freedom must be tempered by responsibility; individual freedom and property rights must have limits, or we will destroy what lets us and our children live on Earth.

The issue is not just America's; it is the world's. Environmentalists are active everywhere, identifying problems, promoting a sense of crisis, and saying what must be done, what behaviors must be controlled, and what freedoms must be limited. They have been successful enough to rouse fears among some far-right political conservatives of a liberal-environmentalist conspiracy to take over the world and impose an antifreedom world government. Similar fears may be shared by more moderate conservatives, but they are rarely voiced explicitly.

In the following selections, Peter W. Huber argues that the environment is best protected by traditional conservation. This puts human concerns before those of what he considers to be the insignificant and unattractive portions of the world that are favored by environmentalists and their "pervasive, manipulative, and intrusive bureaucracy." Paul R. Ehrlich and Anne H. Ehrlich maintain that many objections to environmental protections are essentially self-serving. They assert that antienvironmentalists deny the facts in favor of religious, economic, and political ideologies.

Peter W. Huber

 **YES**

Saving the Environment from the Environmentalists

As a political movement, environmentalism was invented by a conservative Republican. He loved wild animals. He particularly loved to shoot them.

In the spring of 1908, with time running out on his second term, President Theodore Roosevelt held a hugely successful conference on conservation. The report that emerged, T.R. would declare, was "one of the most fundamentally important documents ever laid before the American people." He promptly called a hemispheric conference on the same theme, and was working on a global one when he left office in March 1909.

He had learned his conservation the hard way. After Grover Cleveland defeated the Republicans in 1884, T.R. returned to his Chimney Butte ranch in the Dakota Territory with plans to increase his cattle herd fivefold. Armed neighbors came by to complain. As H. W. Brands recounts in his recent *T.R.: The Last Romantic,* "the potential for overstocking the range weighed constantly on the minds of the ranchers of the plains."

Although Roosevelt faced down his angry neighbors, he also set about finding a political solution to the problem that concerned them, forming and becoming president of the Little Missouri Stockmen's Association. He would only regret not starting earlier. The Dakota pastures were badly overgrazed in the summer of 1886, and many herds, T.R.'s among them, were destroyed in the dreadfully harsh winter that followed.

Occupying the White House two decades later, T.R. and his chief forester, Gifford Pinchot, would be the first to apply the word "conservation" to describe environmental policy. By then, Roosevelt had come to view the misuse of natural resources as "the fundamental problem which underlies almost every other problem of our national life."

The administration of Theodore Roosevelt was certainly not the first to show such concern. Congress had proclaimed Yellowstone a national park in 1872. Yosemite, Sequoia, and General Grant national parks were established in 1890. The first U.S. forest reserve, forerunner of the national forests, was proclaimed in the area around Yellowstone National Park in 1891. Presidents Harrison, Cleveland, and McKinley transferred some 50 million acres of timberland into the reserve system.

T.R.'s distinction was to give conservation its name and, more importantly, to transform it into an enduringly popular political movement. On the way to adding 150 million more acres to the country's forest reserves, he would persuade the great mass of ordinary Americans that conservation was in their own best interests.

What with two world wars and a depression intervening, it would take another six decades to complete a federal legal framework for conservation. In the meantime, much occurred to affect conventional notions of the environment. The radioactive aftermath of Hiroshima taught a first, ghastly lesson about insidious environmental poison. There followed popularized accounts of industrial equivalents of Hiroshima—fallout without the bomb. Rachel Carson defined the new genre in 1962, with the publication of *The Silent Spring,* about the dangers of pesticides.

All this became reflected in law. The Clean Air, Clean Water, and Resource Conservation and Recovery Acts of the 1960's, like the Endangered Species Act passed unanimously by the Senate in 1973, *seemed* to be cut from the same old conservationist cloth woven by T.R. (though they concerned smoke, sewage, and landfills rather than parks and mountains). But even as they completed and somewhat extended the framework for traditional conservation, these laws also quietly launched a new era—the era of environmentalism.

Regulating multifarious forms of pollution—the purpose of the clean-air, clean-water, and landfill acts—required a more elaborate regulatory structure than regulating parks and reserves. President Nixon had to establish a new cabinet-level body, the Environmental Protection Agency (EPA), to take charge. More significantly, each of the laws also included something quite new: an open-ended "toxics" provision, a general invitation to monitor the micro-environment for poisons and regulate them as needed. Even the Endangered Species Act, though written mainly with the likes of cougars in mind, was drafted broadly enough to protect unpleasant rodents like the kangaroo rat, and would soon be amended to prevent not only hunting but also "harming," which a federal court then construed to cover "habitat modification."

A mere statutory afterthought in the 1960's, the micro-environment was getting entire acts of its own a decade later. The Toxic Substances Control Act was promulgated in 1976. Then, in 1980, came Superfund. And thus, somewhere between Vietnam and the discovery of alarming concentrations of chemicals in the soil and groundwater at a town in upstate New York called Love Canal, a legal infrastructure for the new environmentalism slipped into place. Conservation was not abandoned. But politically it was overtaken, subsumed into something bigger. Bigger precisely because it concerned the very small.

⁙

Over time, the distinctions between conservation and environmentalism have been obscured. But they really are two different schools.

Conservation happens in places we can see, and draw on a map. Yellowstone starts here and ends there. Bison, eagles, and rivers are only somewhat harder to track.

T.R. had no trouble seeing the things that made him a conservationist. Forests were being leveled, ranges overgrazed, and game depleted. Hunters and hikers, cattlemen, farmers, and bird-watchers could easily grasp all this, too. The political choices T.R. was urging were based on these considerations. Americans would want to preserve Yellowstone for the same reason they might some day wish to climb Everest: because it was there, because they knew it was there, and because they desired to keep it there.

If conservation happens in places we can see, micro-environmentalism happens everywhere. The microcosm is so populous, the forces of dispersion so inexorable, that in every breath we take we inhale many of the very molecules once breathed by Moses and Caesar. At that level of things, everything gets polluted, even though no one can see it, and it is all too easy to suggest causes and effects. Fish die, frogs are deformed, breast cancers proliferate, immune systems collapse, sperm counts plummet, learning disabilities multiply: every time, invisible toxics are assumed to be the culprit.

To believe wholeheartedly in micro-environmentalism one must either be a savant or put a great deal of trust in savants. In particular, one must put one's trust in computer models. The model is everything. Only the model can say just where the dioxin came from, or how it may affect our cellular protein. Only the model will tell us whether our backyard barbecues (collectively, of course) are going to alter rainfall in Rwanda. Only the model can explain why a relentless pursuit of the invisible—halogenated hydrocarbons, heavy metals, or pesticides —will save birds or cut cancer rates. The cry of the loon gives way to the hum of the computer. T.R. trades in his double-barreled shotgun for a spectrometer.

But precisely because it involves things so very small, the microcosm requires management that is very large. Old-style conservationists maintained reasonably clean lines between private and public space. They may have debated how many Winnebagos to accommodate in Yellowstone, how much logging, hunting, fishing, or drilling for oil to tolerate on federal reserves, but the debates were confined by well-demarcated boundaries. Everyone knew where public authority began and ended. Yellowstone required management of a place, not a populace. Municipal sewer pipes and factory smokestacks may have required more management, but still of a conventional kind. The new models are completely different, so different that they are tended by a new oligarchy, a priesthood of scientists, regulators, and lawyers.

With detectors and computers that claim to count everything everywhere, micro-environmentalism never has to stop. With the right models in hand, it is easy to conclude that your light bulb, flush toilet, and hair spray, your washing machine and refrigerator and compost heap, are all of legitimate interest to the authorities. Nothing is too small, too personal, too close to home to drop beneath the new environmental radar. It is not Yellowstone that has to be fenced, but humanity itself. That requires a missionary spirit, a zealous willingness to work door to door. It requires propagandists at the EPA, lesson plans in public schools, and sermons from the modern pulpit. Children are taught to enlighten —perhaps even to denounce—their backsliding parents.

✦

At this point, environmental discourse often degenerates into a fractious quarrel about underlying facts. One side insists that tetraethyl lead, pseudo-estrogen, and low-frequency electromagnetic radiation seriously harm human health. The other side says they do not. One side says these things will hurt birds, frogs, and forests, and have already done so. The other side says they have not and will not.

One might suppose that science would settle such disputes. But it cannot. In a classic essay from 1972, the nuclear physicist Alvin Weinberg explained why. He coined a term, "trans-science," to describe the study of problems too large, diffuse, rare, or long-term to be resolved by scientific means. It would, for instance, take eight billion mice to perform a statistically significant test of the health effects of radiation at exposure levels the EPA deems to be "safe." The model used to set that threshold may be right, or it may be way off; the only certainty is that no eight-billion-mouse experiment is going to happen.

The same goes for any model of very-low-probability accidents—an earthquake precipitating the collapse of the Hoover dam, say, leading to the inundation of the Imperial Valley of California. Statistical models can be built, and have been, but their critical, constituent parts cannot be tested. And similarly with all the most far-reaching models of micro-environmentalism, a realm of huge populations (molecules, particles) paired with very weak or slow effects. Whether we are talking about global warming, ozone depletion, species extinction, radiation, halogens, or heavy metals, whether the concern is for humans or frogs, redwoods or sandworts, the time frames are too long, the effects too diffuse, the confounding variables too numerous.

You may doubt this if you get your environmental trans-science the way most people do, for the mass media always convey a greater sense of certitude. There is no news in reporting "Dog May or May Not Bite Man; Scientists Waffle." Instead, *Newsweek* gives us: "Meteorologists disagree about the cause and extent of the cooling trend. But they are almost unanimous in the view that the trend will reduce agricultural productivity for the rest of the century." That was in 1975. They were still almost unanimous in 1992, according to Vice President Al Gore; but about what? "Scientists have concluded—almost unanimously—that global warming is real and the time to act is now." (I owe this juxtaposition to the *Economist,* December 20, 1997.) If the papers give you the various sides of the trans-scientific debate at all, they give it in different editions; sometimes, the editions are published twenty years apart.

It is a fair bet that now and again a model will predict things exactly right. It is a fairer bet that much of the time it will not. Indeed, if overall statistics confirm anything, it is that environmental toxins of human origin are not the main cause of anything much. The more industrialized we become, the longer we live and the healthier we grow. There is a model—quite a credible one, in fact —that purports to prove that a steady dose of low-level radiation, like the one you get living in a high-altitude locale like Denver, or at some suitable distance from Chernobyl, actually improves your health.

Nor are these the only problems. Suspect toxins vastly outnumber modelers. The list of things we might reasonably worry about grows faster than new rules can be published in the *Federal Register*. But the axiology of science, its priorities of investigation and research, the criteria for what to study and what not to, are matters of taste, budget, values—everything but science itself. Scientific priorities, Weinberg notes, are themselves trans-scientific. So are all the engineering issues, the practical fixes that regulators prescribe. Science will never tell us just how much scrubber or converter to stick on a tailpipe or smokestack, how much sand and gravel at the end of a sewer pipe, how much plastic and clay around the sides of a dump.

So, in the end, the micro-environmentalist just names his favorite poison, and gets on with making sure that nobody drinks it. The process is arrayed in the sumptuary of science, but the key calls are political. Micro-environmentalism ends up as a pursuit of politics by other means.

◦◦◦

There is nothing wrong with politics, of course—T.R. reveled in them. But here too there is an essential difference between the old conservationism and the new environmentalism.

All the choices old-style conservationists make are conventionally political. The Clinton administration recently designated as a national monument a vast stretch of land in Utah, from Bryce Canyon to the Colorado River, and from Boulder to the Arizona state line. It was a controversial call: the area includes the Kaiparowits plateau, where a Dutch-owned concern was slated to begin mining massive coal formations. T.R. would certainly have understood the controversy over the Kaiparowits plateau, and would likely have approved the decision to conserve.

In the new environmentalism, by contrast, conventional political process decides little. The clauses about toxics that were inserted as an afterthought in the clean-air and clean-water acts, and as the central thought in Superfund, are just a stew of words. They articulate no standard, set no budget, establish no limits. In T.R.'s day they would not even have passed constitutional muster. The Supreme Court would have cited the "nondelegation doctrine," which, then at least, forbade Congress to delegate responsibilities wholesale to the executive branch.

Today the delegation goes a lot further. Though nominally in the hands of the President and overseen by Congress, political authority for micro-environmental matters is now centered in the new trans-scientific oligarchy. The key calls are still stroke-of-the-pen political, at bottom, but no ordinary observer can see to the bottom. The only thing ordinary Americans may dimly realize is that somewhere deep in the EPA it has been deemed wise to spend more money digging up an industrial park in New Jersey than ever was spent conserving a forest in the Adirondacks.

Politicians know how to reward friends and punish enemies, but democratic politics tends, as a whole, to be pretty even-handed. When the old conservationists took your land, they paid you for it, and the money came from taxes and user fees. That was about as fair as the income tax—not very, but fair enough. In the new environmentalism, most of the taxing occurs off the public books. There is a great deal of creeping, uncompensated expropriation, and a freakish rain of ruin on those unlucky enough to discover the wrong rodent, marsh, or buried chemical on their land. Any amount of public environmental good, however small, can entail any private financial burden, however large.

We have likewise lost all pragmatic sense of when enough is enough. Conservation, driven as it must be through normal political channels, can be pushed only so far. The Clinton administration had to trade political chips for the Kaiparowits plateau; nobody feared it would soon seize the rest of Utah. Conservation works, politically, because the boundaries are reasonably well defined and because it targets real estate, not molecules. By contrast, most of the Northeast could be placed in regulatory receivership for its countless microenvironmental derelictions. Whereas hikers and hunters occupy a seat or two at the political table, synthetic estrogens and carbon dioxide have somehow escaped from the coils of politics, and the priesthood can pursue them without restraint.

The "remedial" efforts that emerge from this pursuit end up repelling even the intended beneficiaries. Contact with Superfund has become socially poisonous. The very arrival of the EPA in a community shatters property values, repels new industrial investment, and throws a region's entire future into doubt. Environmental regulation has in effect become a mirror image of the problems it is supposed to solve, leaking into society cancerous plumes of lawyers, administrators, and consultants, the brokers of ignorance, speculation, and uncertainty.

Theodore Roosevelt was no Ralph Waldo Emerson, Henry David Thoreau, or John Muir. These "preservationists" revered wilderness for its own sake. Muir, founder of the Sierra Club, adamantly opposed building the Tuolumne River dam in Yosemite to supply water to San Francisco. T.R. supported it, consistent with his "wise-use" philosophy of conservation. For T.R., the whole point of conserving nature was to continue using it—forests for lumber, ranges for grazing, rivers for electrical power. Hunters, cattlemen, ranchers were to be involved in conservation because it was in their own self-interest. "Despite occasional moments of doubt," writes H. W. Brands, T.R. "passionately believed in the capacity of the ordinary people of America to act in the public welfare, once they were alerted to the true nature of that welfare."

That was the faith that defined the first century of conservationism. Congress had established Yellowstone National Park as a "pleasuring ground" for people. The national parks would include forests, seashores, lakeshores, and scenic trails but also monuments, historical sites, and battlefields—man's creation alongside nature's. T.R.'s distant cousin Franklin, too, was an ardent conservationist, and during his presidency he established his own share of national parks and forests; but he also built roads, bridges, tunnels, airports, and skyscrapers. Like T.R., he believed there was room enough in nature for man.

Today, the preservationist vision is back on top. The quasi-pagan nature worship of the late 19th century has been reworked as the trans-scientific demonology of the late 20th. Those who believe in the new methods and models do not even credit the distinction between conservation and preservation. The computer models can link any human activity, however small, to any environmental consequence, however large—it is just a matter of tracing out small effects through space and time, down the rivers, up the food chains, and into the roots, the egg shells, or the fatty tissue of the breast. This is what chaos theorists call the "butterfly effect," traced out by computer. If you believe in the computer, you must believe that the only way really to "conserve" is not to touch at all.

∽❀∾

Is it possible to change course, and if so, how? The answer comes in two parts, the philosophical and the practical-political.

There was never much high-church philosophy to T.R.'s conservationism. It was inspired by an abiding appreciation for the beauty of nature—that is, by aesthetics. And it was disciplined by a real sense (this may seem a curious thing to say of a man like T.R.) of humility. Not much philosophy there, but enough.

A sense of aesthetics would get us a long way in reforming environmental discourse. It would, to begin with, help us cut through the scientism, the fussy bureaucratic detail. It would let us ignore the priesthood and dispense with its soaring intellectual cathedrals. It would save us the enormous expense and inconvenience of digging up New Jersey and conserving our own trash. It would allow us to spend our energy and dollars on places that are simply beautiful, and oppose things for no fancier reason than that they are ugly.

The aesthetic approach does not mean ignoring the micro-environment completely, still less rejecting every commandment ever prescribed by the priesthood. Priests and propagandists have every right to help shape our aesthetic preferences, for better or worse; they just should not be allowed to palm off their art as science. Purity is beautiful, and industrial byproducts in our drinking water are ugly, even if invisible and harmless. (Fluoride and chlorine in the water are sort of ugly, too, even if they give us healthier teeth and guts.)

There is also an aesthetic case to be made for frugality: we are not going to run out of space for dumps, but garbage is not beautiful, and making do with less often is. By the same token, however, profligate excess in the digging up of dumps is as ugly as profligate excess in the original dumping. T.R.-style conservationists would devote far more energy to parks and forests, to sewage treatment and cleaner smokestacks, and far less to part-per-billion traces of dioxin. Whatever impact pesticides may have, setting aside 100 million acres of forest will likely protect more birds than trying to bankrupt the DuPont corporation through the Superfund. The most beautiful way to purify water is probably the most effective way, too: maintain unspoiled watersheds. While an "almost unanimous" priesthood forecast cooling in 1975, and warming in 1992, the conservationist just went on planting trees, the most pleasant and practical way to suck carbon out of the air, however it may (or may not) affect global climate.

As for a sense of humility, it might usefully take the form of a wariness of grand public works. T.R. endorsed his share of them; FDR endorsed many more. In retrospect, it seems clear that more of the megalithic government projects of those days should have been opposed. They certainly should be as we go forward. Yesterday the federal dollar erected huge dams and drained swamps; today federal money is used to unleash those same rivers, and convert sugar plantations back into swamp. (The swamp programs are doubly expensive because the government also props up the price of sugar.) A consistent conservationism might have blocked more of the before, and thus saved us from having to do much of the after.

A consistent philosophy of moderation and caution could also do much to blunt the vindictive, punitive impulses of the modern environmentalist—and thereby help make things greener. In the aftermath of the Exxon Valdez spill, the multi-billion dollar steam-cleaning of rocks in Prince William Sound did far more harm than good, stripping away the organic seeds of rebirth along with the oil. In places where the cleanup was left to the wind and the waves, "nature," Scientific American would conclude, "fared better on its own." But the frenzied demands that Exxon be made to pay and pay overwhelmed every other impulse, to the point where increasing the damage to the oil company became much more important than abating damage to the Sound.

So much for philosophy. Politically, the most important principle is that whereas the environmentalist mission is exclusionary, the conservationist mission is populist and inclusionary, welcoming humankind as an integral and legitimate part of nature's landscape. Conservationism does not see man as a tapeworm in the bowel of nature. Symbiosis is possible. And when a choice has to be made, as it sometimes must, people come first.

The old conservationists were reluctant collectivists; the new environmentalists, eager ones. Having successfully conflated eagles with snail darters, halogenated hydrocarbons with the mountain peaks of Yosemite, the new environmentalists claim to speak for them all. This is an agenda that fits easily into a left-wing shoe. Running the whole environment—literally, "that which surrounds"—is an opportunity the Left gladly welcomes. The micro-environment is the best part of all, requiring as it does a pervasive, manipulative, and intrusive bureaucracy—for the Left, political ambrosia.

In reply, the Right has nothing better to offer than a long tradition of creating parks, husbanding wildlife, and venerating natural heritages of every kind. Politically speaking, however, that should be enough. It is the old conservation, not the new, that welcomes the family in the camper. It is the old that dispenses with oligarchy and caters to the common tastes of the common man.

It is the old that is the legacy of T.R., a man who so loved to shoot wild animals that he resolved to conserve the vast open spaces in which they live.

Besides, too-eager collectivists never end up conserving anything; only the reluctant ones do. (Behold the land once called East Germany: Love Canal, border to border, perfected by Communists.) The old conservationism, of parks and forests and Winnebagos, advances the green cause *because* of the Winnebago. The man in the Winnebago is enlisted in the cause precisely by an appeal to his own private sense of what is beautiful, and therefore to what he wants for himself and his family.

What is wrong with that?

NO    Paul R. Ehrlich and Anne H. Ehrlich

Brownlash: The New Environmental Anti-Science

Humanity is now facing a sort of slow-motion environmental Dunkirk. It remains to be seen whether civilization can avoid the perilous trap it has set for itself. Unlike the troops crowding the beach at Dunkirk, civilization's fate is in its own hands; no miraculous last-minute rescue is in the cards. Although progress has certainly been made in addressing the human predicament, far more is needed. Even if humanity manages to extricate itself, it is likely that environmental events will be defining ones for our grandchildren's generation —and those events could dwarf World War II in magnitude.

Sadly, much of the progress that has been made in defining, understanding, and seeking solutions to the human predicament over the past 30 years is now being undermined by an environmental backlash. We call these attempts to minimize the seriousness of environmental problems the *brownlash* because they help to fuel a backlash against "green" policies. While it assumes a variety of forms, the brownlash appears most clearly as an outpouring of seemingly authoritative opinions in books, articles, and media appearances that greatly distort what is or isn't known by environmental scientists. Taken together, despite the variety of its forms, sources, and issues addressed, the brownlash has produced what amounts to a body of anti-science—a twisting of the findings of empirical science—to bolster a predetermined worldview and to support a political agenda. By virtue of relentless repetition, this flood of anti-environmental sentiment has acquired an unfortunate aura of credibility.

It should be noted that the brownlash is not by any means a coordinated effort. Rather, it seems to be generated by a diversity of individuals and organizations. Some of its promoters have links to right-wing ideology and political groups. And some are well-intentioned individuals, including writers and public figures, who for one reason or another have bought into the notion that environmental regulation has become oppressive and needs to be severely weakened. But the most extreme—and most dangerous—elements are those who, while claiming to represent a scientific viewpoint, misstate scientific findings to support their view that the U.S. government has gone overboard with regulation, especially (but not exclusively) for environmental protection, and that subtle, long-term problems like global warming are nothing to worry about.

The words and sentiments of the brownlash are profoundly troubling to us and many of our colleagues. Not only are the underlying agendas seldom revealed but, more important, the confusion and distraction created among the public and policymakers by brownlash pronouncements interfere with and prolong the already difficult search for realistic and equitable solutions to the human predicament.

Anti-science as promoted by the brownlash is not a unique phenomenon in our society; the largely successful efforts of creationists to keep Americans ignorant of evolution is another example, which is perhaps not entirely unrelated. Both feature a denial of facts and circumstances that don't fit religious or other traditional beliefs; policies built on either could lead our society into serious trouble.

Fortunately, in the case of environmental science, most of the public is fairly well informed about environmental problems and remains committed to environmental protection. When polled, 65 percent of Americans today say they are willing to pay good money for environmental quality. But support for environmental quality is sometimes said to be superficial; while almost everyone is in favor of a sound environment—clean air, clean water, toxic site cleanups, national parks, and so on—many don't feel that environmental deterioration, especially on a regional or global level, is a crucial issue in their own lives. In part this is testimony to the success of environmental protection in the United States. But it is also the case that most people lack an appreciation of the deeper but generally less visible, slowly developing global problems. Thus they don't perceive population growth, global warming, the loss of biodiversity, depletion of groundwater, or exposure to chemicals in plastics and pesticides as a personal threat at the same level as crime in their neighborhood, loss of a job, or a substantial rise in taxes.

So anti-science rhetoric has been particularly effective in promoting a series of erroneous notions, including:

- Environmental scientists ignore the abundant good news about the environment.
- Population growth does not cause environmental damage and may even be beneficial.
- Humanity is on the verge of abolishing hunger; food scarcity is a local or regional problem and not indicative of overpopulation.
- Natural resources are superabundant, if not infinite.
- There is no extinction crisis, and so most efforts to preserve species are both uneconomic and unnecessary.
- Global warming and acid rain are not serious threats to humanity.
- Stratospheric ozone depletion is a hoax.
- The risks posed by toxic substances are vastly exaggerated.
- Environmental regulation is wrecking the economy.

How has the brownlash managed to persuade a significant segment of the public that the state of the environment and the directions and rates in which it is changing are not causes for great concern? Even many individuals who are sensitive to local environmental problems have found brownlash distortions of global issues convincing. Part of the answer lies in the overall lack of scientific knowledge among United States citizens. Most Americans readily grasp the issues surrounding something familiar and tangible like a local dump site, but they have considerably more difficulty with issues involving genetic variation or the dynamics of the atmosphere. Thus it is relatively easy to rally support against a proposed landfill and infinitely more difficult to impose a carbon tax that might help offset global warming.

Also, individuals not trained to recognize the hallmarks of change have difficulty perceiving and appreciating the gradual deterioration of civilization's life-support systems. This is why record-breaking temperatures and violent storms receive so much attention while a gradual increase in annual global temperatures—measured in fractions of a degree over decades—is not considered newsworthy. Threatened pandas are featured on television, while the constant and critical losses of insect populations, which are key elements of our life-support systems, pass unnoticed. People who have no meaningful way to grasp regional and global environmental problems cannot easily tell what information is distorted, when, and to what degree.

Decision-makers, too, have a tendency to focus mostly on the more obvious and immediate environmental problems—usually described as "pollution" —rather than on the deterioration of natural ecosystems upon whose continued functioning global civilization depends. Indeed, most people still don't realize that humanity has become a truly global force, interfering in a very real and direct way in many of the planet's natural cycles.

For example, human activity puts ten times as much oil into the oceans as comes from natural seeps, has multiplied the natural flow of cadmium into the atmosphere eightfold, has doubled the rate of nitrogen fixation, and is responsible for about half the concentration of methane (a potent greenhouse gas) and more than a quarter of the carbon dioxide (also a greenhouse gas) in the atmosphere today—all added since the industrial revolution, most notably in the past half-century. Human beings now use or co-opt some 40 percent of the food available to all land animals and about 45 percent of the available freshwater flows.

Another factor that plays into brownlash thinking is the not uncommon belief that environmental quality is improving, not declining. In some ways it is, but the claim of uniform improvement simply does not stand up to close scientific scrutiny. Nor does the claim that the human condition in general is improving everywhere. The degradation of ecosystem services (the conditions and processes through which natural ecosystems support and fulfill human life) is a crucial issue that is largely ignored by the brownlash. Unfortunately, the superficial progress achieved to date has made it easy to label ecologists doomsayers for continuing to press for change. At the same time, the public often seems unaware of the success of actions taken at the instigation of the environmental movement. People can easily see the disadvantages of environmental regulations but not the despoliation that would exist without them. Especially resentful are those whose personal or corporate ox is being gored when they are forced to sustain financial losses because of a sensible (or occasionally senseless) application of regulations.

Of course, it is natural for many people to feel personally threatened by efforts to preserve a healthy environment. Consider a car salesperson who makes a bigger commission selling a large car than a small one, an executive of a petrochemical company that is liable for damage done by toxic chemicals released into the environment, a logger whose job is jeopardized by enforcement of the Endangered Species Act, a rancher whose way of life may be threatened by higher grazing fees on public lands, a farmer about to lose the farm because of environmentalists' attacks on subsidies for irrigation water, or a developer who wants to continue building subdivisions and is sick and tired of dealing with inconsistent building codes or U.S. Fish and Wildlife Service bureaucrats. In such situations, resentment of some of the rules, regulations, and recommendations designed to enhance human well-being and protect life-support systems is understandable.

Unfortunately, many of these dissatisfied individuals and companies have been recruited into the self-styled "wise-use" movement, which has attracted a surprisingly diverse coalition of people, including representatives of extractive and polluting industries who are motivated by corporate interests as well as private property rights activists and right-wing ideologues. Although some of these individuals simply believe that environmental regulations unfairly distribute the costs of environmental protection, some others are doubtless motivated more by a greedy desire for unrestrained economic expansion.

At a minimum, the wise-use movement firmly opposes most government efforts to maintain environmental quality in the belief that environmental regulation creates unnecessary and burdensome bureaucratic hurdles which stifle economic growth. Wise-use advocates see little or no need for constraints on the exploitation of resources for short-term economic benefits and argue that such exploitation can be accelerated with no adverse long-term consequences. Thus they espouse unrestricted drilling in the Arctic National Wildlife Refuge, logging in national forests, mining in protected areas or next door to national parks, and full compensation for any loss of actual or potential property value resulting from environmental restrictions.

In promoting the view that immediate economic interests are best served by continuing business as usual, the wise-use movement works to stir up discontent among everyday citizens who, rightly or wrongly, feel abused by environmental regulations. This tactic is described in detail in David Helvarg's book, *The War Against the Greens:*

> To date the Wise Use/Property Rights backlash has been a bracing if dangerous reminder to environmentalists that power concedes nothing without a demand and that no social movement, be it ethnic, civil, or environmental, can rest on its past laurels.... If the anti-enviros' links to the Farm Bureau, Heritage Foundation, NRA, logging companies, resource trade associations, multinational gold-mining companies, [and] ORV manufacturers... proves anything, it's that large industrial lobbies and transnational corporations have learned to play the grassroots game.

Wise-use proponents are not always candid about their motivations and intentions. Many of the organizations representing them masquerade as groups seemingly attentive to environmental quality. Adopting a strategy biologists call "aggressive mimicry," they often give themselves names resembling those of genuine environmental or scientific public-interest groups: National Wetland Coalition, Friends of Eagle Mountain, the Sahara Club, the Alliance for Environment and Resources, the Abundant Wildlife Society of North America, the Global Climate Coalition, the National Wilderness Institute, and the American Council on Science and Health. In keeping with aggressive mimicry, these organizations often actively work *against* the interests implied in their names— a practice sometimes called *greenscamming.*

One such group, calling itself Northwesterners for More Fish, seeks to limit federal protection of endangered fish species so the activities of utilities, aluminum companies, and timber outfits utilizing the region's rivers are not hindered. Armed with a $2.6 million budget, the group aims to discredit environmentalists who say industry is destroying the fish habitats of the Columbia and other rivers, threatening the Northwest's valuable salmon fishery, among others.

Representative George Miller, referring to the wise-use movement's support of welfare ranching, overlogging, and government giveaways of mining rights, stated: "What you have . . . is a lot of special interests who are trying to generate some ideological movement to try and disguise what it is individually they want in the name of their own profits, their own greed in terms of the use and abuse of federal lands."

Wise-use sentiments have been adopted by a number of deeply conservative legislators, many of whom have received campaign contributions from these organizations. One member of the House of Representatives recently succeeded in gaining passage of a bill that limited the annual budget for the Mojave National Preserve, the newest addition to the National Parks System, to one dollar—thus guaranteeing that the park would have no money for upkeep or for enforcement of park regulations.

These same conservative legislators are determined to slash funding for scientific research, especially on such subjects as endangered species, ozone depletion, and global warming, and have legislated for substantial cutbacks in funds for the National Science Foundation, the U.S. Geological Survey, the National Aeronautics and Space Administration, and the Environmental Protection Agency. Many of them and their supporters see science as self-indulgent, at odds with economic interests, and inextricably linked to regulatory excesses.

The scientific justifications and philosophical underpinnings for the positions of the wise-use movement are largely provided by the brownlash. Prominent promoters of the wise-use viewpoint on a number of issues include such conservative think tanks as the Cato Institute and the Heritage Foundation. Both organizations help generate and disseminate erroneous brownlash ideas and information. Adam Myerson, editor of the Heritage Foundation's journal *Policy Review,* pretty much summed up the brownlash perspective by saying: "Leading scientists have done major work disputing the current henny-pennyism about global warming, acid rain, and other purported environmental catastrophes." In reality, however, most "leading" scientists support what Myerson calls henny-pennyism; the scientists he refers to are a small group largely outside the mainstream of scientific thinking.

In recent years, a flood of books and articles has advanced the notion that all is well with the environment, giving credence to this anti-scientific "What, me worry?" outlook. Brownlash writers often pepper their works with code phrases such as *sound science* and *balance*—words that suggest objectivity while in fact having little connection to what is presented. *Sound science* usually means science that is interpreted to support the brownlash view. *Balance* generally means giving undue prominence to the opinions of one or a handful of contrarian scientists who are at odds with the consensus of the scientific community at large.

Of course, while pro-environmental groups and environmental scientists in general may sometimes be dead wrong (as can anybody confronting environmental complexity), they ordinarily are not acting on behalf of narrow economic interests. Yet one of the remarkable triumphs of the wise-use movement and its allies in the past decade has been their ability to define public-interest organizations, in the eyes of many legislators, as "special interests"—not different in kind from the American Tobacco Institute, the Western Fuels Association, or other organizations that represent business groups.

But we believe there is a very real difference in kind. Most environmental organizations are funded mainly by membership donations; corporate funding is at most a minor factor for public-interest advocacy groups. There are no monetary profits to be gained other than attracting a bigger membership. Environmental scientists have even less to gain; they usually are dependent upon university or research institute salaries and research funds from peer-reviewed government grants or sometimes (especially in new or controversial areas where government funds are largely unavailable) from private foundations.

One reason the brownlash messages hold so much appeal to many people, we think, is the fear of further change. Even though the American frontier closed a century ago, many Americans seem to believe they still live in what the great economist Kenneth Boulding once called a "cowboy economy." They still think they can figuratively throw their garbage over the backyard fence with impunity. They regard the environmentally protected public land as "wasted" and think it should be available for their self-beneficial appropriation. They believe that private property rights are absolute (despite a rich economic and legal literature showing they never have been). They do not understand, as Pace University law professor John Humbach wrote in 1993, that "the Constitution does not guarantee that land speculators will win their bets."

The anti-science brownlash provides a rationalization for the short-term economic interests of these groups: old-growth forests are decadent and should be harvested; extinction is natural, so there's no harm in overharvesting economically important animals; there is abundant undisturbed habitat, so human beings have a right to develop land anywhere and in any way they choose; global warming is a hoax or even will benefit agriculture, so there's no need to limit the burning of fossil fuels; and so on. Anti-science basically claims we can keep the good old days by doing business as usual. But the problem is we can't.

Thus the brownlash helps create public confusion about the character and magnitude of environmental problems, taking advantage of the lack of consensus among individuals and social groups on the urgency of enhancing environmental protection. A widely shared social consensus, such as the United States saw during World War II, will be essential if we are to maintain environmental quality while meeting the nation's other needs. By emphasizing dissent, the brownlash works against the formation of any such consensus; instead it has helped thwart the development of a spirit of cooperation mixed with concern for society as a whole. In our opinion, the brownlash fuels conflict by claiming the environmental problems are overblown or nonexistent and that unbridled economic development will propel the world to new levels of prosperity with little or no risk to the natural systems that support society. As a result, environmental groups and wise-use proponents are increasingly polarized.

Unfortunately, some of that polarization has led to ugly confrontations and activities that are not condoned by the brownlash or by most environmentalists, including us. As David Helvarg stated, "Along with the growth of Wise Use/Property Rights, the last six years have seen a startling increase in intimidation, vandalism, and violence directed against grassroots environmental activists." And while confrontations and threats have been generated by both sides—most notably (but by no means exclusively) over the northern spotted owl protection plan—the level of intimidation engaged in by wise-use proponents is disturbing, to say the least....

Fortunately, despite all the efforts of the brownlash to discourage it, environmental concern in the United States is widespread. Thus a public-opinion survey in 1995 indicated that slightly over half of all Americans felt that environmental problems in the United States were "very serious." Indeed, 85 percent were concerned "a fair amount" and 38 percent "a great deal" about the environment. Fifty-eight percent would choose protecting the environment over economic growth, and 65 percent said they would be willing to pay higher prices so that industry could protect the environment better. Responses in other rich nations have been similar, and people in developing nations have shown, if anything, even greater environmental concerns. These responses suggest that the notion that caring about the environment is a luxury of the rich is a myth. Furthermore, our impression is that young people care especially strongly about environmental quality—a good omen if true.

Nor is environmental concern exclusive to Democrats and "liberals." There is a strong Republican and conservative tradition of environmental protection dating back to Teddy Roosevelt and even earlier. Many of our most important environmental laws were passed with bipartisan support during the Nixon and Ford administrations. Recently, some conservative environmentalists have been speaking out against brownlash rhetoric. And public concern is rising about the efforts to cripple environmental laws and regulations posed by right-wing leaders in Congress, thinly disguised as "deregulation" and "necessary budget-cutting." In January 1996, a Republican pollster, Linda Divall, warned that "our party is out of sync with mainstream American opinion when it comes to the environment."

Indeed, some interests that might be expected to sympathize with the wise-use movement have moved beyond such reactionary views. Many leaders in corporations such as paper companies and chemical manufacturers, whose activities are directly harmful to the environment, are concerned about their firms' environmental impacts and are shifting to less damaging practices. Our friends in the ranching community in western Colorado indicate their concern to us every summer. They want to preserve a way of life and a high-quality environment—and are as worried about the progressive suburbanization of the area as are the scientists at the Rocky Mountain Biological Laboratory. Indeed, they have actively participated in discussions with environmentalists and officials of the Department of the Interior to set grazing fees at levels that wouldn't force them out of business but also wouldn't subsidize overgrazing and land abuse.

Loggers, ranchers, miners, petrochemical workers, fishers, and professors all live on the same planet, and all of us must cooperate to preserve a sound environment for our descendants. The environmental problems of the planet can be solved only in a spirit of cooperation, not one of conflict. Ways must be found to allocate fairly both the benefits and the costs of environmental quality.

POSTSCRIPT

Are Environmental Regulations Too Restrictive?

The effects of "wise use" policies can be seen in Douglas Gantenbein's "Old Growth for Sale," *Audubon* (May/June 1998), in which he says that efforts to reduce logging of centuries-old trees on federal lands have failed. Such results would not surprise the Ehrlichs, who, in "Ehrlich's Fables," *Technology Review* (January 1997), write about "a sampling of the myths, or fables, that the promoters of 'sound science' and 'balance' are promulgating about issues relating to population and food, the atmosphere and climate, toxic substances, and economics and the environment."

Which side is right? The debate can be seen in the arguments over whether or not habitat conservation plans, devised as a way to moderate the impact of Endangered Species Act regulations on landowners, actually help endangered species. See Joselyn Kaiser, "When a Habitat Is Not a Home," *Science* (June 13, 1997). Perhaps the answer depends on what one values: human beings or the environment, present prosperity or future survival, past tradition or new understanding.

In the Worldwatch Institute's *State of the World 1999* (W. W. Norton, 1999), Lester R. Brown says, "As we look forward to the twenty-first century, it is clear that satisfying the projected needs of an ever larger world population with the economy we now have is simply not possible.... Human societies cannot continue to prosper while the natural world is progressively degraded." Catastrophe can be avoided, but not if we insist on doing things the way we always have.

Since the 1992 Earth Summit (the UN Conference on Environment and Development) in Rio de Janeiro, the world's environmental problems have actually gotten worse. But according to Christopher Flavin, in "The Legacy of Rio," *State of the World 1997* (W. W. Norton, 1997), the answer does not lie in some centralized world government but "in an eclectic mix of international agreements, sensible government policies, efficient use of private resources, and bold initiatives by grassroots organizations and local governments."

In those nations that have ignored environmental issues and refused to regulate, the problems have grown much worse. See Mike Edwards, "Lethal Legacy: Pollution in the Former USSR," *National Geographic* (August 1994), which begins, "The story on these pages is not a pretty one. It stems from decades of neglect and abuse of a vast and beautiful land.... In their ruthless drive to exploit and industrialize their nation, Soviet leaders gave little thought to the health of the people or to the lands that they ruled."

On the Internet ...

Electromagnetic Fields and Human Health

At this site, John E. Moulder, professor of radiation oncology, radiology, and pharmacology/toxicology at the Medical College of Wisconsin, answers frequently asked questions about the relationship between electromagnetic fields (EMFs) and cancer.

```
http://www.mcw.edu/gcrc/cop/powerlines-cancer-
FAQ/toc.html
```

Food Irradiation

The National Agricultural Library of the U.S. Department of Agriculture makes available for download a number of documents pertaining to the food irradiation controversy.

```
http://www.nal.usda.gov/spevents/pressrel/
preg8003.htm
```

The Foundation for Food Irradiation Education

The Foundation for Food Irradiation Education (FFIE) provides information with the goal of adopting food irradiation where appropriate.

```
http://www.food-irradiation.com
```

The Hampshire Research Institute

The Hampshire Research Institute maintains this site to explain the nature of environmental risk.

```
http://www.hampshire.org/risk01.htm
```

National Institute of Environmental Health Sciences

The National Institute of Environmental Health Sciences studies the health risks of numerous environmental factors, many of which are associated with the use of technology.

```
http://www.niehs.nih.gov
```

PART 3

Health

*M*any people are concerned about new technological and scientific discoveries because they fear their potential impacts on human health. In the past, fears have been expressed concerning nuclear bombs and power plants, the internal combustion engine, medications such as thalidomide and diethylstilbestrol, pesticides and other chemicals, and more. Today people worry about the possible health risks of electromagnetic fields and food irradiation, among other things.

- Are Electromagnetic Fields Dangerous to Your Health?

- Is Irradiated Food Safe to Eat?

ISSUE 7

Are Electromagnetic Fields Dangerous to Your Health?

YES: Paul Brodeur, from *The Great Powerline Coverup: How the Utilities and the Government Are Trying to Hide the Cancer Hazard Posed by Electromagnetic Fields* (Little, Brown, 1993)

NO: Edward W. Campion, from "Power Lines, Cancer, and Fear," *The New England Journal of Medicine* (July 3, 1997)

ISSUE SUMMARY

YES: Writer Paul Brodeur argues that there is an increased risk of developing cancer from being exposed to electromagnetic fields (EMFs) given off by electric power lines and that the risk is significant enough to warrant immediate measures to reduce exposures to the fields.

NO: Physician Edward W. Campion counters that there is no credible evidence that there is any risk of developing cancer from EMF exposure and that it is time to stop wasting research resources on further studies.

Electromagnetic fields (EMFs) are emitted by any device that uses electricity. They weaken rapidly as one gets further from the source, but they can be remarkably strong close to the source. Users of electric blankets, before the blankets were redesigned to minimize EMFs, were among those who were most exposed to EMFs. People who use computers regularly are another highly exposed population. And, since EMF strength depends also on how much electricity is flowing through the source, so are people who live near power lines, especially high-tension, long-distance transmission lines.

Early research shows the difficulties of nailing down any possible side effects of EMF exposure. In 1979 researchers at the University of Colorado Health Center in Denver, Colorado, reported that, in a study of 344 childhood cancer deaths, children whose homes were exposed to higher EMF levels were two to three times more likely to die of leukemia or lymphoma. At the time, however, no one could suggest any mechanism by which EMFs could cause cancer, especially since the body generates its own EMFs of strength similar to those produced in the body by high-tension lines. Some other studies found similar links between EMF exposure and cancer; some did not.

Inconsistency has been the curse of research in this area. Speaking on research into the effects of extremely low frequency (ELF) EMFs on cells in the laboratory (which was performed in an effort to find mechanisms by which EMFs might cause cancer), Larry Cress of the U.S. Food and Drug Administration's Center for Devices and Radiological Health said, "Many researchers have been able to reproduce their effects most, but not all, of the time. And we don't see a dose response, as with some radiation, such as x-ray. Or, one laboratory may see an *increase* in something in a cell when the field is turned on, while another laboratory sees a corresponding *decrease* when the field is turned on." See Dixie Farley, "The ELF in Your Electric Blanket [and Other Appliances]," *FDA Consumer* (December 1992).

In 1992 the Committee on Interagency Radiation Research and Policy Coordination, an arm of the White House's Office of Science and Technology Policy, released *Health Effects of Low Frequency Electric and Magnetic Fields,* a report that concluded, "There is no convincing [published] evidence . . . to support the contention that exposures to extremely low frequency electric and magnetic fields generated by sources such as household appliances, video terminals, and local powerlines are demonstrable health hazards."

However, at about the same time, Swedish researchers announced that a study of leukemic children showed an association between their disease and the distances of their homes from power lines. The researchers also reported finding that the risk of leukemia increases in adults with exposure to EMFs in the workplace. Critics have objected that the correlations in such studies are weak —that they could easily be due to nothing more than coincidence or that they might reflect exposure to something other than EMFs whose levels nevertheless fluctuate in step with EMF levels (perhaps herbicides used to control the growth of vegetation under power lines or vapors given off by electrical insulation).

In 1996 Jon Palfreman, in "Apocalypse Not," *Technology Review* (April 1996), summarized the controversy and the evidence against any connection between cancer and EMFs. On July 3, 1997, *The New England Journal of Medicine* published a report by Martha S. Linet et al. entitled "Residential Exposure to Magnetic Fields and Acute Lymphoblastic Leukemia in Children," in which the authors failed to find any support for such a connection.

Yet the associations are there for scientists, as well as for journalists such as Paul Brodeur, to consider. In July 1990 Brodeur published a long article in *The New Yorker* in which he describes clusters of cancer cases that seemed to be linked to EMFs from power lines and reviews both the evidence and the responses of public utility representatives. In a later article, reprinted here, Brodeur summarizes his earlier report, adds further cases, and urges immediate measures to reduce what he feels are dangerous EMF exposures.

In an editorial that accompanied Linet et al.'s 1997 report, Edward W. Campion argues that there is no credible evidence of cancer risk from EMF exposure. Campion asserts that research has been wasted on trying to find a link between EMF exposure and cancer and that such research provides little insight, merely paranoia.

Paul Brodeur

The Great Powerline Coverup

In my Annals of Radiation about the health hazard posed by the sixty-hertz magnetic fields that are given off by high-current and high-voltage power lines (July 9, 1990) I cited evidence suggesting that a cancer cluster had occurred among residents of Meadow Street in Guilford, Connecticut. During the past twenty years, seven tumors—two malignant brain tumors, two cases of meningioma (a rare and generally nonmalignant tumor of the brain), a malignant eye tumor, an ovarian tumor, and a tumor of the tibia—have been recorded among children and adults living on that street, which is only two hundred and fifty yards long and has only nine houses on it. Because all seven tumors developed in people who were living or had lived for significant periods of time in five of six adjacent houses situated near an electric-power substation and next to some main distribution power lines carrying high current from the substation, I suggested that the cancer among the residents of Meadow Street was associated with chronic exposure to the magnetic fields that are given off by such wires. To support that contention, I cited the fact that during the past decade some two dozen epidemiological studies had been conducted and published in the medical literature of the United States and other parts of the world showing that children and workers exposed to power-line magnetic fields were developing cancer—chiefly leukemia, lymphoma, melanoma, brain tumors, and other central-nervous-system cancers—at rates significantly higher than those observed in unexposed people, and the fact that between 1985 and 1989 no fewer than twelve studies had shown more brain tumors than were to be expected among people exposed to electric and magnetic fields at home or at work.

At a public meeting held in the Guilford Public Library on August 20th, David R. Brown, chief of the Connecticut Department of Health Services' Division of Environmental Epidemiology and Occupational Health, and Sandy Geschwind, an epidemiologist with the division, declared that there was no cancer cluster on Meadow Street. To support their contention, they distributed a document entitled "Guilford Cancer Cluster Preliminary Investigation," claiming that "there was not a cluster of the same kind of tumors on Meadow Street," and that from 1968 through 1988 "Guilford as a whole did not experience a higher than expected number of brain cancer or meningioma cases." The document stated, further, that "mapping of these brain tumor and meningioma cases showed that they did not cluster in a particular area but were scattered throughout the town."

At the meeting, Geschwind gave a presentation in which she said that one of the brain cancers on Meadow Street was not a primary tumor but an esophageal cancer that had metastasized. She also said that the malignant eye tumor in question was a melanoma—a type of cancer that she claimed had never been associated with exposure to electromagnetic fields—and she assured her listeners that meningioma had never been associated with exposure to such fields. Toward the end of her presentation, Geschwind displayed a map showing the location of ten meningiomas and nineteen other brain and central-nervous-system tumors listed by the Connecticut Tumor Registry as having occurred in Guilford between 1968 and 1988, and told the hundred or so members of her audience—they included a dozen newspaper and television reporters—that the map proved that there was "absolutely no clustering" in Guilford and that the state investigation showed "no cancer cluster on Meadow Street."

However, the fact that Guilford as a whole—the town now has a population of twenty thousand five hundred, living in seventy-three hundred dwellings—did not experience a higher than expected number of meningiomas and other brain and nervous-system tumors during those twenty-one years does not address the situation on Meadow Street. Second, while there is no reason to doubt Geschwind's assertion that one of the two brain cancers among Meadow Street residents was not a primary tumor, eye melanoma—the one in question was a malignant tumor involving the optic nerve, an extension of the brain—has been found to be "notably high for electrical and electronics workers," who are known to be exposed to strong magnetic fields. The finding appeared in a highly regarded study entitled "Epidemiology of Eye Cancer in Adults in England and Wales, 1962–1977," which was conducted by Dr. A. J. Swerdlow, a physician at the Department of Community Medicine of the University of Glasgow, in Scotland. Swerdlow reported his findings in 1983, in Volume 118, No. 2, of the *American Journal of Epidemiology*, which is published by the Johns Hopkins University School of Hygiene and Public Health, in Baltimore. Moreover, melanoma of the skin is one of three types of cancer listed by scientists of the Environmental Protection Agency in a recent draft report, "An Evaluation of the Potential Carcinogenicity of Electromagnetic Fields," as being prevalent among workers in electrical and electronic occupations, and thus associated with exposure to magnetic fields.

The conclusion of Brown and Geschwind that there is no cancer cluster among people who have lived on Meadow Street seems disingenuous, to say the least. As Geschwind noted, the Connecticut Tumor Registry recorded ten cases of meningioma and nineteen other primary tumors of the brain and central nervous system among Guilford residents between 1968 and 1988—a span in which the average population of the town was seventeen thousand five hundred. Thus the meningioma rate in Guilford is consistent with the Connecticut statewide incidence, of 2.6 cases per hundred thousand people per year—I was in error when I gave it in my article as one case per hundred thousand—and the incidence of other brain and central-nervous-system tumors in Guilford is also close to the number that would normally be expected. The fact that three of the twenty-nine primary brain and central-nervous-system tumors that occurred in Guilford during those twenty-one years developed among a handful of people who lived in four of five adjacent houses on Meadow Street that are situated near a substation and very close to a pair of high-current distribution lines, called feeders, together with the fact that a malignant eye tumor, involving a tract of brain tissue, occurred in a woman who had lived in a sixth adjacent dwelling, next to a third feeder line, surely suggests that there is a cancer cluster of some significance on Meadow Street.

Finally, and somewhat ironically, further evidence of cancer clustering associated with exposure to power-line magnetic fields can be found in the very map that Geschwind displayed in an effort to persuade the people of Guilford that no cancer cluster existed there. Among those listening to her presentation was Robert Hemstock, a Guilford resident, who, in January of this year, first sounded the alarm about a cluster on Meadow Street. When Geschwind held up the map, Hemstock noticed that three of the twenty-nine cancers on it appeared to have occurred along the route of a feeder line that carried high current from the Meadow Street substation to other towns during the nineteen-sixties, seventies, and early eighties, when the substation was being operated by its owner, the Connecticut Light & Power Company, as a bulk-supply station for large-load areas in Madison and Clinton—neighboring towns with a total population of about twenty thousand during that period. He also noticed that an unusually large proportion of the other brain tumors on the map appeared to have occurred among people living along the routes of other primary distribution lines emanating from the substation.

After the meeting, Hemstock shared his observation with Don Michak, a reporter for the Manchester Enfield *Journal Inquirer,* who on August 23rd asked the Department of Health Services for a copy of the map. As it happened, Brown had displayed the map the day before at a Rotary Club meeting in Guilford, and told the Rotarians that he saw no need for the department to make any further inquiry into the incidence of cancer on Meadow Street. However, Health Services officials refused to release the map to Michak, on the ground that to do so might violate the confidentiality of cancer victims by revealing their addresses. The *Journal Inquirer* reported this development in an article by Michak on September 6th, and on September 10th it published an editorial pointing out that if the withheld map showed that the distribution of cancer cases in Guilford corresponded to the Meadow Street substation and to a power line running north from it "the public's concern might be overwhelming not only in Guilford but throughout Connecticut and even nationally." The editorial went on to question Health Services' rationale for secrecy, declaring that the map "is just a matter of dots superimposed on a map of Guilford; it apparently doesn't include names and addresses," and that "anyone seeking to use the map to find people who have or had cancer would have to knock on doors in the area of the dots on the map and ask such people to identify themselves." After observing that "the health department undermined its own rationale by displaying the map at the public hearing in Guilford in the first place," the editorial concluded by stating that if the department failed to make the map available "the public will have to assume that the department wants to protect something else more than it wants to protect public health."

In September, a reporter for the New Haven *Register* obtained a copy of the map from an assistant to the Guilford health officer. (The assistant later said that she had given it out by mistake.) The *Register* reporter also went to the Connecticut Light & Power Company's office in Madison and obtained a company map of the routes of existing high-current and high-voltage distribution lines in Guilford. On October 3rd, the *Register* published its own map—one combining the locations of the brain tumors and other central-nervous-system tumors with the routes of Connecticut Light & Power's distribution lines. It clearly showed that Hemstock's observation was correct—that an inordinately high number of the meningiomas and other brain and central-nervous-system tumors that had occurred in Guilford over the twenty-one-year period between 1968 and 1988 had developed in people living close to primary distribution wires.

This correlation notwithstanding, Brown and Geschwind denied that the map furnished any evidence of a link between the occurrence of such tumors and proximity to power lines in Guilford. "You can't use the map to show that kind of association," Geschwind told the *Register*. She added that such tumors could be found on streets near main distribution power lines because those streets were densely populated, and heavily populated areas would have proportionally higher cancer rates.

To the contrary, anyone who knows the addresses of the twenty-nine brain-and-other-central-nervous-system-tumor victims in Guilford, and follows the routes of the feeder lines and primary distribution wires leading from the Meadow Street substation, will find not only that there is a strong correlation between the occurrence of these tumors and living close to high-current or high-voltage wires but also that most of the tumors have not occurred in areas of notably dense population. The feeder that carried high current from the substation to Madison and Clinton was abandoned a few years ago; it ran across Meadow Street from the substation and proceeded east for about a mile and a half, to a point near the junction of Stone House Lane, South Union Street, and Sawpit Road. (Up to that point, the poles and the wires of the line remain in place, but they have been removed from the rest of the route—across an uninhabited salt marsh and the East River, which is the eastern boundary of Guilford, to a substation on Garnet Park Road, in Madison.) This feeder line ran for a mile and a half through Guilford, and it passed close—within a hundred and fifty feet or so—to only twelve houses. One of the ten meningiomas and two of the nineteen other brain and central-nervous-system tumors listed by the Tumor Registry as having occurred in Guilford between 1968 and 1988 afflicted people living in three of those twelve dwellings. All three are situated within about forty feet of the high-current wires. Moreover, a former Meadow Street resident who developed eye cancer at the age of forty-four, and has since died of it, lived for fourteen years in one of the twelve houses close to the abandoned feeder line. It is at 56 Meadow, and is situated only about thirty feet from the wires. . . .

All told, seven of the ten meningiomas and ten of the nineteen other brain and central-nervous-system tumors—that is, seventeen of the total of twenty-nine—have afflicted people living near high-current or high-voltage power lines in Guilford. The total combined length of the lines is about forty-five miles, and along this distance some seven hundred and twenty-two out of a total of eight hundred and six houses are situated within a hundred and fifty feet of the wires. It seems obvious that in a town of seventy-three hundred dwellings the occurrence of this proportion of meningiomas and other brain and central-nervous-system tumors in residents of just over eight hundred dwellings strung out along some forty-five miles of roadway cannot be ascribed to heavy population—as the Connecticut Department of Health Services has done. It also seems obvious that people living in houses close to high-current wires and high-voltage transmission lines in Guilford are especially susceptible to developing meningiomas and other brain tumors. Particularly disturbing in this regard is the fact that in March of 1989—too late to be counted among the twenty-nine tumors listed by the Registry on the map that the Connecticut Department of Health Services displayed to reassure the townspeople of Guilford—a seventeen-year-old girl living in a house close to one of the high-current feeder lines was found to be suffering from an astrocytoma, the same type of malignant brain tumor that has afflicted a seventeen-year-old girl living near the same line on Meadow Street.

Instead of continuing to extend the presumption of benignity to power-line magnetic fields, the Connecticut Department of Health Services could require its Division of Environmental Epidemiology and Occupational Health to conduct a thorough study of the apparent strong association between the occurrence of meningiomas and other brain and central-nervous-system tumors, on the one hand, and, on the other, chronic exposure to the magnetic fields given off by high-current and high-voltage power lines in Guilford. Moreover, since Connecticut is one of the few states that have collected data on the occurrence of such tumors over a significant period, the department has a unique opportunity to perform an important service for public health nationwide by conducting a detailed investigation of the seventeen hundred and three meningiomas and the four thousand one hundred and two other brain and central-nervous-system tumors that have been diagnosed among Connecticut residents over the twenty-one years between 1968 and 1988, in order to determine whether, as is clearly the case in Guilford, a disproportionately high percentage of them have developed in people living close to wires giving off strong magnetic fields. If such an association should prevail throughout the state, meningioma and other brain tumors would have to be considered marker diseases for exposure to power-line magnetic fields.

⚬⚭⚬

Later in my article I described a cluster of seven brain cancers that had been reported to have occurred over the past fifteen or twenty years among the residents of Trading Ford and Dukeville—two small communities near Salisbury, in Rowan County, North Carolina—who had either worked at a nearby power-generating plant, owned by the Duke Power Company, or lived in a company village, Dukeville, that was situated close to the plant and adjacent to a large substation and some high-voltage transmission lines giving off strong magnetic fields. I suggested that officials of the North Carolina Department of Environment, Health, and Natural Resources' environmental-epidemiology section were remiss in not having investigated this brain-cancer cluster during the eight and a half months since it was reported in the Salisbury *Post* on July 12 and 18, 1989, especially since one of the officials, Dr. Peter D. Morris, had made a point of stating that such a cluster might be significant if all the cancer victims had worked in the same plant twenty years earlier. I also suggested that the health experience of the three hundred or so people who lived in the company village or worked at the plant, or did both, should be thoroughly investigated, because, in addition to the seven of those people who had died of brain cancer, four others, who simply lived near the plant or the high-voltage transmission lines radiating from it, had died of the disease, and because a preliminary inquiry revealed that there had also been at least eight deaths from leukemia, lymphoma, and other cancers among these people.

In a recent letter to the editor of *The New Yorker* three officials of the environmental-epidemiology section stated that they had evaluated the seven cases of brain cancer, in order to "determine whether or not they should be included in our study of brain cancer in Rowan County from 1980 through 1989," and had found that "two of the seven cases had metastatic brain cancer, a different type of tumor originating in another part of the body and later spreading to the brain." They went on to say that four of the remaining cases were excluded from their study because the diagnoses of two of them were made prior to 1979, an unconfirmed diagnosis of another was made prior to 1979, and one of the victims lived outside Rowan County at the time of diagnosis.

In the final report of their study, which is entitled "Rowan County Brain Cancer Investigation," the North Carolina health officials state that Rowan County did not have a significantly greater incidence of malignant brain cancer between 1980 and 1989 than each of the five surrounding counties. During a press conference at the Rowan County Health Department on October 25th, Dr. Morris told the Salisbury *Post* that brain cancer in the Trading Ford–Dukeville area during the ten-year period "was not studied as a separate cluster."

The rationale of the North Carolina health officials is as faulty as that of their counterparts in Connecticut, because they not only have failed to address the brain-cancer situation in Trading Ford and Dukeville in its entirety but also have submerged the small part they did address in the larger study of Rowan County. In order to understand how flawed their investigation has been, one must remember that the power plant, which was built in 1926, was partly shut down during the nineteen-fifties and sixties, and the eighty-six houses in Dukeville, which were built between 1926 and 1945, were moved elsewhere in 1955. Thus, in addition to the one case of primary brain cancer among Trading Ford and Dukeville residents that the North Carolina officials included in their study, and the four cases of brain cancer that they saw fit to exclude, other people who were exposed to the electric and magnetic fields from the plant, its substation, and its high-voltage transmission lines by virtue of working at the plant or living in the company village during the nineteen-thirties, forties, and fifties may well have developed the disease and died of it before 1979. By deciding not to include brain cancers diagnosed among residents of the Trading Ford–Dukeville area before 1979, the North Carolina health officials decided not to investigate the health experience of people who worked at or lived near the Duke Power Company plant—a decision that makes about as much epidemiological sense as a decision to study the incidence of gray hair in a given population after excluding all those persons in the study group who became gray more than ten years earlier.

⚜

Still later in my article I wrote that cancer among the student population of the Montecito Union School—an elementary school with four hundred pupils in Montecito, California—was "at least a hundred times what might have been expected." This was an error. The incidence of cancer at the school is considerably less than that, though far greater than it should be. Between 1981 and 1988, six cases of cancer are known to have occurred among children who attended the Montecito Union School: two children developed leukemia; three children developed lymphoma; and one child developed testicular cancer. As I wrote in my article, cancer is a rare event in children, occurring annually in about one of ten thousand children per year under the age of fifteen. However, as several readers have pointed out, the child-years at risk should be calculated at eight times four hundred students per year; that comes to thirty-two hundred child-years at risk. Six cases of cancer out of thirty-two hundred child-years translates to 18.75 cases per ten thousand children per year. According to the National Cancer Institute's Surveillance, Epidemiology and End Results (SEER) data, the all-sites cancer rate for white children of both sexes, aged five to nine, between 1983 and 1987 in the San Francisco–Oakland area (the closest metropolitan area to Santa Barbara for which SEER data exist) was 11.9 cases per hundred thousand children per year. Thus the cancer rate over those eight years at the Montecito Union School—18.75 cases per ten thousand—is more than fifteen times the expected rate.

In their assessment of this cancer cluster officials of California's Department of Health Services' environmental-epidemiology-and-toxicology branch have maintained that magnetic-field levels at the school—which is situated within forty feet of a sixty-six-thousand-volt feeder line originating at an adjacent substation—were not unusually high, and that there was no evidence that they posed a health hazard. The fact is, however, that magnetic-field levels measured at the school's kindergarten patio by Enertech, an engineering consulting firm in the Bay Area, were between four and six milligauss; that is, approximately twice the levels that have been associated with a doubling of the expected rate of childhood cancer in three epidemiological studies cited by staff scientists of the Environmental Protection Agency as providing the strongest evidence that there may be a causal relationship between certain forms of childhood cancer—chiefly leukemia, nervous-system cancer, and lymphoma—and exposure to power-line magnetic fields. (Incidentally, on February 26th of this year I measured the magnetic fields at the kindergarten patio of the Montecito Union School, and found them to be about the same as those reported by Enertech.) It is also a fact that the magnetic-field levels at the kindergarten patio are at least equal to, and, for the most part, greater than, the exposure levels of forty-five hundred New York Telephone Company cable splicers, in whom cancer of all types—particularly leukemia—has been found to be higher than expected.

California health officials decided not to include the case of testicular cancer, which occurred in a second-grader, in their assessment of the cancer hazard at the Montecito Union School, and that decision seems arbitrary, in the light of the fact that cancer of all types was elevated in the childhood-cancer studies cited by the E.P.A. and also in the study of the telephone-cable splicers. It seems all the more arbitrary in the light of SEER data that estimate the chances of a seven- or eight-year-old child's developing testicular cancer to be nearly zero in one hundred thousand children per year. Also disturbing is the fact that since the publication of my article a teacher's aide with several years' experience in the kindergarten of the Montecito Union School has developed a brain tumor. This occurrence, together with the fact that four cases of leukemia have been reported among children who attended the Montecito Union School in the late nineteen-fifties, should encourage the California officials to conduct a full-scale investigation of the health experience of all the children who have attended this school during the past thirty-five years, just as the cancer clusters that have been found among the residents of Guilford and Dukeville should occasion in-depth investigations of the health experience of all the people who have lived near high-voltage and high-current power lines in those communities over a similarly appropriate period.

While these studies are in progress, interim preventive measures should be undertaken to reduce the magnetic-field exposure of children in hundreds of schools and day-care centers across the nation which have been built perilously close to high-voltage and high-current power lines. That can be accomplished by rerouting such lines, or burying them in a manner that will prevent hazardous magnetic-field emissions. Needless to say, such measures should be supported by the parents of schoolchildren, by members of parent-teacher associations, and by officials of school districts, of city and state health departments, and of the federal Environmental Protection Agency.

Edward W. Campion  **NO**

Power Lines, Cancer, and Fear

Over the past 18 years, there has been considerable interest in the possible link between electromagnetic fields and cancer, especially leukemia. The story of this highly publicized research has been marked by mystery, contradiction, and confusion. When something as ubiquitous and misunderstood as extremely-low-frequency electromagnetic fields is accused of causing cancer in children, people's reactions may be driven more by passion than by reason.

Each year in this country about 2000 children are given a diagnosis of acute lymphoblastic leukemia (ALL), the most common childhood cancer. Despite the remarkable advances in treatment, ALL still carries a 30 percent mortality. Other than exposure to ionizing radiation, its cause remains a mystery. ALL is more common among whites and children of higher socioeconomic class, and for unclear reasons the incidence of ALL has increased by about 20 percent in the past two decades. [1,2] During the past 50 years, per capita use of electricity has increased more than 10 times. Some investigators have claimed that living close to major power lines causes cancer, particularly leukemia in children.

... Linet et al.[3] report the results of a major study showing that the risk of ALL does not increase with increasing electromagnetic-field levels in children's homes. This study has several strengths. It was large, including 629 children with leukemia and 619 controls, and it included measurements of electromagnetic fields, made by technicians blinded to the case or control status of the subjects, both in the houses where the children had lived and, in 41 percent of cases, in the homes in which their mothers resided while pregnant. Linet et al. also found no relation between the risk of ALL and residential wire-code classifications, again determined by technicians blinded to the children's health status. The wire-code classifications are important, because several of the earlier positive studies relied on these proxy indicators rather than on actual measurements of electromagnetic fields.

This whole saga began when two Denver researchers, puzzled by small clusters of cancer in children, came to believe that living in close proximity to high-voltage power lines was a cause of leukemia.[4] The analysis they published in 1979 was crude and relied on distances from homes to power lines and on wiring configurations rather than on direct measures of exposure to electromagnetic fields. They found that the risk of childhood leukemia was more than doubled among children living near such power lines, a finding that led to more studies and more concern. Soon activists and the media began to spread the word that electromagnetic fields cause cancer.

The hypothesized cause was exposure to extremely-low-frequency magnetic fields generated by the electrical current in power lines. Physicists understand these invisible fields well, but most physicians, parents, and patients do not. The movement of any electrical charge creates a magnetic field that can be measured.[5] Even the 60-Hz residential electric current (50 Hz in Europe) creates a very weak oscillating field, which, like all magnetic fields, penetrates living tissue. These low-frequency electromagnetic fields are known as nonionizing radiation, since the amount of energy in them is far below that required to break molecular bonds such as those in DNA.

One ironic fact about low-frequency electromagnetic fields is that we live and worry about them within the Earth's static magnetic field of 50 μT, which is hundreds of times greater than the oscillating magnetic field produced by 110/220-V current in houses (0.01 to 0.05 μT).[5,6] Even directly under high-voltage transmission lines, the magnetic field is only about 3 to 10 μT, which is less than that in an electric railway car and much weaker than the magnetic field close to my head when I use an electric razor (about 60 μT).

Although most physicists find it inconceivable that power-line electromagnetic fields could pose a hazard to health, dozens of epidemiologic studies have reported weak positive associations between proximity to high-voltage power lines and the risk of cancer.[6,7] The negative or equivocal studies did not end the controversy. Fear of leukemia is a powerful force, and the media response amplified the perception of electromagnetic fields as a health hazard. In 1989 *The New Yorker* published three articles by journalist Paul Brodeur that described in mesmerizing detail how maverick researchers had discovered a cause of cancer that the establishment refused to accept.[8–10] Like many of the epidemiologic studies themselves, these widely quoted articles described biologic mechanisms of action for electromagnetic fields that were hypothetical, even fanciful. Brodeur went so far as to claim that the search for the truth about the hazards of electromagnetic fields was threatened most by the "obfuscation of industry, the mendacity of the military, and the corruption of ethics that industrial and military money could purchase from various members of the medical and scientific community."[8] Suspicion spread to many other wavelengths on the nonionizing electromagnetic spectrum, producing fears about occupational exposure to electricity as well as exposure to microwave appliances, radar, video-display terminals, and even cellular telephones. Dozens of studies looked for associations with brain cancer, miscarriages, fetal-growth retardation, lymphoma, breast cancer, breast cancer in men, lung cancer, all cancers, immunologic abnormalities, and even changes in the behavior of animals.

When people hear that a scientific study has implicated something new as a cause of cancer, they get worried. They get even more worried when the exposure is called radiation and comes from dangerous-looking high-voltage power lines controlled by government and industry, which some distrust deeply. Such exposure seems eerie when people hear that electromagnetic fields penetrate their homes, their bodies, their children. The worried citizens took action.

Frightened people, including parents of children with leukemia, undertook their own epidemiologic studies and fought to get high-power transmission lines moved away from their children. Congress responded with large direct appropriations for wider research on the effects of electromagnetic fields. After a large apparently positive study in Sweden,[7] the Swedish government came close to mandating the relocation of schools to at least 1000 meters from large power lines. But cooler heads prevailed once it became clear that the absolute incremental risk was small at most, the conclusions were based on a tiny fraction of all Swedish children with leukemia, and the increase in risk was found only in relation to some estimates of magnetic fields, not to the actual fields measured in children's homes.

Serious limitations have been pointed out in nearly all the studies of power lines and cancer.[11,12] These limitations include unblinded assessment of exposure, difficulty in making direct measurements of the constantly varying electromagnetic fields, inconsistencies between the measured levels and the estimates of exposure based on wiring configurations, recall bias with respect to exposure, post hoc definitions of exposure categories, and huge numbers of comparisons with selective emphasis on those that were positive. Both study participation and residential wire-code categories may be confounded by socioeconomic factors. Often the number of cases of ALL in the high-exposure categories has been very small, and controls may not have been truly comparable. Moreover, all these epidemiologic studies have been conducted in pursuit of a cause of cancer for which there is no plausible biologic basis. There is no convincing evidence that exposure to electromagnetic fields causes cancer in animals,[6] and electromagnetic fields have no reproducible biologic effects at all, except at strengths that are far beyond those ever found in people's homes.

In recent years, several commissions and expert panels have concluded that there is no convincing evidence that high-voltage power lines are a health hazard or a cause of cancer.[6,13] And the weight of the better epidemiologic studies, including that by Linet et al., now supports the same conclusion. It is sad that hundreds of millions of dollars have gone into studies that never had much promise of finding a way to prevent the tragedy of cancer in children. The many inconclusive and inconsistent studies have generated worry and fear and have given peace of mind to no one. The 18 years of research have produced considerable paranoia, but little insight and no prevention. It is time to stop wasting our research resources. We should redirect them to research that will be able to discover the true biologic causes of the leukemic clones that threaten the lives of children.

References

1. Pui C-H. Childhood leukemias. N Engl J Med 1995; 332: 1618–30.
2. Ries LAG, Miller BA, Hankey BF, Kosary CL, Harras A, Edwards BK, eds. SEER cancer statistics review, 1973–1991: tables and graphs. Bethesda, Md.: National Cancer Institute, 1994. (NIH publication no. 94-2789.)
3. Linet MS, Hatch EE, Kleinerman RA, et al. Residential exposure to magnetic fields and acute lymphoblastic leukemia in children. N Engl J Med 1997; 337: 1–7.

4. Wertheimer N, Leeper E. Electrical wiring configurations and childhood cancer. Am J Epidemiol 1979; 109: 273–84.
5. Hitchcock RT, Patterson RM. Radio-frequency and ELF electromagnetic energies: a handbook for health professionals. New York: Van Nostrand Reinhold, 1995.
6. National Research Council. Possible health effects of exposure to residential electric and magnetic fields. Washington, D.C.: National Academy Press, 1997.
7. Feychting M, Ahlbom A. Magnetic fields and cancer in children residing near Swedish high-voltage power lines. Am J Epidemiol 1993; 138: 467–81.
8. Brodeur P. Annals of radiation: the hazards of electromagnetic fields. I. Power lines. The New Yorker. June 12, 1989: 51–88.
9. *Idem.* Annals of radiation: the hazards of electromagnetic fields. II. Something is happening. The New Yorker. June 19, 1989: 47–73.
10. *Idem.* Annals of radiation: the hazards of electromagnetic fields. III. Video-display terminals. The New Yorker. June 26, 1989: 39–68.
11. Savitz DA, Pearce NE, Poole C. Methodological issues in the epidemiology of electromagnetic fields and cancer. Epidemiol Rev 1989; 11: 59–78.
12. Poole C, Trichopoulos D. Extremely low-frequency electric and magnetic fields and cancer. Cancer Causes Control 1991; 2: 267–76.
13. Oak Ridge Associated Universities Panel. Health effects of low-frequency electric and magnetic fields. Washington, D.C.: Government Printing Office, 1992: V-1-V-18. (Publication no. 029-000-00443-9.)

POSTSCRIPT

Are Electromagnetic Fields Dangerous to Your Health?

Is the EMF scare nothing more than media hype, as suggested by Sid Deutsch in "Electromagnetic Field Cancer Scares," *Skeptical Inquirer* (Winter 1994)? Or do EMFs pose a genuine hazard? If they do, the threat is not yet clear beyond a doubt. However, society cannot always wait for certainty. Gordon L. Hester, in "Electric and Magnetic Fields: Managing an Uncertain Risk," *Environment* (January/February 1992), states that just the possibility of a health hazard from EMFs is sufficient to justify more research into the problem. The guiding principle, says Hester, is " 'prudent avoidance,' which was originally intended to mean that people should avoid fields 'when this can be done with modest amounts of money and trouble.' " H. Keith Florig, in "Containing the Costs of the EMF Problem," *Science* (July 24, 1992), makes a similar point in his discussion of the expenses that utilities, manufacturers, and others are incurring to reduce EMF exposures in the absence of solid evidence that there is a hazard but in the presence of public concern and lawsuits.

And the concern does remain despite the lack of evidence for any real hazard. Researchers Hans Wieser, Michael Fuller, and Jon Paul Dobson reported at the May 1993 meeting of the American Geophysical Union that magnetic fields can affect brain activity, suggesting that the body does respond to EMFs from electrical apparatus. On January 27, 1995, *Science* reported that "the U.S. Navy's 90-kilometer-long Extremely Low Frequency (ELF) antenna, set up [in a Michigan forest] in 1986 to communicate with submarines, is invigorating neighboring plant life"—apparently stimulating tree and algal growth in a way that has led some scientists to consider how ELF EMFs might stimulate the growth of cancer cells.

In August 1995 *Science* published a brief item on a draft report by the National Council on Radiation Protection and Measurements, saying that "some health effects linked to EMFs—such as cancer and immune deficiencies—appear real and warrant steps to reduce EMF exposure," such as not building new housing under high-voltage transmission lines. The final report was promised for 1996. However, in September 1995, *Science* reported a pair of studies that had attempted to confirm work indicating that EMFs could stimulate a cancer gene. Both failed to find any effect. And in November 1996 the National Research Council, in its report *Possible Health Effects of Exposure to Residential Electric and Magnetic Fields,* came down firmly on the "no conclusive and consistent evidence" of hazard side of the question. See Jocelyn Kaiser, "Panel Finds EMFs Pose No Threat," *Science* (November 8, 1996).

When the study by Martha S. Linet et al. appeared, Gary Taubes, in "Magnetic Field-Cancer Link: Will It Rest in Peace?" *Science* (July 4, 1997), said, "It could be the obituary [for the EMF-cancer scare]." "Yet many people will refuse to believe it," says Lawrence Fisher, a toxicologist at Michigan State University in East Lansing, "not on any scientific basis, but because of their emotional involvement with the disease." To such people, the jury will forever be out, just as it was for a scientific panel convened in the summer of 1998 by the Department of Energy and the National Institute of Environmental Health Sciences, which concluded that although the data are hardly adequate for a strong indictment of EMFs, they do—particularly since many exposure assessments are of dubious quality—support calling EMFs a "possible human carcinogen." See "Jury Is Still Out on EMFs and Cancer," *Science News* (August 22, 1998). In May 1999 a National Research Council panel indicated that no further research on the topic was needed. However, Japan's Science and Technology Agency announced that it would fund a major study.

What should society do in the face of weak, uncertain, and even contradictory data? Can we afford to conclude that there is no hazard? Or must we redesign equipment and relocate power lines and homes with no other justification than our fear that there *might* be a real hazard? Many scientists and politicians argue that even if there is no genuine medical risk from exposure to EMFs, there is a genuine impact in terms of public anxiety. See Gary Stix, "Closing the Book," *Scientific American* (March 1998). It is therefore appropriate, they say, to fund further research and to take whatever relatively inexpensive steps to minimize exposure are possible. Failure to do so increases public anxiety and distrust of government and science.

It is worth noting that the EMF scare had a precedent in the late 1800s. See Joseph P. Sullivan, "Fearing Electricity: Overhead Wire Panic in New York City," *IEEE Technology and Society Magazine* (Fall 1995).

ISSUE 8

Is Irradiated Food Safe to Eat?

YES: P. J. Skerrett, from "Food Irradiation: Will It Keep the Doctor Away?" *Technology Review* (November–December 1997)

NO: Hank Hoffman, from "Nukeburgers: The Meat Industry's Solution to E. Coli Is the Big Zap Attack," *The New Haven Advocate* (January 23, 1997)

ISSUE SUMMARY

YES: P. J. Skerrett, a contributing writer for *Technology Review,* maintains that sterilizing food by means of ionizing radiation is an effective way to avoid disease and death due to food-borne bacteria and parasites. Furthermore, the opposition is guilty of "public fear mongering and scare tactics."

NO: Writer Hank Hoffman argues that the studies used to judge the safety of food irradiation are too flawed to trust, the process destroys nutrients, and the technology has the potential to cause widespread environmental contamination. In approving food irradiation, the government is "encouraging a policy that could lead to disaster," he concludes.

It was only a decade after Wilhelm von Roentgen's discovery of X rays in 1895 that the first patents were issued for the use of ionizing radiation (such as X rays) for destroying bacteria in food. During World War II, Massachusetts Institute of Technology (MIT) researchers showed that ground beef could be preserved by exposing it to X rays. Further research followed in the late 1940s and 1950s, when every government agency concerned with nuclear technology sought to free the terms *nuclear* and *radiation* from their powerful connections to death and destruction, as forged by the Hiroshima and Nagasaki explosions that ended World War II. The rhetoric was of "atoms for peace" and "beating swords into plowshares." In 1958, however, the Food and Drug Administration (FDA) defined radiation sources intended for use in food processing as "food additives" and required safety tests before irradiated food could be marketed.

During the 1960s, FDA regulations approved the use of radiation to preserve canned bacon, kill insects in stored wheat and flour, and inhibit potato

148

sprouting. However, when the army asked the FDA in 1968 to approve irradiating canned ham to retard spoilage in tropical areas such as Vietnam, then–FDA commissioner James L. Goddard raised questions about the safety of the process, noting that laboratory animals fed irradiated meat had developed cancers and cataracts and had shown slower reproduction. Shortly after that, the FDA rescinded earlier approvals for food irradiation.

Commercial interest in food irradiation stopped dead until 1980, when an FDA report based on new research said that the only possible hazard of irradiated food lay in "radiolytic products," chemicals formed when radiation strikes chemicals normally present in food. Army researchers had found only six chemicals present in irradiated foods that were not present in nonirradiated foods; furthermore, they found them only in foods exposed to very high doses of radiation (50 kiloGrays). The FDA report concluded that food irradiated at low doses (1 kiloGray) was safe enough not to need extensive tests on laboratory animals.

In 1986, the FDA issued regulations permitting irradiation of fruits, vegetables, and pork at doses under 1 kiloGray and of dried spices and herbs at doses up to 30 kiloGrays and requiring that irradiated foods be appropriately labeled. In 1990, the FDA approved the irradiation of poultry at doses up to 3 kiloGrays.

This approval was welcomed by the poultry industry, for it had suffered bad publicity over bacterial contamination of its products. More recently, similar bad publicity afflicted fast-food chains, and by the end of 1997, the FDA had approved low-dose irradiation of beef with gamma rays.

One might expect that any technological development that promised to end fears of fatal food poisoning attacks would be welcomed with open arms, especially since it produces no detectable difference in the taste of the meat (according to taste tests performed by *USA Weekend,* Sunday supplement [January 23–25, 1998]).

Unfortunately, the critics remain vocal, continuing protests that still keep many food manufacturers and marketers from having anything to do with food irradiation, at least, in the words of Quaker Oats public relations director Ron Bottrell, "until consumer confidence in the process reaches a level where we feel more comfortable with it."

Should the public accept food irradiation as a valuable adjunct to traditional methods of food preservation? P. J. Skerrett is confident that the process is safe and that continuing fears of bacterial food contamination will ensure its acceptance. On the other side, Hank Hoffman stresses that the technology is not trustworthy, both because of what it may do to irradiated food and because of its potential effects on environmental and worker safety.

Food Irradiation: Will It Keep the Doctor Away?

In food we trust. That motto guides us as much as the one that graces our currency. We take for granted the food we buy in grocery stores or eat in restaurants, trusting implicitly that it will satisfy our hunger, build strong bodies 12 ways, and keep us healthy.

That trust may be a bit misplaced. Nearly 200 people in the United States, most of them children or elderly, die each week from illnesses they contract from food. Estimates from the Centers for Disease Control and Prevention in Washington, D.C., suggest that 6 to 33 million people are stricken with food-borne diseases each year. Major outbreaks are grabbing headlines with greater frequency—consider the recent Hudson Foods recall of 25 million pounds of bacteria-tainted beef, contaminated Jack-in-the-Box hamburgers, Odwalla apple juice, and Guatemalan raspberries—while many minor ones go unreported.

Late... spring [1997], President Clinton gave voice to growing concern by public-health officials over our food supply by calling for "new steps using cutting-edge technology to keep our food safe." One of the technologies that Clinton singles out in his proposed $43 million National Food Safety Initiative is food irradiation, a process that has long been lauded by food-safety experts even as it languishes in the backwaters of research and development. "If the president's program takes hold, food irradiation could get the political push it needs," says James Tillotson, director of the Food Policy Institute at Tufts University.

"The benefits of food irradiation are overwhelming," says Richard Lechowich, director of the National Center for Food Safety and Technology at the Illinois Institute of Technology. High-energy radiation kills critters that live in or on food, including the deadly E. coli O157:H7 bacterium and the salmonella and campylobacter species of bacteria found in most uncooked chicken and turkey. "Widespread irradiation of poultry alone in this country could prevent thousands of illnesses and hundreds of deaths every year," concurs Douglas Archer, former deputy director of the Center for Food Safety and Applied Nutrition at the U.S. Food and Drug Administration (FDA).

A major benefit of irradiation is that it can occur after food is packaged and sealed to kill any organisms that may have contaminated the food between production line and plate. "We don't live in a perfect world where we always detect E. coli on a processing line, and where everyone washes their hands and cutting boards and cooks meat and poultry to the proper temperature," says Christine Bruhn, director of the Center for Consumer Research at the University of California at Davis. Food irradiation is like an air bag in a car, she says. Both offer an extra measure of safety in case of carelessness or accident.

More than 40 countries share this view, having authorized irradiation for everything from apples in China and frog legs in France to rice in Mexico, raw pork sausages in Thailand, and wheat in Canada. Irradiation has been endorsed not only by the U.N. World Health Organization and the Food and Agriculture Organization, but also by the U.S. Food and Drug Administration, the American Medical Association, and the American Public Health Association, among others. The process can legally be used in the United States for killing insects in grains, flour, fruits, and vegetables; for preventing stored potatoes, onions, and garlic from sprouting; and for killing microbes, insects, and parasites in spices, pork, and poultry.

But despite such wide-ranging approval, actual use of irradiation in the United States has been limited. Astronauts have eaten irradiated food ever since the Apollo 17 moon shot in 1972, when they carried sandwiches made from irradiated ham, cheese, and bread. Space shuttle crews dine on radiation-treated food, and it will almost certainly show up on space station menus. Some hospitals and nursing homes serve irradiated chicken to people with weakened immune systems, including AIDS patients, burn victims, people undergoing chemotherapy, and patients who have just had a bone marrow or organ transplant. And a few independent grocers carry irradiated produce and poultry. But the vast majority of companies that grow, process, or sell food shy away from this technology.

Why? The food industry has been reluctant partly because of public fear of radiation. In fact, a savvy organization of activists known as Food and Water claims it has held food processors in check simply by threatening to expose any company that dares use the technique. But that may change. Advocates contend that such fears of irradiated food are not only groundless but, with each news report of contaminated food, fading quickly as consumers consider the alternative of ignoring this safeguard. The issue now, they say, is whether the technology is ready for commercial use and can work at reasonable cost.

Roots of Irradiation

Although food irradiation is often referred to as a cutting-edge technology, its beginnings stretch back nearly a century. A few years after radiation was discovered by French physicist Antoine-Henri Becquerel in 1896, Samuel Prescott, professor of biology at MIT, showed that gamma rays from radium destroyed bacteria in food and proposed using radiation to preserve meat, fruit, vegetables, grains, and other foodstuffs. In the 1920s and 1930s, the United States and France awarded patents for radiation-based methods of killing parasites in pork and bacteria in canned food. Some 25 years of research at MIT and U.S. Army research facilities—from 1943 to 1968—further demonstrated its potential for treating and preserving food.

This high-tech cousin of canning, freezing, and fumigating relies on a simple principle that children of the atomic age know by heart: radiation kills, or at least alters, living cells. When gamma rays or other types of ionizing radiation zip through a cell, they knock some electrons out of their orbits, breaking chemical bonds and leaving behind a trail of ions and free radicals— atoms or molecules with an unpaired electron. These highly reactive substances crash into each other and into their nonirradiated neighbors, creating some new compounds and reforming many that had originally been there.

When a cell is exposed to high enough doses of radiation, the maelstrom of chemical reactions inside an irradiated cell inactivates key enzymes, irreparably damages the cell's genetic instructions, and can disrupt its protective outer membrane. The cell either stops growing and fails to reproduce or dies outright. Either of these outcomes destroys organisms that are natural or introduced contaminants of food or other products or prevents them from multiplying.

Examining the Evidence

Though some foods such as cucumbers, grapes, and some tomatoes turn mushy when radiation breaks cell walls and releases enzymes that digest the food and speed up rotting, many others including strawberries, apples, onions, mushrooms, pork, poultry, red meat, and seafood emerge from irradiation intact and edible. But while these foods can legally be irradiated, virtually none of them are.

The problem isn't necessarily radiation itself, because people don't seem to mind that it is used to sterilize half of all sutures, syringes, intravenous lines, and other medical supplies, as well as billions of dollars worth of consumer goods ranging from plastic wrap and milk cartons to tampons and contact lenses. What poses concerns is the juxtaposition of food and irradiation. "Food is a very emotional thing," says Tillotson of Tufts. "We don't want scientists or anyone else mucking around with it, especially not with something that most people link with the atomic bomb."

The activists at Food and Water of Walden, Vt., effectively manipulate this potential reaction. This grassroots group, founded in 1984 to fight hunger, now spends its time fighting food irradiation, genetic engineering, and other technologies used to grow and process food, while advocating a smaller-is-better, back-to-the-land approach.

A willing David to the food industry's Goliath, Food and Water has almost singlehandedly blocked the commercialization of food irradiation. Larger organizations such as Ralph Nader's Public Citizen weigh in on the matter from time to time—"Whenever we need a quote from the big boys," boasts Food and Water's executive director, Michael Colby—but no longer actively campaign against food irradiation because, they say, Food and Water is carrying the ball.

Food and Water charges that irradiation seriously depletes the nutritional value of food, introduces carcinogens, and is essentially a cover-up that allows corporations to sell previously contaminated items. . . . But these charges don't stand up to the evidence or aren't as dire as Food and Water alleges.

It is true that irradiation can alter the nutritional content of food. While no carbohydrates, protein, fats, or minerals are lost, as much as 10 percent of vitamins A, B-1 (thiamine), E, and K can disappear at FDA-approved sterilization doses. But it's also true that similar vitamin losses occur when fresh fruits and vegetables are canned or even when they sit in cold storage.

More important, it does not appear that irradiated food causes cancer. First of all, when a hunk of hamburger is zapped with radiation it does not become radioactive, just as you don't start glowing after an x-ray. At the energy levels used for food, ionizing radiation doesn't have the oomph to knock a neutron away from an atom's nucleus or force an atom to fission. Instead, the radiation leaves behind traces of radiolytic compounds—which merely means broken (lysis) by radiant energy (radio)—that are identical to compounds that naturally occur in the foods we eat every day.

Cancer researcher George Tritsch, now retired from the Roswell Park Cancer Institute in Buffalo, N.Y., and an adviser to Food and Water, points out that some of these radiolytic products are known carcinogens, such as benzene and formaldehyde, and worries that adding more of these products, though measured in parts per billion, will raise cancer rates. This would be a formidable argument if it weren't for the fact that many foods naturally contain much higher levels of these and other cancer-causing agents, says Donald Thayer, research leader for food safety at the U.S. Department of Agriculture's Eastern Regional Research Center. Eggs, for example, contain 100 times more benzene than the highest levels found in food exposed to the maximum doses of sterilizing radiation.

Colby also argues that irradiation may create radiolytic compounds never before identified in food, some of which might cause cancer or other health problems. But he is unable to cite any examples. And, according to Thayer, "in more than 40 years of looking, no one has yet found in foods any compounds unique to the radiation process."

Nor have animal tests turned up any cause for concern. Under the direction of Edward Josephson, professor emeritus of food and nutrition at the University of Rhode Island, researchers at the U.S. Army's Natick (Mass.) laboratories fed irradiated chicken, wheat, oranges, and other foods to four generations of mice, three generations of beagles, and thousands of rats, guinea pigs, and monkeys from the late 1950s to the early 1960s. Even though the radiation doses were 10 to 20 times higher than necessary, he says, the animals eating irradiated foods suffered no more cancer or inherited diseases than animals eating either canned or frozen nonirradiated food.

An inadvertent test of irradiated foods comes from the Paterson Institute for Cancer Research in Manchester, England. For the past 10 years, several thousand mice with impaired immune systems have eaten nothing but radiation-sterilized food. After more than 60 generations, these mice show no more cancers or other diseases than similar mice fed heat-sterilized food.

Finally, the relatively few human studies that have been conducted also suggest that eating irradiated food is safe. In the early 1980s, more than 400 volunteers ate irradiated food for 7 to 15 weeks as part of eight separate studies in China. The volunteers showed no more chromosomal abnormalities—an early warning sign of cancer-causing activity—than those who ate nonirradiated food.

Tougher Testing

Opponents of food irradiation argue that critical tests remain to be done before anyone can say the process is absolutely without risk. Colby argues for standard toxicology tests that would involve irradiating an apple, say, then extracting any radiolytic products that form and feeding those compounds to lab animals at doses hundreds of times higher than that found in irradiated food.

But Josephson, for one, thinks that this exercise is unnecessary. "Why should we feed animals huge doses of these compounds," he says, "when years of animal-feeding studies have already shown that the small amounts that occur in irradiated food don't cause any health or reproductive problems?"

Food and Water adviser Donald Louria, chair of preventive medicine and community health at the University of Medicine and Dentistry of New Jersey, would go one step further than Colby. He says government or industry should fund a study in which volunteers of different ages, races, and socioeconomic backgrounds eat irradiated foods under controlled conditions, and then undergo tests to see if they have higher-than-normal levels of cells with chromosomal abnormalities.

On that score, however, the FDA apparently disagrees. Back in 1958, Congress defined irradiation as an additive rather than a process, even though radiation generates the same sorts of chemical byproducts in food as other processes used to preserve and protect food, including freeze drying, frying, sun drying, and canning. And FDA regulations don't require human studies for food additives, especially when the compounds added are identical to those already found in food, says George Pauli, the FDA's senior food irradiation scientist.

Ironically, neither Food and Water nor any other group is calling for the FDA to reclassify or restudy other techniques that produce the same byproducts. In fact, until the U.S. Army animal experiments, canned food had never been rigorously tested to see if it caused cancer. "People in the canning industry were holding their breath," recalls Josephson, "hoping we weren't going to find that canned food caused problems compared with irradiated food."

Propaganda Campaign

Food and Water's arguments may be shaky, but its public-relations acumen is rock solid, and highly effective. The organization deftly links people's worst fears about radiation to food. For example, one classic Food and Water advertisement shows a mushroom cloud erupting from a freshly cooked hamburger. The message reads: "The Department of Energy has a solution to the problem of radioactive waste. You're going to eat it."

The organization knows how to pressure executives who fear any sort of public controversy. When Food and Water learned that a representative from Hormel Foods attended a 1996 symposium on the benefits of food irradiation, it demanded to know the company's official policy on this technology.

When letters failed, Food and Water sought help from its constituents, which Colby claims total some 100,000, though a recent *Wall Street Journal* article places that figure considerably lower, at around 3,500. Colby asked members of Food and Water's grassroots network to let Hormel know how they felt about irradiation, and supplied preprinted postcards and a listing of Hormel's toll-free phone number.

The organization also ran a full-page ad showing a glowing can of irradiated Spam—one of Hormel's most widely recognized products—in the company's hometown newspaper on the day of its annual stockholder meeting and threatened Hormel officials that it would run the ads nationwide. Copies were sent to 18,000 food-industry executives. Two weeks later, Hormel issued a statement saying that it does not irradiate food. Food and Water suspended the campaign but threatened to resurrect it if Hormel "ever considers using food irradiation in the future."

Colby calls this approach "corporate education" and grassroots activism. Others see it differently. "The organization is shaping the debate and food policy through public fear mongering and scare tactics," says UC Davis's Bruhn.

Technological and Economic Hurdles

Food and Water's anti-irradiation campaign may be the most public obstacle to wider use of food irradiation, but it isn't the only one. "The real barrier is economics and the bottom line" says Martin Stein, president of GrayStar, which is designing a food irradiator that can be installed in existing food-processing plants. In fact, a quick review of the methods the food industry could employ to generate ionizing radiation—using gamma rays from radioactive cobalt-60 or cesium-137, and electron beams or x-rays from linear accelerators—shows that the options have shortcomings that diminish their cost effectiveness, while improved models are still on the drawing board.

Gamma rays: Anyone interested in irradiating food today would probably turn to a cobalt-60-based system like the one in Mulberry, Fla., the first commercial facility dedicated to irradiating food. The heart of the plant, established in 1991, is a shiny rack of 400 gamma-ray-emitting cobalt-60 "pencils," each 18 inches long and the diameter of a fat crayon, housed in a chamber surrounded by a concrete wall 6 feet thick. When not in use, the rack is submerged in a 15-foot-deep pool of cooled water that absorbs and neutralizes the gamma rays. At the push of a button, hydraulic arms lift the cobalt rack out of its protective pool and tall metal boxes packed with food slide into the irradiation chamber on an overhead monorail. The boxes follow a zig-zag pattern around the radioactive rack so gamma rays can reach all sides. Treatment times vary—fresh strawberries pass through in 5 to 8 minutes, frozen chicken takes as long as 20 minutes.

Gamma rays from cobalt-60 can penetrate full boxes of fresh or frozen food. But food must be removed from standard shipping pallets, stacked into metal irradiation boxes, and then returned to the pallets when they emerge from the chamber—all extra labor that increases costs.

A new irradiator now under development by GrayStar promises to address this concern by accepting food loaded onto standard pallets, something "everyone in the food industry says is an absolute must," says Stein. The unit will generate gamma rays using cesium-137, which GrayStar would chemically separate from high-level nuclear waste now stored at several power plants around the country.

The prototype machine—which measures 10 feet wide, 8 feet long, and 28 feet high, 12 of which are underground—is designed to be installed along a meat-packing or food-processing line. After a standard pallet of packaged food rolls into the irradiation chamber, which is constructed from 16-inch steel walls, the operator will seal the doors and instruct a computer to raise the rectangular array of cesium-containing rods from underground for a programmed length of time. Stein is optimistic that the unit will prove attractive to food processors and packers who may be more willing to invest in small, in-house irradiators than build, or contract with, a large central plant to which it must ship food. A working prototype of the compact unit, he says, is still a year away.

Electron beams and x-rays: Linear accelerators can generate ionizing radiation for food processing in the form of electron beams. Like a television set, these devices produce electrons from a heated filament sitting inside a vacuum tube. Magnetic fields accelerate the electrons through the tube until they reach energies as high as 10 million electron volts. At the end of the tube, meat or other food is irradiated as it slides by on a conveyor belt. Turn off the juice and the radiation disappears. A linear accelerator delivers more radiation per second than gamma rays; so it may work more quickly than a cobalt- or cesium-based machine.

"The downside is that electrons don't penetrate more than an inch and a half. Thus electron beams would not be able to handle such items as boxes of fruit or sides of beef. However, says Dennis Olson, a professor of food science at Iowa State University who has been testing this method, "you could handle a product up to about three inches thick, something like hamburger or chicken breasts, if you irradiate from both sides." Electron-beam units for such thin food products could move from the lab to the factory within a year or two at today's pace of development, according to Spencer Stevens, president of Omaha-based APA, Inc., an engineering and consulting firm for the food and meat industry.

Olson and others are also exploring the use of x-rays for irradiating food. While it takes even more energy to make x-rays than it does to generate electron beams, thus lowering the efficiency of the process, x-rays have dramatically better penetrating power and could be used on stacked boxes of fresh or frozen food or on slabs of meat.

The Bottom Line

Economics will play a large role in determining which of these approaches, if any, will ever be widely used in food processing. As commodities go, food is cheap, so even slight increases in processing costs can have a big impact on what consumers pay for certain items. Thus, says Stevens, radiation processing can't cost more than a few cents a pound, a figure that in-house irradiators could soon meet.

But the biggest unknown, of course, is whether consumers will buy irradiated food, even if producers can provide it at an affordable price. A series of surveys from the University of California at Davis, the University of Georgia, and Indiana University suggest the public is ready. "When you ask people if they would ever buy irradiated food, 50 to 60 percent say they would," says UC Davis's Bruhn. "When you mention that irradiation can keep food fresh longer and kill bacteria, the percentage rises to 80."

In-store tests and actual sales from a few independent grocery and produce stores offer real-world evidence that consumers might follow through on what they say. For example, Olson and his colleagues at Iowa State University sold irradiated chicken at a grocery store in Manhattan, Kans. Radiation-treated chicken—clearly labeled with a green symbol called a radura that must legally appear on all irradiated food—was displayed next to the traditionally processed store brand. Whichever one was cheaper sold better. Sales split down the middle when both carried the same price tag. Even when the irradiated chicken cost almost 25 cents a pound more, it still accounted for 20 percent of sales, says Olson.

Carrot Top, a produce store in north-suburban Chicago, also has had success selling irradiated food. Owner Jim Corrigan first introduced irradiated strawberries in 1992 with a two-for-one sale, expecting his customers to buy a box of irradiated strawberries and one of nonirradiated strawberries for comparison. Instead, the berries treated with radiation, which killed the molds normally growing on the fruit, outsold untreated berries ten-to-one because they looked better and lasted far longer. Carrot Top has since expanded its irradiated line to include Vidalia onions, blueberries, chicken, exotic Hawaiian fruits, and any other irradiated foods that are available. "I would carry irradiated hamburger today if it were available, since my customers ask me for it," says Corrigan.

Building Incentives

None of the country's major food companies will publicly acknowledge even a remote interest in food irradiation, yet several developments could push the food industry to adopt irradiation. First, some "traditional" methods for ridding food of pests are under close scrutiny. Methyl bromide, used to fumigate cereal grains, dried fruits and nuts, and fresh fruits and vegetables is scheduled to be banned in the United States as of January 1, 2001. Not only is it toxic to workers—the Environmental Protection Agency classifies it as a Category I acute toxin, the most deadly kind—it also is 50 times more destructive to the ozone layer than chlorine atoms from chlorofluorocarbons. Radiation could offer a reasonable alternative.

Ionizing radiation can also replace ethylene oxide, another widely used toxic fumigant. Radiation kills bacteria and insects more efficiently than the ethylene oxide, says Thomas Mates, general manager of SteriGenics, a California company that owns and operates several medical irradiators. What's more, irradiation doesn't leave behind any residue, and doesn't require any moisture, which can remove some of the volatile chemicals that give spices their smell and taste. SteriGenics recently introduced a line of radiation-treated spices called Purely by Choice.

The changing nature of our food supply may also spur wider use of irradiation. Once upon a time Americans got their food from local growers and neighborhood markets. Today much of our food comes from afar—from across the country and, increasingly, from developing countries. Few of us would eat fruits and vegetables in many of these countries without washing and peeling them. Yet when they are imported and sold in a U.S. store, that concern seems to disappear. "One does not need to leave home to contract traveler's diarrhea caused by an exotic agent," according to a recent editorial in the *New England Journal of Medicine* by Michael Osterholm, head of the Minnesota Department of Health. Food irradiation, he contends, "provides the greatest likelihood of substantially reducing bacterial and parasitic causes of food-borne disease associated with numerous foods, including fresh fruits and vegetables."

Irradiation may get a huge political boost, not to mention funding for further research and development, from the Clinton Administration's food-safety initiative, which is just beginning to wend its way through Congress. Whatever the outcome of the plan, however, the most powerful stimulus for wider use of irradiation is likely to be the ever-larger settlements awarded to people who become sick from eating contaminated food.

A generation ago, individuals felt responsible for the safety of their own food, says Christine Bruhn from UC Davis. Now people blame food growers, processors, and food sellers when they get sick from eating contaminated food, she says. This shift, already seen in million-dollar settlements such as those against Holiday Inn at San Francisco's Fisherman's Wharf and Foodmaster, the parent company of Jack-in-the-Box, is making restaurant owners and grocers take extra steps to make sure the food they deliver or sell is as safe as it can be.

Even though consumers seem willing to buy irradiated food, "it will probably take some truly traumatic E. coli outbreak that causes a number of deaths before government and the food industry get serious about food irradiation," says James Tillotson of Tufts. Without such a crisis, consumers probably wouldn't think of demanding irradiated food and there would be little political push to require leaving companies that explore irradiation open to attack by activist groups such as Food and Water. "No one is willing to get that kind of attention," he says, "even when they might be doing the best thing for consumers."

Nukeburgers: The Meat Industry's Solution to E. Coli Is the Big Zap Attack

Like most patriotic Americans, I love a good cheeseburger, oozing juice and fresh from the grill on a summer's afternoon. Praise the Lord and pass the catsup!

But would I want to die for one? Would you?

In recent years, outbreaks of virulent food poisoning caused by Escherichia coli 0157:H7, a mutant form of the E. coli found in the guts of all mammals, have put that question on the national agenda.

One answer offered by a coterie of government and private researchers, meat industry lobbyists and nuclear power advocates is to zap meat with radiation. That's right: They say they'll make your food safer by nuking it. Ferrying pre-packaged meat past cobalt-60 or cesium-137—or exposing it to an accelerated electron beam equivalent to millions of chest X-rays—kills bugs like E. coli, campylobacter, salmonella, listeria monocytogenes and others by tearing apart the molecular structure of their DNA.

Sounds scary? Don't worry, proponents purr. The meat never touches the radioactive material, nor does the process make the meat radioactive. They claim that decades of study, and feeding irradiated food to astronauts, proves that the food is nutritious and safer to eat than non-irradiated food. The Food and Drug Administration (FDA) and U.S. Department of Agriculture (USDA), they point out, have already approved the irradiation of dry herbs and spices, pork, fruits and vegetables and poultry. And concerns about potential environmental or worker safety hazards from widescale use of irradiation to fight food contamination are pooh-poohed with glowing assurances that the existing medical irradiation industry—which sterilizes medical instruments and uses the same technology that would be used on meat—has a "spotless" record.

But the industry's record is far from spotless. One corporate president went to jail. Workers have ended up in hospitals. Equipment has malfunctioned. And radioactive garbage has contaminated plants and gotten into the environment. Some of the most egregious violators of Nuclear Regulatory Commission (NRC) safety rules are the same firms that have submitted petitions to the FDA for the approval of food irradiation (by law, irradiation is considered a "food additive" subject to FDA regulation). The hollow assurances of the industry's safety cast irradiation champions' other claims of wholesomeness in a dubious light.

Food & Water, Inc., a Vermont-based environmental and nutrition advocacy group, charges that the FDA and the USDA have abdicated their consumer protection role to become cheerleaders for irradiation.

"The USDA is charged with promoting meat products but they're also supposed to be doing oversight. That's a huge conflict of interest," says Food & Water director Michael Colby. "They're in charge of policing this technology but with the other hand they're promoting it."

"Basically, we don't endorse it, we permit it—based on the FDA's assessment that it is safe to irradiate food," says USDA spokesperson Stephen Lombardi.

Don't endorse it? The agency supplies operating funds for an electron-beam irradiator at Iowa State University. It puts out pamphlets presenting a rosy picture of irradiation. And—along with an irradiation company with a history of NRC safety violations—the USDA petitioned its sister agency, the FDA, to approve the irradiation of poultry before the USDA itself approved the process.

♦

The push to irradiate food to kill bacteria and, in the case of fruits and vegetables, insects and other pests, isn't new.

Food irradiation originated as a component of President Dwight Eisenhower's "Atoms for Peace" program, the government's attempt to put a cheerful demeanor on the threatening face of the nuclear weapons establishment. Most research money came from the Army and the Atomic Energy Commission (now the NRC) until 1980. At that point, the USDA, which is responsible for the safety of the country's food supply, took over. The International Atomic Energy Agency has played a key role in hyping the process in global forums. And pro-nuclear agencies have funded most food irradiation research.

"The pressure for food irradiation comes from the DOE [Department of Energy], the USDA, the existing fledgling irradiation industry and its brothers and sisters in the larger nuke industry, and the American Meat Institute. You add it all up and you've got an iron triangle of industry, government and trade association," Colby says. "That's a formidable opponent to a public that opposes irradiation but we've beaten them back, held them off for 10 years."

Indeed, the technology is not yet widely used. Consumer wariness and high-profile pressure from Food & Water—threatened boycotts, radio ads, ads in food industry trade magazines and demonstrations outside stores and plants—have given most food companies and supermarket chains the willies. But while they haven't cast their lot with irradiation today, many companies and trade associations are hedging their bets for tomorrow by funding consumer research into how shoppers might be convinced to buy nukeburgers and bankrolling organizations like the Council for Agricultural Science and Technology (CAST), which produces a steady drumbeat of pro-irradiation issue papers.

Permission to irradiate red meat—beef—is the Holy Grail for which the irradiation industry is crusading; a petition has been before the FDA since August 1994.

The only plant constructed specifically to irradiate foods, the Food Technology Services (FTS) facility in Mulberry, Florida, has been limping along the past several years irradiating spices. A hoped-for bonanza of Florida produce to irradiate has never materialized due to fear of consumer outcry. Poultry irradiation is hung up on FDA approval of the packaging tray (meats are processed in their consumer packaging to stave off recontamination). FTS, formerly known as Vindicator, has survived through cash infusions from Nordion International, Inc., its Canadian supplier of cobalt-60 and irradiation equipment.

"The irradiation industry will be established processing meats," says Harley Everett, FTS's executive vice president. "Irradiating fruits and vegetables extends shelf life. That makes money but it doesn't save lives."

Providing the red meat petition is approved by the FDA, Dennis Olson, a researcher at Iowa State University who oversees the electron beam irradiator, says two likely factors will determine the success of the food irradiation industry: another large outbreak of E. coli poisoning and the extent of the resulting liability damages companies would have to pay.

"In our day and age of litigation and huge damages, companies don't want to expose themselves to that kind of threat," Olson says. "That may be enough to have them go to irradiation."

"We don't think anyone questions that there is a problem with contamination of meat, and it's getting worse. But we differ as to what to do about it," says Michael Colby. "We don't think zapping is the solution. It just creates additional problems."

Opponents of food irradiation, such as Food & Water, and skeptics—including the consumer group the Center for Science in the Public Interest (CSPI) and Safe Tables Our Priority (STOP, an E. coli poisoning victims advocacy group)—charge that irradiation of red meat is a shortcut, an attempt to avoid cleaning up the food production process. Inadequate plant sanitation and antiquated and under-staffed inspection processes, they say, are to blame for problems.

"Irradiation is an end-of-the-line technique to improve food safety that doesn't address the underlying question of why these products become contaminated in the first place," says Caroline Smith DeWaal, director of food safety for CSPI. "I don't believe consumers want feces on their meat or poultry products."

"I challenge you to find fecal matter on beef," counters Janet Riley, a spokesperson for the American Meat Institute (AMI), the chief lobbying arm for the meat and poultry industry. "The USDA has a zero tolerance policy. You have to trim any visible contamination."

But, as Rainer Mueller, president of STOP, notes, E. coli 0157:H7 can cause illness with only 10 cells. "There's no way an inspector can see E. coli cells," declares Mueller, whose 13-year-old son Eric died of E. coli poisoning from a tainted cheeseburger in 1993. CSPI's Smith DeWaal notes, "If you have cases of E. coli in beef products there has been some manure contact at some point to get there. It may be an insignificant or small amount."

According to Riley, AMI is "supportive" of meat irradiation, but "we don't see it as the be-all, end-all of food safety either." She says that—contrary to charges that irradiation is a substitute for cleaning up farms, feedlots, slaughter-houses, and processing plants—the meat industry is pursuing safety from farm to table.

"Have you seen a plant?" she asks me. (I haven't.) "They're like operating rooms. I'm amazed at the precautions they take, it's incredible. The problem is the visual images people have of processing plants are visions of yesteryear."

If meat processors are so clean then why do they need irradiation? Iron-ically, the analogy that Iowa State's Dennis Olson uses is also to operating rooms.

"Even in hospital operating rooms people get infections," Olson says. "You're never going to have processing plants like operating rooms. There's bacteria everywhere."

While AMI roots for irradiation, some meat processors have doubts that go beyond issues of consumer acceptance. Gary Michaelson, a spokesperson for International Beef Processors, Inc. (IBP), says the company does not irradiate its product and has no plans to do so. "We contracted for an evaluation with outside laboratories and it showed that current irradiation procedures affect meat flavor and color stability," Michaelson says.

CSPI and STOP have no official position on irradiation, but Food & Water's Colby blasts it as a "radical and dangerous technology."

Food & Water's specific concerns:

- The bombardment of foods with enormous amounts of ionizing radia-tion—more than enough to kill human beings—disrupts the molecular structure and creates "radiolytic products," new chemicals formed as a result of the irradiation process. Some of these are known carcinogens.
- Irradiation significantly depletes some key nutrients and vitamins.
- Wide-scale use of irradiation to process food would be an environmen-tal and worker safety disaster.

That radiolytic products exist isn't in dispute, only whether they are sig-nificant. Food & Water says the creation of toxic chemicals such as benzene, formaldehyde and formic acid presents a potential health risk—including cancer—that has not been sufficiently researched.

A hotly disputed study conducted in India in the 1970s found significant numbers of intrauterine deaths and depression in immune response in rats and mice fed freshly irradiated wheat. There was also an increase in polyploid cells, a chromosomal abnormality, in the bone marrow of rats and mice and the blood of children and monkeys fed freshly irradiated wheat. Similar results were not obtained from non-irradiated wheat or irradiated wheat that had been stored for three months prior to feeding.

One of the researchers, Dr. Vijaylaxmi, a geneticist now at the University of Texas, "strongly suspects there are radiolytic products which are problematic in these studies."

"In regard to polyploid cells, we do not know the significance of these cells so we expressed a note of caution, but scientific studies have shown that they are associated with cancer—whether polyploid cells cause cancer or cancer produces polyploid cells, we don't know," Dr. Vijaylaxmi says. "But we do know the significance of intrauterine death and depressed immune response and I would consider that a strong factor in whether one chooses to eat irradiated food. If the choice was given to me, I wouldn't eat irradiated food."

Radiation proponents dismiss concerns over radiolytic products, equating them with similar changes that occur from cooking. They contend that, in fact, studies prove irradiated food is safe.

Olson, the Iowa State University researcher, says the FDA "didn't find anything that would suggest an unsafe condition."

"While Food & Water tries to take the debate to the public, where they need to go if they have credible evidence is the FDA," Olson argues. "They can scare people by saying it produces benzene and benzene is carcinogenic and they can debate it in the newspapers but the real judge is the FDA."

How the FDA has performed in its role as a judge, though, is a point of contention. From the late 1960s, when the FDA rescinded its approval of an Army petition to irradiate bacon because the agency concluded the data didn't prove the process was safe, until the early 1980s, FDA skepticism stalled growth of food irradiation. But in 1980, the FDA executed a turnaround and, following the lead of a committee organized by the International Atomic Energy Agency, declared food irradiated up to a dose of 100,000 rads safe and in need of no further testing. In short order, the FDA gave thumbs-up to the irradiation of herbs and spices (1983), pork (1985) and—petitioning itself!—fruits and vegetables (1986).

Out of 441 studies of the effects of food irradiation, the FDA concluded that "only five... were considered by agency reviewers to be properly conducted, fully adequate by 1980 toxicological standards, and able to stand alone in the support of safety."

Dr. Donald Louria, chairman of the Department of Preventive Medicine at the New Jersey Medical School, reviewed the five studies cited by the FDA. His conclusion? "The FDA studies did not document safety." Writing in the *Bulletin of Atomic Scientists* in 1990, Louria stated that two studies were methodologically flawed (and one of those two suggested an adverse effect on older animals) and in a third FDA-cited study, "animals fed a diet of irradiated food experienced weight loss and miscarriage." According to Louria, the other two studies appeared to be conducted adequately but dealt with food irradiated at doses lower than the FDA allows.

Louria acknowledges that "a lot of good scientists are for [irradiation]" but he is adamant that more testing is needed.

"People in the industry will not settle the issues," he states. "They should do a chromosome study on people given irradiated food." Louria thinks it's likely such tests would show irradiated food to be harmless, "but they won't do it."

Louria also believes irradiation advocates have been dismissive of concerns over vitamin loss in irradiated foods.

Studies by the USDA's Agricultural Research Service (ARS) have documented nutrient depletion in a host of irradiated foods. Thiamin content, for example, is particularly vulnerable to radiation. As in the case of radiolytic products, irradiation's defenders point out that nutrients are lost in other processes, including cooking. However, irradiation is not a substitute for cooking. Furthermore, an ARS study on bacon indicated that "when irradiated bacon was fried, a greater amount of thiamin was lost than would be predicted if the loss was strictly additive."

Louria wants all irradiated foods to be tested for vitamin content before and after the recommended irradiation dose and the results printed on the package's label.

"They want to sell to everybody—young kids, people in poverty who may already be vitamin-deficient," he argues. "It shouldn't be let into the marketplace without this information and these tests."

⋅⋅⊙⋅⋅

Faced with the claims of dueling scientists, how is the layperson to know whom to believe? In the case of food irradiation, the questions of environmental contamination and worker safety may be the best yardstick by which to decide the issue.

Irradiation advocates respond to such questions with honeyed paeans to the safety record of the existing medical irradiation industry. The analogy makes sense. Not only is the technology for food irradiation the same as that used to sterilize medical instruments—cobalt-60 and, less frequently, cesium-137 gamma radiation exposure or electron-beam irradiation—but, in fact, it is primarily medical irradiation companies that are seeking approval for the irradiation of food in a bid to open new markets.

Janet Riley of the American Meat Institute says she has heard of no accidents or safety concerns associated with medical irradiation. Harley Everett of Food Technology Services declares, "Irradiation with cobalt has a spotless environmental record in this country." A pro-irradiation report by CAST, "Radiation Pasteurization of Food," states, "Many commercial irradiation plants exist in the United States and they have established an excellent safety record." Question number seven in a USDA pamphlet, "Ten Most Commonly Asked Questions About Food Irradiation," asks "will my risks of radiation exposure increase significantly if I live next to an irradiator?" The pamphlet's answer? No, because "the use and transportation of radioactive materials... is closely monitored by the Nuclear Regulatory Commission, state agencies and the Department of Transportation."

But serious accidents and even deliberate violations of NRC safety regulations have occurred at medical irradiators. Workers have suffered life-threatening exposures to radiation (at least two workers have died in other countries) and radiation has leaked into the environment.

The most notorious case involved the firm Radiation Technology, Inc. [RTI] and its president Martin Welt. RTI, which has since been purchased by SteriGenics, operated four irradiators in the 1980s, two in New Jersey and one

each in Arkansas and North Carolina. Welt, who wrote the FDA petitions for approval of irradiation of poultry, seafood and spices, served prison time after his conviction in 1988 on six out of seven criminal counts, including conspiracy to defraud the United States, lying to NRC investigators and intentionally violating the Atomic Energy Act. Welt also obstructed FDA attempts to inspect his plants (the FDA had jurisdiction because of RTI's irradiation of medical instruments and spices).

In order to increase production, Welt ordered the deliberate bypassing of safety features designed to prevent worker exposure to unshielded cobalt-60. He directed RTI's Rockaway, New Jersey, plant to run unattended on weekends to process more product. He also illegally irradiated food before it had been approved by the FDA, bringing it into the Rockaway plant on weekends in unmarked U-Haul trucks to be zapped by himself and another employee for cash. The NRC forced Welt out of his association with RTI but he is still active in the irradiation business as a consultant.

The late George Giddings wrote the pending petition for red meat irradiation as a consultant for Isomedix, Inc., an irradiator firm with plants in New Jersey and Massachusetts. Food & Water reports that in 1974, radioactive water was flushed down toilets in Isomedix's New Jersey plant, contaminating pipes leading to sewers. Also that year, a worker received a near-lethal radiation dose. According to a document downloaded from the NRC's website, the NRC proposed a "substantial civil penalty" against Isomedix in 1987 for "serious violation of safety requirements." The company had deliberately bypassed the radiation monitor interlock systems and also "installed jumper cables to bypass ventilation system interlocks which were designed to automatically protect individuals from noxious gases produced by irradiation." Isomedix is currently negotiating with a municipality in Hawaii to build an irradiator for the processing of fresh fruits.

Use of cesium-137 was seriously set back by an accident at Radiation Sterilizers, Inc. in Georgia in 1988. Leaking cesium-137 capsules contaminated the water storage pool, resulting in the closure of the facility. The Department of Energy (DOE) was forced to take over the cleanup at a cost to taxpayers of over $30 million. Under its Byproducts Utilization Program, DOE has sought for over a decade to find commercial uses for its large store of cesium-137, a more dangerous isotope than cobalt-60. Food & Water's Michael Colby believes that if food irradiation becomes accepted by the public, "You can bet the farm that it won't be long before cesium-137 comes back on the table."

Lax safety procedures continue in the industry. Earlier this month, the NRC proposed an $8,000 fine against a 3M medical irradiator facility in South Dakota for operating a cobalt-60 irradiator without an operator in attendance. Fortunately, although the conveyor jammed and stopped on two occasions, the irradiator's cobalt-60 source withdrew as designed into its underwater holder, preventing any radiation exposure.

Because irradiation of food on a wide scale would require the siting of many more such plants, the potential for threats to the public would multiply. As in any industry, financially strapped firms would be tempted to cut corners.

Additionally, increased traffic in cobalt-60 and/or cesium-137 would raise the possibility of transport accidents.

✦

None of this apparently concerns either the FDA or the USDA.

Dr. George Pauli, Director of the FDA's Division of Product Policy, says environmental or safety issues associated with food irradiation technology are "not something we dwell on from our standpoint." Asked whether Isomedix's safety lapses concern him, Pauli says, "Any company in business will have an accident at some time or other varying from isolated to serious. The radiation business is more closely regulated than others so the smallest thing would be cited so I wouldn't be surprised if any company had an accident. Our regulations don't apply to a specific company; our approvals are generic."

The USDA had petitioned the FDA to approve irradiation of poultry with Radiation Technology, Inc., the company started by Martin Welt. USDA spokesperson Dan Engeljohn says the USDA knew of Welt's history, but adds, "Related to the one individual with a documented history of non-compliance, he was not in a position of authority in the company when we petitioned to approve the process."

Engeljohn echoes Pauli, saying oversight of the operation of irradiators is the province of the NRC.

"We do believe those operators are in business to put out a product that is safe and can do so without jeopardizing the environment or public health," Engeljohn says. "But as with every industry there can be some who are not as concerned with safety. Fortunately, there is a lot of government oversight to make sure that does not happen and to assess penalties."

However, at the point where the nuclear industry and the food supply intersect, the government isn't so much exercising oversight as looking the other way. Or, worse yet, encouraging a policy that could lead to disaster.

POSTSCRIPT

Is Irradiated Food Safe to Eat?

Shortly after the FDA approved the use of food irradiation in poultry, Jacques Leslie wrote in "Food Irradiation," *The Atlantic* (September 1990) that "Most opposition... starts from the assumption that radiation, frequently a lethal agent, cannot possibly affect food in safe ways.... [T]he dispute thus chiefly pits experts who support food irradiation against laymen who oppose it. Instead of grappling with the details of scientific inquiry, the coalition of anti-nuclear activists, organic-food advocates, and holistic-health practitioners who compose the organized opposition to food irradiation habitually make startling but invariably hollow claims of conspiracy.... Of the hundreds of scientists in this country who have done extensive research on the wholesomeness of food irradiation, only a few have publicly expressed opposition to it, and the several other scientists who are actively against food irradiation are not experienced in the field.... [T]he preponderance of evidence refutes the opposition's claims." The article is well worth reading for its detailed refutations of several objections to food irradiation, including some mentioned by Donald B. Louria in "Zapping the Food Supply," *Bulletin of the Atomic Scientists* (September 1990). See also Richard L. Worsnop, "Food Irradiation," *CQ Researcher* (June 12, 1992).

However, refutations have had little effect on the opposition, whose activities, covered in Larry Katzenstein, "Good Food You Can't Get," *American Health* (December 1992), have hardly stopped. In the April 1993 issue of *American Family Physician,* James Mason wrote "Food Irradiation: Let's Move Ahead." It had been two years since Fritz Kaferstein, head of the United Nations' World Health Organization, had said that food irradiation "is a perfectly sound food preservation technology badly needed in a world where food-borne disease is on the increase." It had been endorsed by the FDA and numerous scientific groups and institutes, and 36 nations had approved its use, but the opposition, "citing discredited research, [had] voiced unfounded fears often enough to make some consumers think twice."

Is the issue of food irradiation one of public safety or public anxiety? Most risk analysts say that it does not matter, at least from the point of view of those responsible for processes or products that provoke public concern. No matter how safe irradiated food may be, no one will build irradiation facilities, process irradiated food, or stock it in stores if the public refuses to buy the product. Those who try will likely go out of business. It is the public's perception of risk—pointed out by Michael Fumento in "Food Irradiation's Hysteria Industry," *Washington Times* (February 19, 1999)—that matters and must be dealt with by educating the public, modifying the process or product, or turning to alternatives.

On the Internet . . .

National Aeronautics and Space Administration

At this site, you can find out the latest information on the Pathfinder mission—including Mars surface photos—as well as other NASA projects.

http://www.nasa.gov

Center for Mars Exploration

This is the starting point for an exploration of the history of Mars, with links to the Whole Mars Catalog and information about the Mars Pathfinder and Mars Global Surveyor missions.

http://cmex-www.arc.nasa.gov

The SETI Institute

The SETI Institute serves as a home for scientific research in the general field of life in the universe, with an emphasis on the search for extraterrestrial intelligence (SETI).

http://www.seti-inst.edu

The SETI League

The SETI League, Inc., is dedicated to the electromagnetic (radio) search for extraterrestrial intelligence.

http://seti1.setileague.org

PART 4

Space

*M*any interesting controversies arise in connection with technologies that are so new that they often sound more like science fiction than fact. Some examples are technologies that allow the exploration of outer space, the search for extraterrestrial intelligence, and genetic engineering. Such advances offer capabilities undreamed of in earlier ages, and they raise genuine, important questions about what it is to be a human being, the limits on human freedom in a technological age, and the place of humanity in the broader universe. They also raise questions of how we should respond: Should we accept the new devices and abilities offered by scientists and engineers? Or should we reject them?

- Can Humans Go to Mars Now?

- Is It Worthwhile to Continue the Search for Extraterrestrial Life?

ISSUE 9

Can Humans Go to Mars Now?

YES: John Tierney, from "Martian Chronicle," *Reason* (February 1999)

NO: Neil de Grasse Tyson, from "Space: You Can't Get There from Here," *Natural History* (September 1, 1998)

ISSUE SUMMARY

YES: John Tierney, a columnist for *The New York Times,* argues that it is technically and economically possible to establish a human presence on Mars.

NO: Neil de Grasse Tyson, the Frederick P. Rose Director of New York City's Hayden Planetarium, counters that space travel is an impractical dream.

The dream of conquering space has a long history. The pioneers of rocketry —the Russian Konstantin Tsiolkovsky (1857–1935) and the American Robert H. Goddard (1882–1945)—both dreamed of exploring other worlds, although neither lived long enough to see the first artificial satellite, Sputnik, go up in 1957. That success sparked a race between America and the Soviet Union to be the first to achieve each step in the progression of space exploration. The next steps were to put dogs (the Soviet Laika was the first), monkeys, chimps, and finally humans into orbit. Communications, weather, and spy satellites were then designed and launched. And on July 20, 1969, the U.S. Apollo Program landed the first men on the Moon. See Buzz Aldrin and Malcolm McConnell, *Men from Earth* (Bantam, 1989).

There were a few more Apollo landings, but not many. The United States had achieved its main political goal of beating the Soviets to the Moon and, in the minds of the government, demonstrating American superiority. Thereafter, the United States was content to send automated spacecraft (computer-operated robots) to observe Venus, Mars, and the rings of Saturn; to land on Mars and study its soil; and even to carry recordings of Earth's sights and sounds past the distant edge of the solar system, perhaps to be retrieved in the distant future by intelligent life from some other world.

Humans have not left near-Earth orbit for two decades, though space technology has continued to develop through communications satellites, space shuttles, space stations, and independent robotic explorers such as the Mariners and Vikings and—landing on Mars on July 4, 1997—the Pathfinder craft (now the Sagan Memorial Station) and its tiny robot rover, Sojourner.

Why has human space exploration gone no further? One reason is that robots are now extremely capable and much cheaper; see David Callahan, "A Fork in the Road to Space," *Technology Review* (August/September 1993). Although some robot spacecraft have failed partially or completely, there have been many grand successes that have added enormously to humanity's knowledge of the earth and other planets.

Another reason for the reduction in human space travel seems to be the fear that astronauts will die in space. This point was emphasized by the explosion of the space shuttle *Challenger* in January 1986, which killed seven astronauts and froze the entire shuttle program for over two-and-a-half years. Still another is money: Lifting robotic explorers into space is expensive, but lifting people into space—along with all the food, water, air, and other supplies necessary to keep them alive for the duration of a mission—is much more expensive. And there are many people in government and elsewhere who cry that there are many better ways to spend the money on Earth.

In the following selections, John Tierney states that it is already technically possible to establish a human presence on Mars and that there are several practical ways to raise the necessary funds. Furthermore, he adds, to go to Mars —or even to dream of doing so—serves the cause of human liberty. Neil de Grasse Tyson argues that space travel is an impractical dream. To go to Mars —or elsewhere in the universe—will require enormous technical breakthroughs, he concludes.

John Tierney

 **YES**

Martian Chronicle

A couple of years ago, after hearing an engineer named Robert Zubrin rhapsodize about his plan for a privately financed expedition to Mars, I tried out the idea on America's masters of marketing. I sent an outline of the scheme to Bill Gates, Ted Turner, Barry Diller, Peter Uberroth, television executives such as ABC's Roone Arledge and NBC's Don Ohlmeyer, the leaders of DreamWorks, and a long list of other people whose names tend to be accompanied by the word visionary. I wasn't asking for money, just for their thoughts on how humanity's interplanetary adventure could be packaged profitably, but most of them didn't even want to think about it. Except for a few enthusiasts, they couldn't imagine how you could make the trip interesting enough to pay the bills. How could you hold the audience for such a long trip to such a desolate place?

"Personally," Barry Diller explained, "I don't care about going to Mars."

Personally, I did. But I didn't presume to know as much about the mass audience as Diller and his fellow moguls. They knew how short the public's attention span could be; they remembered how quickly people had gotten bored with the Apollo program. What, really, was the point of going to Mars? If the idea made any commercial sense, why wasn't someone working on it? I wondered if Zubrin was hopelessly unrealistic—until this past summer, when he managed to get 700 people from 40 countries to travel to Boulder, Colorado.

Officially, it was the founding convention of the Mars Society. Unofficially, it was the Woodstock of Mars, a horde of scientists, entrepreneurs, schoolteachers, lawyers, writers, engineers, college students, musicians, computer geeks, and assorted hustlers wearing "MARS OR BUST" buttons. They ranged from space hobbyists to the president of a company working on a privately financed mission to survey an asteroid. They debated the cost of spaceships and whether to power the Mars land rover with a nuclear reactor. They bought Mars trinkets and pictures. They analyzed details ranging from the proper Martian calendar (there are dozens of competing systems) to the mechanics of creating a breathable atmosphere on Mars.

And they cheered Zubrin, who is one of the more riveting engineer-orators in history. A short man with intense dark eyes and a passionate speaking style—

he can bring to mind Savonarola—he railed at the stagnation that would afflict humans without a frontier to conquer. He extolled the Europeans who crossed the Atlantic 500 years ago to find freedom in the New World and the Africans who left the comforts of the tropics 50,000 years ago for the cold, harsh regions where they were forced to develop the tools that made civilization possible. "Humans did not leave paradise because they ate of the tree of knowledge," he proclaimed. "They ate of the tree of knowledge because they left paradise." The audience gave him a two-minute standing ovation.

In some ways it was reminiscent of the passion for space back in the 1960s, but not even the moon landings had ever aroused such a zealous corps of volunteer mission planners. These people wanted much more than another Apollo program, whose achievements they dismissed as "flags and footprints." Their heroes were from earlier eras of exploration: Columbus, the Pilgrims, Lewis and Clark, the settlers of the American West. As they put it in their society's founding declaration, "The settling of the Martian New World is an opportunity for a noble experiment in which humanity has another chance to shed old baggage and begin the world anew."

They were dangerously close to utopianism—which at first seemed odd, given that Zubrin and a good many of the others are libertarians. Ordinarily, libertarians are too busy opposing politicians' utopian schemes to be preaching their own. But as they fantasized about casting off the chains of earthly governments, the Mars-libertarian connection began to make sense. Mars gives libertarians a rare chance to be *for* something, to present a grand vision of freedom instead of merely trying to fend off the latest excesses of big government. Building the future is a splendid alternative to the drudgery of deregulating and privatizing the present. Spaceships and extraterrestrial colonies evoke the sort of emotions inspired by cathedrals in the Middle Ages—or, to use a more recent example, by modern architecture in *The Fountainhead*.

Libertarians can appreciate Mars in a way that Barry Diller and his fellow moguls can't. A desolate planet free of earthly institutions is more appealing to libertarians than it is to the corporate elite, just as the New World was more appealing to the Pilgrims and other contrarians than it was to the European aristocracy. It will take some doing to settle Mars, but libertarians have a crucial advantage. They're not expecting government bureaucrats to do the job. They know better than to count on NASA.

Four decades after the Lewis and Clark expedition, the American West had been mapped by trappers and was being rapidly settled by farmers. It has now been nearly four decades since the first explorers went into space, and what do we have to show for it? Chiefly two government programs that have created lots of jobs and produced massive cost overruns: the space shuttle and the space station. Rick Tumlinson, the president of the Space Frontier Foundation, is grateful that NASA did not exist in Thomas Jefferson's day.

"Suppose," Tumlinson says, "that when Lewis and Clark returned from their trip, Jefferson had told them, 'Mr. Clark, you develop a Conestoga shuttle.

Mr. Lewis, I want you to build a national cabin.' And 30 years later they had three or four Conestoga shuttles, and they were just beginning to build the national cabin. That's where we are today."

Admittedly, space poses more logistical challenges than the American West. But NASA has shown a genius for complicating those challenges. It is burdened not only by bureaucratic inefficiency and pork barrel politics (every superfluous job means votes in someone's congressional district) but also by the public's aversion to risk. Private explorers can afford to fail and risk lives; NASA's leaders are expected by politicians and the press to prevent any loss of life or damage to "national prestige." They're forced to avoid another *Challenger* disaster at all costs.

"The cost of space travel ought to be declining with new technology, but it's not," says Edward L. Hudgins, director of regulatory studies at the Cato Institute. "About three decades after the Wright brothers' flight, the commercially viable DC-3 was flying. But today the cost of placing payloads into orbit on the shuttle is 10 times higher than it was during the Apollo program. By contrast, in the past 20 years the cost of airline tickets per passenger mile has dropped by 30 percent, and the cost of shipping oil has dropped 80 percent."

NASA's profligacy became absurdly obvious in 1989, when the agency was asked by President Bush to plan a mission to Mars. It responded with a $400 billion proposal to build a 1,000-ton interplanetary spaceship the length of a football field, which would have carried all the fuel for the return voyage. It would have been assembled in orbit because it was too large to be launched from Earth—"the battlestar *Galactica*," as Zubrin dubbed it. At the time he was an engineer at Martin Marietta Astronautics and a member of an informal group called the Mars Underground that met occasionally to dream of interplanetary travel. He and a colleague at Martin Marietta, Donald Baker, came up with an alternative to NASA's battlestar *Galactica* by adopting the philosophy of Roald Amundsen, the entrepreneurial Norwegian who explored the polar regions early this century.

Besides winning the race to the South Pole, Amundsen was the first person to sail the Northwest Passage, which he accomplished by avoiding the mistakes of the British Navy. As the NASA of its day, the Royal Navy in the 19th century sent one lavishly provisioned expedition after another in search of the Northwest Passage, but the large ships kept getting stuck in the Arctic ice, and when the food ran out the men had to return home (or perish, as many of them did). Amundsen, who was financing his own expedition, bought a small fishing boat and took a crew of just six. Unable to bring huge stores of food, he learned to live off the land by hunting caribou as he maneuvered the small boat through the ice all the way from the Atlantic to the Pacific.

"Amundsen's expedition was a brilliant example of a small group of explorers succeeding on a shoestring budget," Zubrin says. "Lewis and Clark's was another. Before their journey, armies with big baggage trains had failed to make any significant penetration in the American West. But Lewis and Clark managed to cross the continent with just 25 men."

To reach Mars, Zubrin proposed replacing NASA's huge ship with a vessel small and light enough to be launched directly from Earth. It would not need to carry fuel for the return trip because the Martian explorers, like Amundsen, would exploit local resources: the carbon dioxide in the Martian atmosphere, which when combined with hydrogen brought from Earth, could be converted to methane and liquid oxygen to fuel the return voyage. Zubrin built a machine to demonstrate how easily it could be done, and eventually NASA adopted his idea. It redesigned the Mars mission, lowering the cost estimate from $400 billion to $55 billion, and is contemplating a trip sometime after 2010.

But Zubrin, who's now the president of his own firm in Boulder, Pioneer Astronautics, has pared down NASA's plans to come up with a still cheaper mission. He figures that within a decade a private entrepreneur could get to Mars and back for a mere $5 billion. He's been promoting this idea in lectures and in a book, *The Case for Mars,* that has been translated into half a dozen languages and attracted letters from thousands of Mars enthusiasts around the world. (See "Spaceship Enterprise," *Reason,* April 1997.)

Other engineers estimate the cost of a private mission might be more like $10 billion, maybe up to $20 billion, but even at those prices the trip is not an absurdly extravagant dream. NASA's budget for a single year is $13 billion. For the estimated cost of building and operating the space station, $100 billion, you could send a fleet of Zubrin's ships to Mars. By NASA standards, the cost of a private Mars mission is chump change.

⁂

But by venture capital standards, it's a lot of money for a highly speculative endeavor. To pay for the mission, Zubrin and members of the Mars Society have been analyzing the financing techniques of pre-NASA explorers and looking for new ideas. Some possibilities:

The Mars Prize   Zubrin tried selling this idea during a dinner with then–House Speaker Newt Gingrich, who got so enthusiastic that the meal lasted for four hours. But Gingrich never followed through on the proposal, which calls for Congress to promise $20 billion to the first explorers who reach Mars and return. In case that prize isn't enough to interest entrepreneurs in such a risky all-or-nothing venture, Zubrin also envisions offering smaller bonuses for achieving technical milestones along the way, like sending the equipment for making fuel to Mars.

Prizes have been used in the past to spur public-private ventures in exploration. Fifteenth-century Spanish and Portuguese rulers offered financial inducements to captains who ventured down the African coast and across the Atlantic. In the 19th century, the British Parliament offered cash awards for reaching the North Pole and for venturing westward into the Arctic ice: a prize of £5,000 for reaching 110 degrees west, double that for reaching 130 degrees, and triple that for 150 degrees.

For politicians, the most appealing aspect of the Mars Prize is that they could reap the publicity of announcing it without having to pay for it immediately. They could present themselves as both patrons of exploration and opponents of make-work government programs. NASA would surely object to the proposal, and so might libertarian purists, who could argue that there's no need for the public to finance any kind of Martian adventure. But to some extent, the knowledge gained from Martian exploration would be a public good; so would the national glory, for whatever that's worth. And there's always the preservation-of-the-species argument: By supporting the exploration of a potential new home, the public is buying insurance against Earth's becoming uninhabitable.

The Mars Prize would certainly be more defensible than NASA's current monopoly on public funds for space exploration. Still, there's no reason the trip must be financed by the government. Entrepreneurial explorers have long profited from the fortunes and egos of . . .

Rich Patrons   In 1911, William Randolph Hearst offered a $50,000 prize to the first person to fly across America in less than 30 days. Calbraith Perry Rodgers immediately set out to win it in a plane called the *Vin Fiz,* named after a carbonated grape drink manufactured by his sponsor, the Armour Meat Packing Company. He endured 15 accidents on the way from New York to Los Angeles, one of which landed him in the hospital for a month. He didn't meet the deadline—it took him 84 days—but he did complete the trip. Other prizes have been offered for human-powered flight (a $200,000 award claimed in 1978, when the *Gossamer Albatross* flew a mile) and for the first manned, completely reusable spaceship (a $10 million award, announced in 1996 by the X Prize Foundation, that has yet to be claimed).

The Mars Prize would be an expensive proposition, but modern-day Hearsts such as Bill Gates could afford to offer it. Or they could directly finance expeditions, the way wealthy gentlemen supported polar exploration at the start of the century. Robert Peary, for instance, was bankrolled by the Peary Arctic Club, a group of businessmen who paid for the privilege of basking in his company and achieving geographic immortality. Peary and other polar explorers named mountains and glaciers after the American, British, and Norwegian plutocrats who financed the discoveries. Mars' most prominent features, like its 18-mile-high volcano and 2,800-mile-long version of the Grand Canyon, have already been named, but the first explorers there—and certainly the first settlers —could exercise their prerogative to assign new names.

The patrons of Arctic expeditions also sometimes paid to tag along for part of the trip. Peary brought wealthy sponsors on his ship; Frederick C. Cook was accompanied by a sportsman who wanted to hunt. The Mars mission—six months traveling there, two years on the surface, and six months back—might be too grueling a vacation for the typical billionaire. But plenty of other people would pay for a chance to go along, and there's a clever way to get hold of their money.

The Mars Lottery   Perhaps the most promising new idea at the conference in Boulder came from someone outside the aerospace industry. Alex Duncan, a local resident with experience in the commodities business, proposed an international Mars Lottery, modeled on the lottery based in Lichtenstein that raises funds internationally for the Red Cross. A Mars Lottery could be headquartered anywhere and reach a global audience through the Internet.

Besides the usual cash prizes, which could be awarded fortnightly or monthly, the Mars Lottery would have two big selling points. First, participants would know that a portion of the proceeds was going to support a private expedition to Mars. Second, and more important, participants would be buying a chance to go themselves. Duncan proposed that all the winners of the regular drawings become eligible for a grand prize: a berth on the first ship to Mars, assuming that the winner of this grand drawing met the physical and mental requirements for the voyage. Duncan figures that the proceeds from this lottery could pay for the whole Mars mission within three to five years.

A variation on his scheme would be to give the winner of each regular drawing the option of trying out for the mission at the explorers' training camp, which would probably be in the Arctic (to simulate the frigid conditions on Mars). The leader of the crew could evaluate dozens, maybe hundreds, of different winners and choose one or two for the trip. This system would produce a better crew and also increase the appeal of the lottery, because each winner would be getting an Arctic adventure in addition to the cash prize.

Media and Marketing   The Summer Olympics last just three weeks and generate more than $2 billion in fees from television networks and corporate sponsors. The three-year Mars mission has the potential to make much more money, possibly enough to pay for itself, solely with the revenue from media rights and corporate tie-ins.

Just as Henry Morton Stanley charged the expenses of his African journeys to the *New York Herald,* just as Sir Ernest Shackleton paid for his Antarctic voyages with best-selling books and international lecture tours, the Mars explorers could tap into the global appetite for adventure stories. And just as Shackleton exploited the new media of his day—at his lectures in 1910 he showed the first movies from the Antarctic—the Mars explorers could reach a paying audience through new cable channels and Web sites. The media coverage of the mission would attract the same kind of sponsors who pay to be part of the Olympics. Outdoor gear makers and high-technology firms would have a special incentive to have their logos and products associated with the adventure.

Although some sponsors would be reluctant to get involved with a project that could fail spectacularly and fatally, others (especially those selling products to young males) would be attracted by the aura of danger. But the dangers must seem worthwhile; the mission shouldn't come off as a pointless stunt. If the trip appeared to be just a longer version of *Apollo 11,* another enterprise that left nothing but flags and footprints, it would be less appealing to the audience —and therefore to potential sponsors. That's one reason that Zubrin and his disciples focus on analogies with Columbus instead of Neil Armstrong. The vision of Mars as the New World lends the first trip gravitas.

But why would anyone, especially a libertarian devoted to free markets, believe that a Mars colony would be a good investment? The first humans on Mars will encounter horrific dust storms, temperatures of minus 70 degrees Fahrenheit, and an unbreathable atmosphere. If they stood on the Martian surface without a pressurized suit, their blood would expand and burst out of their veins. Why would it pay to stick around?

At first glance, Mars has none of the commercial opportunities that drew the first Europeans to America. Columbus, who was financed by merchants as well as by Queen Isabella, crossed the Atlantic with the intention of making money. Even after his first goal, a trade route to the Orient, proved unattainable, there were other attractions for investors. The Spanish conquered the natives and took home gold; the French and Dutch set up trading posts in North America to acquire furs.

Mars offers no such inducements, unless you count the souvenir value of its rocks. Otherwise the minerals in its crust appear to be of little value. Science fiction writers like to imagine humans profitably mining asteroids and other planets, but there's no looming scarcity of minerals on Earth. The prices of metals and most other natural resources have been falling for millennia. Unless the prices here rise dramatically, or the cost of interplanetary shipping plummets, space miners won't be able to profitably export Mars' resources in the foreseeable future.

But Mars does have some resources of local value: water, carbon dioxide, and real estate. It contains as much dry land as all the continents on Earth, and the leaders of the Mars Society have big plans for it. They want to "terraform" Mars by injecting chlorofluorocarbons into its atmosphere and setting off a runaway greenhouse effect. As the planet thawed, the atmosphere would thicken with carbon dioxide released from melting ice caps and soil. Add some trees and plants to convert the carbon dioxide into oxygen, and before long humans could be breathing comfortably as they strolled in shirt sleeves on the green planet.

This scheme sounds outlandish today, but there was a time when Europeans couldn't imagine settling the American wilderness either. The Spanish and French leaders, as well as the officials of the Dutch West India Company, didn't initially emphasize permanent settlements of families. They sent mainly single men—soldiers, traders, and trappers—on temporary assignments to extract resources. America was a nice place to exploit, but you wouldn't want to live there.

"From the Spanish point of view," Zubrin says, "the only parts of the Americas that were valuable were the places with civilized Indians that could be taxed. They dismissed the rest as a howling wilderness. The British had a different notion of where wealth comes from. They created farms and towns in New England, turning the wilderness into a domain where social reproduction could occur."

The British settlers, motivated by a yearning for religious freedom, eventually outnumbered and expelled the Spanish, French, and Dutch from most of North America. Isolated from Europe, they created new kinds of communities with new kinds of liberties. "Humanity needs room to play and experiment with ideas in human governance," Zubrin says. "In 1776 Thomas Paine wrote, 'We hold it in our power to begin the world anew.' So they did, and so do we. People will endure the risk and hardships of emigrating to Mars if, like the colonists in America, they can find a higher level of freedom." . . .

Already a few entrepreneurs are looking to launch their own missions into space. Two companies, hoping to tap the adventure travel market, have announced plans to build space planes that will take customers for a brief ride just outside the atmosphere. Another firm, Space Dev, has raised $20 million as part of its plan to send scientific instruments to survey an asteroid and sell the data to scientists. But the Mars mission requires investment of another order of magnitude, and even enthusiasts like Zubrin aren't sure the private sector will take the risk anytime soon. As he hopes for a private mission, he's also lobbying for an old-fashioned NASA program.

"I'm a hard libertarian about rights on Mars, but not about getting there," he says. "With something as risky as Mars, it would be useful for the government to absorb some of the up-front costs. Spanish merchants weren't willing to back Columbus' first trip without royal involvement. Lewis and Clark were funded by the U.S. government—and then, as soon as they came back and said there's beaver there, John Jacob Astor's people did their own private exploration that ultimately was much more extensive than the government's. The American government also stimulated the private sector by setting up forts in the frontier, which attracted peddlers who established trade routes in the area. If the government set up a research base on Mars, it would stimulate private competition to lower the costs of delivering cargo."

⠂⠶⠶⠂

Once the cost of transport to Mars dropped, real estate speculators might begin to see the planet's potential. One member of the Mars Society, Richard Allen Brown, has proposed that a private company divide Mars into a million plots, each 25,000 acres, and sell bonds giving a 100-year option on each plot. By charging $20,000 for each bond, the company could raise $20 billion. It would invest this capital conservatively and use the income, about $1 billion a year, to finance the exploration and settlement of Mars over the course of a century. If you bought a bond and the land eventually became valuable, you (or your heir) could exercise the option to trade in the bond for a deed to the land. If after 100 years the option still hadn't been exercised, your heir could redeem the bond for the original capital investment of $20,000.

Mars bonds would not be for the timid investor. Even if the land did become valuable, there's no guarantee that your deed to the land would be recognized, because for now there's no internationally recognized method of claiming land in outer space. The vagaries of space property law make another great topic of discussion among Mars Society members. (See "A Little Piece of Heaven," *Reason*, November 1998). But then, the first investors in the New World did not have secure property rights either.

"People in England were buying and selling Kentucky back in the 1600s, when it might as well have been Mars," Zubrin says. "No British citizen had been there, and it wasn't clear that British law would prevail—the French and Spanish had claims there too. But the king of England would sell patents to a nobleman, who would sell pieces to capitalists willing to speculate on the British. They'd hire someone to survey it, and then, if there were good prospects, they'd sell the land at a profit or start developing it by sending in settlers."

... [It is] the largest real estate project in history, and it illustrate[s] why Mars is a no-lose proposition for libertarians. If colonizing the Red Planet ever becomes a practical possibility, we should be ready to get there before anyone else starts writing the rules. And even if colonization never becomes practical, even if Mars never becomes a free new world, just imagining it is good for the libertarian soul.

NO

Neil de Grasse Tyson

Space: You Can't Get There from Here

From listening to space enthusiasts talk about space travel, or from watching blockbuster science fiction movies, you might think that sending people to the stars is inevitable and will happen soon. Reality check: It's not and it won't—the fantasy far outstrips the facts.

A line of reasoning among those who are unwittingly wishful might be, "We invented flight when most people thought it was impossible. A mere sixty-five years later, we went to the Moon. It's high time we journeyed among the stars. The people who say it isn't possible are ignoring history."

My rebuttal is borrowed from a legal disclaimer often used by the investment industry: "Past performance is not an indicator of future returns." Analysis of the problem leads to a crucial question: What does it take to pry money out of a population to pay for major initiatives? A quick survey of the world's famously funded projects reveals three common motivations: praise of person or deity, economics, and war. Expensive investments in praise include the Great Pyramids, the Taj Mahal, and opulent cathedrals. Expensive projects launched in the hope of economic return include Columbus's voyage to the New World and Magellan's round-the-world voyage. Expensive projects with military or national defense incentives include the Great Wall of China, which helped keep out the Mongols; the Manhattan Project, which designed and built the first atomic bomb; and the Apollo space program.

When it comes to extracting really big money from an electorate, pure science—in this case, exploration for its own sake—doesn't rate. Yet during the 1960s, a prevailing rationale for space travel was that space was the next frontier; we were going to the Moon because humans are innate explorers. In President Kennedy's address to a joint session of Congress on May 25, 1961, he waxed eloquent on the need to reach the next frontier. The speech included these oft-quoted lines:

> I believe that this nation should commit itself to achieving the goal, before the decade is out, of landing a man on the moon and returning him safely to the earth. No single space project in this period will be more impressive to mankind, or more important for the long-range exploration of space; and none will be so difficult or expensive to accomplish.

These words inspired the explorer in all of us and reverberated throughout the decade. But nearly all of the astronauts were being drawn from the military—a fact I could not reconcile with the rhetoric.

Only a month before Kennedy's Moon speech, Soviet cosmonaut Yuri Gagarin had become the first human to be launched into Earth orbit. In a rarely replayed portion of the same address, Kennedy adopts a military posture:

> If we are to win the battle that is now going on around the world between freedom and tyranny, the dramatic achievements in space which occurred in recent weeks should have made clear to us all, as did Sputnik in 1957, the impact of this adventure on the minds of men everywhere who are attempting to make a determination of which road they should take.

Had the political landscape been different, Americans (Congress in particular) would have been loath to part with the money (more than $200 billion in 1998 dollars) that accomplished the task. In spite of Kennedy's persuasive phrases, the debates that followed on the floor of Congress demonstrated that funding for Apollo was not a foregone conclusion.

A trip to the Moon through the vacuum of space had been in sight, even if technologically distant, ever since 1926, when Robert Goddard perfected liquid-fuel rockets. This advance in rocketry made flight possible without the lift provided by air moving over a wing. Goddard himself realized that a trip to the Moon was finally possible but that it might be prohibitively expensive. "It might cost a million dollars," he once mused.

Calculations that were possible the day after Isaac Newton introduced his law of universal gravitation show that an efficient trip to the Moon—in a craft escaping Earth's atmosphere at a speed of seven miles per second and coasting the rest of the way—takes about a day and a half. Such a trip has been taken only nine times—all between 1968 and 1972. Otherwise, when NASA sends astronauts into "space," a crew is launched into Earth orbit a few hundred miles above our 8,000-mile-diameter planet. Space travel, this isn't.

What if you had told John Glenn, after his historic three orbits and successful splashdown in 1962, that in thirty-seven years, NASA was going to send him into space once again? You can bet he would never have imagined that the best we could offer was to send him into Earth orbit again.

Space. Why can't we get there from here?

Let's start with money. If we can send somebody to Mars for less than $100 billion, then I say, let's go for it. But I have a friendly bet with Louis Friedman, the executive director of the Planetary Society (a membership-funded organization founded by the late Carl Sagan, and others, to promote the peaceful exploration of space), that we are not going to Mars any time soon. More specifically, I bet him that there will be no funded plan by any government before the year 2005 to send a manned mission to Mars. I hope I am wrong. But I will only be wrong if the cost of modern missions is brought down considerably, compared with those of the past. The following note on NASA's legendary spending habits was forwarded to me by a Russian colleague:

THE ASTRONAUT PEN
During the heat of the space race in the 1960s, the U.S. National Aeronautics and Space Administration [NASA] decided it needed a ballpoint pen to write in the zero gravity confines of its space capsules. After considerable research and development, the Astronaut Pen was developed at a cost of approximately $1 million U.S. The pen worked and also enjoyed some modest success as a novelty item back here on earth. The Soviet Union, faced with the same problem, used a pencil.

Unless there is a reprise of the geopolitical circumstances that dislodged $200 billion for space travel from taxpayers' wallets in the 1960s, I will remain unconvinced that we will ever send *Homo sapiens* anywhere beyond Earth's orbit. I quote a Princeton University colleague, J. Richard Gott, a panelist who spoke a few years ago at a Hayden Planetarium symposium that touched upon the health of the manned space program: "In 1969, [space flight pioneer] Wernher von Braun had a plan to send astronauts to Mars by 1982. It didn't happen. In 1989, President George Bush promised that we would send astronauts to Mars by the year 2019. This is not a good sign. It looks like Mars is getting farther away!"

To this I add that, as we approach the millennium, the only correct prediction from the 1968 sci-fi classic *2001: A Space Odyssey* is that things can go wrong.

Space is vast and empty beyond all earthly measure. When Hollywood movies show a starship cruising through the galaxy, they typically show points of light (stars) drifting past like fireflies at a rate of one or two per second. But the distances between stars in the galaxy are so great that for these spaceships to move as indicated would require traveling at speeds up to 500 million times faster than the speed of light.

The Moon is far away compared with where you might go in a jet airplane, but it sits at the tip of your nose compared with anything else in the universe. If Earth were the size of a basketball, the Moon would be the size of a softball some ten paces away—the farthest we have ever sent people into space. On this scale, Mars (at its closest) is a mile away. Pluto is 100 miles away. And Proxima Centauri, the star nearest to the Sun, is a half million miles away.

Let's assume money is no object. In this pretend-future, our noble quest to discover new places and uncover scientific truths has become as effective as war for drumming up funds. If a spaceship sustained the speed needed to escape Earth—seven miles per second—a trip to the nearest star would last a long and boring 100,000 years. Too long, you say? Energy increases as the square of your speed, so if you want to double your speed, you must invest four times as much energy. A tripling of your speed requires nine times as much energy. No problem. Let's just assemble some clever engineers who will build us a spaceship that can magically summon as much energy as we want.

How about a spaceship that travels as fast as *Helios B,* the U.S.-German solar probe that was the fastest-ever unmanned space probe? Launched in 1976, it was clocked at nearly 42 miles per second (150,000 miles per hour) as it accelerated toward the Sun. (Note that this is only one-fiftieth of one percent of the speed of light.) This craft would cut the travel time to the nearest star down to a mere 15,000 years—three times the length of recorded human history.

What we really want is a spaceship that can travel near the speed of light. How about 99 percent the speed of light? All you would need is 700 million times the energy that thrust the Apollo astronauts on their way to the Moon. Actually, that's what you would need if the universe were not described by Einstein's special theory of relativity. But as Einstein correctly predicted, while your speed increases, so too does your mass, forcing you to spend even more energy to accelerate your spaceship to near the speed of light. A back-of-the-envelope calculation shows that you would need at least 10 billion times the energy used for our Moon voyages.

No problem. These are very clever engineers we've hired. But now we learn that the closest star known to have planets is not Proxima Centauri but one that is about fifteen light-years away. Einstein's theory of special relativity shows that, while traveling at 99 percent of the speed of light, you will age at only 14 percent the pace of everybody back on Earth, so the round-trip for you will last not thirty years but about four. On Earth, however, thirty years actually do pass by, and everybody has forgotten about you.

The distance to the Moon is 10 million times greater than the distance flown by the original *Wright Flyer,* built by the Wright brothers. But the Wright brothers were two guys with a bicycle repair shop. *Apollo 11,* the first moon landing, was two guys with $200 billion and ten thousand scientists and engineers and the mandate of a beloved, assassinated president. These are not comparable achievements. The cost and effort of space travel are a consequence of space's being supremely hostile to life.

You might think that the early explorers had it bad, too. Consider Gonzalo Pizarro's 1540 expedition from Quito across Peru in search of the fabled land of oriental spices. Oppressive terrain and hostile natives ultimately led to the death of half Pizarro's expedition party of more than 4,000. In the classic account of this ill-fated adventure, *History of the Conquest of Peru,* William H. Prescott describes the state of the expedition party a year into the journey:

> At every step of their way, they were obliged to hew open a passage with their axes, while their garments, rotting from the effects of the drenching rains to which they had been exposed, caught in every bush and bramble, and hung about them in shreds. Their provisions spoiled by the weather, had long since failed, and the livestock which they had taken with them had either been consumed or made their escape in the woods and mountain passes. They had set out with nearly a thousand dogs, many of them of the ferocious breed used in hunting down the unfortunate natives. These they now gladly killed, but their miserable carcasses furnished a lean banquet for the famished travelers.

On the brink of abandoning all hope, Pizarro and his men built from scratch a boat large enough to take half the remaining men along the Napo River in search of food and supplies:

> The forests furnished him with timber; the shoes of the horses which had died on the road or had been slaughtered for food, were converted into nails; gum distilled from the trees took the place of pitch; and the tattered garments of the soldiers supplied a substitute for oakum.... At the end of two months, a brigantine was completed, rudely put together, but strong and of sufficient burden to carry half the company.

Pizarro transferred command of the makeshift boat to Francisco de Orellana, a cavalier from Trujillo, and stayed behind to wait. After many weeks, Pizarro gave up on Orellana and returned to the town of Quito, taking yet another year to get there. Pizarro later learned that Orellana had successfully navigated his boat down the Napo River to the Amazon and, with no intention of returning, had continued along the Amazon until he emerged in the Atlantic. Orellana and his men then sailed to Cuba, where they subsequently found safe transport back to Spain.

Does this story have any lessons for would-be star travelers? Suppose one of our spacecraft with a shipload of astronauts crash-lands on a distant, hostile planet—the astronauts survive, but the spacecraft is totaled. The crew adopts the spirit of our sixteenth-century explorers. Problem is, hostile planets tend to be considerably more dangerous than hostile natives. The planet might not have air. And what air it does have may be poisonous. And if the air is not poisonous, the atmospheric pressure may be 100 times higher than on Earth. If the pressure is okay, then the air temperature may be 200° below zero. Or 500° above zero. None of these possibilities bode well for our astronaut explorers, but perhaps they can survive for a while on their reserve life-support system. Meanwhile, all they would need to do is mine the planet for raw materials; build another spacecraft from scratch, along with its controlling computers (using whatever spare parts are musterable from the crash site); build a rocket fuel factory; launch themselves back into space; and then fly back home.

I needn't dwell on the absurdity of this scenario.

Perhaps what we really need to do is to engineer life-forms that can survive the stress of space and still conduct scientific experiments. Actually, such "life" forms have already been created. They are called robots. You don't have to feed them. They don't need life support. And most importantly, they won't be upset if you don't bring them back to Earth. People, however, generally want to breathe, eat, and eventually come home.

It's probably true that no city has yet held a ticker-tape parade for a robot. But it's probably also true that no city has ever held a ticker-tape parade for an astronaut who was not the first (or the last) to do something or go somewhere. Can you name the two *Apollo 16* astronauts who walked on the Moon? Probably not. It was the second-to-last moon mission. But I'll bet you have a favorite picture of the cosmos taken by the orbiting robot known as the *Hubble Space Telescope*. I'll bet you remember the images from the Mars robotic lander, *Pathfinder*, and its deployed rover, *Sojourner*, which went "six-wheeling" across the Martian terrain. I'll further bet that you remember the *Voyager*'s images of the Jovian planets and their zoo of moons from the early 1980s.

In the absence of a few hundred billion dollars in travel money, and in the presence of hostile cosmic conditions, what we need is not wishful thinking and science fiction rhetoric inspired by a cursory reading of the history of exploration. What we need, but may never have, is a breakthrough in our scientific understanding of the structure of the universe, so that we might exploit shortcuts through the space-time continuum—perhaps through wormholes that connect one part of the cosmos to another. Then, once again, reality will become stranger than fiction.

POSTSCRIPT

Can Humans Go to Mars Now?

In 1996, a team of researchers, led by Everett Gibson of NASA's Johnson Space Center, reported that in the interior crevices of meteorite ALH 84001—blasted from the surface of Mars some 14–18 million years ago, crashed on the ice of Antarctica 13,000 years ago, and found in Antarctica's Allan Hills in the mid-1980s—are structures that look much like fossils from the dawn of life here on Earth.

Current thinking is that the Martian "fossils" are simply mineral formations. But the possibility that there might be—or might have been—life on Mars has been enough to increase the level of interest in sending scientists to Mars to see for themselves. And perhaps it would be possible to do so without bankrupting the nation, as Robert Zubrin and Richard Wagner suggest in *The Case for Mars: The Plan to Settle the Red Planet and Why We Must* (The Free Press, 1996). Another recent book on Mars is Jay Barbree and Martin Caidin with Susan Wright, *Destination Mars: In Art, Myth, and Science* (Penguin Studio, 1997).

Interest in Mars expeditions is hardly new. During the Bush administration, the Synthesis Group of the White House Science Office, given the task of finding the best way to go to Mars, concluded that the benefits of such a mission would include, besides simply getting to Mars, job creation, investment in science and technology, and stimulated innovation.

The Synthesis Group's report included a call for the development of a new "Heavy Lift Launch Vehicle" (HLLV) to reduce the cost and difficulty of getting materials into orbit. Such a cargo vehicle has been discussed for years as a supplement to the Space Shuttle, with a great deal of emphasis on its value for constructing space stations as well as interplanetary spaceships. The dream continues—see Stanley Schmidt and Robert Zubrin, eds., *Islands in the Sky: Bold New Ideas for Colonizing Space* (Wiley, 1996)—but an HLLV has never been approved, and it seems very unlikely that NASA will be able to find funds for any major new launch system that would make a Mars mission possible.

Do we need to send people to Mars? Won't robots do? These questions are timely, for 1997 was the year when humans finally returned—two decades after the robotic Vikings—to Mars with the Pathfinder lander and its accompanying Sojourner rover. The prospects for a renewal of manned space exploration, much less a trip to Mars, seem dim. Much more likely may be combining robot explorers with a "virtual reality" feature that would let Earth-bound humans "ride along"; see John Merchant, "A New Direction in Space," *IEEE Technology and Society Magazine* (Winter 1994).

ISSUE 10

Is It Worthwhile to Continue the Search for Extraterrestrial Life?

YES: Frank Drake and Dava Sobel, from *Is Anyone Out There? The Scientific Search for Extraterrestrial Intelligence* (Delacorte Press, 1992)

NO: A. K. Dewdney, from *Yes, We Have No Neutrons: An Eye-Opening Tour Through the Twists and Turns of Bad Science* (John Wiley, 1996)

ISSUE SUMMARY

YES: Professor of astronomy Frank Drake and science writer Dava Sobel argue that the search for radio signals from extraterrestrial civilizations has only just begun and that scientists must continue to search because contact will eventually occur.

NO: Computer scientist A. K. Dewdney maintains that although there may indeed be intelligent beings elsewhere in the universe, there are so many reasons why contact and communication are unlikely that searching for them is not worth the time or the money.

In the 1960s and early 1970s the business of listening to the radio whispers of the stars and hoping to pick up signals emanating from some alien civilization was still new. Few scientists held visions equal to Frank Drake, one of the pioneers of the search for extraterrestrial intelligence (SETI) field. Drake and scientists like him utilize radio telescopes—large, dish-like radio receiver-antenna combinations—to scan radio frequencies (channels) for signal patterns that would indicate that the signal was transmitted by an intelligent being. In his early days, Drake worked with relatively small and weak telescopes out of listening posts that he had established in Green Bank, West Virginia, and Arecibo, Puerto Rico. See Carl Sagan and Frank Drake, "The Search for Extraterrestrial Intelligence," *Scientific American* (May 1975).

There have been more than 50 searches for extraterrestrial radio signals since 1960. The earliest ones were very limited. Later searches have been more ambitious, culminating in the 10-year program known as the High Resolution

Microwave Survey (HRMS). The HRMS, which began on Columbus Day of 1992, uses several radio telescopes and massive computers to scan 15 million radio frequencies per second. This has been the most massive SETI to date and the one with the greatest hope of success.

At the outset, many people thought—and many still think—that SETI has about as much scientific relevance as searches for Loch Ness Monsters and Abominable Snowmen. However, to Drake and his colleagues, it seems inevitable that with so many stars in the sky, there must be other worlds with life upon them, and some of that life must be intelligent and have a suitable technology and the desire to search for alien life too.

Writing about SETI in the September–October 1991 issue of *The Humanist,* physicist Shawn Carlson compares visiting the National Shrine of the Immaculate Conception in Washington, D.C., to looking up at the stars and "wondering if, in all [the] vastness [of the starry sky], there is anybody out there looking in our direction.... [A]re there planets like ours peopled with creatures like us staring into their skies and wondering about the possibilities of life on other worlds, perhaps even trying to contact it?" That is, SETI arouses in its devotees an almost religious sense of mystery and awe, a craving for contact with the *other.* Success would open up a universe of possibilities, add immensely to human knowledge, and perhaps even provide solutions to problems that our interstellar neighbors have already defeated.

SETI also arouses strong objections, partly because it challenges human uniqueness. Many scientists have objected that life-bearing worlds such as Earth must be exceedingly rare because the conditions that make them suitable for life as we know it—composition and temperature—are so narrowly defined. Others have objected that there is no reason whatsoever to expect that evolution would produce intelligence more than once or that, if it did, the species would be similar enough to humans to allow communication. Still others say that even if intelligent life is common, technology may not be so common. Richard C. Teske, for example, in "Is This the E.T. to Whom I Am Speaking?" *Discover* (May 1993), argues that the geological processes that have supplied humans with the raw materials of technology—metals—are too unlikely to have been repeated elsewhere. A similar criticism is that technology may occupy such a brief period in the life of an intelligent species that there is virtually no chance that it would coincide with Earth scientists' current search. Whatever their reasons, SETI detractors agree that listening for extraterrestrial signals is futile.

In the selections that follow, Drake and Dava Sobel discuss Drake's first search for messages from distant stars (Project Ozma). Today's technology, the authors note, has made it possible to duplicate all of Ozma's work in a fraction of a second, making it that much more probable that Earth will soon make contact with extraterrestrials. A. K. Dewdney discusses several reasons why listening for extraterrestrial signals is a waste of time and money.

Frank Drake and Dava Sobel  **YES**

No Greater Discovery

$\mathbf{M}$y scientific colleagues raise their eyebrows when I speculate on the appearance of extraterrestrials. But about 99.9 percent of them agree wholeheartedly that other intelligent life-forms do exist—and furthermore that there may be large populations of them throughout our galaxy and beyond.

Personally, I find nothing more tantalizing than the thought that radio messages from alien civilizations in space are passing through our offices and homes, right now, like a whisper we can't quite hear. In fact, we have the technology to detect such signals *today,* if only we knew where to point our radio telescopes, and the right frequency for listening.

I have been scanning the stars in search of extraterrestrial intelligence (an activity now abbreviated as SETI, and pronounced *SET-ee*) for more than thirty years. I engineered the first such effort in 1959, at the National Radio Astronomy Observatory in Green Bank, West Virginia. I named it "Project Ozma," after a land far away, difficult to reach, and populated by strange and exotic beings. I used what would now be considered crude equipment to listen for signals from two nearby, Sunlike stars. It took two months to complete the job. With the marvelous technological advances we have made in the intervening years, we could repeat the whole of Project Ozma today in a fraction of a second. We could scan for signals from a *million* stars or more at a time, at distances of at least a *thousand* light-years from Earth....

Until the late 1980s, the fact that we had not yet found another civilization, despite continued global efforts and better equipment, simply meant we had not looked long enough or hard enough. No knowledgeable person was disappointed by our inability to detect alien intelligence, as this in no way proved that extraterrestrials did not exist. Rather, our failure simply confirmed that our efforts were puny in relation to the enormity of the task—somewhat like hunting for a needle in a cosmic haystack of inconceivable size. The way we were going about it, with our small-scale attempts, was like looking for the needle by strolling past the haystack every now and then. We weren't embarked on a search that had any real chance of success.

Then many people began to grasp the nature and scope of the challenge, the consequent investment required to succeed, and the importance of success

---

to all humanity. They pushed relentlessly for a serious search. And won. The National Aeronautics and Space Administration (NASA) committed $100 million to a formal SETI mission spanning the decade of the 1990s, making the work a priority for the space agency and guaranteeing that coveted telescope time will be devoted to the search.

Now, after all our efforts over the past three decades, I am standing with my colleagues at last on the brink of discovery.... I see a pressing need to prepare thinking adults for the outcome of the present search activity—the imminent detection of signals from an extraterrestrial civilization. This discovery, which I fully expect to witness before the year 2000, will profoundly change the world....

I want to show that we need not be afraid of interstellar contact, for unlike the primitive civilizations on Earth that were overpowered by more advanced technological societies, we cannot be exploited or enslaved. The extraterrestrials aren't going to come and eat us; they are too far away to pose a threat. Even back-and-forth conversation with them is highly unlikely, since radio signals, traveling at the speed of light, take *years* to reach the nearest stars, and many *millennia* to get to the farthest ones, where advanced civilizations may reside. But one-way communication is a different story. Just as our radio and television transmissions leak out into space, carrying the news of our existence far and wide, so similar information from the planets of other stars has no doubt been quietly arriving at Earth for perhaps billions of years. Even more exciting is the likelihood of *intentional* messages beamed to Earth for our particular benefit. As we know from our own efforts at composing for a pangalactic audience, reams of information about a planet's culture, history, and technology—the entire thirty-seven-volume set, if you will, of the "Encyclopedia Galactica"—could be transmitted (and received) easily and cheaply.

As a scientist, I'm driven by curiosity, of course. I want to know what's out there. But as a human being, I persevere in this pursuit because SETI promises answers to our most profound questions about who we are and where we stand in the universe. SETI is at once the most technical of scientific subjects, and also the most human. Every tactical problem in the search endeavor rests on some age-old philosophical conundrum: *Where did we come from? Are we unique? What does it mean to be a human being?...*

[W]e have only just begun to search.

So many individuals I meet seem to think that we have already searched the sky completely and continuously over the past thirty years. The deed is done, they assume. And since we found nothing out there, to search further is to beat a dead horse. But in fact, the combinations of frequencies and places to look have hardly been touched.

In my historical analysis; the search for extraterrestrial intelligence divides itself into four eras. The first dates back at least three thousand years, to the time when people started contemplating the universe....

I trace the start of the second era to the coming of the Copernican Revolution in the sixteenth century. That was when astronomers such as Kepler and Galileo, who used a real telescope, recognized that some of the other objects in the Solar System were planets similar to the Earth. Scientific observations could now support the philosophical argument in favor of other life in the cosmos—and perhaps even within the Solar System....

The third era began in 1959–60, when scientists first employed quantitative measures to compute the strength of possible signs of life crossing interstellar space. In other words, we made precise calculations of the detectability of alien signals, and acted on them. Projects—beginning with [Cornell physics professors Philip] Morrison and [Giuseppe] Cocconi's proposal to search for radio waves and my strategy for Project Ozma—sprang from a greater knowledge of the universe and a real sense of the numbers involved. For the first time, SETI embodied philosophical, qualitative, *and* quantitative elements. Scientists conducted some sixty "third era" extraterrestrial searches in the 1960s, 1970s, and 1980s. Most of these, however, were low-budget productions, done with leftover funds in borrowed time on equipment built for other purposes.

The fourth era, which starts now, is not only quantitative, it is also, finally, *thorough.* The projects of the 1990s represent the most exhaustive probing to date of the cosmic haystack. Here I am referring especially to the NASA SETI project....

My involvement in SETI activities has actually increased over the years, because SETI itself has grown so much. It occupies more people than ever before, and demands more of their time. Jill Tarter, for example, is the first astronomer to work full-time as a SETI scientist. When she isn't fully engaged in her role as project scientist, the senior scientific position in the NASA SETI project, she is in Washington, explaining the project to congressional representatives. Paul Horowitz runs a close second in activity. Despite his teaching duties at Harvard, Paul has had one search or another in progress since 1977. In some years he devotes nearly 100 percent of his time to these efforts—masterminding a new project and then personally soldering the thousands of joints that hold the equipment together....

I finally got my turn to meet Paul in 1977, when he was already a full professor of physics at Harvard....

A short time later,... Paul accepted a 1981–82 NASA Ames fellowship, which enabled him to work on SETI at the Ames Research Center and at Stanford University. He joined the Ames-Stanford group trying to create a SETI machine that could analyze a huge number of separate channels—128,000 of them, more than anyone had ever been able to monitor simultaneously....

The sheer number of channels in this multichannel analyzer was a big advance in itself, but Paul also made the components portable, so they could be packed up in three small boxes and hand-carried to any observatory, anywhere in the world. The system, which he dubbed "Suitcase SETI," traveled first to Arecibo [Ionospheric Observatory in northern Puerto Rico, home of the largest radio telescope ever built]. After examining 250 stars with it, Paul took it back to Harvard in 1983. He hooked it up to the same telescope I had partially built and calibrated in my student days—the one I had used to observe the Pleiades for my doctoral thesis. Suitcase SETI's rambling days were over at that point. Portable though it was, it never ventured out of Harvard's Oak Ridge Observatory again. A new name, Project Sentinel, recognized the fact that Paul's multichannel analyzer was now connected to a dedicated telescope, with funding from The Planetary Society to run a permanent SETI facility.

In time, Sentinel begat "META-SETI"—the Megachannel ExtraTerrestrial Assay—which boosted the number of channels from 128,000 to more than 8 million. . . . Paul needed the extra channels, he said, to respond to a new concept put forward by Phil Morrison, who had reminded him in a letter that everything in the universe is in motion. . . .

Intelligent radio signals from distant civilizations could [therefore] be expected to arrive shifted in frequency, just as the starlight from distant suns is shifted toward the red or the blue end of the optical spectrum by stellar motions. There was no way to predict which way a signal's frequency would shift without knowing how its home star was moving. Thus a message transmitted on the hydrogen frequency could wind up far above or far below that frequency by the time it reached a radio telescope on Earth.

With META, Paul could scrutinize myriad frequencies in the vicinity of the hydrogen line and sift through them, narrow bandwidth by narrow bandwidth, on millions of channels at once to detect the displaced signals.

In 1991 Paul set up a second META, also financed by The Planetary Society, called META II, in the Southern Hemisphere, at the Instituto Argentino de Radioastronomia in Villa Elisa, Argentina. This allowed Argentinian astronomers led by Raul Colombo to observe the portion of the southern sky that's not visible from Cambridge. META II opened up very important new regions of the Milky Way as well as a clear line of sight to the two galaxies that are the Milky Way's nearest neighbors: the Magellanic Clouds. Now, with META and META II thriving, Paul is already dreaming of BETA. This would be a new system ("It'll be *betta* than META," he promises), with one hundred million channels.

Paul has obviously done more searching, with more sensitivity, than anybody who preceded him, so it shouldn't be too surprising to learn that he's actually heard things through his systems. Indeed, Paul has records of about sixty signals that are all excellent candidates for being the real thing. But Paul's searches run themselves, automatically. By the time he recognizes the candidates in the recorded data, hours or days later, it's too late to check them. Looking for them later proves fruitless, as they are no longer where they were. No doubt the civilizations are still there—if that's what made the signal—but they've stopped talking, at least for the moment. . . . If only Paul's strategy included a human operator who could double-check the signals on the spot! However, Paul has severe budget constraints, and I know that he can't afford to pay someone to sit there through the long nights and wait.

The new NASA SETI Microwave Observing Project will change all that, because I'll be sitting there myself. Or Jill will, or some other radio astronomer who will be able to react immediately to chase down a candidate signal the moment it appears. This project, which has been in various stages of planning and development since 1978, is just now beginning its methodical hunt. Because of its great power and sensitivity, it outstrips all previous search activities combined. Three days' operation can accomplish more than was done in the preceding three decades. Indeed, it gives me a strange chill to acknowledge that it takes this new setup only one one-hundredth of a second to duplicate what Project Ozma did in its full two hundred hours. . . .

What does NASA SETI have that no other search had? The short answer is "everything." It has everything that early searches had, and everything we could think of that had never been done before.

Like Ozma, NASA SETI scrutinizes a group of relatively close, Sun-like stars for signs of intelligent life. But where Ozma had only two targets, NASA SETI has one thousand. This much more extensive "targeted search," however, is still only half the mission. The other half is an "all-sky survey" that repeatedly scans the whole grand volume of outer space for alien signals from any star, anywhere. Our dual search strategy deals with two alternate possibilities for our cosmic neighbors: Either the easiest aliens to detect are right nearby (targeted search), or they are very far away but very bright (all-sky survey and targeted search).

Like the Ohio State project, NASA SETI is an ongoing endeavor that will run for years. But unlike the low-cost efforts that preceded it, this project fought for and won a total of more than $100 million in federal funding. While other searches started up and faded out without so much as a nod from NASA, this one enjoys the same position as a mission to send a small spacecraft to another planet. Mission status means that SETI is supported all through NASA management, right up to the topmost level.

Like META and META II, NASA SETI spans the globe and the heavens. It utilizes at least five telescopes—at Arecibo, Green Bank, the Observatoire de Nançy in France, the Goldstone Tracking Station in California, and an identical NASA tracking station at Tidbinbilla, Australia. It is the first truly global cooperative effort to search for interstellar signals.

Unlike . . . Suitcase SETI, NASA SETI is no backseat or part-time visitor. It constitutes the largest single program running at Arecibo and will soon dominate a fully dedicated telescope at Green Bank. It employs more than one hundred people, including a rotating team of radio astronomers who stand ready to respond to candidate signals in real time.

Most American searches until now have sought narrow-band signals on magic frequencies, such as the hydrogen line. We call them "magic" because they seem to have some real rationale for being logical channels of communication. Part of their magic is that they occupy quiet regions of the electromagnetic spectrum. What's more, the hydrogen line, considered the most magical frequency of all, is such a fertile field for making general discoveries in radio astronomy that scientists of all civilizations probably keep close tabs on it. Thus, a signal on that particular frequency should have the greatest chance of being detected. The hydrogen line is the frequency Morrison and Cocconi suggested in their original paper, and the actual frequency searched in Project Ozma. . . .

Magic frequencies have special appeal, but even human beings disagree as to which ones are best. . . . The point is, any search based on a magic frequency assumes first of all that extraterrestrials are broadcasting on a chosen frequency, and furthermore that we can know what that frequency is.

The NASA SETI project makes no such assumptions. It scans most of the frequencies in the waterhole that penetrate the Earth's atmosphere. This means we'll have a much greater chance than ever before to detect a message, whether the aliens choose a frequency for convenience' sake or some numerology of their own. Our new equipment frees us from the need to select just one or two frequencies from among the vast field of possibilities. . . .

META set a world's record with 8 million channels, but NASA SETI has 28 million. At the core of its hardware is a device called a multichannel spectrum analyzer (MCSA in NASA's beloved alphabet soup), which divides the incoming radio noise into 14 million narrow-band channels. The MCSA also combines the signals from several adjacent channels to create another 14 million broader bandwidths, just in case the extraterrestrials use them.

The MCSA relies on ultra-advanced software to make sense out of the millions of data points pouring in every second. Software analyzes the data, looking for patterns that reveal intelligence—and that could not possibly be intercepted as fast or as well by human intelligence. The human operator, whose presence is so important to me, steps in *after* computers sound the alarm that a candidate signal has just been detected. . . .

In the course of gushing about the great power of NASA SETI compared to any and all of its predecessors, I've dropped several huge numbers, referring to everything from frequencies and sensitivities to dollars and cents. That said, do I really need one more quantitative comparison to make my point? Would it really clarify things further to say that NASA SETI is a ten-millionfold improvement over past efforts? Maybe not. Maybe the more important thing to say now is that the magnitude of our current efforts creates so much promise that we find ourselves contemplating what we should do when we actually receive signal evidence of extraterrestrial life. When and how do we inform the people of Earth?

John Billingham [a former aerospace physician with England's Royal Air Force] has probably given more thought to this delicious dilemma than anyone else. Working with other members of the SETI committee of the International Academy of Astronautics (IAA), he has drawn up a "Declaration of Principles Concerning Activities Following the Detection of Extraterrestrial Intelligence." It lists all the steps to be taken to verify the authenticity of a signal and inform the proper authorities that extraterrestrial word has been heard.

This document has been approved or endorsed by every major, international, professional space society, including the IAA, the International Institute of Space Law, the Committee on Space Research, Commission 51 of the International Astronomical Union, and Commission J of the Union Radio Scientifique Internationale. In essence, Billingham's protocol says, *Make sure you've got something; then tell EVERYBODY.*

I've spoken at some length about how one goes about checking a candidate signal for authenticity—how to establish extraterrestrial origin, and how the special hallmarks of artificiality can distinguish a signal as being of intelligent design. But to announce to the world at large that you've made the greatest discovery in the history of astronomy—perhaps in history, period—takes an even wider margin of certainty.

On the NASA SETI project, you probably can't ask another observatory to help you verify your findings. If the long-awaited signal is intercepted at Arecibo, and it is weak, which is the most likely possibility, then no other observatory in the world could make the desired verification. This is because Arecibo has the greatest collecting area of any telescope, as well as the Gregorian feed and other specialized equipment. Even the other participants in NASA SETI, in France and Australia, will not match Arecibo's wide range of frequency coverage. And if the signal did fall within their frequency range, they might lack the sensitivity to hear it. Arecibo is so much more sensitive than the others—ever so much more capable of picking a faint, fragile *"We are here!"* out of a welter of cosmic noise.

In lieu of interobservatory checks and balances, the people at Arecibo (I hope I'm one of them when this happens) will have to spend several days checking and rechecking their data, locating the signal, if possible, a second, third, and fourth time rather than risk setting off a false alarm. After several days, however, repeated observations would build up a chink-free wall of evidence that would justify going public....

Hard upon detection of an intelligent signal, there follows the delicate matter of a reply to the civilization that sent it. I've thought a lot, of course, about what to say in that happy situation. I have waited a lifetime for the opportunity, and the waiting has not diminished my confidence or my enthusiasm. I can't be specific about it, though, because when you really think about it, the only answer to the question "What do you say?" is "It depends."

It depends on the nature of the signal and what it's telling us. It depends on the world's reaction. It depends on the distance the message traveled, because we couldn't establish true dialogue with civilizations far removed from us—only lengthy monologues, crossing each other eternally in the interstellar mail. It depends on whether we can understand it. Certainly no stock reply, prepared in advance and stashed in someone's file cabinet, could match more than one of the infinite possibilities for the message's content. Certainly any reply should be crafted on a worldwide basis, and only after lengthy deliberation by knowledgeable individuals.

I have a recurring dream in which we receive our much-anticipated intelligent signal from across the Galaxy. The signal is unambiguous. It repeats over and over, allowing us to get a fix on its source, some twenty thousand light-years away. The signal is . . . apparently dense with information content. It is so full of noise, however, that we can't extract any information from it. And so we know only that another civilization exists. We cannot decipher the message itself.

If this dream becomes real, such documented detection of alien signals will, of course, be big news in itself. It will be a call to action, too, beckoning us to do whatever is required—build a much larger radio-telescope system, for example—to obtain information about that civilization, to learn whatever secrets the extraterrestrials will share with us.

Indeed, our response to a message from an alien civilization may thus be a response to the *situation* instead of an actual reply to the senders. We will tell the world at large what has happened, and that we're taking the next step by building better equipment to understand the message we've received. How I would love to have to go to Congress with a budget request for that project. I don't imagine I'd encounter much opposition. . . .

I do not wonder *whether* this will happen. My only question is *When?*

The silence we have heard so far is not in any way significant. We still have not looked long enough or hard enough. We've not explored a large enough chunk of the cosmic haystack. I could speculate that "they" are watching us to see if we are worth talking to. Or perhaps the ethic exists among them that rules, "There is no free lunch in the Galaxy." If we want to join the community of advanced civilizations, we must work as hard as they must. Perhaps they will send a signal that can be detected only if we put as much effort into receiving it as they put into transmitting it. NASA SETI is the beginning of the first truly meaningful effort to demonstrate the sincerity of our intentions.

Thus, the lesson we have learned from all our previous searching is that the greatest discovery is not a simple one to make. If there were once cockeyed optimists in the SETI endeavor, there aren't any now. In a way, I am glad. The priceless benefits of knowledge and experience that will accrue from interstellar contact should not come too easily. To appreciate them, we should expect to devote a substantial portion of our resources, our assets, our intellectual vigor, and our patience. We should be willing to sweat and crawl and wait.

The goal is not beyond us. It is within our grasp.

A. K. Dewdney

 **NO**

Surfing the Cosmos: The Search for Extraterrestrial Intelligence

It was noon, April 8, 1960. The recently completed 85-foot radio telescope dish at Green Bank, West Virginia, had just lost the star Tau Ceti below the horizon. Steering motors hummed and the great dish swung grandly to the south along the horizon until, like a great ear, it listened to another star, Epsilon Eridani. Up in the control room, radio astronomer Frank Drake and his colleagues listened eagerly to sounds coming from a loudspeaker. The sounds enabled the astronomers to hear the signals being intercepted by the dish.

Gathered in the 85-foot parabolic surface, electromagnetic waves, some of them from Epsilon Eridani and some from much further away, reflected to the focus of the dish where a large cylindrical housing sheltered a precisely tuned amplifier. The signals from the amplifier were fed to a chart recorder in the control room and, of course, to the speaker. It was a propitious day, the dawn of Drake's dream of intercepting messages from an alien civilization.

Called Project Ozma, the dream reflected Drake's conviction that somewhere out there, alien intelligences were transmitting helpful messages to less developed civilizations or, failing that, were at least inadvertently broadcasting their radio and television programs. Given the air of anticipation that surrounded the inaugural evening of Project Ozma, Drake and his colleagues can perhaps be forgiven for what happened next:

> [S]carcely five minutes had passed before the whole system erupted. WHAM! A burst of noise shot out of the loudspeaker, the chart recorder started banging off the scale, and we were all jumping at once, wild with excitement. Now we had a signal—a strong, unique pulsed signal. Precisely what you'd expect from an extraterrestrial intelligence trying to attract attention.

To check that the source of the signal really was Epsilon Eridani, Drake had the telescope taken off the target. The sound disappeared, meaning that this star (or a planet near it) may actually have been the source. Unfortunately, when they returned the telescope to track the star, the noise had disappeared.

An even more significant incident followed on the heels of the first one: One of the telescope operators told a friend about the signal and the friend contacted a newspaper. Before Drake knew it, he was deluged by calls from the media demanding to know what had happened.

"Have you really detected an alien civilization?"

"We're not sure. There's no way to know."

This answer could not have been better calculated to raise curiosity about the incident still further, guaranteeing a great deal of publicity for Project Ozma. A better answer would have been, "As far as we know, the anomalous signal originated right here on Earth." Both responses are true, of course, but the second would have a more chilling effect on the media. Drake, after all, was no stranger to anomalous signals.

At the tender age of twenty-six, he had been observing the Pleiades star group when a new signal suddenly appeared on his chart recorder. Drake recalls:

> It was a strikingly regular signal—too regular, in fact, to be of natural origin. I had never seen it before, though I had repeated the spectrum measurement countless times. Now, all of a sudden, the spectrum had sprouted this strong added signal that looked unusual and surely of intelligent design....
> I still can't adequately describe my emotions at that moment. I could barely breathe from excitement, and soon after my hair started to turn white.

Drake never succeeded in recapturing the signal and today suspects that it may have been a military aircraft.

Since the exciting early days of extraterrestrial probing, Project Ozma has been succeeded by SETI, the search for extraterrestrial intelligence. Sponsored by NASA, the National Aeronautics and Space Administration, the SETI project, along with similar schemes, has absorbed over a billion dollars in congressional appropriations. Is the money well spent? The project has had and continues to have many critics, but few have gone to the heart of the matter.

As I will show in a later section, the problem with SETI lies at the very beginning of the scientific method—the hypothesis. Not only is it unavoidably geocentric, it is essentially nonfalsifiable. There is a troublesome formula, moreover, that is supposed to make the hypothesis seem more reasonable. As I will also show, the formula is a two-edged sword that actually argues against the hypothesis.

At this writing, none of the SETI projects have revealed so much as a whisper of alien intelligence. This has not stopped Drake from going out on a limb. He seems eager to "prepare thinking adults for the outcome of the present search activity—the imminent detection of signals from an extraterrestrial civilization. This discovery, which I fully expect to witness before the year 2000, will profoundly change the world."

When confronted with the failure of SETI programs up to this point, Drake wisely opines, "Absence of evidence is not evidence of absence."

Scanning the Skies

Radio telescopes supplement ordinary optical telescopes by giving us a picture of the cosmos by the light of radio waves. I say "light" because radio waves are just another part of the great electromagnetic [EM] spectrum, which also includes light waves. . . .

Many of the stars that appear as sharp points in the light telescope map also show up as blobs in the radio telescope map. This means that such stars not only emit light, they emit radio waves. By the same token, some of the radio sources that show up in the radio maps have no visual counterparts, or if they do, turn out to be clouds of gas, regions of violent galactic activity. Radio telescopy has been an invaluable tool in learning more about the structure of our own galaxy and that of other galaxies, not to mention a string of amazing discoveries such as pulsars and quasi-stellar objects, or quasars.

Nevertheless, the relatively long length of radio waves makes it very difficult to get much resolution out of a single telescope. Indeed, the signal from a radio telescope is essentially one-dimensional, like a sound track. The signal from an optical telescope is, of course, two-dimensional—a picture. These days, radio astronomers squeeze more resolution from their instruments by using several receivers at widely separated locations, as if to construct an effective dish that has the same dimensions relative to radio waves that optical mirrors do in relation to light waves.

Consider a typical dish as it tracks a distant star. Radio waves pour onto the dish from all directions. Some of the radiation comes from the Earth itself, stray radio or television broadcasts, ham radio operators, taxi dispatchers, truckers on CB radios, cellular phone callers, direct-to-home-satellite broadcasts, and so on. These signals, the only evidence we have of intelligent life so far, all come from the planet Earth. They sometimes bedevil the life of normal radio astronomers.

Electromagnetic waves of more natural origin arrive from the ionosphere, where energetic particles from the Sun collide with molecules of air at the very top of the Earth's atmosphere. Electromagnetic waves also come from radio sources in our own solar system, such as Jupiter and the Sun. From beyond the solar system, faint waves arrive from other stars in our own galaxy, from pulsars, and from stellar clouds. Other ripples, ancient and feeble, arrive at the great dish from other galaxies, not to mention those primordial sources, the unimaginably remote quasars.

Life is nevertheless relatively easy for the normal radio astronomer who has techniques for eliminating many kinds of interference from earthly sources. He or she may listen largely undisturbed for the random hiss of ancient stars and galaxies or the repetitive clicking of a pulsar. But the radio astronomer who searches for intelligent life must stand this rationale on its head, listening for the whispers of intelligent transmission amid a welter of natural electromagnetic hisses, clicks, chirps, and buzzes. The SETI astronomer is even more bedeviled by earthly signals. They tend to sound just like the thing he or she is searching for.

Is it just possible that somewhere, among all the radiation flooding the dish from a myriad of sources, one or two indescribably faint signals amount to whispers from distant and ancient civilizations? Perhaps the signals patiently repeat the recipes for astounding scientific and technical breakthroughs, as some SETI enthusiasts have dreamed.

In the meantime, even as radiation from a multitude of sources pours onto the dish, a kind of reverse process goes on. All of those television and radio signals that interfere with the radiation from outer space are themselves zooming away from Earth in all directions at the speed of light. In their entirety, the signals form a vast, expanding ball of radiation. Since radio broadcasts began about ninety years ago, the radius of that ball of radiation is now about ninety light years. It is large enough to contain a few hundred stars in our near galactic neighborhood, albeit still tiny compared to our galaxy as a whole. It is nevertheless possible, of course, that a technological civilization on Alpha Centauri or Ophiuchus has picked up our broadcasts, including enough episodes of *The Three Stooges* to place the Earth in a state of permanent galactic quarantine.

The point of that rapidly expanding sphere of programming has certainly not escaped the SETI theorists. Other civilizations with the ability to monitor electromagnetic radiation should be able, sooner or later, to hear our signals, however faint. Should we not, by the same token, be able to pick up the signals of other civilizations? The prospect has an unquestioned fascination about it. Imagine what an alien signal might be like, the very stuff of science fiction! But is it science? Or is it fiction? In particular, is Drake behaving like an apprentice?

In this case, it all depends on the hypothesis and your opinion of it. As the well-known astronomer Carl Sagan once speculated, the sheer numbers of stars in our galaxy lends enormous weight to even the most slender estimates of probability for the evolution of technological civilizations elsewhere: What is the chance of Earth-like planets? What is the chance of life spontaneously emerging on such a planet? Even small probabilities, when multiplied by the enormous number of stars out there, turn into something almost definite. The hypothesis is this: Given the near-ubiquity of life in our galaxy, some life forms have surely developed intelligence, including the ability to communicate by radio waves. Such waves should be detectable by suitable receivers right here on Earth.

There are a few minor flaws in this hypothesis and one major one. The minor flaws involve unstated assumptions that enter the hypothesis....

The hypotheses of the theoretical physicist or cosmologist "work" because the model is precise and one can tell, almost as soon as new observational evidence arrives, whether it confirms the model or not. If the speculation was far-fetched to begin with, the physicist should not be too surprised if further observations fail to confirm the model. ...[A] hypothesis must be falsifiable.

Consider now the scientist who looks up at the night sky and asks the age-old question, Is there anyone out there? The question seems perfectly reasonable. It means, Is there another race of beings, living somewhere else, whom we would call intelligent? Apart from the fact that we as yet have no formal scientific definition of intelligence..., most people think they know intelligence when they see it, at least among fellow human beings.

Perhaps the best laboratory in which to consider alien cultures is right here on Earth. Consider a country that is dominated by Zen Buddhism, for example. Many people would say that the Zen monk represents a very high level of human development (without being exactly sure what that means). If the world were full of Zen monks, however, we would be very unlikely to have radio. The technology would contribute very little to the insights necessary on the fivefold way, and one could argue that the technology and its development would constitute a completely unnecessary distraction from the real work of the monk, which is to rid himself of attachments to things of the world. As for advice from beyond, Zen monks have all they can handle in advice from the teacher.

With the peculiar myopia that characterizes Western culture, we have come to regard our own development as more or less inevitable, an extension of the Darwinian imperative into the technocultural realm.

The real question is What is the chance of a Western-style scientific-technological civilization developing out there? The "Western" qualifier is crucial, for we in the Western world may be living in a spell, trapped in yet another aberrant vision of our place in the universe, one no less misleading than the pre-Copernican idea of a central Earth. If the sorcerer is under a spell, he will hardly do better than the apprentice!

Live by the Formula, Die by the Formula

The unquestioned pioneer of the SETI project is the well-respected radio astronomer Frank Drake. Early in his career as a radio astronomer, Drake developed an interest in the possibility of life on other planets, particularly intelligent life. He became intrigued, some might say obsessed, with the prospect of intelligent beings broadcasting radio signals into space, signals that we on Earth might intercept—to our infinite advantage.

Intuitively, Drake understood that with 200 billion stars in our galaxy, there might be a very good chance that someone out there was already sending the very signals he dreamed of receiving. To put the project on a quantitative footing, Drake devised the equation below. To some people it may appear complicated, but mathematically speaking, it could hardly be simpler. The right-hand side of the equation consists merely of a bunch of variables all multiplied together:

$$N = R^* \times Fp \times Ne \times Fl \times Fi \times Fc \times L$$

The equation attempts to estimate the number N of "radio civilizations" in our galaxy. A radio civilization is simply a race of intelligent beings that have developed the ability to broadcast and receive messages via electromagnetic radiation, and do so on a regular basis. The equation estimates the number N by taking into account a variety of factors in the product:

R^*: number of new stars that form in our galaxy each year

Fp: fraction of stars having planetary systems

Ne: average number of life-supporting planets per star

Fl: fraction of those planets on which life develops

Fi: fraction of life forms that become intelligent

Fc: fraction of intelligent beings that develop radio

L: average lifetime of a communicating civilization

At first glance, the equation seems perfectly definite. If you happen to know the value of each variable, you can come up with a pretty good estimate for N. If the estimate you arrive at is reasonably large, you may use the equation to squeeze endless amounts of money out of Congress to support a search for intelligent life. The equation, after all, is mathematical, and that means real science.

An estimate of the number R^* is based on an assumed rate of star formation of about ten a year. This is an extremely crude estimate based on current observations of regions where stars appear to be forming in our galaxy. The actual number has undoubtedly varied enormously over time, particularly in the remote past. For the Drake formula, it's all uphill from this point on.

The fraction Fp of stars having planetary systems is completely unknown. Although a few relatively nearby stars are suspected of having very large Jupiter-like companions or planets that are nearly stars in their own right, we have yet to observe a single star with a planetary system even remotely like our own. Period. It follows that we haven't the slightest idea what the real value of Fp might be, and any "estimates" would better be called wild guesses.

If we haven't a clue how many stars have planetary systems, then we're even more in the dark about the average number Ne of life-supporting planets per star. Some of them may well have such planets. Perhaps they all do. Perhaps our sun is the only such star. We simply have no idea.

Will a "life-supporting planet" ever develop life? I'm not sure how a planet could support life if it didn't already have it. The Earth has oxygen, for example, only because photosynthesizing organisms evolved here a long time ago and eventually filled the atmosphere with this (for us) vital gas. Perhaps the rather silly variable Fl should be set equal to 1 and simply dropped from the equation.

As you will see from a glance at the remaining variables, it gets worse.

The fraction Fi of life forms that become intelligent is even less well known, if that is possible, than the previous variables. What do we mean by "intelligent," anyway? As you may have already discovered . . . , we're not even sure what we mean by our own "intelligence"! Once again, my guess for this variable is as good as Frank Drake's.

The fraction Fc of intelligent life forms that develop radio is likewise completely unknown and pointless to estimate. Finally, the lifetime L of the average radio civilization is the only variable about which we have any information, and that information may be about to improve. We know, for example, that our own radio civilization has existed for about ninety years. There is a real possibility that it may reach one hundred. In any case, this sample of one is our only basis for an estimation of L.

How do Drake and his disciples use the formula? Here are two examples that have appeared in popular magazine articles on the subject. I have no doubt that the guesses come directly from the SETI school.

$$N = 10 \times 0.3 \times 1 \times 0.1 \times 0.5 \times 0.5 \times 10^6 = 125{,}000$$
$$N = 10 \times 1 \times 1 \times 1 \times 0.01 \times 0.1 \times L = 0.01 \times L$$

In the first guess, L was given a value of 10^6, or one million years. The second guess refused to assign a definite value to L, which is strange, considering that we already know more about L than the other variables. Nevertheless, using the value for L from the first equation in the second, we get a more conservative estimate:

$$N = 10,000$$

That's still quite a few radio civilizations. Why haven't we heard from any of them yet? We might find the answer by taking a closer look at ourselves, in particular, and our probable destiny as a radio civilization. It is not nuclear holocaust that will seal our fate as a spherical broadcaster of invaluable cultural and scientific information to the cosmos, but the incredible inefficiency of antenna broadcasting!

As every radio engineer knows, broadcasting electromagnetic waves in all directions at once is an enormously wasteful way to transmit information. Although the emissions from standard mast antennas can be directed somewhat in the form of lobes, only the tiniest fraction of broadcast energy ever reaches receiving antennas. The evidence is now very clear that the Earth is rapidly fading as a source of electromagnetic energy. Increasingly, we transmit radio and television signals by cable, not to mention the exponentially increasing Internet traffic on phone lines and fiber-optic cables. An even more powerful trend involves the broadcast of television signals toward Earth from satellites, signals that are completely absorbed by the ground. The Earth may be about to vanish as a radio source.

If this is true, then 100 might be taken as a perfectly reasonable estimate for the crucial variable L. In this case, plugging the new value for L into the last equation..., we get

$$N = 0.01 \times 100 = 1$$

That must be us.

Another implication of current developments in the dissemination of information points up another minor flaw in the Drake hypothesis. Increasingly, radio signals between points in deep space will be beamed ever more precisely at the target receivers, somewhat like a laser beam. This would make their reception by nontargeted civilizations increasingly less likely. Can anyone believe that these vastly "superior" alien civilizations would themselves employ any method so incredibly wasteful as spherical broadcasting to communicate with each other? The implications for SETI enthusiasts are clear: Don't hold your breath waiting for that magic signal.

Finally, there may well be radio signals that SETI will eventually intercept but the signals will present us with an enormous headache. Seemingly intelligent, they will only be meaningful to beings of a similar mindset, whatever that might mean. Neither I nor anyone in the SETI team can imagine what a distinctly inhuman mentality might be like.

POSTSCRIPT

Is It Worthwhile to Continue the Search for Extraterrestrial Life?

The modern, high-tech version of SETI, the High Resolution Microwave Survey (HRMS), almost never came to pass. As Donald Tarter of the International Space University, in "Treading on the Edge: Practicing Safe Science With SETI," *Skeptical Inquirer* (Spring 1993), writes, "SETI's recent history has been one of fighting for scientific respect and then fighting for funding.... SETI has been so frequently ridiculed and singled out as [a program that could be eliminated by budget-cutting congressional members] that officially SETI no longer exists." He then notes that, shortly before NASA began its current search for extraterrestrial intelligence, the name was changed to HRMS.

However, the name change did not solve the problem. A year after HRMS was born, the budget was cut. By October 12, 1993, the $1 million a month needed to sustain it had been eliminated from the budget by a House-Senate conference committee. It was not the sort of arguments raised by critics such as Dewdney that defeated HRMS; it was image. SETI smacked too much of science fiction and Hollywood. It might not be terribly expensive—the cost of a single space shuttle flight could pay SETI's bills for several years—but whatever it cost seemed to the budget cutters pure waste when compared to the many other programs and problems requiring funds.

Yet SETI was not dead. Many scientists—including nonastronomers such as David M. Raup of the University of Chicago's Department of Geophysical Sciences and Committee on Evolutionary Biology—disagree with those who believe that humans are probably alone in the universe and who say that the search for intelligent extraterrestrials is not worth the effort. So do many nonscientists. The private SETI Institute (http://www.seti-inst.edu) has raised millions of dollars, much of it from leaders of California's computer industry.

Another effort worth noting is that of the SETI League http://www.setileague.org, which is recruiting owners of obsolete satellite TV dishes (3–5 meters in diameter; new dishes are much smaller) to connect the dishes to home computers and let them listen to the sky as part of Project Argus. See Marcus Chown, "The Alien Spotters," *New Scientist* (April 19, 1997). Still another is SETI@home (http://www.setiathome.ssl.berkeley.edu), which has turned the project into a computer screensaver. It sends the raw signal recordings out to over 500,000 personal computer (PC) owners (as of June 1999), whose computers analyze the data whenever they are not busy with other tasks. The hope is that the massed power of so many thousands of home PCs will prove more sensitive than the supercomputers used elsewhere.

On the Internet . . .

CDT Privacy Issues Page

At this site, the Center for Democracy and Technology (CDT) demonstrates how easy it is for people to find out about you by using the Internet as a research tool.

`http://www.cdt.org/privacy/`

The Electronic Frontier Foundation

The Electronic Frontier Foundation is concerned with protecting individual freedoms and rights such as privacy as new communications technologies emerge.

`http://www.eff.org`

Project Gutenberg

Project Gutenberg is an ongoing project to convert the classics of literature into digital format.

`http://www.gutenberg.net`

Hans Moravec

From here, take a peek at Hans Moravec's new book *Universal Robots: Object to Person to Spirit* (Oxford University Press, 1998).

`http://www.frc.ri.cmu.edu/~hpm/`

PART 5

The Computer Revolution

*F*ans *of computers are sure that the electronic wonders offer untold benefits to society. When the first personal computers appeared in the early 1970s, they immediately brought unheard-of capabilities to their users. Ever since, those capabilities have been increasing. Today children command more sheer computing power than major corporations did in the 1950s and 1960s. Computer users are in direct contact with their fellow users around the world. Information is instantly available and infinitely malleable.*

Some observers wonder about the purported untold benefits of computers. Specifically, will such benefits be outweighed by threats to children (by free access to pornography), civil order (by free access to sites that advocate racism and violence), traditional institutions (will books, for example, become an endangered species?), or to human pride (a computer has already outplayed the human world chess champion)? Also, scientists debate quite seriously whether or not there will ever be a computer that genuinely thinks like a person.

- Should the Internet Be Censored?

- Is Microsoft's Dominance of the Personal Computer Market About to End?

- Are Computers Hazardous to Literacy?

- Will It Be Possible to Build a Computer That Can Think?

ISSUE 11

Should the Internet Be Censored?

YES: John Carr, from "It's Time to Tackle Cyberporn," *New Statesman* (February 20, 1998)

NO: Raymond W. Smith, from "Civility Without Censorship: The Ethics of the Internet—Cyberhate," *Vital Speeches of the Day* (January 15, 1999)

ISSUE SUMMARY

YES: John Carr, an Internet consultant to NCH Action For Children, contends that children must be protected from exposure to hazardous Internet materials.

NO: Raymond W. Smith, chairman of the Bell Atlantic Corporation, argues that the commitment to free speech must always take precedence over fear.

From its beginning in e-mail, bulletin board systems, and newsgroups—long before the invention of the World Wide Web—the Internet has been a favorite haunt of extremists on both the right and the left, pornographers, adolescent males, and others who revel in exchanging unapproved information. Not surprisingly, this has alarmed those who feel certain kinds of information—such as pornography, anarchist manifestoes, and bomb-making instructions—should be kept from public view.

Such alarm is not new. It long predates the Internet:

- In 1792, Thomas Paine's *The Rights of Man* got him indicted for treason.
- Nineteenth-century censors banned the use of the mails to transmit birth control information.
- In the 1930s, censors banned James Joyce's *Ulysses*.
- Every year—still!—various groups try to have classic works by Mark Twain, Shakespeare, and many more removed from school libraries on the grounds of obscenity, racism, and alcohol and abuse advocacy.

But the Internet makes all these works, and many more, widely and easily available. Anyone with an Internet connection can download anything that has been posted anywhere in the world. Children are not limited to what they can find at the school or town library. Nor are adults, and Saudi Arabia, Serbia, and China have all made the news for restricting access within their borders to information that they deem inconsistent with their preferred religion, ideology, or view of current events. See Seydou Amadou Oumarou and Rene Lefort, "The Web, the Spider and the Fly," *UNESCO Courier* (September 1998).

In the United States, state and federal legislators have repeatedly passed laws restricting pornographic books and magazines, generally on the grounds that they offend against "community standards." Laws attempting to restrict a broader array of materials have not survived their court tests, at least in the United States. Jonathan D. Wallace, in "Pervasive Problem: The 1978 Supreme Court Decision Allowing Censorship of Dirty Words on Radio Threatens Free Speech in Cyberspace," *Reason* (October 1998), discusses the "pervasiveness" doctrine established by the Supreme Court in 1978; this doctrine, originally directed toward radio and TV, may threaten the Internet as well.

Legislative efforts such as the Communications Decency Act (CDA), which passed in 1996, and the Child Online Protection Act (COPA or CDA II), which passed in 1998, have tried to prevent people from making offensive material available via the Internet. The CDA targeted "indecent" material (including both obscenity and sober discussions of sex-related matters). The COPA had a broader aim, for it made it a federal crime to knowingly communicate for commercial purposes any material considered harmful to minors. Not surprisingly, both the CDA and the COPA have proved controversial, as have software programs that have been devised to detect and block access to offensive Internet sites. The American Civil Liberties Union (ACLU), the Electronic Frontier Foundation (EFF), and the Electronic Privacy Information Center (EPIC), with others, have filed suits in federal courts, and the Internet community has provided testimony, witnesses, and attorneys. The same groups have also sued to block state laws censoring the Internet.

Like the proponents of the CDA and COPA bills, John Carr argues that children must be protected from exposure to hazardous Internet materials such as pornography. "Anxieties about illiberal abuse of the Internet," he states, "are . . . at best misplaced and at worst paranoid, reckless or self-serving." Raymond W. Smith focuses less on pornography than on violence and bigotry, but he shares the belief of the critics of the CDA and the COPA that the commitment to free speech must always take precedence over fear.

John Carr

 **YES**

It's Time to Tackle Cyberporn

The Great Internet Freedom Debate is rolling forward. At issue is the balance to be struck between "free speech" and the ability of families, employers, schools or other organisations to protect themselves against the receipt of material that is unwanted, illegal or both. The responsibility for striking the balance —and providing mechanisms to enforce it—is, however, increasingly seen not as a job for governments, legislatures or police forces, but for private citizens and the private companies that own and run the Internet industry.

There is a tenacious cyber-myth that the Internet is a vast, anarchic forum, beyond the reach of any government or authority, uncontrolled and uncontrollable. The reality is that for all parts of the Internet there are several potential points of control, and for the typical UK cybernaut one of them has been in operation for a while. So this debate is not about whether some sacred principle of non-regulation or freedom from censorship should be breached: that point was passed some time ago. Now we are discussing practical questions of degree: the ways in which intervention or regulation might occur; the level at which a censorship option might be feasible or appropriate.

If you link up to the Internet with any of the big UK-based Internet service providers (ISPs), such as AOL, MSN, Compuserve, Poptel or LineOne, you already do not enjoy full and unrestricted access to the superhighway. Even Demon, the ISP that represents the liberal wing in this debate, does not allow its subscribers to access everything that is "out there". Most of what is kept from you is illegal material, principally child pornography. There are ways of circumventing the barriers, but you have to know first that you are being "deprived"; second, how to get around the obstacles; and third, you have to find an unrestricted source that will let you in. The last bit in particular is not easy.

It is only in the past two years that the ISPs operating in Britain have chosen to restrict what they provide as part of their standard service. They have done so as a result of a combination of threats from police and the last government, administrative convenience and their own sense of civic responsibility (all foreign-owned ISPs come within the jurisdiction of UK courts for their operation in this country).

The UK Internet industry also established the Internet Watch Foundation (IWF), on whose policy board I sit as an unpaid member. The IWF runs a hotline facility, which allows people who find potentially illegal material on the Internet to report it. Once a report is verified two things will happen: if the material is housed on a server owned by a British-based ISP it will be removed forthwith and the police will be notified. The deal between the industry, the IWF and police, however, is that, whereas possession of certain types of illegal material is normally a crime, if the material is removed promptly the police will not prosecute the service provider.

The IWF's remit covers all illegal material on all parts of the Net, but it has prioritised child pornography, which is principally exchanged through newsgroups, occasionally is found on websites, and increasingly is being spread and procured through chat rooms.

Similar hotlines are springing up all over the world and the EU [European Union] recently announced its intention to support their development as part of an ambitious package of measures aimed at making the Internet a safer, more congenial place.

However, the IWF and the police are powerless to do anything about a huge body of material which, though not illegal, is highly offensive to some (hardcore pornography, for instance) or else dangerous or undesirable (say, information about bomb-making). It is not simply a matter of overprotecting the frail or faint-hearted: anyone may by accident or through curiosity stumble on unwanted matter. Debate is now focused on what might be done about this type of material: in the US it is a topic of urgent public concern.

There is no legal basis for banning these categories; neither will the newsagents' answer to printed pornography work: the physical barrier a "top shelf" policy offers to children and customers who don't want to stand and stare at porn mags simply cannot be replicated on the Net.

Instead the buzz phrase is "ratings systems", a concept akin to film or video classification, although necessarily rather more complex. A ratings system is an agreed set of criteria for describing material to be published on the Internet. The originator or publisher of the material provides the rating, which appears as a label attached to the article or site, giving a brief standardised description of its content. As the system is based on self-assessment, there may eventually need to be a set of sanctions for misrating and methods for policing, but these are not yet in place. The idea is that the ratings labels are picked up and read by filtering programmes that work with your browser. The user will have told the filtering programme what to allow through and what to block. Those who do not want any material filtered will still be able to set that option on their computer.

There is no jurisprudentially savvy software available on the market that would filter out only illegal material. You have to describe categories or types of material you do not want to see. Thus if you do not want to access anything with violent images or bad language, you could programme accordingly; alternatively you might find "PG"-type levels acceptable.

It is easy to foresee the emergence of third-party ratings systems; so for instance if you are a devout Catholic, you might put your trust in "Vatican

Net", a subscription service which, if it is ever formed, will only allow material through that would not trouble the Pontiff. Different ratings levels can also be set for different users of the same computer or network, allowing parents to set different access levels for their children than for themselves.

There is already one type of ratings system in widespread use, built into Internet Explorer. That system was established and is managed by RSACi (Recreational Software Advisory Council on the Internet), a not-for-profit body linked to the Massachusetts Institute of Technology. However, the current RSACi criteria are too narrowly American and their system is too crude. The UK's IWF has been trying to work out a better alternative and will shortly be consulting on its proposals, with a view to co-operating eventually with RSACi and other interests in the formulation of a global system. Some day a Baptist minister in the US Bible Belt, a liberal atheist in Amsterdam and a party official in Beijing should all be able to use the same means to decide whether or not their nine year olds can visit this or that website or newsgroup.

Not everyone welcomes the prospect, however. There is vocal opposition to the development of ratings systems, most forcibly expressed by the American Civil Liberties Union (ACLU) in its paper *Fahrenheit 451.2—Is Cyberspace Burning?* In ratings systems the cyber-libertarians see not enhanced consumer choice but new tools being fashioned to allow authoritarian interests to "lock out" unpopular views, or otherwise to control the content of the Internet by requiring all ISPs, for example, to run it on their servers. They fear that minority opinions or tastes will be excluded.

These anxieties about illiberal abuse of the Internet through ratings and similar technologies are, I believe, at best misplaced and at worst paranoid, reckless or self-serving. The days are over when the Internet was the private preserve of academics and computer geeks. Now that its trajectory is to become an integral part of our living-room mass media (with a projected 200 million users worldwide by 2001), the rules simply have to change.

If we do nothing to curb some of the more rampant excesses, the Internet as we know it will cease to exist in the not-too-distant future. It will be replaced by (at least) two Internets: one which is safe, homogenised, dull, highly commercialised and accessible by subscription only, and another which will be for the poor: free and wild, but most definitely a place to go only at your own risk.

The anti-censorship lobby has had an early but significant victory in this battle. In 1996 the US government tried to legislate against offensive Internet material. The Communications Decency Act (CDA) was fatally undermined during its passage through Congress when the religious right sought to widen its ambit. The ACLU sued and in June last year the Supreme Court struck down the relevant provisions as being contrary to the first amendment protection of free speech.

Its strategy in tatters, in July the White House reiterated its intention to make the Internet "family-friendly", but stressed that it would look to the industry to take the initiative. Self-regulation was the new approach, but with the clear warning that inaction would lead to renewed legislative efforts. As Al Gore said at the time, "Hands off does not mean indifference."

In December the US Internet industry gathered in Washington, DC, to deliver its response. Many in the industry fully share their government's aims. Steve Case, president of AOL, declared: "Let's face it, many of us are parents and we want to work in an industry we can feel proud of."

All the major ISPs announced they were supporting ratings systems. The owners of some of the bigger Internet search services—Yahoo, Lycos and Excite —said they were considering in future allowing into their directories only material that had been rated. The ISPs also announced that they are going to amend their standard terms of contract to allow them to withdraw service from anyone found misusing their Internet connection by, for instance, soliciting or offering child pornography.

The conference also announced other initiatives being researched, notably to place greater requirements on distributors of hardcore porn not to sell to underage viewers; to make it easier to identify visitors to chat rooms; and to try to end the practice of anonymous e-mailing.

Disney and Time Warner announced they are establishing "whitelisting services": Internet subscription services that give you access not to the whole of the Net but only to the parts they have vetted. For "Vatican Net" read "Donald Duck Net." We are soon likely to see an explosion of similar whitelists here, especially aimed at the schools audience. BT's "Campus World" already exists and is being marketed as a safe haven.

Janet Reno, the US Attorney General, told the Washington conference that last year alone there were roughly 200 convictions for child pornography and other forms of paedophile activity where the Internet played a major part. She did not tell us how many arrests there had been, how many cases were awaiting trial or how many perpetrators escaped prosecution on technical grounds. The UK's IWF, in its first, under-publicised year of operation, received more than a thousand complaints, of which 300-plus were adjudged to contain illegal material, the great bulk of them relating to child pornography.

The Internet is far from a stable or mature technology. Advances are made almost daily, some of which can have profound and immediate consequences for the medium. It serves no one's interests to pretend we are on the brink of some last-ditch defence of democracy and free speech when we engage in this debate. Instead we should all recognise that almost all of us are looking, in good faith, for new answers to the new problems thrown up by the new technology.

In doing so I trust we will all give at least equal weight to the right of a child to grow up unmolested by paedophiles as we do to the rights of the rugged cyberfrontiersmen who pose as defenders of liberty in a medium that almost no one had even heard of six years ago.

Civility Without Censorship

I've been using the "bully pulpit" to alert various civil rights leaders and organizations (like Martin Luther King III and the NAACP) of the dangers posed by cyberhate. If not for the early groundbreaking work by the Simon Wiesenthal Center, I doubt whether I would have even known of this growing threat. Thank you for warning us—and now, for showing us—how extremists are using the Internet for their own purposes.

When thinking about this... topic, I can't help but mention a cartoon that recently appeared in the newspapers. Through the doorway, a mother calls out to her teenager—who is surrounded by high-tech equipment—"I hope you're not watching sex stuff on the Internet!" To which her son replies, "Naw, I'm getting it on TV!"

Until recently, the chief concern of parents was pornography—kids' access to it over the Web and the fear of sexual predators cruising cyberspace. Now, we're worried about hate mongers reaching out to our children in digital space.

As we have just seen and heard, Neo-Nazis and extremists of every political stripe who once terrorized people in the dead of night with burning crosses and painted swastikas are now sneaking up on the public—especially our kids—through the World Wide Web.

As cyberhate is nothing less than the attempt to corrupt public discourse on race and ethnicity via the Internet, many people see censorship of web sites and Net content as the only viable way to meet this growing threat.

I disagree.

Instead of fearing the Internet's reach, we need to embrace it—to value its ability to connect our children to the wealth of positive human experience and knowledge. While there is, to quote one critic, "every form of diseased intelligence" in digital space, we must remember that it comprises only a small fraction of cyberspace. The Internet provides our children unlimited possibilities for learning and education—the great libraries, cities and cultures of the world also await them at just the click of a mouse key.

In short, we need to think less about ways to keep cyberhate off the screen, and more about ways to meet it head on: which translates into fighting destructive rhetoric with constructive dialogue—hate speech with truth—restrictions with greater Internet access.

This morning, then, I would like to discuss with you the options that are available to combat cyberhate that don't endanger our First Amendment guarantees—and that remain true to our commitment to free speech.

That people and institutions should call for a strict ban on language over the Web that could be considered racist, anti-Semitic or bigoted is totally understandable. None of us was truly prepared for the emergence of multiple hate-group web sites (especially those geared toward children), or the quick adoption of high technology by skinheads and others to market their digital cargo across state lines and international date lines at the speed of light.

One possible reason some people feel inclined to treat the Internet more severely than other media is that the technology is new and hard to understand. Also, the Internet's global reach and ubiquitous nature makes it appear ominous. As Justice Gabriel Bach, of Israel, noted, this ability makes it especially dangerous. "I'm frightened stiff by the Internet," he said, "billions of people all over the world have access to it."

My industry has seen all this before.

The clash between free speech and information technology is actually quite an old one. Nearly a century ago, telephone companies, courts, and the Congress debated whether "common carriers" (public phone companies) were obligated to carry all talk equally, regardless of content. And in the end—though some believed that the phone would do everything from eliminate Southern accents and increase Northern labor unrest—free speech won out in the courts.

Whatever the technology, be it the radio or the silver screen, history teaches us that white supremacists, anti-Semites and others will unfortunately come to grasp, relatively early on, a new medium's potential.

We simply can't condemn a whole technology because we fear that a Father Coughlin or a Leni Riefenstahl (early pioneers in the use of radio and film to advance anti-Semitism or Hitler's Reich) is waiting in the wings to use the latest technology to their own advantage. Nor can we expect the Congress, the federal government or an international regulatory agency to tightly regulate cyberspace content in order to stymie language we find offensive.

The wisdom of further empowering such organizations and agencies like the FCC or the United Nations aside, it is highly doubtful even if they had the authority, that they would have the ability to truly stem the flow of racist and anti-Semitic language on the World Wide Web.

Anybody with a phone line, computer and Internet connection can set up a web site—even broadcast over the Net.

Even if discovered and banned, on-line hate groups can easily jump Internet service providers and national boundaries to avoid accountability. I think cyber guru Peter Huber got it right when he said, "To censor Internet filth at its origins, we would have to enlist the Joint Chiefs of Staff, who could start by invading Sweden and Holland."

Then there is the whole matter of disguise. Innocent sounding URLs (handles or Web site names) can fool even the most traveled or seasoned "cybernaut."

As for efforts on Capitol Hill and elsewhere to legislate all so-called "offensive" language off the Internet, here again, we can expect the courts to knock down any attempts to curtail First Amendment rights on the Internet. As the Supreme Court ruled last year when it struck down legislation restricting the transmission of "indecent" material on-line: (To Quote) "Regardless of the strength of the government's interest, the level of discourse reaching a mailbox simply cannot be limited to what is suitable for a sandbox."

In short, although the temptation is great to look to legislation and regulation as a remedy to cyberhate, our commitment to free speech must always take precedence over our fears.

So, cyberhate will not be defeated by the stroke of a pen.

Now, this is not to say that, because we place such a high value on our First Amendment rights, we can't do anything to combat the proliferation of hate sites on the Internet or protect young minds from such threatening and bigoted language.

Law enforcement agencies and state legislators can use existing laws against stalking and telephone harassment to go after those who abuse e-mail... parents can install software filtering programs (such as the Anti-Defamation League's HateFilter, or the one Bell Atlantic uses, CyberPatrol) to block access to questionable Internet sites... schools and libraries can protect children by teaching them how to properly use the Internet and challenge cyberhate... and Internet Service Providers can voluntarily decline to host hate sites. (Bell Atlantic Internet Services, for instance, reserves the right to decline or terminate service which "espouses, promotes or incites bigotry, hatred or racism.")

Given that today's panel has representatives from state government, law enforcement, the courts and the Internet industry, we can discuss these initiatives later in more detail. The point is, there are other ways besides empowering national or international oversight agencies, or drafting draconian legislation, to lessen the impact of cyberhate.

Freedom, not censorship, is the only way to combat this threat to civility. In short, more speech—not less—is needed on the World Wide Web.

In fact, the best answer to cyberhate lies in the use of information technology itself. As a reporter for the Boston Globe recently concluded, (quote) "the same technology that provides a forum for extremists, enables civil rights groups and individuals to mobilize a response in unprecedented ways."

We totally agree.

Our prescription to cyberhate is therefore rather simple, but far reaching in its approach:

The first component is access: if we're to get to a higher level of national understanding on racial and ethnic issues—and strike at the very roots of cyberhate—we must see that no minority group or community is left out of cyberspace for want of a simple Internet connection or basic computer.

At Bell Atlantic, we've been working very hard to provide the minority communities we serve with Internet access. Across our region, thousands of inner-city schools, libraries, colleges and community groups are now getting connected to cyberspace through a variety of our foundation and state grant programs. Also, our employees have been in the forefront of volunteering their time and energy to wire schools to the Internet during specially designated "Net" days.

Internet access alone, however, won't build bridges of understanding between people—or level the playing field between cyber-haters and the targets of their hate.

The second thing we must do is make sure the Web's content is enriched by minority culture and beliefs, and that there are more Web sites and home pages dedicated to meeting head-on the racist caricatures and pseudo history often found in cyberspace.

While cyberhate cannot be mandated or censored out of existence, it can be countered by creating hundreds of chat-lines, home pages, bulletin boards and Web sites dedicated to social justice, tolerance and equality—for all people regardless of race, nationality or sexual orientation.

Over the past two years, Bell Atlantic has helped a number of minority and civil rights groups launch and maintain their Web sites (like the NAACP, the Leadership Council on Civil Rights, and the National Council of La Raza), and we've done the same for dozens of smaller cultural organizations (like the Harlem Studio Museum and El Museo del Barrio).

We believe that kind of moral leadership can have a tremendous impact. Quite simply, we need more Simon Wiesenthal Centers, Anti-Defamation Leagues, and Southern Poverty Law Centers monitoring and responding to cyberhate.

If we're to bring the struggle for human decency and dignity into cyberspace, we must see that the two most powerful revolutions of the 20th century—those of civil rights and information technology—are linked even closer together.

Finally, we need to drive real-time, serious dialogue on the religious, ethnic, and cultural concerns that divide us as a nation—a task for which the Internet is particularly suited.

Precisely because it is anonymous, the Internet provides a perfect forum to discuss race, sexual orientation and other similar issues. On the Internet, said one user, "you can speak freely and not have fears that somebody is going to attack you for what comes out of your heart." It's this kind of open and heartfelt discussion that we need to advance and sponsor on-line.

Already, a number of small groups and lone individuals are meeting the cyberhate challenge through simple dialogue between strangers. I'm talking about Web sites run by educators to inform parents about on-line hate materials... sites operated by "recovering" racists to engage skinheads and other misguided kids in productive debate... web sites run by concerned citizens to bridge the gap in ignorance between ethnic, racial and other communities.

The "Y? forum," also known as the National Forum on People's Differences, is a wonderful example of a Web site where readers can safely ask and follow discussions on sensitive cross-cultural topics without having to wade through foul language or "flame wars."

As a columnist from the Miami Herald described the appeal of these kinds of sites: "As long as we are mysteries, one to another, we face a perpetuation of ignorance and a feeding of fear. I'd rather people ask the questions than try to make up the answers. I'd rather they ask the questions than turn to myth and call it truth."

In closing, my company recognizes that the Internet doesn't operate in a vacuum. We agree that those who profit from information technology have a special responsibility to see that its promise is shared across class, race and geographic boundaries.

That's why we're working with the public schools and libraries in our region to see that they're all equipped with the pens, pencils and paper of the 21st century... why we're helping to further distance learning and telemedicine applications that serve the educational and health needs of the disabled and isolated... why we're helping minority groups and civil rights organizations use information technology to spread their vision and their values to the millions of people electronically linked to the global village.

And that's the way it should be.

Let me leave you with a personal story...

When growing up, my Jewish friends and I often swapped theology—tales from the Hassidic Masters for stories from the Lives of the Saints. I remember from these discussions that one of the great Rabbis noted that the first word of the Ten Commandments is "I" and the last word is "neighbor." In typical Talmudic fashion, the Rabbi was telling us that if we want to incorporate the Commandments into our lives, we must move from a focus on ourselves to others.

At Bell Atlantic, the more we grow—in both scale and scope—the greater the emphasis we place on being a good corporate citizen, and the more we're driven to see that digital technology is used for purposes of enlightenment and education.

The Internet will fundamentally transform the way we work, learn, do commerce. It will also, if properly used and rightly taught, help bridge the gap in understanding between communities—becoming not a tool of hate, but one of hope.

POSTSCRIPT

Should the Internet Be Censored?

So far, the courts have supported those who, like Smith, believe that free speech is more important than censorship. In June 1996, the U.S. District Court for the Eastern District of Pennsylvania found the CDA unconstitutional on grounds that it violated rights of free speech, with Judge Stewart Dalzell writing, "Just as the strength of the Internet is chaos, so the strength of our liberty depends upon the chaos and cacophony of the unfettered speech the First Amendment protects." A year later, the U.S. Supreme Court agreed, with Justice John Paul Stevens writing for the majority: "As a matter of constitutional tradition, in the absence of evidence to the contrary, we presume that governmental regulation of the content of speech is more likely to interfere with the free exchange of ideas than to encourage it. The interest in encouraging freedom of expression in a democratic society outweighs any theoretical but unproven benefit of censorship." See Glenn E. Simon, "Cyberporn and Censorship: Constitutional Barriers to Preventing Access to Internet Pornography by Minors," *Journal of Criminal Law and Criminology* (Spring 1998).

The censors did not give up, however. Many people feel that children must be sheltered from much of what is available on the Internet; see John W. Kennedy, "Profamily Groups Demand More Cyberporn Prosecutions," *Christianity Today* (February 1998). Even before the CDA had been declared unconstitutional, legislators had begun work on the COPA in hopes that the bill would avoid some of the CDA's weaknesses. See Max Hailperin, "The COPA Battle and the Future of Free Speech," *Communications of the ACM* (January 1999). Immediately, Judge Lowell Reed of the U.S. District Court for the Eastern District of Pennsylvania issued an injunction prohibiting enforcement of the act, saying that it was overly broad and would unreasonably limit the Internet to material suitable for children.

Some people believe filtering software is a better approach, for it permits access to be blocked to selected topics. See Marjorie Heins, "Screening out Sex: Kids, Computers, and the New Censors," *The American Prospect* (July 1998). There appears to be no legal obstacle to use of such programs by parents and schools (where they are very popular), but libraries are another matter. In Loudoun County, Virginia, the public library installed filtering software on all of its computers, used by both children and adults to access the Internet. In November 1998, Judge Leonie M. Brinkema of the U.S. District Court for the Eastern District of Virginia declared that usage unconstitutional, saying, "Mandatory blocking constitutes 'prior restraint'—an extreme form of censorship that few courts have allowed" and "Any library policy that censors adults in the guise of protecting minors is unconstitutional." See http://www.aclu.org/news/n112398a.html.

219

ISSUE 12

Is Microsoft's Dominance of the Personal Computer Market About to End?

YES: Robert Berger, from "Microscared: The Challenge of Open Source Software," *Linux Magazine* (Spring 1999)

NO: Michael Dertouzos and Bill Gates, from "Titans Talk Tech: Bill G. and Michael D.," *Technology Review* (May/June 1999)

ISSUE SUMMARY

YES: Robert Berger, president of Internet Bandwidth Development, argues that the open source software (OSS) movement poses a potentially fatal threat to Microsoft's Windows operating systems.

NO: In an interview with Massachusetts Institute of Technology's (MIT's) Michael Dertouzos, Bill Gates, founder and president of Microsoft, argues that the continuing need for innovation and consistency ensures that Microsoft will remain a major player in the software field.

Microsoft began its phenomenal rise when IBM—reacting to the success of the first Apple computer—was preparing to bring out its first PC (personal computer). Bill Gates licensed QDOS (Quick and Dirty Operating System) for $50,000 and renamed it PC-DOS 1.0 in 1981. With improvements, PC-DOS became MS-DOS. It came with every IBM PC, and soon with every "clone" marketed by other companies; it made operating these computers relatively simple and straightforward, but it did require users to remember and type in seemingly arbitrary, cryptic, and sometimes elaborate commands.

At about the same time, Apple was borrowing the graphical user interface developed by Xerox's Palo Alto Research Center; the result was the Macintosh computer. When it proved popular, Microsoft developed the very similar Windows 1.0, which evolved to become Windows 3.1x, 95, 98, and NT. When the Internet became popular, Microsoft developed its Internet Explorer browser program. Since these programs also came with virtually every non-Apple PC, Microsoft grew rapidly. Today it is one of the largest corporations on the planet, and Bill Gates is a very, very rich man.

Unfortunately, Microsoft did not achieve its near-monopoly status solely by offering computer users a quality product. The U.S. Justice Department has brought a major antitrust suit against the company, alleging that it used unfair tactics such as requiring PC makers to "install its browser, Internet Explorer (IE), as a condition for receiving licenses for Windows 95." See Stuart J. Johnston, "A Microsoft Decade: Writing and Rewriting History," *Information Week* (February 16, 1998) and "Microsoft Accused: Play Nicely, or Not at All," *The Economist* (May 23, 1998). Some people criticize the "quality" of the product as well; the Windows operating systems can be slow (earning them the nickname of "Windoze") and are infamous for freezing up or "crashing," thus stopping computers in their tracks.

Still others have objected to the commercialism and exclusivity of Microsoft (and other software companies). Richard Stallman's "The GNU Manifesto" first appeared in 1985 (see M. David Ermann, Mary B. Williams, and Michele S. Shauf, eds., *Computers, Ethics, and Society,* 2d. ed. [Oxford University Press, 1997]) to announce what would become the open source software (OSS) movement. Today thousands of computer programmers work at improving GNU (Gnu's Not Unix) programs, sending their contributions to central locations for incorporation into the canonical versions of the programs. For an example of how these programs work, see Eric Raymond, "The Cathedral and the Bazaar" at http://www.tuxedo.org/esr/writings/cathedral-bazaar/.

The open source operating system is Linux, developed by Linus Torvalds; it has established a reputation for speed and for being far more crashproof than Windows, and its popularity has been growing with remarkable speed. Its partisans are extremely enthusiastic—see Jeff Prothero, "The Last Dinosaur and the Tarpits of Doom: How Linux Smashed Windows" at http://muq.org/cynbe/rants/lastdino.htm—and they may be right when they forecast the death of Microsoft.

In the following selections, Robert Berger argues that the open source software movement—prominently represented by the Linux operating system— poses a potentially fatal threat to Microsoft's Windows operating systems. Bill Gates, however, does not seem worried. Interviewed by Michael Dertouzos, he contends that there is a place for open source software, but the market demands more innovation and consistency than it can provide. Microsoft will remain a major player in the software field, he concludes.

Robert Berger

Microscared: The Challenge
of Open Source Software

Microsoft. Sun. Bitter enemies with only one thing in common—their hatred for each other. Until recently, that is. Lately they have come to share something else: a fear of Linux. And they are not alone. Throughout the software industry, companies of all shapes and sizes have been asking themselves, "How will the open source movement affect our business?" Or, "Can we embrace open source without destroying our traditional businesses at the same time?"

Pondering these questions is causing the fear level to rise at every software company whose profits depend on the proprietary closed source revenue model. They are having difficulty adjusting to the open source paradigm for the creation and distribution of software. The Linux OS [operating system] represents the ultimate manifestation of this movement.

What many people seem to be overlooking in the middle of all the hype is that open source is not really a new paradigm at all. It has been around for at least as long as all of the companies that now fear it. This begs an interesting question: if open source has been around all this time, how come it is only now becoming a threat to the entrenched players in the software industry?

To answer this question, we first need to briefly explore the history of the open source movement, and look at some of the differences in the underlying economic philosophies of the open and closed software camps.

Closed source software relies upon the economic principle of scarcity. If there is only a single source for a product, then consumers are at the mercy of that source. Thus, the source has ultimate control over the direction and price of that product. Open source software (of which Linux is the prime example) relies upon the economic principle of abundance. Which is to say, the more you share something, the more valuable it becomes. No one source has complete control over the direction or price of an open source product.

The Roots of Open Source

In the late '70s, Richard Stallman was one of the first programmers to assert the need for hackers to have free access to source code whenever they needed it. Stallman began to articulate the fact that software is different from physical resources, like oil or manpower. It is something that you can share while never reducing your own possessions.

In fact, just the opposite occurs. When you share your software as source code with other programmers and users, it enables them to debug, enhance, and modify your code. This creates an environment with an inherent positive feedback loop that accelerates growth as more sharing occurs. Such shared efforts are necessarily dynamic in nature and are thus quickly adaptable to any need. With the rapid rate of change that exists in high technology, such flexibility is a valuable asset. The founders of Sun Microsystems recognize this.

> "Speaking as someone who started the open systems idea (by the way the most criticized part of the SUN business plan), it seems like open source is the next logical evolution of offering each user or set of users just what they need and not everything everybody might want.
> "Change isn't an event anymore (version 2,3 . . .)—it's a process. Adaptability and evolution are far more important goals for systems, as opposed to the old goal of optimization (I could give you a whole dissertation on this). Open source and Linux have fortunately fallen into this new paradigm and are benefiting from rapid evolution, incremental changes, and modularity which also implies customization and personalization."

> — Vinod Khosla, founding CEO of Sun Microsystems, and a partner in the Venture Capital Firm of Kleiner, Perkins, Caufield, and Byer

Richard Stallman went on to found the Free Software Foundation (FSF) whose motto is "All software should be free." But what does that mean? According to them, "free software" is a matter of liberty, not price. To understand the concept, you should think of "free speech," not "free beer."

The FSF set as its goal to create an entire freely distributable operating environment, modeled after UNIX. The FSF's system would also be licensed under terms that made it impossible to redistribute any part of the system without supplying full source code with it. To highlight the differences between themselves and the commercial Unices, the FSF named their system GNU, which stands for "GNU's Not UNIX" (it's a recursive acronym). The license, which guarantees redistribution of source code, they named The GNU Public License, or GPL (it's also sometimes referred to as a "copyleft"). Software written under this license is often referred to as having been GPL'd.

Meanwhile, at the same time Stallman was working on GNU, another important example of openness based on the assumption of abundance was beginning to emerge. This was the ARPANET, which in the early '80s moved from being a Military R&D [research and development] project to an academic network of researchers funded by the National Science Foundation and called the Internet. The ARPANET developers dreamed of protocols that allowed for robust and unlimited communications. The protocols were described independently of the implementation and were made available to anyone who wanted them. An environment evolved that fostered interoperability and sharing at the hardware, software, and human levels.

Open consensus, and result-driven processes organically evolved into the Internet Engineering Task Force (found at http://www.ietf.org/tao.html). The IETF, which had no centralized authority, or legal foundation, nevertheless became the incubator within which the standards were grown. Interop became the forum where the interoperability between implementations and devices was tested, debugged and proven.

At each stage the "common wisdom" of the day said that it would be impossible to use the model of "rough consensus and running code" to make a system that would be robust and scalable. When AT&T was approached by ARPA [United States Advanced Research Project Agency] to implement the original network, the AT&T engineers told ARPA that they had already proven that packet switching would not work. The International Telecommunications Union (made up of the world's telephone monopolies) mocked the "unprofessionalism" of the IETF process and spent decades creating the OSI [open system interconnection] family of protocols which in the end was abandoned by most of the world in favor of the "unprofessional" but robust, scalable and ubiquitous Internet Protocols.

If you are familiar with the evolution of Linux, this may sound eerily familiar....

> "To me it [open source] is no different than ARPA funding developments, like TCP/IP, and granting them to the world at large. In the case of Linux the money/resources came from personal donations, instead of being washed by the goverment. People make money when they create something others want badly enough to buy it. Linux is not a charity case. It produces useful stuff or it vanishes.
>
> "Microsoft is a mechanism for creating, distributing and servicing software. It has been extremely successful. One could almost say it got started with free software. Didn't they pay something like 50K for Qdos? And they have done well for themselves and for the world. IBM sure as hell would not have made computing as pervasive as MS has done. And for the same reasons people were mad at IBM, people are mad at MS—they squelch innovation by virtue of their real monopoly. So something like Linux has a chance. But will it be squandered like UNIX was, due to loads of squabbling? Remains to be seen. Open interfaces promote diversity. Money is a great example of that. But money is rather sterile. Linux is more fecund."
>
> — Dan Lynch, founder of Interop and CyberCash, as well as private investor board member in several key Internet companies.

Interestingly enough, it was the intersection of the Internet and the GNU Free Software concepts that gave rise to Linux in the early '90s. Linus Torvalds, then a computer science student in Finland, got sick of not having an OS that he could explore, learn from and freely extend. So he put out some messages onto the Internet through the comp.os.minix newsgroup (Minix was an early, not quite free, not quite UNIX clone) and asked for input and help on creating a free OS....

This began a group collaboration via the Internet that grew into Linux. Linus recruited volunteer software developers from around the world to work on a GPL'd UNIX kernel clone. Others integrated the work being done with the

FSF's GNU software that neatly surrounded and supported the Linux kernel. The fact that all of this software was developed under the GPL was key to keeping the work done by all these volunteers in the public domain. The Internet, which has a complementary philosophy of open standards, acted as a medium to foster a distributed development team and an environment allowing thousands of developers and hundreds of thousands, if not millions, of testers and users to cooperate in ways never before seen.

> "The open source model of 'development at a distance' is a compelling solution to complexity management in software creation. It forces modularity, resulting in code that is generally more elegant, more secure, and more reliable than alternative techniques of software development."
>
> — Hal Varian, Dean of the School of Information Management
> and Systems at the University of California at Berkeley,
> and co-author, with Carl Shapiro, of *Information
> Rules* from Harvard Business School Press.

Not surprisingly, GNU, Linux and other Open Source projects have given back to the Internet in the form of many of the servers and services that make the Internet run. From the most popular web server on the Internet—Apache—to BIND (which is the software that allows the Internet's Domain Name System to work), to Sendmail, which moves and delivers the bulk of the Internet mail, open source software has become the backbone of the Internet. Most recently the GNU/Linux operating environment has emerged as an extremely robust, portable, and scalable platform for the next wave of open source software and services to be built upon.

[Recently], GNU/Linux and open source in general has emerged from universities, ISPs [Internet service providers], and programmer's workshops. It has achieved significant mindshare alongside commercial OSes. Besides its already dominant position as a platform for ISPs and business web servers, Linux has recently been injected into corporate enterprise networks. System administrators who had used the system for software development or other purposes quickly saw its flexibility and robustness, and were sick and tired of having to come in and reboot the Windows NT servers at all times of the day and night. Additionally, with the development of Samba (http://www.samba.org/), Linux became a better file and print server for Windows than Windows NT.

"Linux snuck in the back-door, and corporate IT [information technology] often doesn't know it's there," says Dan Kusnetzky, an analyst at International Data Corporation. At first management doesn't know that anything has changed except that their network is more reliable and performs higher. Eventually the system administrators get brave enough to show management what they've implemented, along with the dramatic cost savings that a Linux server delivers.

> "Compare the costs of a file and print server for a 25-person group using Linux or NT: NT Server has a street price of $809, including a license for five clients. Two more 10-client packs, at $1,129 apiece, brings the total to $3,067.
>
> "A copy of Linux from Red Hat—one of several companies that offer Linux support—costs $49.95, and the cost doesn't go up if clients have to

use the server. If you have a fast Internet connection, it doesn't cost you anything to download it. If you want to install the same copy of Linux on another server, or five other servers, or 50 other servers, it's the same price. And Linux lets you do the job with hardware that Microsoft and Intel have declared obsolete."

— Dan Kusnetzky

This brief history of Open Source software and Linux brings us to the present. Until recently, Open Source software kept a low profile. It was simply the stuff in the background that made the whole Internet work. Now, however, cheap computing power and widespread Internet access have created a huge grassroots movement around Open Source and Linux, accompanied by a surge in media recognition. Its widespread popularity has brought Linux into direct competition with a number of major commercial OS vendors.

The Beginning of the End of Closed Source as We Know It

With the US Department of Justice anti-trust court case underway, Microsoft has tried to paint Linux as a competitor, particularly in the more public forums (like the trial itself) as shown in this excerpt from the testimony of Paul Maritz, Sr. VP of Microsoft:

> "Linux is rapidly emerging as a major competitor to Windows. Indeed, the number of developers working on improving Linux vastly exceeds the number of Microsoft developers working on Windows NT."

But in the more private trade journals the story gets twisted back to the usual Microsoft PR message: "For IT personnel, the up-front cost of the operating system is a relatively minor component of the total cost of ownership of a system," a Microsoft spokesman said. "Microsoft sees Linux as a competitor, and we see that as good for the market," the spokesman said. But Linux competes more with other UNIX systems, the spokesman said. "It's unlikely someone would move from NT to Linux. It's more likely they'd move from an unexposed system to a Linux-based system."

Microsoft is the ultimate example of a company with too much invested in proprietary systems to seriously consider the open source model. Faced with this threat to its revenue stream, Microsoft has been carefully weighing its options vis-a-vis the open source movement and specifically Linux.

An internal Microsoft memo detailing their feelings on this subject was posted to the Internet on October 31, 1998 and for that reason is referred to as "the Halloween document." It can be found on the web at `http://www.opensource.org/halloween.html`. One of the most interesting points in the memo relates to Microsoft's inability to effectively respond to Linux. Because there is no single company for them to target and compete with, they are unsure of how to respond to this perceived threat.

Faced with this dilemma, they have been considering options ranging from creating fear, uncertainty, and doubt (FUD) around Linux in the marketplace to taking legal action against Linux and/or Open Source software, but it is unclear how they would execute such strategies. It is precisely these predatory tactics that have led to the government's aforementioned anti-trust suit.

No matter what the outcome of that case, it has already had a beneficial side effect for Open Source software. By tying Microsoft's hands in court, many of Microsoft's partners and customers have been granted enough breathing room to allow them to act without the fear of instant retaliation. Many of them (Intel, Dell, Compaq, IBM, etc.) have used this breathing room to embrace Linux.

"Linux threatens commercial operating systems and provides a model for freeware development. Previously confined to the fringe of the computer industry, Linux is breaking out, with a huge potential impact," says Tom Kucharvy an analyst for Summit Strategies. "Even if it does not capture the operating system market, Linux serves as a model for open source software and is thereby laying the seeds for a revolution in the software industry."

Hardware system vendors who only a few months ago would not even acknowledge an alternative to Windows 98 and NT are now trying to outdo each other with their Linux announcements. This will soon be mirrored by peripheral manufacturers: video cards, cameras, scanners, etc.

"Demand for applications and support for Linux is growing rapidly. Customers appreciate the ease and reliability of purchasing integrated Internet-based solutions through the Hewlett-Packard Covision program, and through our alliance with Red Hat, they will now have the flexibility to select solutions built on the Linux operating-system platform."

— Greg Mihran, head of Internet Business
Development for HP's Personal Systems Group.

All I Needed to Know I Learned from Open Source

One cannot overstate how important it is to the open source community not to repeat the mistakes made by Netscape Communications. They confronted Microsoft on Microsoft's home turf and lost their competitive edge by treading there. Netscape made its original giant leap ahead by creating a new paradigm in an area where Microsoft was not a powerful force. They were well on their way to creating a defendable new marketplace. By directly challenging Microsoft, Netscape stopped focusing on doing exciting new things, and instead focused first on competing with Microsoft and then with not getting steamrolled by it.

It is also important that we learn from the mistakes of the UNIX Wars of the '80s, where petty differences, arrogance, ignorance and greed stopped the first attempt at open systems and paved the way for mediocre monopolies to fill the void. Stop and think before you flame a KDE [K Desktop Environment] person if you're into GNOME [GNU Network Object Model Environment], or a BSDI [Berkeley Software Design, Inc.] guy if you're into Linux, or even a

Microsoft addict if you're into open source. "Religious" wars always lead to unnecessary conflict—much different than a healthy competition.

The positive approach for the open source community is to stay focused on creating and extending open source software. It is important that we continue to observe and learn what makes GNU/Linux and open source such a successful movement. We must also continue to study why the Internet continues to defy logic in growth, capabilities, reach and valuations, and how new technologies snowball and expand our horizons and possibilities. As more and more traditional software companies embrace open source, we must remember our roots. We must remember that the closed source model inspires both fear and scarcity, creating a vicious cycle that leaves everyone worse off. In contrast, the open source model inspires creativity, leading to accelerated growth and better products.

The problem for Microsoft, Sun and all the others is that people are beginning to discover this for themselves. No marketing campaign in the world can change that.

Titans Talk Tech: Bill G. and Michael D.

DERTOUZOS: It is ironic to me that in the United States, the bastion of capitalism, where people have given of their work lives and capital to create a huge industrial economy, we are now asked to surrender the very same factors of production—our labor and our capital—to develop software that will be open and free for all. I do see some qualified benefits to open software, but I wanted to get your views on the big picture before going any deeper.

GATES: Most of the people and companies that create intellectual property will continue to want to get some payment for it, as with any creative area. The beauty of all intellectual property compared to physical property is that there is no marginal cost of production. The world benefits immensely from this, whether it's from a great book or a new drug or a new piece of software. There are fixed costs, so most work will cost something, but for software sold on a high-volume low-price model the price is very small compared to the value.

There's always been a role for open-source software, and there always will be. Free software has been around for a long time. Likewise there is commercial software where the source is easy to access so the pricing and the source availability are two different things. Ideally, software should be componentized enough that you could extend it without having to read and rebuild the source code of the product.

For any software to gain widespread acceptance and use—to be popular with consumers and corporate customers—it has to possess the infrastructure and support that make it efficient and easy to deploy. So just as the car became popular only when there was a network of gas stations, repair shops, dealerships, paved roads and so on, the same is true for software and most other products.

The role of common standards in intellectual property is central here. Thanks to a common operating system standard—Windows—a whole industry got created, one that employs more than five million people worldwide. When both hardware companies and independent software vendors have a common standard to work with, the end result is enormous choice for consumers.

Open-source software's strength is massive customization but this works against consistency. Consumers don't know what to expect when they load the software; corporate customers find it hard to stay current as each version is customized; developers don't get a volume market because there are multiple flavors of the same product.

A lot of software that started out as university software—like browsers—transitioned to become commercial software when customers asked for rich features and broad support. In the case of browsers they stayed free because of the advertising value and additional demand for complementary products that they create.

DERTOUZOS: I agree with you that there is a role for all three—commercial, open, and free software—and add to the list another important benefit of open software: It accumulates for everyone's use code contributed by many programmers. But what of commercial software, that has the potential of becoming a standard for millions of people? To be used widely, it will be given away initially, and sold later when it has taken hold. In the long term, after the software has stabilized and returned its development cost and a good profit, software developers may find it increasingly difficult to charge for it. I suspect that such software, and maybe most software, will, after a commercial period, become very low-cost, and in some cases, even free. Do you think this is likely?

GATES: One of the key characteristics of the software industry is that, because of incredibly rapid technological change, products must be continuously modified to reflect innovations. For example, software will need to change to support speech input, which will be fantastic for users. So development costs are ongoing. With the high-volume, low-cost model adopted by Microsoft and the PC software industry, such costs are spread widely, so consumers pay a very low price to benefit from billions of dollars of R&D [research and development].

The key is in value and utility—if consumers get both, they will be willing to pay for them and, if the software is good enough, it will be used widely from the outset. So the world you are describing already exists: Consumers already get an amazing amount of functionality from their software at a very low cost. Contrast the old proprietary computing model, where software accounted for a high proportion of system cost, with the PC model, where software is only a tiny percentage of overall cost. That comparison makes much of today's PC software seem almost free.

DERTOUZOS: In the commercial period, when the software is still evolving, a successful strategy for maintaining revenue is, increasingly, the annual upgrade, which, incidentally, adds to the "feature shock" of users. This practice, together with an evolving Web, suggests that we'll move from buying shrink-wrapped software to simply buying upgrades through periodic downloads at a monthly fee. Do you see Microsoft and other software developers becoming such "service" organizations?

GATES: Regular upgrades are clearly necessary in an industry that is changing as fast as the software business—just as they are in, say, the auto industry. I can't ever imagine a time when software will not continue to evolve in this way. With the high-volume, low-cost model, you have to make the software as attractive as possible to as many computer users as possible, and that means lots of features. And clearly not all of them will be used by every buyer. But in general I think you are right that, in order to "hide" the complexity and adapt-ability of software from the average user, upgrades will increasingly be carried out transparently and automatically, without users having to do anything.

So rather than having to ensure that your software is always up-to-date, the software will do it for you—you'll wake up in the morning and the latest version of the software will have been installed overnight. To that extent, soft-ware will evolve into even more of a service business than it already is, and in the long term there will probably be a move toward a subscription-style model.

DERTOUZOS: Browsers and operating systems will merge in functionality, simply because people need to have the same commands for dealing with in-formation, regardless of whether it is local or distant. On this, you and I agree. However, we disagree on how to get there: I dream of a system built from scratch that gets rid of layers of old software and brings a new truly easy-to-use metaphor to the Web-centric world, as important as the desktop was earlier. I believe that you want to get there gradually, by upgrading Windows. Recall that the Web itself was created by a small team of people, yet ended up on mil-lions of computers. Could something like that happen here, with a new system that might spring out of nowhere? Would you consider replacing your own baby, ahead of a competitive threat, with a brand-new, simple, super-efficient browser-operating system?

GATES: Whenever a new word is added to a computer language or a new feature to an operating system there is a question of whether it would be better to start from scratch. We actually did start from scratch with Windows NT and I am sure we will do so again. In the meantime, we are evolving every version of our operating system. We have made the browser and HTML the primary display language, replacing the old style help and folder display. There are new operating systems that integrate the browser like BeOS but none have done as much as Windows has.

For every new advance there will be many new competitors, including people who compete with a whole new operating system and people who com-pete using middleware to run on top of the operating system. If we do our job well, giving people the new capabilities and compatibility, we can make a big contribution.

With Windows running on well over 200 million computers worldwide, we constantly think about the customer base and how we get them from here to there. A lot of the "layers of old software" you refer to do get eliminated—we're constantly stripping out redundant code or replacing it with faster ways of doing what the old code did.

DERTOUZOS: The millions of users of all operating systems and browsers, worldwide, appreciate the need for system stability. Yet the incremental changes that have ensured it have also led to today's difficult-to-use systems—and I mean the systems of all software developers, without exception. Novices and experts alike kneel (I sometimes even cry) as we try to fend off a tangle of intertwined lizards and thousands of moving parts within these systems and the many ap-plications that use them—until we luck in on a fix. We'll have to clean up this mess if we are to provide the true ease of use that will enable people to achieve the 300 percent productivity gains we envision in the 21st century. People will have to rise above battling low-level details, to access the knowledge they need, collaborate with others, customize their systems to their own human needs and automate their own repetitive tasks. I think the time has come to bridge local and distant computation and support these much-needed capabilities in a new breed of system; applications will then be freed up to use all this new power in medicine, education, business, recreation, commerce and so on. I can't see us getting there incrementally.

GATES: The danger here is that we may simply dismiss the progress that the computer software and hardware industries have already made. Twenty years ago nobody used a computer unless they were a hobbyist or employed by a corporate IT [information technology] department. Now, even a child can use a PC to carry out computing tasks that were actually beyond the capabilities of those 1970s IT departments. We've already seen huge gains in productivity as a result of the PC, and enormous strides in education, medicine, recreation and commerce. Four years ago you couldn't buy a book online; now you can buy almost anything online. And the gulf between remote and local computers is already being bridged, both by the Web and by other networking technologies. Clearly, we're only at the start of the Digital Age, and our future progress will undoubtedly dwarf our past achievements. But we shouldn't underestimate how far we've already come.

We also shouldn't underestimate how much work remains to be done. Simplicity is a key goal, but it's a constantly moving target. Both hardware and software are constantly becoming ever more sophisticated, we want to add more and different types of devices to our computers, and we want all this to work perfectly and easily—and be simple to upgrade too. Plus we're trying to drive computer usage toward less-technical consumers—deep into the mass market. And that's a huge challenge for the industry, but one we undoubtedly have to meet if we are to drive future growth.

DERTOUZOS: The Agrarian Revolution with its plow, the Industrial Revolution with its steam engine and the Information Revolution with its computer have all improved our economic lives. Maybe the time has come for a new revolution, not about things, but about the most precious resource on this planet—ourselves? What role and purpose do you see for human beings in the Information Age?

GATES: I'm very optimistic about the role of human beings in the Information Age, because this is an era where people—their knowledge, and their ability to put that knowledge to work—will be more important than ever before. There are great dangers to thinking that just because manual labor—whether on the land or in factories—is playing a relatively smaller role in wealth creation, then people are also playing a smaller role. In fact, the Information Age is enabling people who were previously forced to pursue a single means of wealth creation —those, for example, who lived in remote areas had no option but to work on the land—to choose from a far wider range of work. Technology such as the PC, the Internet and cheap telecommunications have brought amazing mobility to the factors of production.

The Information Age has brought people together in even more fundamental ways. The increasing speed and flow of information has opened up closed economies and helped democratize the most repressive regimes. You can close geographic borders but you can't build effective borders in cyberspace. So technology is giving people more freedom, and the power to do more with that freedom. And technology will never replace the wonders of human interaction —no matter how good PCs get at recognizing voice or handwriting, they'll never read body language or smile back at you.

DERTOUZOS: I fully share your views and optimism on human beings and the future uses of the technologies we are developing. However, I am concerned about a split that started 300 years ago in the Enlightenment that busted up faith and reason, man and nature, which until that time were united. The liberation of reason caused science to blossom and led to the Industrial Revolution, which made our part of the world wealthy. By now, this split has taken hold, and each of us goes through life in a compartment, labeled technologist or humanist, rational or spiritual, logical or emotional. I don't see the Information Revolution curing this split. It may even aggravate it by increasing our reliance on virtual encounters and machine knowledge. Meanwhile, the world around us is becoming explosively complex with a myriad of intertwined challenges and problems that straddle these divisions and cannot be handled with such partial mindsets. To cope with this new world, but also to enrich ourselves, I believe we need to unite our divided selves and try to become whole again. That's what I mean by a fourth revolution aimed at understanding, beyond things, ourselves. Any thoughts along these lines?

GATES: If the Information Revolution did lead to a reliance on virtual encounters and machine knowledge, then I would agree with you. In reality, though, the computer is increasingly a gateway to knowledge, to the arts, to new cultures, and so on, that were simply not accessible before. It is creating communities that, far from being mere virtual entities, serve as the foundation for real relationships. So to the extent that the computer can link people with knowledge and cultures and each other more efficiently than any other past technology, it can help push them toward healing the rift you see. But technology is only a tool—and, like all tools, its effectiveness depends on the skill and intentions of the user. In the end, you have to put your faith in human nature. If you think the invention of the book was bad, then you will feel the same way about the changes that are coming. If the book was a good thing, then these advances carry the empowerment even further.

DERTOUZOS: I agree with you on this last point: The angels and the devils are definitely within us, not within the machines we use. And so are our divided selves. That's why I view this as a human problem in need of a human revolution. Speaking of human problems, I believe that left to its own devices, the new world of information will increase the gap between rich and poor people, simply because computers make the rich more productive and hence richer, while the poor are standing still. Do you agree?

GATES: The power of cheap software and cheap computing has brought enormous economic power to millions of people who in the past lacked it. It has helped democratize nations and economies around the world. It is bringing about the death of distance, as high-speed telecommunications link people, companies and countries faster and cheaper than ever before. And while this Information Revolution hasn't yet reached deeply into the poorest regions of the world, it will—look at what is happening in India and China, for example. The Industrial Age did in many ways bypass poorer countries; the Information Age actually gives those countries a chance to compete on equal footing with richer countries. In fact many of the poorer countries have a comparative advantage in that they can now leverage their cheaper labor around the world—not just locally—using the power of the PC, the Internet and cheap telecommunications. The poor are not standing still; they are catching up faster than they ever did in the Industrial Age.

DERTOUZOS: I share the view that the poor could rise out of poverty, by using the new world of information to learn how to read and write, take care of their health, cultivate the land, and acquire language and other skills that they may use to sell services in the information marketplace. However, for this to happen, the poor will need communications, workstations and training—all of which cost a great deal, and therefore cannot materialize spontaneously. The people you allude to, in Bangalore and elsewhere, who deliver software services over the Net, speak English and know how to program. They are but a drop in the ocean of six billion people on Earth, barely 2 percent of whom are interconnected. My point is that all the benefits that we envision will not become available to the poor if we leave the Information Revolution to its own devices. We need to take an active role as individuals, companies and governments of the industrially rich world to help the poor ascend along this path. How can you disagree, in light of all you have done along these lines?

GATES: Unfortunately, the benefits of every new technology tend to trickle down slowly. Even the earliest tools of the communications revolution—the auto, the airplane, the telephone—have yet to benefit some poorer parts of the world. But what will clearly help the spread of information technology is the amazing speed at which computing costs have dropped, along with information technology's ability to break down borders. We're already seeing examples of how cheap PCs can transform companies and government agencies in poorer countries, and the benefits of these changes feed directly to the population. But generally, you are right: companies and individuals in rich countries will have to contribute technology and cash to kick-start a truly global Information Revolution.

　　I am a big believer in philanthropy, and I'm excited about the impact it can have. I think it is also important to consider priorities. I have chosen to focus on making sure that children in poor countries get access to vaccines so they can live a healthy life. This has to come before making sure they have access to computers. I have put more than $6 billion into my two foundations because of my enthusiasm for taking the great advances in medicine and information technology and giving more people access. We can do some great things here.

DERTOUZOS: I wish other people and organizations would follow your philanthropic lead. And thanks for this enjoyable and informative discussion.

POSTSCRIPT

Is Microsoft's Dominance of the Personal Computer Market About to End?

In June 1999 Linux hit two significant milestones. The magazine *PC World* gave Linux its "Most Promising Software Newcomer" award for 1999, and Red Hat, a company that offers Linux as a free download via the Internet or, for a price, as a package with instructions and technical support, announced that it would soon offer the public $96.6 million worth of stock shares. So far, computer companies IBM, Intel, Netscape, and Oracle have invested money in Red Hat, and analysts say that this stock offering is only the first of many for Linux-related companies.

Should Microsoft be worried? In March 1999, Microsoft executive Ed Muth told *PC Week Online* that Linux had fundamental flaws and had little chance of satisfying PC users. However, in the "Halloween memo" mentioned by Berger (http://www.fr.debian.org/OpenSource/halloween.html), Vinod Valloppillil, a Microsoft engineer who analyzes the competition, had already said that OSS "poses a direct, short-term revenue and platform threat to Microsoft.... The intrinsic parallelism and free idea exchange in OSS has benefits that are not replicable with our current licensing model.... OSS is long-term credible.... Linux and other OSS advocates are making a progressively more credible argument that OSS software is at least as robust—if not more—than commercial alternatives.... Linux has been deployed in mission critical, commercial environments with an excellent pool of public testimonials.... The ability of the OSS process to collect and harness the collective IQ of thousands of individuals across the Internet is simply amazing. More importantly, OSS evangelization scales with the size of the Internet much faster than our own evangelization efforts appear to scale."

At its federal antitrust trial, Microsoft has called witnesses to claim that Linux is a strong competitor, but a Justice Department witness has called such claims self-serving and irrelevant. According to the June 4 *Newsbytes*, "Massachusetts Institute of Technology Professor Franklin M. Fisher argued that the growing popularity of the Linux operating system... would have little impact on Microsoft's monopoly in the PC operating system market. He called Linux 'a niche operating system.'... Fisher said the reason he believes Linux will not be a significant competitor to Windows in the foreseeable future is that there are not very many consumer software programs that run on Linux."

Yet there was a time when one could say the same thing about Windows. But the GNOME (GNU Network Object Model Environment) graphical (desktop) interface for Linux is available, with simple word processor, database, and spreadsheet programs; see Charles C. Mann, "Programs to the People," *Technology Review* (January/February 1999). Corel is already marketing WordPerfect for Linux (`http://linux.corel.com/linux8/index.htm`) and promising Linux versions of the other components of its office suite. The number of other consumer applications that run under Linux is growing rapidly. There are even "emulator" programs that permit one to run Windows programs. See `http://www.ssc.com/linux/apps/index.html`.

Should Microsoft be worried? The personal computer industry is only three decades old, but in that short time it has seen many companies die, hardware disappear (Has anyone seen an external hard drive lately? a 5.25" floppy disk? a daisywheel printer?), and software vanish (Electric Pencil, AllWrite, and XyWrite were once popular word processors.) Rapid, drastic change is so normal in the industry that it seems foolish for anyone, even a Bill Gates, to feel complacent.

Microsoft is not in trouble yet, but Linux is getting a lot of attention and growing very rapidly. Indeed, David Bollier, in *The Power of Openness: Why Citizens, Education, Government and Business Should Care about the Coming Revolution in Open Source Code Software* (Berkman Center for Internet and Society, `http://cyber.law.harvard.edu` [March 10, 1999]), says it amounts to "a growing grassroots movement on a global scale [that] is challenging proprietary models of software development by generating superior, more reliable software that is far cheaper and even free. The implications are not just technical but economic, political and cultural."

ISSUE 13

Are Computers Hazardous to Literacy?

YES: Sven Birkerts, from *The Gutenberg Elegies: The Fate of Reading in an Electronic Age* (Faber & Faber, 1994)

NO: Wen Stephenson, from "The Message Is the Medium: A Reply to Sven Birkerts and *The Gutenberg Elegies*," *Chicago Review* (Winter 1995–1996)

ISSUE SUMMARY

YES: Author Sven Birkerts argues that electronically presented information (i.e., via computer screens) threatens traditional conceptions of literacy, the literary culture, and the sense of ourselves as individuals.

NO: Wen Stephenson, editor of the *Atlantic Monthly*'s online edition, argues that the essence of literature, literacy, and the literary culture will survive the impact of computers.

When personal computers first came on the market in the 1970s, they were considered useful tools, but their memory was limited to only a few thousand bytes, hard drives were expensive add-ons, and the Internet was a distant dream (though something similar was already connecting university and government mainframe computers). By the 1980s some people had begun to realize that computer disks could hold as much information as a book, were smaller, took less postage to mail, and could be recycled. By this time Project Gutenberg, founded in 1971 by Michael Hart at the University of Illinois, had already been converting works of classic literature into digital form and making them available on disk for a number of years. By 1990 several small companies—including Soft Press, Serendipity Systems, and High Mesa Publishing—were trying to turn this insight into profitable businesses. All are now gone.

The approach failed partly because people seemed to find paper books more congenial for reading than computer screens. But then the Internet came along, and the early 1990s saw an explosion of activity exploiting this new ability to put information of all kinds—including poetry, fiction, and nonfiction of precisely the sort one used to find only on paper—onto "Web pages" that Internet users could access for free. Digital publishing boomed and companies such as Mind's Eye Fiction (http://tale.com) now sell their wares to be downloaded via the Internet. This is not the first time that the nature of publishing has changed. Five centuries ago the printing press greatly increased the availability of books, including Bibles, and contributed to the Protestant Reformation and the American and French Revolutions. See Rudi Volti, *Society and Technological Change*, 3rd ed. (St. Martin's Press, 1995), chapter 11. The printing press also utterly destroyed the primacy of the scroll and delivered the first hard blow to literacy as a distinguishing characteristic of the social elite. There were, of course, protests aimed at the way this new technology was threatening handwritten text and undermining the social order.

In the twentieth century, the invention of cheap paper ("pulp") made possible a profusion of magazines (the "pulps") and cheap novels ("dime novels") that made reading for entertainment and information accessible to vast numbers of people and did a great deal to create the modern publishing industry. It also led to loud cries of protest because the greatly increased demand for material meant that "literary quality" suffered; today, *pulp literature* is still a term of derision. Many of the protests came from those who felt that the pulps were dealing a final blow to literacy as a distinguishing characteristic of a social elite.

More recently, radio and television seemed to be restoring a kind of balance by drawing many people away from reading. Among the first to decry that change were Marshall McLuhan and Quentin Fiore, in *The Medium Is the Message* (Random House, 1967). And now we have the computer and the Internet, which promise to replace the traditional linear absorption of information—as in scrolls, books, radio and TV programs, and even storytellers—with an ever-branching web of interconnections often referred to as "hypertext" (indeed, Web pages are written in a special computer programming language known as "hypertext mark-up language," or "html").

A great many people think that the Internet and the vastly increased access to information of all sorts that it provides is an astonishing gift. Some, however, object to the way it seems to threaten the old order of things. In the following selections, Sven Birkerts argues that computer-presented information threatens traditional conceptions of literacy, the literary culture, and the sense of ourselves as individuals, among other things. Wen Stephenson, on the other hand, argues that the essence of literature, literacy, and the literary culture will survive the impact of the computer, just as it did the advent of the pulps, radio, and television.

Into the Electronic Millenium

Think of it. Fifty to a hundred million people (maybe a conservative esti-mate) form their ideas about what is going on in America and in the world from the same basic package of edited images—to the extent that the image it-self has lost much of its once-fearsome power. Daily newspapers, with their long columns of print, struggle against declining sales. Fewer and fewer people un-der the age of fifty read them; computers will soon make packaged information a custom product. But if the printed sheet is heading for obsolescence, people are tuning in to the signals. The screen is where the information and entertain-ment wars will be fought. The communications conglomerates are waging bitter takeover battles in their zeal to establish global empires. As Jonathan Crary has written in "The Eclipse of the Spectacle," "Telecommunications is the new ar-terial network, analogous in part to what railroads were for capitalism in the nineteenth century. And it is this electronic substitute for geography that cor-porate and national entities are now carving up." Maybe one reason why the news of change is not part of the common currency is that such news can only sensibly be communicated through the more analytic sequences of print.

To underscore my point, I have been making it sound as if we were all abruptly walking out of one room and into another, leaving our books to the moths while we settle ourselves in front of our state-of-the-art terminals. The truth is that we are living through a period of overlap; one way of being is pushed athwart another. Antonio Gramsci's often-cited sentence comes in-evitably to mind: "The crisis consists precisely in the fact that the old is dying and the new cannot be born; in this interregnum a great variety of morbid symptoms appears." The old surely is dying, but I'm not so sure that the new is having any great difficulty being born. As for the morbid symptoms, these we have in abundance.

The overlap in communications modes, and the ways of living that they are associated with, invites comparison with the transitional epoch in ancient Greek society, certainly in terms of the relative degree of disturbance. Historian Eric Havelock designated that period as one of "proto-literacy," of which his fellow scholar Oswyn Murray has written:

> To him [Havelock] the basic shift from oral to literate culture was a slow process; for centuries, despite the existence of writing, Greece remained

essentially an oral culture. This culture was one which depended heavily on the encoding of information in poetic texts, to be learned by rote and to provide a cultural encyclopedia of conduct. It was not until the age of Plato in the fourth century that the dominance of poetry in an oral culture was challenged in the final triumph of literacy.

That challenge came in the form of philosophy, among other things, and poetry has never recovered its cultural primacy. What oral poetry was for the Greeks, printed books in general are for us. But our historical moment, which we might call "proto-electronic," will not require a transition period of two centuries. The very essence of electronic transmissions is to surmount impedances and to hasten transitions. Fifty years, I'm sure, will suffice. As for what the conversion will bring—and mean—to us, we might glean a few clues by looking to some of the "morbid symptoms" of the change. But to understand what these portend, we need to remark a few of the more obvious ways in which our various technologies condition our senses and sensibilities.

I won't tire my reader with an extended rehash of the differences between the print orientation and that of electronic systems. Media theorists from Marshall McLuhan to Walter Ong to Neil Postman have discoursed upon these at length. What's more, they are reasonably commonsensical. I therefore will abbreviate.

The order of print is linear, and is bound to logic by the imperatives of syntax. Syntax is the substructure of discourse, a mapping of the ways that the mind makes sense through language. Print communication requires the active engagement of the reader's attention, for reading is fundamentally an act of translation. Symbols are turned into their verbal referents and these are in turn interpreted. The print engagement is essentially private. While it does represent an act of communication, the contents pass from the privacy of the sender to the privacy of the receiver. Print also posits a time axis; the turning of pages, not to mention the vertical descent down the page, is a forward-moving succession, with earlier contents at every point serving as a ground for what follows. Moreover, the printed material is static—it is the reader, not the book, that moves forward. The physical arrangements of print are in accord with our traditional sense of history. Materials are layered; they lend themselves to rereading and to sustained attention. The pace of reading is variable, with progress determined by the reader's focus and comprehension.

The electronic order is in most ways opposite. Information and contents do not simply move from one private space to another, but they travel along a network. Engagement is intrinsically public, taking place within a circuit of larger connectedness. The vast resources of the network are always there, potential, even if they do not impinge on the immediate communication. Electronic communication can be passive, as with television watching, or interactive, as with computers. Contents, unless they are printed out (at which point they become part of the static order of print) are felt to be evanescent. They can be changed or deleted with the stroke of a key. With visual media (television, projected graphs, highlighted "bullets") impression and image take precedence over logic and concept, and detail and linear sequentiality are sacrificed. The pace is rapid, driven by jump-cut increments, and the basic movement is laterally associative rather than vertically cumulative. The presentation structures the reception and, in time, the expectation about how information is organized.

Further, the visual and nonvisual technology in every way encourages in the user a heightened and ever-changing awareness of the present. It works against historical perception, which must depend on the inimical notions of logic and sequential succession. If the print medium exalts the word, fixing it into permanence, the electronic counterpart reduces it to a signal, a means to an end.

Transitions like the one from print to electronic media do not take place without rippling or, more likely, reweaving the entire social and cultural web. The tendencies outlined above are already at work. We don't need to look far to find their effects. We can begin with the newspaper headlines and the millennial lamentations sounded in the op-ed pages: that our educational systems are in decline, that our students are less and less able to read and comprehend their required texts, and that their aptitude scores have leveled off well below those of previous generations. Tag-line communication, called "bite-speak" by some, is destroying the last remnants of political discourse; spin doctors and media consultants are our new shamans. As communications empires fight for control of all information outlets, including publishers, the latter have succumbed to the tyranny of the bottom line; they are less and less willing to publish work, however worthy, that will not make a tidy profit. And, on every front, funding for the arts is being cut while the arts themselves appear to be suffering a deep crisis of relevance. And so on.

Every one of these developments is, of course, overdetermined, but there can be no doubt that they are connected, perhaps profoundly, to the transition that is underway.

Certain other trends bear watching. One could argue, for instance, that the entire movement of postmodernism in the arts is a consequence of this same macroscopic shift. For what is postmodernism at root but an aesthetic that rebukes the idea of an historical time line, as well as previously uncontested assumptions of cultural hierarchy. The postmodern artifact manipulates its stylistic signatures like Lego blocks and makes free with combinations from the formerly sequestered spheres of high and popular art. Its combinatory momentum and relentless referencing of the surrounding culture mirror perfectly the associative dynamics of electronic media.

One might argue likewise, that the virulent debate within academia over the canon and multiculturalism may not be a simple struggle between the entrenched ideologies of white male elites and the forces of formerly disenfranchised gender, racial, and cultural groups. Many of those who would revise the canon (or end it altogether) are trying to outflank the assumption of historical tradition itself. The underlying question, avoided by many, may be not only whether the tradition is relevant, but whether it might not be too taxing a system for students to comprehend. Both the traditionalists and the progressives have valid arguments, and we must certainly have sympathy for those who would try to expose and eradicate the hidden assumptions of bias in the Western tradition. But it also seems clear that this debate could only have taken the form it has in a society that has begun to come loose from its textual moorings. To challenge repression is salutary. To challenge history itself, proclaiming it to be simply an archive of repressions and justifications, is idiotic.

Then there are the more specific sorts of developments. Consider the multibillion-dollar initiative by Whittle Communications to bring commercially sponsored education packages into the classroom. The underlying premise is staggeringly simple: If electronic media are the one thing that the young are at ease with, why not exploit the fact? Why not stop bucking television and use it instead, with corporate America picking up the tab in exchange for a few minutes of valuable airtime for commercials? As the *Boston Globe* reports:

> Here's how it would work:
>
> Participating schools would receive, free of charge, $50,000 worth of electronic paraphernalia, including a satellite dish and classroom video monitors. In return, the schools would agree to air the show.
>
> The show would resemble a network news program, but with 18- to 24-year old anchors.
>
> A prototype includes a report on a United Nations Security Council meeting on terrorism, a space shuttle update, a U2 music video tribute to Martin Luther King, a feature on the environment, a "fast fact" ('Arachibutyrophobia is the fear of peanut butter sticking to the roof of your mouth') and two minutes of commercial advertising.

"You have to remember that the children of today have grown up with the visual media," said Robert Calabrese [Billerica School Superintendent]. "They know no other way and we're simply capitalizing on that to enhance learning."

Calabrese's observation on the preconditioning of a whole generation of students raises troubling questions: Should we suppose that American education will begin to tailor itself to the aptitudes of its students, presenting more and more of its materials in newly packaged forms? And what will happen when educators find that not very many of the old materials will "play"—that is, capture student enthusiasm? Is the what of learning to be determined by the how? And at what point do vicious cycles begin to reveal their viciousness?

A collective change of sensibility may already be upon us. We need to take seriously the possibility that the young truly "know no other way," that they are not made of the same stuff that their elders are. In her *Harper's* magazine debate with Neil Postman, Camille Paglia observed:

> Some people have more developed sensoriums than others. I've found that most people born before World War II are turned off by the modern media. They can't understand how we who were born after the war can read and watch TV at the same time. But we can. When I wrote my book, I had earphones on, blasting rock music or Puccini and Brahms. The soap operas—with the sound turned down—flickered on my TV. I'd be talking on the phone at the same time. Baby boomers have a multilayered, multitrack ability to deal with the world.

I don't know whether to be impressed or depressed by Paglia's ability to disperse her focus in so many directions. Nor can I say, not having read her book, in what ways her multitrack sensibility has informed her prose. But I'm baffled by what she means when she talks about an ability to "deal with the world." From the context, "dealing" sounds more like a matter of incessantly repositioning the self within a barrage of onrushing stimuli.

Paglia's is hardly the only testimony in this matter. A *New York Times* article on the cult success of Mark Leyner (author of *I Smell Esther Williams* and *My Cousin, My Gastroenterologist*) reports suggestively:

> His fans say, variously, that his writing is like MTV, or rap music, or rock music, or simply like everything in the world put together: fast and furious and intense, full of illusion and allusion and fantasy and science and excrement.

Larry McCaffery, a professor of literature at San Diego State University and co-editor of *Fiction International,* a literary journal, said his students get excited about Mr. Leyner's writing, which he considers important and unique: "It speaks to them, somehow, about this weird milieu they're swimming through. It's this dissolving, discontinuous world." While older people might find Mr. Leyner's world bizarre or unreal, Professor McCaffery said, it doesn't seem so to people who grew up with Walkmen and computers and VCR's, with so many choices, so much bombardment, that they have never experienced a sensation singly.

The article continues:

> There is no traditional narrative, although the book is called a novel. And there is much use of facts, though it is called fiction. Seldom does the end of a sentence have any obvious relation to the beginning. "You don't know where you're going, but you don't mind taking the leap," said R. J. Cutler, the producer of "Heat," who invited Mr. Leyner to be on the show after he picked up the galleys of his book and found it mesmerizing. "He taps into a specific cultural perspective where thoughtful literary world view meets pop culture and the TV generation."

My final exhibit—I don't know if it qualifies as a morbid symptom as such —is drawn from a *Washington Post Magazine* essay on the future of the Library of Congress, our national shrine to the printed word. One of the individuals interviewed in the piece is Robert Zich, so-called "special projects czar" of the institution. Zich, too, has seen the future, and he is surprisingly candid with his interlocutor. Before long, Zich maintains, people will be able to get what information they want directly off their terminals. The function of the Library of Congress (and perhaps libraries in general) will change. He envisions his library becoming more like a museum: "Just as you go to the National Gallery to see its Leonardo or go to the Smithsonian to see the Spirit of St. Louis and so on, you will want to go to libraries to see the Gutenberg or the original printing of Shakespeare's plays or to see Lincoln's hand-written version of the Gettysburg Address."

Zich is outspoken, voicing what other administrators must be thinking privately. The big research libraries, he says, "and the great national libraries and their buildings will go the way of the railroad stations and the movie palaces of an earlier era which were really vital institutions in their time... Somehow folks moved away from that when the technology changed."

And books? Zich expresses excitement about Sony's hand-held electronic book, and a miniature encyclopedia coming from Franklin Electronic Publishers. "Slip it in your pocket," he says. "Little keyboard, punch in your words and it will do the full text searching and all the rest of it. Its limitation, of course, is that it's devoted just to that one book." Zich is likewise interested in the possibility of memory cards. What he likes about the Sony product is the portability: one machine, a screen that will display the contents of whatever electronic card you feed it.

I cite Zich's views at some length here because he is not some Silicon Valley research and development visionary, but a highly placed executive at what might be called, in a very literal sense, our most conservative public institution. When men like Zich embrace the electronic future, we can be sure it's well on its way.

Others might argue that the technologies cited by Zich merely represent a modification in the "form" of reading, and that reading itself will be unaffected, as there is little difference between following words on a pocket screen or a printed page. Here I have to hold my line. The context cannot but condition the process. Screen and book may exhibit the same string of words, but the assumptions that underlie their significance are entirely different depending on whether we are staring at a book or a circuit-generated text. As the nature of looking—at the natural world, at paintings—changed with the arrival of photography and mechanical reproduction, so will the collective relation to language alter as new modes of dissemination prevail.

Whether all of this sounds dire or merely "different" will depend upon the reader's own values and priorities. I find these portents of change depressing, but also exhilarating—at least to speculate about. On the one hand, I have a great feeling of loss and a fear about what habitations will exist for self and soul in the future. But there is also a quickening, a sense that important things are on the line. As Heraclitus once observed, "The mixture that is not shaken soon stagnates." Well, the mixture is being shaken, no doubt about it. And here are some of the kinds of developments we might watch for as our "proto-electronic" era yields to an all-electronic future:

1. Language Erosion.   There is no question but that the transition from the culture of the book to the culture of electronic communication will radically alter the ways in which we use language on every societal level. The complexity and distinctiveness of spoken and written expression, which are deeply bound to traditions of print literacy, will gradually be replaced by a more telegraphic sort of "plainspeak." Syntactic masonry is already a dying art. Neil Postman and others have already suggested what losses have been incurred by the advent of telegraphy and television—how the complex discourse patterns of the nineteenth century were flattened by the requirements of communication over distances. That tendency runs riot as the layers of mediation thicken. Simple linguistic prefab is now the norm, while ambiguity, paradox, irony, subtlety, and wit are fast disappearing. In their place, the simple "vision thing" and myriad other "things." Verbal intelligence, which has long been viewed as suspect as the act of reading, will come to seem positively conspiratorial. The greater part of any articulate person's energy will be deployed in dumbing-down her discourse.

Language will grow increasingly impoverished through a series of vicious cycles. For, of course, the usages of literature and scholarship are connected in fundamental ways to the general speech of the tribe. We can expect that curricula will be further streamlined, and difficult texts in the humanities will be pruned and glossed. One need only compare a college textbook from twenty years ago to its contemporary version. A poem by Milton, a play by Shakespeare —one can hardly find the text among the explanatory notes nowadays. Fewer and fewer people will be able to contend with the so-called masterworks of literature or ideas. Joyce, Woolf, Soyinka, not to mention the masters who preceded them, will go unread, and the civilizing energies of their prose will circulate aimlessly between closed covers.

2. Flattening of Historical Perspectives.   As the circuit supplants the printed page, and as more and more of our communications involve us in network processes —which of their nature plant us in a perpetual present—our perception of history will inevitably alter. Changes in information storage and access are bound to impinge on our historical memory. The depth of field that is our sense of the past is not only a linguistic construct, but is in some essential way represented by the book and the physical accumulation of books in library spaces. In the contemplation of the single volume, or mass of volumes, we form a picture of time past as a growing deposit of sediment; we capture a sense of its depth and dimensionality. Moreover, we meet the past as much in the presentation of words in books of specific vintage as we do in any isolated fact or statistic. The database, useful as it is, expunges this context, this sense of chronology, and admits us to a weightless order in which all information is equally accessible.

If we take the etymological tack, history (cognate with "story") is affiliated in complex ways with its texts. Once the materials of the past are unhoused from their pages, they will surely mean differently. The printed page is itself a link, at least along the imaginative continuum, and when that link is broken, the past can only start to recede. At the same time it will become a body of disjunct data available for retrieval and, in the hands of our canny dream merchants, a mythology. The more we grow rooted in the consciousness of the now, the more it will seem utterly extraordinary that things were ever any different. The idea of a farmer plowing a field—an historical constant for millennia—will be something for a theme park. For, naturally, the entertainment industry, which reads the collective unconscious unerringly, will seize the advantage. The past that has slipped away will be rendered ever more glorious, ever more a fantasy play with heroes, villains, and quaint settings and props. Small-town American life returns as "Andy of Mayberry"—at first enjoyed with recognition, later accepted as a faithful portrait of how things used to be.

3. The Waning of the Private Self. We may even now be in the first stages of a process of social collectivization that will over time all but vanquish the ideal of the isolated individual. For some decades now we have been edging away from the perception of private life as something opaque, closed off to the world; we increasingly accept the transparency of a life lived within a set of systems, electronic or otherwise. Our technologies are not bound by season or light— it's always the same time in the circuit. And so long as time is money and money matters, those circuits will keep humming. The doors and walls of our habitations matter less and less—the world sweeps through the wires as it needs to, or as we need it to. The monitor light is always blinking; we are always potentially on-line.

I am not suggesting that we are all about to become mindless, soulless robots, or that personality will disappear altogether into an oceanic homo- geneity. But certainly the idea of what it means to be a person living a life will be much changed. The figure-ground model, which has always featured a solitary self before a background that is the society of other selves, is romantic in the extreme. It is ever less tenable in the world as it is becoming. There are no more wildernesses, no more lonely homesteads, and, outside of cinema, no more emblems of the exalted individual.

The self must change as the nature of subjective space changes. And one of the many incremental transformations of our age has been the slow but steady destruction of subjective space. The physical and psychological distance be- tween individuals has been shrinking for at least a century. In the process, the figure-ground image has begun to blur its boundary distinctions. One day we will conduct our public and private lives within networks so dense, among so many channels of instantaneous information, that it will make almost no sense to speak of the differentiations of subjective individualism.

We are already captive in our webs. Our slight solitudes are transected by codes, wires, and pulsations. We punch a number to check in with the an- swering machine, another to tape a show that we are too busy to watch. The strands of the web grow finer and finer—this is obvious. What is no less obvi- ous is the fact that they will continue to proliferate, gaining in sophistication, merging functions so that one can bank by phone, shop via television, and so on. The natural tendency is toward streamlining: The smart dollar keeps finding ways to shorten the path, double-up the function. We might think in terms of a circuit-board model, picturing ourselves as the contact points. The expansion of electronic options is always at the cost of contractions in the private sphere. We will soon be navigating with ease among cataracts of organized pulsations, putting out and taking in signals. We will bring our terminals, our modems, and menus further and further into our former privacies; we will implicate our- selves by degrees in the unitary life, and there may come a day when we no longer remember that there was any other life.

While I was brewing these somewhat melancholy thoughts, I chanced to read in an old *New Republic* the text of Joseph Brodsky's 1987 Nobel Prize accep- tance speech. I felt as though I had opened a door leading to the great vault of the nineteenth century. The poet's passionate plea on behalf of the book at once corroborated and countered everything I had been thinking. What he upheld in faith were the very ideals I was saying good-bye to. I greeted his words with an agitated skepticism, fashioning from them something more like a valediction. Here are four passages:

> If art teaches anything ... it is the privateness of the human condition. Being the most ancient as well as the most literal form of private enterprise, it fosters in a man, knowingly or unwittingly, a sense of his uniqueness, of individuality, of separateness—thus turning him from a social animal into an autonomous "I."

> The great Baratynsky, speaking of his Muse, characterized her as possessing an "uncommon visage." It's in acquiring this "uncommon visage" that the meaning of human existence seems to lie, since for this uncommonness we are, as it were, prepared genetically.

> Aesthetic choice is a highly individual matter, and aesthetic experience is always a private one. Every new aesthetic reality makes one's experience even more private; and this kind of privacy, assuming at times the guise of literary (or some other) taste, can in itself turn out to be, if not a guarantee, then a form of defense, against enslavement.

> In the history of our species, in the history of Homo sapiens, the book is an anthropological development, similar essentially to the invention of the wheel. Having emerged in order to give us some idea not so much of our origins as of what that sapiens is capable of, a book constitutes a means of transportation through the space of experience, at the speed of a turning page. This movement, like every movement, becomes flight from the common denominator ... This flight is the flight in the direction of "uncommon visage," in the direction of the numerator, in the direction of autonomy, in the direction of privacy.

Brodsky is addressing the relation between art and totalitarianism, and within that context his words make passionate sense. But I was reading from a different vantage. What I had in mind was not a vision of political totalitariansim, but rather of something that might be called "societal totalism" —that movement toward deindividuation, or electronic collectivization, that I discussed above. And from that perspective our era appears to be in a headlong flight from the "uncommon visage" named by the poet.

Trafficking with tendencies—extrapolating and projecting as I have been doing—must finally remain a kind of gambling. One bets high on the validity of a notion and low on the human capacity for resistance and for unpredictable initiatives. No one can really predict how we will adapt to the transformations taking place all around us. We may discover, too, that language is a hardier thing than I have allowed. It may flourish among the beep and the click and the monitor as readily as it ever did on the printed page. I hope so, for language is the soul's ozone layer and we thin it at our peril.

NO

Wen Stephenson

The Message Is the Medium

I have before my eyes a page, and on the page, typewritten in a serif font, is a poem. It is an ode written in 1819 by John Keats. I read the first words aloud to myself, slowly, pronouncing each syllable as though it were a musical note or a percussive beat: "Thou still unravish'd bride of quietness, / Thou foster-child of silence and slow time." As I continue down the page, I linger over certain phrases and rhymes; I go back and re-read, taking the stanzas apart and putting them back together again in my mind. The words fall into their order, and I feel their rhythm somewhere in my chest, the resonance of language uttered by a human voice in solitude. I am forced back into myself by the words on the page, my mind pushed deeper and deeper into a realm of images and associations, and emotion that did not exist a moment before is conjured from some mysterious wellspring.

I repeat the last lines of the poem—an indecipherable pronouncement on the relation of art to life—and then a noise from outside draws my attention to the open window; the spell is broken. It is a sultry Sunday afternoon over the rooftops of Boston's Back Bay, and through the window of my office a humid breeze rustles the papers strewn across my desk. I notice the clock: nearly five hours have elapsed since I sat down to read, and in that time I've wandered through a collection of British poetry. It seemed like no time at all. As I stand up to stretch, there's the sensation of floating that I often experience after long immersion in literature. But the pressure of the world returns, and its gravity pulls me back. The shock of reentering the temporal zone leaves me a little dazed, disoriented. I am still inside that Keats poem. Or it is inside me—the experience proved upon my pulse, which, by the way, is beating somewhat more rapidly than normal.

Where have I been? What has happened to the sense of time and space that governed my consciousness before I came upon that text? Something has happened, something connecting me across space and time to another human being, perhaps untold others—some experience of language that is ageless, primal, and indefinable. Perhaps I have had what some would call an authentic aesthetic experience of the art of poetry. If so, then I have experienced it directly through the digital channels of the Internet, on "pages" of the World

From Wen Stephenson, "The Message Is the Medium: A Reply to Sven Birkerts and *The Gutenberg Elegies*," *Chicago Review*, vol. 41, no. 4 (Winter 1995-1996). Copyright © 1995 by *Chicago Review*. Reprinted by permission.

Wide Web, through the circuitry of an Apple computer and the cathodes of a Sony monitor, at some 28,000 bytes per second.

⋅✿⋅

If imitation is the sincerest form of flattery, then I hope Sven Birkerts will take the preceding paragraphs not only as a rebuttal but as a compliment. His most recent collection of essays, *The Gutenberg Elegies: The Fate of Reading in an Electronic Age,* is one of the most engrossing, engaging, provocative, and frustrating books I've come across in a long while. Published in December, 1994, on the cusp of the millennial hype surrounding the so-called "online revolution," it has become one of the most talked about literary events of the past year. There should be nothing mysterious about its notoriety. At a time when the subject of the Internet and the new media it has spawned is everywhere you look—not just in the pages of *Wired* magazine but on the covers and in the headlines of the very print publications these new media are said to be replacing—Birkerts strikes deeply and often convincingly to the core of an anxiety felt by many in our postmodern literary culture. The strategy is simple and rather brilliant: to explore the relationship between a reader and an imaginative text at a time when serious literature is increasingly marginalized by the communications technologies that are transforming mass media and mass culture.

And yet, as one of a growing number of people with a foot in both the worlds of traditional literary publishing and the emerging online media, I can't help wondering how Birkerts could be so closed-minded to the possibilities the new media present for serious literary activity. Reading the book, especially his descriptions of the reading experience itself, I often felt as though Birkerts and I should be allies; but time and again I found myself fundamentally at odds with him, baffled by his condescension toward all forms of electronic media. Here's a typical statement in *The Gutenberg Elegies:* "[circuit and screen] are entirely inhospitable to the more subjective materials that have always been the stuff of art. That is to say, they are antithetical to inwardness."[1] Elsewhere he has elaborated on the idea that the Internet is barren of serious thought and writing. "What the wires carry is not the stuff of the soul," he said in the August, 1995, Forum in *Harper's.* Afraid of what he calls a "creeping shallowness," Birkerts complained in another context, "If I could be convinced that the Net and its users had a genuine purchase on depth, on the pursuit of things which are best pursued in stillness, in dread, and by way of patiently articulated language, then I would open wide my heart. I just don't see it." The fact that this last comment was made in the course of a live *online* conference hosted by *The Atlantic Monthly* on the America Online network (in which, I must confess, I participated as an editor), complicates things and adds perhaps more than just a touch of irony. I can only ask, as a worker in the "shallow" domain of cyberspace: should I be concerned, or merely insulted?

It isn't just that Birkerts is less than optimistic about the prospects for serious literature in cyberspace—his misgivings go well beyond a reasoned critical skepticism toward new forms of literary activity springing up on the World Wide Web and in other multimedia applications. The magnitude of his subject is spelled out in the opening pages of *The Gutenberg Elegies.* While Birkerts is hardly the first in recent years to see a "total metamorphosis" of our culture brought on by the revolution in communications technology, his stance in regard to the effects on literature and the consequences for Western culture is, I believe, radical. "Suddenly," he says,

> it feels like everything is poised for change.... The stable hierarchies of the printed page... are being superseded by the rush of impulses through freshly minted circuits. The displacement of the page by the screen is not yet total.... But, living as we do in the midst of innumerable affiliated webs, we can say that changes in the immediate sphere of print refer outward to the totality; they map on a smaller scale the riot of societal forces.(3)

At the vortex of this tranformative riot is for Birkerts the printed page. Not only is the "formerly stable system" of literary publishing being undermined and eroded, but as "the printed book, and the ways of the book—of writing and reading—are modified, as electronic communications assert dominance, the 'feel' of the literary engagement is altered. Reading and writing come to mean differently; they acquire new significations" (6). Pondering what he calls the "elegiac exercise" of reading a serious book, Birkerts concludes that "profound questions must arise about our avowedly humanistic values, about spiritual versus material concerns, and about subjectivity itself" (6). Clearly, there's more at stake here than the fate of the traditional publishing industry. For Birkerts, it is never merely a question of whether we get our reading material via the Internet or from a bookstore; what matters is how we experience what we read: "I speak as an unregenerate reader, one who still believes that language and not technology is the true evolutionary miracle.... That there is profundity in the verbal encounter itself... and that for a host of reasons the bound book is the ideal vehicle for the written word" (6). I follow along fine until his insistence on the bound book and the primacy of print stops me cold. Birkerts raises his devotion to the printed word to a nearly religious level: the book as holy relic, the page a fetish embodying everything he holds sacred.

Nowhere does Birkerts provide better insight into the underlying reasons for this devotion to print than, of all places, the inaugural issue of the electronic magazine *FEED*. As one of four participants in *FEED*'s first hypertext roundtable "Dialog," called "Page versus Pixel" (June 1995), Birkerts gets top billing and is allowed to fire off the first shot. Thus, with the kind of irony that has come to characterize so much of the self-reflexive discourse on media, Birkerts offers the crux of his argument in favor of print in the context of a hip new e-zine on the World Wide Web:

> I do not accept the argument that a word is a word is a word is a word no matter where it appears. There is no pure 'word' that does not inhabit

context inextricably. I don't think the medium is absolutely the message, but I do think that the medium conditions the message considerably. A word incised in stone (to be extreme) asks to be read as a word incised; a word skywritten (to be extreme again) asks to be looked at as such. A word on the page at some level partakes of—participates in—the whole history of words on pages, plays in that arena. Reading it, we accept certain implicit notions: of fixity, of hierarchy, of opacity. By 'opacity' I mean that the physical word dead-ends on the page and any sense of larger resonance must be established in the reader and by the reader.

Inexplicably, for the same words to be displayed on a computer screen, in Birkerts's reasoning, causes their presence to disintegrate, and with that loss so goes the entire hierarchy they represent: the whole culture disintegrates into random bits of digital information as soon as the words disappear from the screen, as if irretrievably. The image strikes me as an apt metaphor for the chaos that has been unleashed in literary studies by deconstruction and the linguistic indeterminacy associated with postmodernism. It's as though Birkerts fears for the stability and efficacy of language itself, and I begin to imagine him as Dr. Johnson's hapless lexicographer, who in the preface to his dictionary laments the vanity of the wish that language "might be less apt to decay, and that signs might be permanent, like the things which they denote."[2] Like Johnson, Birkerts appears to suffer an acute discomfort over the mutabilities of meaning and the transience of cultural values.

It is not surprising, then, that the fixity of words printed on page, and bound in a book, becomes Birkerts's last best hope for Western civilization. What's at stake for Birkerts is nothing less than the tradition of Western humanism dating back to the Renaissance and rooted in Hellenic civilization. Books are the repository of that tradition. It all rests on the stability of print. "For, in fact," he says in *The Gutenberg Elegies,* "our entire collective subjective history —the soul of our societal body—is encoded in print.... If a person turns from print ... then what happens to that person's sense of culture and continuity?" (20). Birkerts observes how the narrative and syntactical structures afforded by print are for the most part linear, whereas in electronic media everything from the jump-cut in film and video to the lateral and tangential movements of hypertext works against our traditional notions of time and historical progression. That Western culture is threatened both by these technologies and by the intellectual and artistic movements associated with postmodernity is to Birkerts no mere coincidence:

> Transitions like the one from print to electronic media do not take place without rippling or, more likely, reweaving the entire social and cultural web.... One could argue, for instance, that the entire movement of postmodernism in the arts is a consequence of this same macroscopic shift. For what is postmodernism at root but an aesthetic that rebukes the idea of an historical time line, as well as previously uncontested assumptions of cultural hierarchy. The postmodern artifact manipulates its stylistic signatures like Lego blocks and makes free with combinations from the formerly sequestered spheres of high and popular art. Its combinatory momentum

and relentless referencing of the surrounding culture mirror perfectly the associative dynamics of electronic media. (123)

Postmodernism's "relentless referencing" of mass culture and its rebuke of the historical time line are closely related, in Birkerts's picture, to the electronic media that are undermining the "stable hierarchies" upon which both narrative history and the novel are based. In the midst of these rioting forces, can there be any doubt that Birkerts would prefer for the spheres of high and popular art to remain sequestered? It would seem that the fate of literature in the electronic age depends upon the extent to which they do.

Accordingly, Birkerts feels the decline of print most acutely in the accompanying eclipse of the "serious" or "literary" novel as a form wielding cultural authority. Its eclipse, the direct result of the rise of electronic culture at the expense of print, represents for Birkerts no less than the death of literature itself, or at least the possibility of its death.... It is here that Birkerts's position begins to come into clearer focus, and we see a nostalgic modernist overwhelmed by the currents of postmodernism carried on the tide of electronic media. In response, Birkerts erects the physical certainty and materiality of the printed word as a levee against the flood.

Knowing as he does that the levee cannot hold—or, more likely, that it has long since broken—at least Birkerts shows a sense of humor (if a somewhat perverse one) as he takes his stand. In the final essay of *The Gutenberg Elegies*, an eerie coda titled "The Faustian Pact," we find our champion of high-modernist print culture resisting the temptations of a cyber-pop Mephistopheles decked out in the "bold colors, sans serif type fonts, [and] unexpected layouts" (210) of *Wired* magazine. Appropriately, one of Birkerts's rare bows to popular art takes the form of the blues refrain he intones from the chapter's first sentence onward: "I've been to the crossroads and I've seen the devil there" (210). He pauses. "Or is that putting it too dramatically? What I'm really saying is that I've been to the newsstand, again, to plunk down my money for *Wired*. You must have seen it—that big, squarish, beautifully produced item, that travel guide to the digital future" (210). Evidently it's not too dramatic for Birkerts; he develops the theme thoroughly before returning to it on the climactic last page. The image would be more humorous if not for the distinct impression that Birkerts is only half joking:

> Yes, I've been to the crossroads and I've met the devil, and he's sleek and confident, ever so much more 'with it' than the nearest archangel. He is causal and irreverent, wears jeans and running shoes and maybe even an earring, and the pointed prong of his tail is artfully concealed. Slippery fellow. He is the sorcerer of the binary order, jacking in and out of terminals, booting up, flaming, commanding vast systems and networks with an ease that steals my breath away. (211)

You can almost hear Birkerts pronouncing these (to him) exotic terms of the digital present, distrusting them, not quite sure what to make of them, superstitious of the mystical powers they seem to hold, as though they're poised to steal our souls—or, as Birkerts would say, "our subjective individualism" (228).

He goes on to lament the inevitable loss of this individualism in the midst of an increasing "electronic tribalism," or "hive life," and he identifies the consequences of our Faustian contract in the realization of his "core fear"—"that we are, as a culture, as a species, becoming shallower" (228). In our embrace of technology and its transformation of our culture we have sacrificed depth, "adapting ourselves to the ersatz security of a vast lateral connectedness" (228). Woven into this expanding web—pervading our academic institutions and trickling down into the mass media by way of high-brow journalism, film, and now, he fears, the Internet—is a nihilistic "postmodern culture" with its "vast fabric of competing isms," chief among them a terrorizing "absolute relativism" (228). Birkerts's answer is to resist the reflex response that all is "business as usual," and to see through the illusions that our wired Mephisto would weave seductively before our eyes. Birkerts won't be fooled: "The devil no longer moves about on cloven hooves, reeking of brimstone. He is an affable, efficient fellow. He claims to want to help us all along to a brighter, easier future, and his sales pitch is very smooth. I was, as the old song goes, almost persuaded" (229). From somewhere deep in his "subjective self," Birkerts summons his courage and with his final words heeds the inner voice that says, "Refuse it."

It's a dramatic ending, to be sure—the work of a skilled evangelist. Yet, as it turns out, in his rhetorical flourish Birkerts has inverted the meaning of the "old song," the traditional evangelical hymn in which the speaker is, as the title says, "Almost Persuaded" to respond to the call of salvation but is ultimately too late. The hymn is supposed to strike fear and contrition into the hearts of sinful listeners, and using it the way he does is a telling maneuver on Birkerts's part, turning it around so that it's the voice of an electronic-age Devil rather than the voice of God that nearly persuades him. To be honest, he almost persuades me that my soul is in danger, nearly convinces me of my shallowness—almost, but not quite.

The truth is that, like many in Birkerts's target audience, I'm susceptible to the alarm. Like the fretful soul in the revival tent I am vulnerable to the message, and the heightened passion of its delivery makes inroads where reason cannot. I recognize myself in his portrait of the "unregenerate reader." Here's my confession, my creed. Yes, I believe. I believe in aesthetic experience and in the need for literature to communicate something otherwise unknowable—and in that communication to achieve some connection with other human beings, however slight and fleeting, and however compromised by the indeterminacies of signs and the structures of meaning and power imposed by our cultural contexts. I make my own refusal: a refusal to accept that such communication is impossible. I take the very existence of . . . literary journal[s] as evidence that others share a need for this kind of communication, within and across personal and cultural boundaries. A postmodern pilgrim, I struggle to maintain my faith in the ability of language to transmit not just what one culture calls beauty (though that, too, is an important function) but more so, to communicate what people recognize across time and space as human experience. If I truly believed that any of this is threatened with extinction by the new electronic media, I would gladly cast my modem down the sea's throat and never look back. But, in fact, the picture I see looks considerably different, considerably less frightening.

To be fair, there are glimpses of hope even in the midst of Birkerts's apocalyptic visions, though they are rarely pursued. These are the occasions, usually at the end of a chapter, upon which he rises to affirm the possibility that language itself, even literary language, might survive despite the decline of print. "We may discover, too," he concedes, "that language is a hardier thing than I have allowed. It may flourish among the beep and the click and the monitor as readily as it ever did on the printed page" (133). Yet these moments are few and far between. The conclusion forever reached is that our literary culture and our civilization rest on print, and that the fate of our individual and collective souls depends upon the solidity of ink and paper.

It is hard to believe, despite his statements about words incised in stone versus words written in the sky, that Birkerts really accepts the McLuhanesque determinism embodied in the ubiquitous cliché about the medium being the message. What if the medium in question is language? Then what does the message become? At the end of his chapter called "Close Listening," in which he describes his experiences with books on tape, Birkerts confesses to having had an epiphanic moment, one that may suggest an answer. He recalls driving down a stretch of open road after visiting Walden Pond, near Concord, Massachusetts —a good place for a transcendental experience—and popping in a cassette of Thoreau's *Walden,* spoken by Michael O'Keefe. The effect is that Birkerts seems momentarily transformed into an all-encompassing, all-hearing ear:

> The words streamed in unmediated, shot like some kind of whiskey into my soul. I had a parenthesis of open country, then came the sentence of the highway. But the state held long enough to allow a thought: In the beginning was the Word—not the written or printed or processed word, but the spoken word. And though it changes its aspect faster than any Proteus, hiding now in letter shapes and now in magnetic emulsion, it remains. It still has the power to lay us bare. (150)

I remember first encountering that passage and putting down the book, thinking, "Precisely! I rest my case!" I can only hope that Birkerts has more experiences like this one. For he as much as admits that the essence of literature might actually survive in the valley of its saying, even outside the precincts of print.

Given such a revelation, the absence of poetry from Birkerts's discussion of literature's fate becomes all the more conspicuous. In *The Gutenberg Elegies,* he has given us a moving paean to the achievements of great prose stylists, such as Flaubert, whose *mots justes* represent the essence of what Birkerts fears we are losing. But what of the poets? How is it that they do not figure into his scheme of things? After all, sound as much as sense is the essence of poetry, and verse may bring us closer than any other use of language to that primal "Word" Birkerts communed with on the road from Walden. And that is just the point. Poetry does not fit into the design of his argument. For unlike prose, and especially the kind of prose narrative Birkerts is so keen to salvage, poetry has long been comfortable outside of print. Poetry, in many of its forms, comes much closer to the kind of aesthetic Birkerts describes as characterizing postmodern, electronic culture. And where much is made of the non-linear, cinematic techniques employed in prose narrative, so we would do well to remind ourselves that poets have been using those techniques since the first invocation of the Muse.

... [N]o matter how the words of a literary work are reproduced and transmitted, the essential qualities of the language, the sounds and meanings, survive.... Language is more than content; it is itself a medium—the medium of literature—and it transcends print, paper, silicon, electricity, even the human voice.

⁂

So, where does this leave literature—or, more to the point, literary language and the kind of communication it allows—in the computer age, and in a future of rapidly expanding online networks? One place to look is the emergence of literary publishing on the Internet. If we venture beyond the too-easy opposition of print and pixel, we might find that literature will take to the digital environment more naturally than many would expect. For one thing, computers themselves, and the experience of cyberspace, can appeal to our imaginations in ways similar to the aesthetic experience of literary language. As Robert Pinsky wrote in *The New York Times Book Review*, ... in an essay titled "The Muse in the Machine: Or, the Poetics of Zork," poetry and computers may have something uniquely in common, sharing what he identifies as "a great human myth or trope, an image that could be called the secret passage: the discovery of large, manifold channels through a small, ordinary-looking or all but invisible aperture."[3] Pinsky appears to be tantalized, rather than threatened, by the possibilities implied in the comparison. "This opening up," he continues in the same essay, "the discovery of much in little, seems to be a fundamental resonance of human intelligence. Perhaps more than the interactive or text-shuffling capacity of the machine, this passage to vast complexities is at the essence of what writing through the machine might become. The computer, like everything else we make, is in part a self-portrait; it smells of our human souls." From hypertext and archival databases, to advanced language experimentation, to the increasingly sophisticated descendants of early computer text-adventure games such as Zork, the "peculiar terrain of literature-for-the-monitor" offers a vision of what the digital future may hold for the literary imagination.

Not long after that essay appeared I had the opportunity, as the moderator of another online conference for *The Atlantic Monthly*, to ask Pinsky if he would elaborate on his thoughts about poetry and its potential life in cyberspace. He confirmed a qualified optimism, emphasizing certain practical advantages of the new medium over the old, while leaving no doubt as to where, he believes, the message is to be found. "The medium of poetry—real poetry, for me —is ultimately breath," he typed (broadcasting the words to a live audience), "one person's breath shaped into meaning by our larynx and mouth. So like print, the computer is still a servant or a conduit—not the ultimate scene of poetry, which is in the ear." He then declined to predict what might be the most promising applications of computer technology to literature, opting instead to point out perhaps the most significant aspect of electronic publishing, not only for poetry but for literary activity in general: "the capacity to download what used to require a publisher, a bookstore, etc. . . . That compression and availability have amazing potential for freeing individuals from control, from the treatment of people as masses. In that, poetry (an ancient technology) and new technologies are potential allies in the service of individual creativity, orneriness, imagination." A few hours browsing on the World Wide Web will more than bear Pinsky out. What he tentatively projects is in fact taking shape, albeit in an infantile form, on the Internet, especially across the multimedia landscape of the Web. . . .

It is becoming clearer that the Internet has vast potential to expand the audience for works of the literary imagination; and not only to expand access but also opportunities for interactivity, and for building communities of creative minds that could not exist otherwise. It's a lovely picture, one I'd like to believe in. But I know it is more likely that the Internet will become a vast cyberspace mall, every bit as commercialized as any other mass medium in a free-market society. And yet, if it's true, as [the poet W. H.] Auden put it, that "poetry makes nothing happen"—at least not within the realm of an expanding and virtually untapped marketplace—it is nevertheless also true that individuals do make things happen. And I will maintain—surely Birkerts would agree with me here—that literature, as a means of communication, has the power to make something happen within individuals. For this reason, it is all the more important that we do not surrender cyberspace and the new media to the purely market-driven forces of late-twentieth-century multinational capitalism. There are other values—values which cannot be measured in monetary units—that will survive only if we vigilantly carve out a space for them to breathe.

Notes

1. Sven Birkerts, *The Gutenberg Elegies: The Fate of Reading in an Electronic Age* (Boston: Faber and Faber, 1994), p. 193. Page numbers of subsequent quotations are indicated parenthetically.

2. Samuel Johnson, "Preface to a Dictionary of the English Language," in Frank Brady and W. K. Wimsatt, eds., *Samuel Johnson: Selected Poetry and Prose* (University of California Press, 1977), p. 280.

3. Robert Pinsky, "The Muse in the Machine: Or, the Poetics of Zork," *The New York Times Book Review* (March 19, 1995): 3.

POSTSCRIPT

Are Computers Hazardous to Literacy?

In at least one sense, Birkerts is correct when he says that computers and the Internet threaten traditional conceptions of literacy and the literary culture. If we try to summon up an image to go with those conceptions, we might come up with a library reading room, vast shelves of dusty tomes, human figures slowly paging through books spread across long oak tables, silence but for a buzzing fly or two, and fingers coated with gray dust. The new order carries a very different image: modern and technological and fast, sleek casings surrounding glowing screens, and clicking mice. To a huge extent this image has already won—card catalogs in libraries have almost been completely replaced by computerized databases—and anyone with a fondness for the old image is bound to object.

Birkerts developed his objections at length and stirred up considerable controversy in some circles. But he also struck a chord. Mike Shahin, in "Internet: Boon or Bane for Literacy?" *The Ottawa Citizen* (September 8, 1996), writes, "Literacy workers, social scientists and computer nerds are beginning to realize that the Internet has the potential to radically alter the way we use and understand language, and the way we define literacy." Also, the National Literacy Secretariat and the Literacy Section of the Ontario Ministry of Education and Training are funding *CONNECT: A National Newsletter on Technology in Adult Literacy* to promote the appropriate use of technology in literacy programs.

On the other hand, Dean Blobaum, of the University of Chicago Press, reviewed Birkerts's *Gutenberg Elegies* online, saying, "Birkerts's take on electronic media follows a well-trodden path—a rehash of media theory and broad generalizations about the effects of electronic media, making it the whipping boy for the ills of western society—the decline in education, literacy, and literate culture; the financial straits of publishers; postmodernism in the arts; and the fight over the canon in literature. His thoughts on electronic media lack focus and originality." The Internet, he added, actually fulfills the 1932 call of literary giant Bertolt Brecht for a radio medium that permits the receiver of information to communicate with the provider.

Media theorist Paul Levinson, in *Wired, Analog, and Digital Writings* (Pulpless.com, 1999), tries "to disentangle the extent to which our attachment to books is based on real advantages in performance versus rosy nostalgia." Levinson concludes that digital texts have genuine advantages (such as hypertext features) but that books have enough advantages of their own that they will remain with us for the foreseeable future.

ISSUE 14

Will It Be Possible to Build a Computer That Can Think?

YES: Hans Moravec, from "The Universal Robot," in *Vision-21: Interdisciplinary Science and Engineering in the Era of Cyberspace* (National Aeronautics and Space Administration, 1993)

NO: John Searle, from "God, Mind, and Artificial Intelligence: An Interview With John Searle," *Free Inquiry* (Fall 1998)

ISSUE SUMMARY

YES: Research scientist Hans Moravec describes the necessary steps in what he considers to be the inevitable development of computers that match and even exceed human intelligence.

NO: Professor of philosophy John Searle argues that computers merely manipulate symbols, while biological brains have a consciousness that allows for the interpretation and understanding of symbols. Therefore, computers will not be able to achieve or exceed the level of consciousness of the human brain.

T he first primitive digital computers were instantly dubbed "thinking machines" because they were able to perform functions—initially only arithmetic—that had always been considered part of the uniquely human ability to think. Some critics of the "thinking machine" label, however, objected that arithmetic is so much simpler than, say, poetry or philosophy (after all, it is only a matter of following a few simple rules) that computers were not thinking at all. Thinking, they said, is for humans only. In fact, if a machine can do it, then it cannot possibly be real thinking.

In 1950 Alan Turing (1912–1954), an English mathematician and logician, devised a test to determine whether or not a machine was intelligent. Turing's test entailed whether or not one could converse with a person and a computer (through a teletype so that neither could be seen nor could the human be heard) and, after a suitable period, tell which was which. If the computer could pass for an intelligent conversationalist, Turing felt, then it would have to be considered intelligent.

Over the next two decades, computer scientists learned how to program their machines to play games such as chess, solve mathematical theorems, parse sentences (break them down into their grammatical components), and perform a number of other tasks that had once been thought doable by thinking humans only. In most cases the machines were not as good at these tasks as humans, but many artificial intelligence (AI) researchers believed that it was only a matter of time before the machines matched and even exceeded their creators.

The closest any machine has come to passing the Turing test may have been in the early 1970s, when Kenneth Mark Colby, then a Stanford University psychiatrist and computer scientist, programmed a computer to imitate the conversational style of paranoid humans. This was much easier than programming a computer to imitate a nonparanoid human's conversational style because paranoid individuals tend to be very rigid and predictable in their responses. When Colby had psychiatrists interview the programmed computer and a human paranoid (through a teletype, per Turing's criteria), only half could correctly distinguish between computer and human. That is, the computer did indeed come close to passing the Turing test. On the other hand, it was not trying to pass as an average human being, whose thought processes are far freer and more flexible than those of a paranoid person.

Will a computer ever be able to imitate a normal human being? And if it can, will that mean it is really "thinking" or really "intelligent" or really "conscious"? Many computer scientists believe that it is still just a matter of time before a computer passes the Turing test with flying colors and that that machine will be truly intelligent. Indeed, many even say that the human mind is nothing more than a program that runs on a biological machine.

Others argue that machines cannot have emotions or appreciate beauty and that computers cannot be self-aware or conscious, no matter how intelligent they may seem to an interrogator. They therefore can never be intelligent in a human way.

Hans Moravec asserts that true artificial intelligence can be achieved. It will require computers that are much more powerful than any that exist today, he predicts, and the process of achieving intelligence will involve a series of evolutionary stages.

In contrast, John Searle argues that consciousness is achieved by the biological brain only. Computers, he says, do no more than manipulate symbols while the brain can interpret symbols and attach meaning to them.

Hans Moravec

 **YES**

The Universal Robot

Abstract. Our artifacts are getting smarter, and a loose parallel with the evolution of animal intelligence suggests one future course for them. Computerless industrial machinery exhibits the behavioral flexibility of single-celled organisms. Today's best computer-controlled robots are like the simpler invertebrates. A thousand-fold increase in computer power in the next decade should make possible machines with reptile-like sensory and motor competence. Properly configured, such robots could do in the physical world what personal computers now do in the world of data—act on our behalf as literal-minded slaves. Growing computer power over the next half-century will allow this reptile stage to be surpassed, in stages producing robots that learn like mammals, model their world like primates and eventually reason like humans. Depending on your point of view, humanity will then have produced a worthy successor, or transcended some of its inherited limitations and so transformed itself into something quite new.

Introduction: State of the Art

Instincts which predispose the nature and quantity of work we enjoy probably evolved during the 100,000 years our ancestors lived as hunter-gatherers. Less than 10,000 years ago the agricultural revolution made life more stable, and richer in goods and information. But, paradoxically, it requires more human labor to support an agricultural society than a primitive one, and the work is of a different, "unnatural" kind, out of step with the old instincts. The effort to avoid this work has resulted in domestication of animals, slavery and the industrial revolution. But many jobs must still be done by hand, engendering for hundreds of years the fantasy of an intelligent but soulless being that can tirelessly dispatch the drudgery. Only in this century have electronic sensors and computers given machines the ability to sense their world and to think about it, and so offered a way to fulfill the wish.

As in fables, the unexpected side effects of robot slaves are likely to dominate the resulting story. Most significantly, these perfect slaves will continue to develop, and will not long remain soulless. As they increase in competence they will have occasion to make more and more autonomous decisions, and so will

From National Aeronautics and Space Administration. Office of Management. Scientific and Technical Information Program. *Vision-21: Interdisciplinary Science and Engineering in the Era of Cyberspace.* (NASA Conference Publication 10129; 1993). References omitted.

slowly develop a volition and purposes of their own. At the same time they will become indispensable. Our minds were evolved to store the skills and memories of a stone-age life, not the enormous complexity that has developed in the last ten thousand years. We've kept up, after a fashion, through a series of social inventions—social stratification and division of labor, memory aids like poetry and schooling, written records, stored outside the body, and recently machines that can do some of our thinking entirely without us. The portion of absolutely essential human activity that takes place outside of human bodies and minds has been steadily increasing. Hard working intelligent machines may complete the trend.

Serious attempts to build thinking machines began after the second world war. One line of research, called Cybernetics, used simple electronic circuitry to mimic small nervous systems, and produced machines that could learn to recognize simple patterns, and turtle-like robots that found their way to lighted recharging hutches. An entirely different approach, named Artificial Intelligence (AI), attempted to duplicate rational human thought in the large computers that appeared after the war. By 1965, these computers ran programs that proved theorems in logic and geometry, solved calculus problems and played good games of checkers. In the early 1970s, AI research groups at MIT (the Massachusetts Institute of Technology) and Stanford University attached television cameras and robot arms to their computers, so their "thinking" programs could begin to collect their information directly from the real world.

What a shock! While the pure reasoning programs did their jobs about as well and about as fast as college freshmen, the best robot control programs took hours to find and pick up a few blocks on a table. Often these robots failed completely, giving a performance much worse than a six month old child. This disparity between programs that reason and programs that perceive and act in the real world holds to this day. In recent years Carnegie Mellon University produced two desk-sized computers that can play chess at grandmaster level, within the top 100 players in the world, when given their moves on a keyboard. But present-day robotics could produce only a complex and unreliable machine for finding and moving normal chess pieces.

In hindsight it seems that, in an absolute sense, reasoning is much easier than perceiving and acting—a position not hard to rationalize in evolutionary terms. The survival of human beings (and their ancestors) has depended for hundreds of millions of years on seeing and moving in the physical world, and in that competition large parts of their brains have become efficiently organized for the task. But we didn't appreciate this monumental skill because it is shared by every human being and most animals—it is commonplace. On the other hand, rational thinking, as in chess, is a newly acquired skill, perhaps less than one hundred thousand years old. The parts of our brain devoted to it are not well organized, and, in an absolute sense, we're not very good at it. But until recently we had no competition to show us up.

By comparing the edge and motion detecting circuitry in the four layers of nerve cells in the retina, the best understood major circuit in the human nervous system, with similar processes developed for "computer vision" systems that allow robots in research and industry to see, I've estimated that it would take a billion computations per second (the power of a world-leading Cray 2 supercomputer) to produce the same results at the same speed as a human retina. By extrapolation, to emulate a whole brain takes ten trillion arithmetic operations per second, or ten thousand Crays worth. This is for operations our nervous systems do extremely efficiently and well.

Arithmetic provides an example at the other extreme. In 1989 a new computer was tested for a few months with a program that computed the number pi to more than one billion decimal places. By contrast, the largest unaided manual computation of pi was 707 digits by William Shanks in 1873. It took him several years, and because of a mistake every digit past the 527th was wrong! In arithmetic, today's average computers are one million times more powerful than human beings. In very narrow areas of rational thought (like playing chess or proving theorems) they are about the same. And in perception and control of movement in the complex real world, and related areas of common-sense knowledge and intuitive and visual problem solving, today's average computers are a million times less capable.

The deficit is evident even in pure problem solving AI programs. To this day, AI programs exhibit no shred of common sense—a medical diagnosis program, for instance, may prescribe an antibiotic when presented a broken bicycle because it lacks a model of people, diseases or bicycles. Yet these programs, on existing computers, would be overwhelmed were they to be bloated with the details of everyday life, since each new fact can interact with the others in an astronomical "combinatorial explosion." [A ten year project called Cyc at the Microelectronics and Computer Consortium in Austin, Texas, is attempting to build just such a common-sense data base. They estimate the final result will contain over one hundred million logic sentences about everyday objects and actions.]

Machines have a lot of catching up to do. On the other hand, for most of the century, machine calculation has been improving a thousandfold every twenty years, and there are basic developments in research labs that can sustain this for at least several decades more. In less than fifty years computer hardware should be powerful enough to match, and exceed, even the well-developed parts of human intelligence. But what about the software that would be required to give these powerful machines the ability to perceive, intuit and think as well as humans? The Cybernetic approach that attempts to directly imitate nervous systems is very slow, partly because examining a working brain in detail is a very tedious process. New instruments may change that in the future. The AI approach has successfully imitated some aspects of rational thought, but that seems to be only about one millionth of the problem. I feel that the fastest progress on the hardest problems will come from a third approach, the newer field of robotics, the construction of systems that must see and move in the physical world. Robotics research is imitating the evolution of animal minds, adding capabilities to machines a few at a time, so that the resulting sequence of machine behaviors resembles the capabilities of animals with increasingly complex nervous systems. This effort to build intelligence from the bottom up is helped by biological peeks at the "back of the book"—at the neuronal, structural, and behavioral features of animals and humans.

The best robots today are controlled by computers which are just powerful enough to simulate the nervous system of an insect, cost as much as houses, and so find only a few profitable niches in society (among them, spray painting and spot welding cars and assembling electronics). But those few applications are encouraging research that is slowly providing a base for a huge future growth. Robot evolution in the direction of full intelligence will greatly accelerate, I believe, in about a decade when the mass-produced general purpose, universal robot becomes possible. These machines will do in the physical world what personal computers do in the world of data—act on our behalf as literal-minded slaves.

The Dumb Robot (ca. 2000–2010)

To be useful in many tasks, the first generation of universal robots should navigate efficiently over flat ground and reliably and safely over rough terrain and stairs, be able to manipulate most objects, and to find them in the nearby world. There are beginnings of solutions today. In the 1980s Hitachi of Japan developed a mobility system of five steerable wheels, each on its own telescoping stalk that allows it to accommodate to rises and dips in uneven terrain, and to climb stairs, by raising one wheel at a time while standing stably on the other four. My laboratory at Carnegie Mellon University in Pittsburgh has developed a navigation method that enables a robot equipped with sonar range measuring devices and television cameras to build probabilistic maps of its surroundings to determine its location and plan routes. An elegant three-fingered mechanical hand at the Massachusetts Institute of Technology can hold and orient bolts and eggs and manipulate a string in a humanlike fashion. A system called 3DPO from SRI International in Menlo Park, California, can find a desired part in a jumble seen by a special range-finding camera. The slow operation of these systems suggests one other element needed for the universal robot, namely a computer about one thousand times as powerful as those found on desks and in robots today. Such machines, able to do one billion computations per second, would provide robots approximately the brain power of a reptile, and the personality of a washing machine.

Universal robots will find their first uses in factories, where they will be cheaper and more versatile than the older generation of robots they replace. Eventually they will become cheap enough for some households, extending the reach of personal computers from a few tasks in the data world to many in the physical world. . . .

Learning (2010–2020)

Useful though they will be, the first generation of universal robots will be rigid slaves to simple programs. If the machine bangs its elbow while chopping beef in your kitchen making Stroganoff, you will have to find another place for the robot to do its work, or beg the software manufacturer for a fix. Second generation robots with more powerful computers will be able to host a more flexible kind of program able to adjust itself by a kind of conditioned learning.

First generation programs will consist primarily of sequences of the type "Do step A, then B, then C...." The programs for the second generation will read "Do step A1 or A2 or A3... then B1 or B2 or B3... then C1 or C2 or C3...." In the Beef Stroganoff example, A1 might be to chop with the right hand of the robot, while A2 is to use the left hand. Each alternative in the program has a "weight," a number that indicates the desirability of using it rather than one of the other branches. The machine also contains a "pain" system, a series of programs that look out for problems, such as collisions, and respond by reducing the weights of recently invoked branches, and a "pleasure" system that increases the relevant weights when good conditions, such as well charged batteries or a task efficiently completed, are detected. As the robot bangs its elbow repeatedly in your kitchen, it gradually learns to use its other hand (as well as adapting to its surroundings in a thousand other ways). A program with many alternatives at each step, whose pain and pleasure systems are arranged to produce a pleasure signal on hearing the word "good" and a pain message on hearing "bad" could be slowly trained to do new tasks, like a small mammal. A particular suite of pain- and pleasure-producing programs interacting with a robot's individual environment would subtly shape its behavior and give it a distinct character.

Imagery (2020–2030)

Adaptive robots will find jobs everywhere, and the hardware and software industry that supports them could become the largest on earth. But teaching them new tasks, whether by writing programs or through punishment and reward, will be very tedious. This deficiency will lead to a portentous innovation, a software world-modeler (requiring another big increase in computer power), that allows the robot to simulate its immediate surroundings and its own actions within them, and thus to think about its tasks before acting. Before making Beef Stroganoff in your kitchen, the new robot would simulate the task many times. Each time its simulated elbow bangs the simulated cabinet, the software would update the learning weights just as if the collision had physically happened. After many such mental run-throughs the robot would be well trained, so that when it finally cooks for real, it does it correctly. The simulation can be used in many other ways. After a job, the robot can run though its previous actions, and try variations on them to improve future performance. A robot might even be configured to invent some of its own programs by means of a simpler program that can detect how nearly a sequence of robot actions achieves a desired task. This training program would, in repeated simulations, provide the "good" and "bad" indications needed to condition a general learning program like the one of the previous section.

It will take a large community of patient researchers to build good simulators. A robot entering a new room must include vast amounts of not directly perceived prior knowledge in its simulation, such as the expected shapes and probable contents of kitchen counters and the effect of (and force needed for) turning faucet knobs. It needs instinctive motor-perceptual knowledge about the world that took millions of years of evolution to install in us, that tells us instinctively when a height is dangerous, how hard to throw a stone, or if the animal facing us is a threat. Robots that incorporate it may be as smart as monkeys.

Reasoning (2030–2040)

In the decades while the "bottom-up" evolution of robots is transferring the perceptual and motor faculties of human beings into machinery, the conventional Artificial Intelligence industry will be perfecting the mechanization of reasoning. Since today's programs already match human beings in some areas, those of 40 years from now, running on computers a million times as fast as today's, should be quite superhuman. Today's reasoning programs work from small amounts of clear and correct information prepared by human beings. Data from robot sensors such as cameras is much too voluminous and too noisy for them to use. But a good robot simulator will contain neatly organized data about the robot and its world. For instance, if a knife is on a countertop, or if the robot is holding a cup. A robot with a simulator can be married to a reasoning program to produce a machine with most of the abilities of a human being. The combination will create beings that in some ways resemble us, but in others are like nothing the world has seen before.

First Generation Technicalities

Both industrial robot manipulators and the research effort to build "smart" robots are twenty five years old. Universal robots will require at least another decade of development, but some of their elements can be guessed from the experience so far. One consideration is weight. Mobile robots built to work in human sized spaces today weigh too many hundreds of pounds. This dangerously large mass has three major components: batteries, actuators and structure. Lead-acid batteries able to drive a mobile robot for a day contribute about one third of the weight. But nickel-cadmium aircraft batteries weigh half as much, and newer lithium batteries can be half again as light. Electric motors are efficient and precisely controllable, but standard motors are heavy and require equally heavy reducing gears. Ultrastrong permanent magnets can halve the weight and generate high torque without gears. Robot structure has been primarily aluminum. Its weight contribution can be cut by a factor of four by substituting composite materials containing superstrength fibers of graphite, aramid or the new material Spectra. These innovations could be combined to make a robot with roughly the size, weight, strength and endurance of a human.

The first generation robot will probably move on wheels. Legged robots have advantages on complicated terrain, but they consume too much power. A simple wheeled robot would be confined to areas of flat ground, but if each wheel had a controlled suspension with about a meter of travel, the robot could slowly lift its wheels as needed to negotiate rough ground and stairs. The manipulation system will consist of two or more arms ending in dexterous manipulators. There are several designs in the research labs today, but the most elegant is probably that of the so-called Stanford-JPL hand (mentioned above, now found at MIT), which has three fingers each with three controlled joints.

The robot's travels would be greatly aided if it could continuously pinpoint its location, perhaps by noting the delay from a handful of small synchronized transmitters distributed in its environment. This approach is used in some terrestrial and satellite navigation systems. The robot will also require a sense of its immediate surroundings, to find doors, detect obstacles and track objects in its workspace. Research laboratories, including my own, have experimented with techniques that do this with data from television cameras, scanning lasers, sonar transducers, infrared proximity sensors and contact sensors. A more precise sensory system will be needed to find particular work objects in clutter. The most successful methods to date start with three dimensional data from special cameras and laser arrangements that directly measure distance as well as lateral position. The robot will thus probably contain a wide angle sensor for general spatial awareness, and a precise, narrow angle, three dimensional imaging system to find particular objects it will grasp.

Research experience to date suggests that to navigate, visually locate objects, and plan and control arm motions, the first universal robots will require a billion operations per second of computer power. The 1980s have witnessed a number of well publicized fads that claim to be solutions to the artificial intelligence or robot control problem. Expert systems, the Prolog logical inference language, neural nets, fuzzy logic and massive parallelism have all had their spot in the limelight. The common element that I note in these pronouncements is the sudden enthusiasm of groups of researchers experienced in some area of computer science for applying their methods to the robotics problems of perceiving and acting in the physical world. Invariably each approach produces some simple showcase demonstrations, then bogs down on real problems. This pattern is no surprise to those with a background in the twenty five year research robotics effort.

Making a machine to see, hear or act reliably in the raw physical world is much, much more difficult than naive intuition leads us to believe....

Mind Children (2050+)

The fourth robot generation and its successors, with human perceptual and motor abilities and superior reasoning powers, could replace human beings in every essential task. In principle, our society could continue to operate increasingly well without us, with machines running the companies and doing the research as well as performing the productive work. Since machines can be designed to work well in outer space, production could move to the greater resources of the solar system, leaving behind a nature preserve subsidized from space. Meek humans would inherit the earth, but rapidly evolving machines would expand into the rest of the universe.

This development can be viewed as a very natural one. Human beings have two forms of heredity, one the traditional biological kind, passed on strands of DNA, the other cultural, passed from mind to mind by example, language, books and recently machines. At present the two are inextricably linked, but the cultural part is evolving very rapidly, and gradually assuming functions once the province of our biology. In terms of information content, our cultural side is already by far the larger part of us. The fully intelligent robot marks the point where our cultural side can exist on its own, free of biological limits. Intelligent machines, which are evolving among us, learning our skills, sharing our goals, and being shaped by our values, can be viewed as our children, the children of our minds. With them our biological heritage is not lost. It will be safely stored in libraries at least; however its importance will be greatly diminished.

What about life back on the preserve? For some of us the thought of being grandly upstaged by our artificial progeny will be disappointing, and life may seem pointless if we are fated to spend it staring stupidly at our ultra-intelligent progeny as they try to describe their ever more spectacular discoveries in baby-talk that we can understand. Is there any way individual humans might join the adventure?

You've just been wheeled into the operating room. A robot brain surgeon is in attendance, a computer waits nearby. Your skull, but not your brain, is anesthetized. You are fully conscious. The robot surgeon opens your brain case and places a hand on the brain's surface. This unusual hand bristles with microscopic machinery, and a cable connects it to the computer at your side. Instruments in the hand scan the first few millimeters of brain surface. These measurements, and a comprehensive understanding of human neural architecture, allow the surgeon to write a program that models the behavior of the uppermost layer of the scanned brain tissue. This program is installed in a small portion of the waiting computer and activated. Electrodes in the hand supply the simulation with the appropriate inputs from your brain, and can inject signals from the simulation. You and the surgeon compare the signals it produces with the original ones. They flash by very fast, but any discrepancies are highlighted on a display screen. The surgeon fine-tunes the simulation until the correspondence is nearly perfect. As soon as you are satisfied, the simulation output is activated. The brain layer is now impotent—it receives inputs and reacts as before but its output is ignored. Microscopic manipulators on the hand's surface excise this superfluous tissue and pass them to an aspirator, where they are drawn away.

The surgeon's hand sinks a fraction of a millimeter deeper into your brain, instantly compensating its measurements and signals for the changed position. The process is repeated for the next layer, and soon a second simulation resides in the computer, communicating with the first and with the remaining brain tissue. Layer after layer the brain is simulated, then excavated. Eventually your skull is empty, and the surgeon's hand rests deep in your brainstem. Though you have not lost consciousness, or even your train of thought, your mind has been removed from the brain and transferred to a machine. In a final, disorienting step the surgeon lifts its hand. Your suddenly abandoned body dies. For a moment you experience only quiet and dark. Then, once again, you can open your eyes. Your perspective has shifted. The computer simulation has been disconnected from the cable leading to the surgeon's hand and reconnected to a shiny new body of the style, color, and material of your choice. Your metamorphosis is complete.

Your new mind has a control labeled "speed." It had been set at 1, to keep the simulations synchronized with the old brain, but now you change it to 10,000, allowing you to communicate, react, and think ten thousand times faster. You now seem to have hours to respond to situations that previously seemed instantaneous. You have time, during the fall of a dropped object, to research the advantages and disadvantages of trying to catch it, perhaps to solve its differential equations of motion. When your old biological friends speak with you, their sentences take hours—you have plenty of time to think about the conversations, but they try your patience. Boredom is a mental alarm that keeps you from wasting your time in profitless activity, but if it acts too soon or too aggressively it limits your attention span, and thus your intelligence. With help from the machines, you change your mind-program to retard the onset of boredom. Having done that, you will find yourself comfortably working on long problems with sidetracks upon sidetracks. In fact, your thoughts routinely become so involved that you need an increase in your memory. These are but the first of many changes. Soon your friends complain that you have become more like the machines than the biological human you once were. That's life.

God, Mind, and Artificial Intelligence

John R. Searle, the Mills Professor of the Philosophy of Mind at the University of California, Berkeley, is one of the pre-eminent philosophers of our time. His many books include *The Rediscovery of the Mind*; *Minds, Brains, and Science* and *The Construction of Social Reality*. In the following interview with FREE INQUIRY Deputy Editor Matt Cherry, Searle explains his views on the philosophy of mind, as well as discussing religion and ethics and his latest work on the role of reason in constructing our social world.

FREE INQUIRY: We're a secular humanist magazine, which means that we like to think of ourselves as the children of the Enlightenment. So we must ask—do you personally believe in God?

JOHN SEARLE: I don't. Actually, the best remark made about this was by Bertrand Russell at a dinner I attended when I was an undergraduate. Russell was 85 years old. We were all a bunch of kids, and we thought, he's not going to live much longer, and he's a famous atheist, so let's really put it to him. So we asked him, What would happen if you were wrong about the existence of God? What would you say to *Him*? That is, suppose you died and you went to heaven and there you were in front of Him—what would you say? Russell didn't hesitate a second. He said, "I would say, 'You didn't give us enough evidence.'" And I think that's my attitude. On the available evidence we have about how the world works, we have to say that we're alone, there is no God, we don't have a cosmic friend, we're on our own. I might be wrong about that, but on the available evidence, that's the situation we're in. So I guess that makes me a kind of agnostic.

FI: And you have no belief in the supernatural?

SEARLE: None. But you see, there's something else that is, in a way, more important in this issue of the supernatural. Intellectuals in our culture have become so secularized, there's a sense in which the existence of the supernatural wouldn't matter in the way that it mattered a hundred years ago. Suppose we discovered that we're wrong, that there really is this divine force in the universe. Well then, most intellectuals would say, okay, that's a fact of physics like any other—instead of just four forces in the universe we have a fifth force. In this sense, our attitude about the existence of God wouldn't be as important because the world has already become demystified for us. Essentially our world-view would remain even if we discovered that we had been wrong, that God did exist.

FI: Would you call yourself a secular humanist?

SEARLE: Well, I've not bothered to worry too much about labels. I'm always reluctant to use these pigeonholes. But I suppose I do fit this description, which I first saw discussed in a book 25 years ago by an old friend of mine, Paul Kurtz.

FI: Could you summarize your views on consciousness?

SEARLE: Consciousness simply consists of our inner states and processes of sentience or awareness. By "inner" I just mean inside the brain. These states go on all day until you fall into dreamless sleep or become otherwise uncon-scious. Dreams are a form of consciousness, too, so these states can happen even in sleep. There is a qualitative difference between dreams and ordinary, wide-awake consciousness.

But the important thing to remember about consciousness is that it's a bi-ological phenomenon. We're talking about the capacity of human and animal brains to produce consciousness in the same way that biological systems pro-duce digestion. Consciousness is caused by operations in the brain, it goes on in the brain, and in my view there's nothing mysterious about it or metaphysical about consciousness—it's just part of the ordinary biological world.

FI: So what is your view on the mind/body problem?

SEARLE: Well that's it, actually, I just solved it for you. The traditional ques-tion known as the mind/body problem is, how does the mind relate to the body? And the answer I'm proposing to that is (a) the essence of the mental is conscious states, (b) these conscious states are caused by processes in the brain —they're caused by neurobiological processes, and (c) they are higher level fea-tures of the brain—they're features of the brain in the way that the solidity of the table is a feature of the table even though it's caused by the behavior of the particles.

Now, there's a hard question that we don't know the answer to, namely, how exactly does the brain do it? I don't know the answer to that, and neither does anybody else. But if we know anything about how the world works, we know that the brain does produce consciousness.

FI: Some people believe that we can draw an analogy between the mind and computers. That is, they want to say that the mind is just the software that your brain runs. So would you say that the mind and mental processes are equivalent to software?

SEARLE: No, I wouldn't. I think that's one of the dumbest analogies that has ever cropped up in this whole debate, because the relationship between the brain and consciousness is one of *causation*. Brain processes have to *cause* con-sciousness, but the relationship between the computer—the hardware—and the software is one of implementation, not of causation. That is, with computers, it's a matter of implementing a certain symbolic sequence in a set of hardware processes.

The key point is this: the computer processes are computational processes —they are defined purely in virtue of their symbolic, or their formal or syntactical properties. That is, the implemented program consists purely of syntactical or symbolic processes, usually thought of as sequences of zeros and ones, but any symbols will do. Now, we know that something more than that goes on in the brain because we know that our thought processes have more than uninterpreted formal symbols. They actually have mental contents. As I often explain it, the *syntax* of the computer program isn't sufficient for the *semantics* of actual human thought processes.

Years ago I gave a proof of that—called the "Chinese room argument"—and the way it works is this: just imagine that you're the computer, and you're carrying out the steps in a program for something you don't understand. I don't understand Chinese, so I imagine I'm locked in a room shuffling Chinese symbols according to a computer program, and I can give the right answers to the right questions in Chinese, but all the same, I don't understand Chinese. All I'm doing is shuffling symbols. And now, and this is the crucial point: if I don't understand Chinese on the basis of implementing the program for understanding Chinese, then neither does any other digital computer on that basis because no computer's got anything I don't have. It's the simplest argument in history, but you'd be surprised how many people have fits about it.

FI: Do you think there ever could be an artificial intelligence that has consciousness?

SEARLE: I don't see why not. If we knew how the brain produced consciousness, we could eventually produce it artificially. Let's suppose that we actually discover that consciousness is produced by a certain electrical sequence in the brain, and we build a machine that would have that electrical sequence. Such an achievement might be medically useful because if my brain was starting to decay they might be able to replace it with these electrical gimmicks. So I don't have any difficulty in principle with the idea of building artificial intelligence. But if you're talking about actual conscious thought processes, you can't do it with a computer.

FI: Not even a very sophisticated, very fast computer?

SEARLE: Well, it depends on your definition of computation. I'm going with the definition of computation used now, which was essentially [Alan] Turing's definition. Computation is defined in terms of mathematics and mapping inputs onto outputs according to a certain set of procedures or a certain set of computational rules. But, of course, you can redefine computation any way you want to. You can say that we're going to redefine computation to mean the brain processes that produce consciousness. Then, trivially, you've solved your problem. But now as we understand computers—whether they're the machines that you and I normally use or these so-called connectionist machines—computation is defined independently of the underlying medium. It's defined in terms of formal, abstract symbolic processes, and those will never be enough to produce a mind because they're not enough to cause consciousness or intentionality. That's what the Chinese room argument shows.

FI: So however complex computers get, there will never be an emergence of conscious thought?

SEARLE: That's right. You see, the point is, there might be some other reason why a computer has consciousness: maybe God decides he's going to make all Macintoshes conscious. I can't argue with that. But what I'm going to say is it doesn't matter how complex the program is, or what state of technology you're at, or how fast the processors are. The program—defined in terms of syntactical processes—would never be sufficient to guarantee the presence of consciousness because the processes are defined independently of consciousness, purely in terms of symbolic manipulation. Now the system might be conscious for some other reason, but the consciousness wouldn't be guaranteed by the program, and it doesn't matter whether the program's simple or complex. It doesn't matter if it runs fast or slow; it's all the same. Syntax is not enough to guarantee the presence of semantics. That's the basic idea.

FI: There has been a lot of progress in the field of artificial intelligence and the neuro-sciences in general. And it's fed into a lot of philosophical debate. What do you think has been the most important development in these areas in the last 10 years as it relates to the study of the mind?

SEARLE: Well, as you probably know, I am a cognitive scientist, a member of the Cognitive Science Group at Berkeley. From this perspective, I make a distinction between cognitive neurobiology and computational cognitive science. I think computational cognitive science is useful as a tool; it's a useful device to perform thought experiments, test hypotheses, and so on. So I have no objection to artificial intelligence so construed. But to my mind, if we include neurobiology within cognitive science, the greatest advances in the past 10 years have been in our advanced knowledge of the brain. I think that this is the most exciting area of scientific research right now. This knowledge is incremental. It's not that we've had some fantastic breakthroughs, but if you look at the textbooks today and compare them with the textbooks of 20 years ago, we just know a whole lot more than we used to know. Now, there's a whole lot of other stuff going on that I think is pretty useful too, and this is not at the level of neurobiology, but at a higher level. We are, for example, understanding perception better. To me these two areas are the most exciting.

FI: Looking forward a bit, if we have this interview in 10 years time, what would you anticipate as being the most likely area for new discovery?

SEARLE: I think that substantial progress will be made in the study of the brain. My brain scientist friends are always frustrated by how slow it is. But I'm a philosopher; we've been at this 2,000 years. I don't expect a solution overnight. It would be wonderful if we knew in 10 years time how the brain caused consciousness. I don't think we will. And I'm afraid probably not in our lifetime. But just to get closer to understanding it would be a tremendous achievement.

FI: What excites you the most in your own work?

SEARLE: I just finished a book called *The Construction of Social Reality*. It's about how conscious agents create an objective reality of money, property, government, marriage, universities, language, and institutions. I think there ought to be more research in this area, and I hope to do a lot of that work.

Another area about which I'm writing a book is rationality. I think that it's kind of a scandal that philosophers regard rationality as so important yet don't really have a good theory of it. I'm trying to work on that, but again it's slow going, and I may not succeed. I have been working on that for some years.

FI: What would a theory of rationality involve?

SEARLE: It would involve answering such questions as: what is the nature of the human capacity to think and act rationally? To what extent is it dependent on language? To what extent is it constituted by linguistic phenomena, by semantic phenomena? Is it a separate faculty like the faculty of perception or the faculty of acquiring a language that children have, or is it already built into the structure of those faculties? Why is it we don't have a formal logic of practical rationality in the way that classical logic seems to give us the formal logic of theoretical rationality? So it is a whole pile of questions that I'm working on. I think it's an exciting field because I believe that our traditions handed down from Aristotle have been mistaken.

FI: Mistaken? Can you elaborate on that?

SEARLE: Well, it's difficult to summarize, but it's something like this: in practical rationality, essentially we have thought that practical reasoning—reasoning about what to do—was in the end reasoning about how to satisfy desires. So, as Hume says, reason is and ought to be the slave of the passions. Aristotle says reasoning is always about a means to an end. There are a whole lot of slogans in our traditions that articulate this idea. In any case, rationality is always about satisfying desires.

Now Kant labored mightily to overcome this tradition, and it's a hell of an effort. The guy was fantastic, but I don't think he succeeded. And what I want to suggest is that there's a much simpler answer to at least a part of the question, though it doesn't answer the whole question. A part of the answer is that we have this remarkable capacity to create desire-independent reasons for action. The classic case of course is promising, where you can do something now that will create a reason for you to do something in the future, even if in the future you'd rather not do it. Anyway, I think that's a kind of entering wedge for me into cracking the whole tradition of practical rationality.

POSTSCRIPT

Will It Be Possible to Build a Computer That Can Think?

Science fiction has played with the idea of "thinking machines" for decades, but is this idea nothing but science fiction? Some scientists do not think so, although they are quick to grant that the technology is not yet nearly ready to produce a convincing example. Still, they are trying, at least in restricted subsets of human intelligence such as game playing. A program called Chinook, for example, is the current world checkers champion. See Ivars Peterson, "Silicon Champions of the Game," *Science News* (August 2, 1997). In February 1996 IBM's "Deep Blue," a chess-playing supercomputer, won and drew games against the human world champion, Garry Kasparov. Although it lost the six-game match, it still demonstrated a skill at something that most people are willing to call "thinking." See Monty Newborn, *Kasparov Versus Deep Blue: Computer Chess Comes of Age* (Springer-Verlag, 1996).

In May 1997 an improved Deep Blue topped its own performance by defeating Kasparov 2–1, with 3 draws, and sent the news media into a frenzy. We are, wrote Charles Krauthammer in *The Weekly Standard,* "creating a new and different form of being. And infinitely more monstrous: creatures sharing our planet who not only imitate and surpass us in logic, who have even achieved consciousness and free will, but are utterly devoid of the kind of feelings and emotions that, literally, humanize human beings. Be afraid." See also Donald Michie, "Slaughter on Seventh Avenue," *New Scientist* (June 7, 1997).

Is chess playing a kind of thinking? When the idea of artificial intelligence was new, workers in the field agreed that it was and set out to achieve it. Even partial success was enough to rouse critics who said that if a machine could do it, it could not be "real" thinking. Deep Blue's complete success, however, seems to have many people *afraid* that chess playing is real thinking and that human primacy in a very fundamental area—in fact, human identity—is now seriously threatened. Moravec, of course, does not feel threatened at all. He develops his ideas at much greater length in his book *Mind Children* (Harvard University Press, 1988) and its successor *Robot, Being: Mere Machine to Transcendent Mind* (Oxford University Press, 1998). In these books, Moravec focuses on the development of motor and sensory apparatus for robots, forecasts the transfer of human minds into immensely capable machines, and speculates on the replacement of biological intelligence by machine intelligence. He also discusses some of the ideas behind the growing field of "artificial life." Also see Steven Levy, *Artificial Life* (Pantheon, 1992).

Moravec's speculations reach far into the future, culminating in a time when humans will exist as streamlined minds residing in "cyberspace," a world simulated within computers, and when the very definition of "reality" must be changed to encompass the new conditions of human life. For an interesting discussion along the same lines, see Frederick Pohl and Hans Moravec, "Souls in Silicon," *Omni* (November 1993).

Not everyone is willing to go as far as Moravec. Searle laid out his argument at length in "Is the Brain's Mind a Computer Program?" *Scientific American* (January 1990). His essay was paired with Paul M. and Patricia Smith Churchland's "Could a Machine Think?" The Churchlands "reject the Turing test as a sufficient condition for conscious intelligence [because it is] very important... that the right sorts of things be going on inside the artificial machine." Unlike Searle, however, the Churchlands believe that true "artificial intelligence, in a nonbiological but massively parallel machine, remains a compelling and discernible prospect."

Searle is by no means alone in objecting to the idea of the mind as a computer program (also known as "strong AI"). Roger Penrose, a renowned physicist and mathematician at the University of Oxford in England, attacks the idea of strong AI vigorously and at length in *The Emperor's New Mind: Concerning Computers, Minds, and the Laws of Physics* (Penguin Books, 1991) and concludes, "Is it not 'obvious' that mere computation cannot evoke pleasure or pain; that it cannot perceive poetry or the beauty of an evening sky or the magic of sounds; that it cannot hope or love or despair; that it cannot have a genuine autonomous purpose?... Perhaps when computations become extraordinarily complicated they can begin to take on the more poetic or subjective qualities that we associate with the term 'mind.' Yet it is hard to avoid an uncomfortable feeling that there must always be something missing from such a picture."

On the Internet ...

The Foundation for Biomedical Research

The Foundation for Biomedical Research promotes public understanding and support of the ethical use of animals in scientific and medical research.

http://www.fbresearch.org

The Nature of Wellness

The Nature of Wellness aims to inform the public about the medical and scientific invalidity of animal experimentation and testing and to demonstrate that reliance on animal experimentation and testing is destroying the health care system, the environment, and the economy.

http://home.earthlink.net/~supress/

National Center for Genome Resources

The National Center for Genome Resources (NCGR) is a not-for-profit organization created to design, develop, support, and deliver resources in support of public and private genome research.

http://www.ncgr.org

Office of Health and Environmental Research Biology Information Center

The Department of Energy's Office of Health and Environmental Research's Biology Information Center is a listing of Internet-accessible resources for biology and other related areas of research or development.

http://www.er.doe.gov/production/ober/
bioinfo_center.html

Center for Bioethics: Bioethics Internet Project

The mission of the Center for Bioethics is to advance scholarly and public understanding of ethical, legal, social, and public policy issues in health care.

http://www.med.upenn.edu/bioethics/index.shtml

The Roslin Institute

The Roslin Institute—where Dolly the sheep was cloned—is the major center for research on molecular and quantitative genetics of farm animals and poultry science in the United Kingdom.

http://www.ri.bbsrc.ac.uk

PART 6

Ethics

*S*ociety's standards of right and wrong have been hammered out over millennia of trial, error, and (sometimes violent) debate. Accordingly, when science and technology offer society new choices to make and new things to do, debates are renewed over whether or not these choices and actions are ethically acceptable. Today there is vigorous debate over such topics as the use of animals in research, genetic engineering, performing experiments on human beings, and cloning.

- Is the Use of Animals in Research Justified?

- Should Genetic Engineering Be Banned?

- Is It Ethical to Sell Human Tissue?

- Is It Ethically Permissible to Clone Human Beings?

ISSUE 15

Is the Use of Animals in Research Justified?

YES: Elizabeth Baldwin, from "The Case for Animal Research in Psychology," *Journal of Social Issues* (1993)

NO: Steven Zak, from "Ethics and Animals," *The Atlantic Monthly* (March 1989)

ISSUE SUMMARY

YES: Elizabeth Baldwin, research ethics officer of the American Psychological Association's Science Directorate, argues that animals do not have the same moral rights as humans do, that their use in scientific research is justified by the resulting benefits to both humans and animals, and that their welfare is protected by law.

NO: Research attorney Steven Zak maintains that current animal protection laws do not adequately protect animals used in medical and other research and that, for society to be virtuous, it must recognize the rights of animals not to be sacrificed for human needs.

$\mathbf{M}$odern biologists and physicians know a great deal about how the human body works. Some of that knowledge has been gained by studying human cadavers and tissue samples acquired during surgery and through "experiments of nature" (strokes, for example, have taught a great deal about what the various parts of the brain do; extensive injuries from car accidents and wars have also been edifying). Some knowledge of human biology has also been gained from experiments on humans, such as when brain surgery patients agree to let their surgeons stimulate different parts of their brains electrically while the brains are exposed or when cancer patients agree to try experimental treatments.

The key word here is *agree*. Today it is widely accepted that people have the right to consent or not to consent to whatever is done to them in the name of research or treatment. In fact, society has determined that research done on humans without their free and informed consent is a form of scientific misconduct. However, this standard does not apply to animals, experimentation on which has produced the most knowledge of the human body.

Are mammals special?

Although animals have been used in research for at least the last 2,000 years, during most of that time, physicians who thought they had a workable treatment for some illness commonly tried it on their patients before they had any idea whether or not it worked or was even safe. Many patients, of course, died during these untested treatments. In the mid-nineteenth century, the French physiologist Claude Bernard argued that it was sensible to try such treatments first on animals to avoid some human suffering and death. No one then questioned whether or not human lives were more valuable than animal lives.

Today millions of animals are used in research. Geneticists generally study fruit flies, roundworms, and zebra fish. Physiologists study mammals, mostly mice and rats but also rabbits, cats, dogs, pigs, sheep, goats, monkeys, and chimpanzees. Experimental animals are often kept in confined quarters, cut open, infected with disease organisms, fed unhealthy diets, and injected with assorted chemicals. Sometimes the animals suffer. Sometimes the animals die. And sometimes they are healed, albeit often of diseases or injuries induced by the researchers in the first place.

Not surprisingly, some observers have reacted with extreme sympathy and have called for better treatment of animals used in research. This "animal welfare" movement has, in turn, spawned the more extreme "animal rights" movement, which asserts that animals—especially mammals—have rights as important and as deserving of regard as those of humans. In its most extreme form, this movement insists that animals are persons in every moral sense. Thus, to kill an animal, whether for research, food, or fur, is the moral equivalent of murder.

This attitude has led to important reforms in the treatment of animals, to the development of several alternatives to using animals in research, and to a considerable reduction in the number of animals used in research. See Alan M. Goldberg and John M. Frazier, "Alternatives to Animals in Toxicity Testing," *Scientific American* (August 1989), Wade Roush, "Hunting for Animal Alternatives," *Science* (October 11, 1996), and Erik Stokstad, "Humane Science Finds Sharper and Kinder Tools," *Science* (November 5, 1999). However, it has also led to hysterical objections to in-class animal dissections, terrorist attacks on laboratories, the destruction of research records, and the theft of research materials (including animals). In 1989 an undersecretary of the Department of Health and Human Services, in attacking the animal rights movement, said, "We must not permit a handful of extremists to deprive millions of the life-sustaining and life-enhancing fruits of biomedical research."

In the following selections, Elizabeth Baldwin argues in the same vein: animals are of immense value with regard to medical, veterinary, and psychological research, but they do not have the same moral rights as humans. Our obligation, she maintains, is not to treat them as persons but to treat them humanely, and there is a sufficient number of laws and regulations to ensure that this is done. In opposition, Steven Zak states that morality requires society to recognize the right of animals not to be made to suffer at all for the benefit of humans. Therefore, researchers should always find alternative modes of research.

Elizabeth Baldwin  **YES**

The Case for Animal Research
in Psychology

*Animal liberationists do not separate out the human animal. A rat is a
pig is a dog is a boy.*

> — Ingrid Newkirk, Director, People for the
> Ethical Treatment of Animals.

The shock value of this quote has made it a favorite of those defending
the use of animals in research. It succinctly states the core belief of many animal rights activists who oppose the use of animals in research. Although some
activists work for improved laboratory conditions for research animals, recent
surveys suggest that most activists would like to eliminate animal research entirely (Plous, 1991). These activists believe animals have rights equal to humans
and therefore should not be used as subjects in laboratory research.

The debate over animal research can be confusing unless one understands the very different goals of animal welfare organizations and animal
rights groups. People concerned with animal welfare seek to improve laboratory conditions for research animals and to reduce the number of animals
needed. These mainstream goals encompass traditional concerns for the humane treatment of animals, and most researchers share these goals. In contrast,
the views of animal rights activists are *not* mainstream, since there are few
people who would agree with the above quote from Ingrid Newkirk. Indeed,
in a national poll conducted by the National Science Foundation, half the re-
spondents answered the following question affirmatively: "Should scientists be
allowed to do research that causes pain and injury to animals like dogs and
chimpanzees if it produces new information about human health problems?"
(National Science Board, 1991). These findings are particularly impressive given
the explicit mention of "pain and injury" to popular animals such as dogs
and chimpanzees. My own position is that animals do not have rights in the
same sense that humans do, but that people have a responsibility to ensure the
humane treatment of animals under their care. Animals have played a pivotal
role in improving the human condition, and in return, society should strive to
treat them well.

From Elizabeth Baldwin, "The Case for Animal Research in Psychology," *Journal of Social Issues,*
vol. 49, no. 1 (1993). Copyright © 1993 by The Society for the Psychological Study of Social Issues.
Reprinted by permission of Blackwell Publishers. References omitted.

Background

The modern animal rights movement is intellectual and spiritual heir to the Victorian antivivisection movement in Britain (Sperling, 1988). This 19th-century movement was a powerful force in Britain and arose in part from accelerating changes brought about by science and technology (and the resulting challenges to the prevailing view of humanity's relationship to nature).

The British movement peaked in 1876 with the passage of the Cruelty to Animals Act. This compromise legislation required licenses for conducting animal research, but recognized the societal value of continuing to use animals in research. It was about this time that the scientific community began to organize a defense of animal research. Several challenges to animal research were made in the ensuing 20 years, but in the end, the medical and scientific community were able to successfully protect their interests. The Victorian antivivisection movement, however, did bring about the regulation of research and helped prevent outright abuse (Sperling, 1988).

The beginning of the modern animal rights movement is generally dated to the 1975 publication of *Animal Liberation* by philosopher Peter Singer. Although Singer himself is not an advocate of animal "rights," he provided the groundwork for later arguments that animals have rights—including the right not to be used in research. Most animal rights activists believe animals have a right not to be used for research, food, entertainment, and a variety of other purposes. An inordinate amount of attention is devoted to animal research, however, even though far fewer animals are used for research than for other purposes (Nicoll & Russell, 1990).

There has been a phenomenal growth in the animal rights movement since the publication of Singer's book. People for the Ethical Treatment of Animals (PETA), the leading animal rights organization in the United States, has grown from 18 members in 1981 to more than 250,000 members in 1990. (McCabe, 1990). By any standard, the animal rights movement is a force to be reckoned with.

Philosophical Issues

There are two basic philosophies that support the animal rights movement, although activists are often unable to articulate them (Sperling, 1988). These two positions are summarized by Herzog (1990) as the *utilitarian* argument and the *rights* argument.

The utilitarian position is that the greatest good is achieved by maximizing pleasure and happiness, and by minimizing suffering and pain. Although traditionally applied only to humans, Singer argues that animals should be included when considering the greatest good. He states, "No matter what the nature of the being, the principle of equality requires that its suffering be counted equally with the like suffering—insofar as rough comparisons can be made—of any other being" (Singer, 1990, p. 8). Utilitarians would thus argue that animals have an interest equal to that of humans in avoiding pain and suffering, and should therefore not be used in experiments that could cause them harm. Two problems with this philosophy are that (1) it is hard to draw a line between creatures that suffer and creatures that do not, and (2) the argument does not address *qualitative* differences in pain and pleasure across species (Herzog, 1990).

The rights position states that animals possess certain rights based on their inherent value. This philosophy, first developed by Tom Regan (1983), argues that animals have a right not to be used by humans in research (and for many other purposes). Major problems with this position arise in deciding just what rights are and in determining who is entitled to hold them (Herzog, 1990).

While the above positions have been developed relatively recently, the alternative view of animals as qualitatively different from humans has a long history in Judeo-Christian thought. Traditionally, humans were believed to have been created in the image of God and to have dominion over animals. Robb (1988) uses this perspective in arguing that humans are unique by virtue of their capacity for moral choice. Because of this capacity, humans can be held responsible for their choices, and can therefore enter into contractual agreements with binding rights and responsibilities for *both* parties. Robb acknowledges that some animals have human capacities in certain areas, but he argues that this does not make them morally equal to humans or give them rights that take precedence over human needs.

The most persuasive argument for using animals in behavioral research, however, is the untold benefit that accrues to both humans and animals. The benefits of behavioral research with animals have been enumerated by such authors as Miller (1985) and King and Yarbrough (1985), and for most people, these benefits are the reason that they support the continued use of animals in research. This argument—which is basically utilitarian—is the one most often cited by the research community in defense of animal research. In contrast to Singer's utilitarianism, however, animals are not given the same degree of consideration as people.

In conclusion, both sides in the animal rights debate have philosophical underpinnings to support their position, but what often emerges in the rhetoric is not reasoned debate but emotion-laden charges and personal attacks. This is not surprising, given the strong passions aroused in the discussion.

Framing the Debate

In the 1980s, activists targeted certain researchers or areas of research that they viewed as vulnerable to attack, and researchers were forced to assume a defensive posture. Unfortunately, activists were right about the vulnerability of individual scientists; little or no institutional defense was mounted against these early attacks. The prevailing attitude was to ignore the activists in hopes that they would go away, and thus attract less attention from the public and the press. This passivity left the early targets of animal rights activists in the position of a man asked, "Why do you beat your wife?" No matter how researchers responded, they sounded defensive and self-serving. It took several years for the research community to realize that animal rights activists were not going away, and that the activists' charges needed to be answered in a systematic and serious manner.

This early failure on the part of the research community to communicate its position effectively left the public with little information beyond what was provided by the animal rights activists. Framing the debate is half the battle, and the research community was left playing catch-up and answering the question, "Why do you abuse your research animals?"

The research community also faced the daunting task of explaining the use of animals in research to a public whose understanding of the scientific method was almost nil. The most difficult misconception to correct was the belief that every research project with animals should produce "useful" results (Orem, 1990). Social scientists who have received Senator William Proxmire's "Golden Fleece Award" are well aware of this line of thinking—a line of thinking that displays a complete misunderstanding of how science works, and ignores the vast amount of basic research that typically precedes each "useful" discovery.

It is difficult for scientific rationales to compete with shocking posters, catchy slogans, and soundbites from the animal rights movement. The most effective response from the scientific community has been to point out innumerable health advances made possible by the use of animals as research models. This approach is something that most people can relate to, since everyone has benefited from these advances.

The early defensive posture of scientists also failed to allay public concerns about the ability of researchers to self-regulate their care and use of research animals. Unlike the participation of humans in research (who are usually able to speak in their own defense and give consent), there seemed to be no one in the system able to "speak" for the animals. Or so people were encouraged to believe by animal rights activists. As discussed below, there are elaborate federal regulations on the use of animals in research, as well as state laws and professional guidelines on the care and use of animals in research.

Restoring Trust

Scientists, research institutions, and federal research agencies finally came to realize that the charges being leveled by animal rights activists needed to be publicly—and forcefully—rebutted. Dr. Frederick Goodwin, former Administrator of the Alcohol, Drug Abuse, and Mental Health Administration (ADAMHA), was one of the first federal officials to defend animal research publicly, and point out the difference between animal welfare and animal rights (Booth, 1989). Recently, many more federal officials and respected researchers have publicly spoken on the importance of animal research (Mervis, 1990).

Countering Misinformation

Animal rights literature often uses misleading images to depict animal research —images such as animals grimacing as they are shocked with electricity. These descriptions lead readers to believe animals are routinely subjected to high volt-age shocks capable of producing convulsions (e.g., Singer, 1990, pp. 42–45). Such propaganda is far from the truth. In most cases, electric shock (when used at all) is relatively mild—similar to what one might feel from the discharge of static electricity on a cold, dry day. Even this relatively mild use of shock is care-fully reviewed by Institutional Animal Care and Use Committees before being approved, and researchers must demonstrate that alternate techniques are not feasible. Stronger shock *is* used in animal research, but it is used to study med-ical problems such as epilepsy (a convulsive disorder). It is also used to test the effectiveness and side effects of drugs developed to control such disorders. It is not within the scope of this article to refute the myriad charges issued against animal research in general, specific projects, and individual researchers. Suffice it to say that such allegations have been persuasively refuted (Coile & Miller, 1984; Feeney, 1987; Johnson, 1990; McCabe, 1986).

Benefits to Animals

Animal rights activists often fail to appreciate the many benefits to animals that have resulted from animal research. Behavioral research has contributed to improvements in the environments of captive animals, including those used in research (Novak & Petto, 1991). The list of benefits also includes a host of veterinary procedures and the development of vaccines for deadly diseases such as rabies, Lyme disease, and feline leukemia. Research in reproductive biology and captive breeding programs are also the only hope for some animals on the brink of extinction (King et al., 1988).

Regulations and Guidelines   *Discuss – they should know this*

It is clear that many people concerned about the use of animals in research are not aware of the elaborate structure that exists to regulate the care and use of animals in research. This system includes federal regulations under the Animal Welfare Act (U.S. Department of Agriculture, 1989, 1990, 1991), Public Health Service (PHS) policy (Office for Protection from Research Risks, 1986), and state laws that govern the availability of pound animals for research.

The Animal Welfare Act, most recently amended in 1985, is enforced by the USDA's Animal and Plant Health Inspection Service (APHIS). The regula-tions connected with this law include 127 pages of guidelines governing the use of animals in research. It also includes unannounced inspections of animal research facilities by APHIS inspectors who do nothing but inspect research facilities. Their inspections are conducted to ensure compliance with regula-tions that include everything from cage size, feeding schedules, and lighting to exercise requirements for dogs and the promotion of psychological well-being among nonhuman primates.

In addition to APHIS inspectors who make unannounced inspections of animal research facilities, there are local Institutional Animal Care and Use Committees (IACUCs) that review each proposed research project using ani-mals. Research proposals must include a justification for the species used and the number of animals required, an assurance that a thorough literature review has been conducted (to prevent unnecessary replication of research), and a consideration of alternatives if available. IACUCs are also responsible for inspecting local animal research facilities to check for continued compliance with state protocols.

Each grant proposal received by a PHS agency (National Institutes of Health, and the Centers for Disease Control) that proposes using animals must contain an assurance that it has been reviewed by an IACUC and been approved. IACUCs must have no less than five members and contain at least one veterinarian, one practicing scientist experienced in research involving animals, one member who is primarily concerned in nonscientific matters (e.g., a lawyer or ethicist), and one member who is not affiliated with the institution in any way and is not an immediate family member of anyone affiliated with the institution (Office for Protection from Research Risks, 1986; USDA, 1989).

Beyond federal animal welfare regulations, PHS policy, and the PHS Guidelines (National Research Council, 1985), there are professional guidelines for the care and use of research animals. Examples include the American Psychological Association's (APA) *Ethical Principles of Psychologists* (1990) and *Guidelines for Ethical Conduct in the Care and Use of Animals* (1993), and the Society for Neuroscience's Handbook (Society for Neuroscience, 1991).

The APA also has a Committee on Animal Research and Ethics (CARE) whose charge includes the responsibility to "review the ethics of animal experimentation and recommend guidelines for the ethical conduct of research, and appropriate care of animals in research." CARE wrote the APA's *Guidelines for Ethical Conduct in the Care and Use of Animals,* and periodically reviews it and makes revisions. These guidelines are widely used by psychologists and other scientists, and have been used in teaching research ethics at the undergraduate and graduate level. The APA's Science Directorate provided support for a conference on psychological well-being of nonhuman primates used in research, and published a volume of proceedings from that conference (Novak & Petto, 1991). The APA also helps promote research on animal welfare by membership in and support for such organizations as the American Association for the Accreditation of Laboratory Animal Care (AAALAC).

AAALAC is the only accrediting body recognized by the PHS, and sets the "gold standard" for animal research facilities. To receive AAALAC accreditation, an institution must go beyond what is required by federal animal welfare regulations and PHS policy. AAALAC accreditation is highly regarded, and those institutions that receive it serve as models for the rest of the research community.

Even with all these safeguards in place, some critics question the ability of the research community to self-regulate its use of animals in research. The system can only be considered self-regulating, however, if one assumes that researchers, institutional officials, members of IACUCs (which must include a member not affiliated with the institution), USDA inspectors, animal care and lab technicians, and veterinarians have identical interests. These are the individuals with the most direct access to the animals used in research, and these are the specialists most knowledgeable about the conditions under which animals are used in research.

In several states, animal rights activists have succeeded in gaining access to IACUC meetings where animal research proposals are discussed. On the whole, however, research institutions have fought—and are still fighting —to keep these meetings closed to the general public. There is a very real fear among researchers that information gleaned from such meetings will be used to harass and target individual researchers. Given the escalating nature of illegal break-ins by such organizations as the Animal Liberation Front, this is a legitimate concern. Indeed, on some campuses "reward posters" offer money to individuals who report the abuse of research animals.

Even though IACUC meetings are generally closed to the public, the elaborate system regulating animal research is by no means a closed one. The most recent animal welfare regulations were finalized after five years of proposals recorded in the *Federal Register;* comments from the public, research institutions, professional associations, animal welfare groups, and animal rights groups; the incorporation of these comments; republication of the revised rules; and so forth. Neither researchers nor animal rights groups were entirely pleased with the final document, but everyone had their say. Although certain elements of the regulatory system rely on researchers, it is hard to imagine a workable system that would fail to use their expertise. The unspoken assumption that researchers cannot be trusted to care for their research animals is not supported by the records of APHIS inspections. Good science demands good laboratory animal care, and it is in a researcher's best interest to ensure that laboratory animals are well cared for.

The Benefits of Behavioral Research With Animals

The use of animals in psychological and behavioral research was an early target of animal rights activists. This research was perceived as a more vulnerable target than biomedical research, which had more direct and easily explained links to specific human health benefits. Psychological and behavioral research also lacked the powerful backing of the medical establishment (Archer, 1986).

There is, of course, a long list of benefits derived from psychological research with animals. These include rehabilitation of persons suffering from stroke, head injury, spinal cord injury, and Alzheimer's disease; improved communication with severely retarded children; methods for the early detection of eye disorders in children (allowing preventive treatment to avoid permanent impairment); control of chronic anxiety without the use of drugs; and improved treatments for alcoholism, obesity, substance abuse, hypertension, chronic migraine headaches, lower back pain, and insomnia (Miller, 1985). Behavioral research with nonhuman primates also permits the investigation of complex behaviors such as social organization, aggression, learning and memory, communication, and growth and development (King et al., 1988).

The nature of psychological and behavioral research makes the development and use of alternatives difficult. It is the behavior of the whole organism, and the interaction among various body systems, that is examined. Computer models may be used, but "research with animals will still be needed to provide basic data for writing computer software, as well as to prove the validity and reliability of computer alternatives" (U.S. Congress, Office of Technology Assessment, 1986). The alternative of using nonliving systems may be possible with epidemiologic data bases for some behavioral research, but chemical and physical systems are not useful for modeling complex behaviors. Likewise, in vitro cultures of organs, tissues, and cells do not display the characteristics studied by psychologists.

Conclusion

Research psychologists have been asked to eschew emotionalism, and bring logic and reason to the debate over animal research (Bowd, 1990). This is certainly the style most researchers are comfortable with—yet they have also been advised to quit trying to "apply logic and reason in their responses [to animal rights activists]" (Culliton, 1991). Culliton warns that while "animal rights people go for the heart, the biologists go for the head" and are losing the public in the process.

Which path is best? A reasoned approach draws high marks for civility, but will it help scientists in their trench warfare with animal rights activists?

Do animals have rights that preclude their use in laboratory research? I, and the psychologists I help represent, would say no. But researchers do have responsibilities to the animals they use in their research. These responsibilities include ensuring the humane care of their research animals, using the minimum number of animals necessary, and seeing to it that all laboratory assistants are adequately trained and supervised. As stated in the APA's *Ethical Principles,* "Laws and regulations notwithstanding, an animal's immediate protection depends upon the scientist's own conscience" (APA, 1990).

Researchers and others concerned with animal welfare can engage in a useful dialogue as standards of care and use evolve. This dialogue has proven fruitless with animal rights activists, though, since they seem unwilling to compromise or consider other viewpoints. What is the middle ground for a discussion with someone whose goal is the elimination of all research on animals?

The collective decision society has made is that the benefits derived from animal research far outweigh the costs. As public opinion polls indicate, most people are willing to accept these costs but want assurances that animals are humanely cared for. Yes, I'm "speciesist" in the eyes of Ingrid Newkirk—I will never believe my son is a dog is a pig is a rat.

Ethics and Animals

In December of 1986 members of an "animal-liberation" group called True Friends broke into the Sema, Inc., laboratories in Rockville, Maryland, and took four baby chimpanzees from among the facility's 600 primates. The four animals, part of a group of thirty being used in hepatitis research, had been housed individually in "isolettes"—small stainless-steel chambers with sealed glass doors. A videotape produced by True Friends shows other primates that remained behind. Some sit behind glass on wire floors, staring blankly. One rocks endlessly, banging violently against the side of his cage. Another lies dead on his cage's floor.

The "liberation" action attracted widespread media attention to Sema, which is a contractor for the National Institutes of Health [NIH], the federal agency that funds most of the animal research in this country. Subsequently the NIH conducted an investigation into conditions at the lab and concluded that the use of isolettes is justified to prevent the spread of disease among infected animals. For members of True Friends and other animal-rights groups, however, such a scientific justification is irrelevant to what they see as a moral wrong; these activists remain frustrated over conditions at the laboratory. This conflict between the NIH and animal-rights groups mirrors the tension between animal researchers and animal-rights advocates generally. The researchers' position is that their use of animals is necessary to advance human health care and that liberation actions waste precious resources and impede the progress of science and medicine. The animal-rights advocates' position is that animal research is an ethical travesty that justifies extraordinary, and even illegal, measures.

The Sema action is part of a series that numbers some six dozen to date and that began, in 1979, with a raid on the New York University Medical Center, in which members of a group known as the Animal Liberation Front (ALF) took a cat and two guinea pigs. The trend toward civil disobedience is growing. For example, last April members of animal-rights groups demonstrated at research institutions across the country (and in other countries, including Great Britain and Japan), sometimes blocking entrances to them by forming human chains. In the United States more than 130 activists were arrested, for offenses ranging from blocking a doorway and trespassing to burglary.

Not correct

To judge by everything from talk-show programs to booming membership enrollment in animal-rights groups (U.S. membership in all groups is estimated at 10 million), the American public is increasingly receptive to the animal-rights position. Even some researchers admit that raids by groups like True Friends and the ALF have exposed egregious conditions in particular labs and have been the catalyst for needed reforms in the law. But many members of animal-rights groups feel that the recent reforms do not go nearly far enough. Through dramatic animal-liberation actions and similar tactics, they hope to force what they fear is a complacent public to confront a difficult philosophical issue: whether animals, who are known to have feelings and psychological lives, ought to be treated as mere instruments of science and other human endeavors....

Animal-rights activists feel acute frustration over a number of issues, including hunting and trapping, the destruction of animals' natural habits, and the raising of animals for food. But for now the ALF considers animal research the most powerful symbol of human dominion over and exploitation of animals, and it devotes most of its energies to that issue. The public has been ambivalent, sometimes cheering the ALF on, at other times denouncing the group as "hooligans." However one chooses to characterize the ALF, it and other groups like it hold an uncompromising "rights view" of ethics toward animals. The rights view distinguishes the animal-protection movement of today from that of the past and is the source of the movement's radicalism.

"They All Have a Right to Live"

Early animal-protection advocates and groups... seldom talked about rights. They condemned cruelty—that is, acts that produce or reveal bad character. In early-nineteenth-century England campaigners against the popular sport of bull-baiting argued that it "fostered every bad and barbarous principle of our nature." Modern activists have abandoned the argument that cruelty is demeaning to human character ("virtue thought") in favor of the idea that the lives of animals have intrinsic value ("rights thought"). Rights thought doesn't necessarily preclude the consideration of virtue, but it mandates that the measure of virtue be the foreseeable consequences to others of one's acts.

"Michele" is thirty-five and works in a bank in the East. She has participated in many of the major ALF actions in the United States. One of the missions involved freeing rats, and she is scornful of the idea that rats aren't worth the effort. "These animals feel pain just like dogs, but abusing them doesn't arouse constituents' ire, so they don't get the same consideration. They all have a right to live their lives. Cuteness should not be a factor."

While most people would agree that animals should not be tortured, there is no consensus about animals' right to live (or, more precisely, their right not to be killed). Even if one can argue, as the British cleric Humphrey Primatt did in 1776, that "pain is pain, whether it be inflicted on man or on beast," it is more difficult to argue that the life of, say, a dog is qualitatively the same as that of a human being. To this, many animal-rights activists would say that every morally relevant characteristic that is lacking in all animals (rationality

— Is philosophically sound, but still not justification

might be one, according to some ways of defining that term) is also lacking in some "marginal" human beings, such as infants, or the senile, or the severely retarded. Therefore, the activists argue, if marginal human beings have the right to live, it is arbitrary to hold that animals do not. Opponents of this point of view often focus on the differences between animals and "normal" human beings, asserting, for instance, that unlike most human adults, animals do not live by moral rules and therefore are not part of the human "moral community."

The credibility of the animal-rights viewpoint, however, need not stand or fall with the "marginal human beings" argument. Lives don't have to be qualitatively the same to be worthy of equal respect. One's perception that another life has value comes as much from an appreciation of its uniqueness as from the recognition that it has characteristics that are shared by one's own life. (Who would compare the life of a whale to that of a marginal human being?) One can imagine that the lives of various kinds of animals differ radically, even as a result of having dissimilar bodies and environments—that being an octopus feels different from being an orangutan or an oriole. The orangutan cannot be redescribed as the octopus minus, or plus, this or that mental characteristic; conceptually, nothing could be added to or taken from the octopus that would make it the equivalent of the oriole. Likewise, animals are not simply rudimentary human beings, God's false steps, made before He finally got it right with us.

Recognizing differences, however, puts one on tentative moral ground. It is easy to argue that likes ought to be treated alike. Differences bring problems: How do we think about things that are unlike? Against what do we measure and evaluate them? What combinations of likeness and difference lead to what sorts of moral consideration? Such problems may seem unmanageable, and yet in a human context we routinely face ones similar in kind if not quite in degree: our ethics must account for dissimilarities between men and women, citizens and aliens, the autonomous and the helpless, the fully developed and the merely potential, such as children or fetuses. We never solve these problems with finality, but we confront them. . . .

Both advocates and opponents of animal rights also invoke utilitarianism in support of their points of view. Utilitarianism holds that an act or practice is measured by adding up the good and the bad consequences—classically, pleasure and pain—and seeing which come out ahead. There are those who would exclude animals from moral consideration on the grounds that the benefits of exploiting them outweigh the harm. Ironically, though, it was utilitarianism, first formulated by Jeremy Bentham in the eighteenth century, that brought animals squarely into the realm of moral consideration. If an act or practice has good and bad consequences for animals, then these must be entered into the moral arithmetic. And the calculation must be genuinely disinterested. One may not baldly assert that one's own interests count for more. Animal researchers may truly believe that they are impartially weighing all interests when they conclude that human interests overwhelm those of animals. But a skeptical reader will seldom be persuaded that they are in fact doing so. . . .

I don't agree

Even true utilitarianism is incomplete, though, without taking account of rights. For example, suppose a small group of aboriginal tribespeople were captured and bred for experiments that would benefit millions of other people by, say, resulting in more crash-worthy cars. Would the use of such people be morally acceptable? Surely it would not, and that point illustrates an important function of rights thought: to put limits on what can be done to individuals, even for the good of the many. Rights thought dictates that we cannot kill one rights-holder to save another—or even more than one other—whether or not the life of the former is "different" from that of the latter.

Those who seek to justify the exploitation of animals often claim that it comes down to a choice: kill an animal or allow a human being to die. But this claim is misleading, because a choice so posed has already been made. The very act of considering the taking of life X to save life Y reduces X to the status of a mere instrument. Consider the problem in a purely human context. Imagine that if Joe doesn't get a new kidney he will die. Sam, the only known potential donor with a properly matching kidney, himself has only one kidney and has not consented to give it—and his life—up for Joe. Is there really a choice? If the only way to save Joe is to kill Sam, then we would be unable to do so—and no one would say that we chose Sam over Joe. Such a choice would never even be contemplated.

In another kind of situation there *is* a choice. Imagine that Joe and Sam both need a kidney to survive, but we have only one in our kidney bank. It may be that we should give the kidney to Joe, a member of our community, rather than to Sam, who lives in some distant country (though this is far from clear—maybe flipping a coin would be more fair). Sam (or the loser of the coin flip) could not complain that his rights had been violated, because moral claims to some resource—positive claims—must always be dependent on the availability of that resource. But the right not to be treated as if one were a mere resource or instrument—negative, defensive claims—is most fundamentally what it means to say that one has rights. And this is what members of the ALF have in mind when they declare that animals, like human beings, have rights.

Where, one might wonder, should the line be drawn? Must we treat dragonflies the same as dolphins? Surely not. Distinctions must be made, though to judge definitively which animals must be ruled out as holders of rights may be impossible even in principle. In legal or moral discourse we are virtually never able to draw clear lines. This does not mean that drawing a line anywhere, arbitrarily, is as good as drawing one anywhere else.

The line-drawing metaphor, though, implies classifying entities in a binary way: as either above the line, and so entitled to moral consideration, or not. Binary thinking misses nuances of our moral intuition. Entities without rights may still deserve moral consideration on other grounds: one may think that a dragonfly doesn't quite qualify for rights yet believe that it would be wrong to crush one without good reason. And not all entities with rights need be treated in precisely the same way. This is apparent when one compares animals over whom we have assumed custody with wild animals. The former, I think, have rights to our affirmative aid, while the latter have such rights only in certain circumstances. Similar distinctions can be made among human beings, and also between human beings and particular animals. For example, I recently spent $1,000 on medical care for my dog, and I think he had a right to that care, but I have never given such an amount to a needy person on the street. Rights thought, then, implies neither that moral consideration ought to be extended only to the holders of rights nor that all rights-holders must be treated with a rigid equality. It implies only that rights-holders should never be treated as if they, or their kind, didn't matter.

Animals, Refrigerators, and Can Openers

The question of man's relationship with animals goes back at least to Aristotle, who granted that animals have certain senses—hunger, thirst, a sense of touch— but who held that they lack rationality and therefore as "the lower sort [they] are by nature slaves, and ... should be under the rule of a master." Seven centuries later Saint Augustine added the authority of the Church, arguing that "Christ himself [teaches] that to refrain from the killing of animals ... is the height of superstition, for there are no common rights between us and the beasts...." Early in the seventeenth century René Descartes argued that, lacking language, animals cannot have thoughts or souls and thus are machines.

One may be inclined to dismiss such beliefs as archaic oddities, but even today some people act as if animals were unfeeling things. I worked in a research lab for several summers during college, and I remember that it was a natural tendency to lose all empathy with one's animal subjects. My supervisor seemed actually to delight in swinging rats around by their tails and flinging them against a concrete wall as a way of stunning the animals before killing them. Rats and rabbits, to those who injected, weighed, and dissected them, were little different from cultures in a petri dish: they were just things to manipulate and observe. Feelings of what may have been moral revulsion were taken for squeamishness, and for most of my lab mates those feelings subsided with time.

The first animal-welfare law in the United States, passed in New York State in 1828, emphasized the protection of animals useful in agriculture. It also promoted human virtue with a ban on "maliciously and cruelly" beating or torturing horses, sheep, or cattle. Today courts still tend to focus on human character, ruling against human beings only for perpetrating the most shocking and senseless abuse of animals....

Most states leave the regulation of medical research to Washington. In 1966 Congress passed the Laboratory Animal Welfare Act, whose stated purpose was not only to provide humane care for animals but also to protect the owners of dogs and cats from theft by proscribing the use of stolen animals. (Note the vocabulary of property law; animals have long been legally classified as property.) Congress then passed the Animal Welfare Act [AWA] of 1970, which expanded the provisions of the 1966 act to include more species of animals and to regulate more people who handle animals. The AWA was further amended in 1976 and in 1985.

The current version of the AWA mandates that research institutions meet certain minimum requirements for the handling and the housing of animals, and requires the "appropriate" use of pain-killers. But the act does not regulate research or experimentation itself, and allows researchers to withhold anesthetics or tranquilizers "when scientifically necessary." Further, while the act purports to regulate dealers who buy animals at auctions and other markets to sell to laboratories, it does little to protect those animals. . . .

The 1985 amendments to the AWA were an attempt to improve the treatment of animals in laboratories, to improve enforcement, to encourage the consideration of alternative research methods that use fewer or no animals, and to minimize duplication in experiments. One notable change is that for the first time, research institutions using primates must keep them in environments conducive to their psychological well-being; however, some animal-rights activists have expressed skepticism, since the social and psychological needs of primates are complex, and the primary concern of researchers is not the interests of their animal subjects. Last September [1988] a symposium on the psychological well-being of captive primates was held at Harvard University. Some participants contended that we lack data on the needs of the thirty to forty species of primates now used in laboratories. Others suggested that the benefits of companionship and social life are obvious.

The U.S. Department of Agriculture is responsible for promulgating regulations under the AWA and enforcing the law. Under current USDA regulations the cages of primates need only have floor space equal to three times the area occupied by the animal "when standing on four feet"—in the words of the USDA, which has apparently forgotten that primates have hands. The 1985 amendments required the USDA to publish final revised regulations, including regulations on the well-being of primates, by December of 1986. At this writing the department has yet to comply, and some activists charge that the NIH and the Office of Management and Budget have delayed the publication of the new regulations and attempted to undermine them.

One may believe that virtue thought—which underlies current law—and rights thought should protect animals equally. After all, wouldn't a virtuous person or society respect the interests of animals? But virtue thought allows the law to disregard these interests, because virtue can be measured by at least two yardsticks: by the foreseeable effects of an act on the interests of an animal or by the social utility of the act. The latter standard was applied in a 1983 case in Maryland in which a researcher appealed his conviction for cruelty to animals after he had performed experiments that resulted in monkeys' mutilating their hands. Overturning the conviction, the Maryland Court of Appeals wrote that "there are certain normal human activities to which the infliction of pain to an animal is purely incidental"—thus the actor is not a sadist—and that the state legislature had intended for these activities to be exempt from the law protecting animals.

The law, of course, is not monolithic. Some judges have expressed great sympathy for animals. On the whole, though, the law doesn't recognize animal rights. Under the Uniform Commercial Code, for instance, animals—along with refrigerators and can openers—constitute "goods."

Alternatives to Us-Versus-Them

Estimates of the number of animals used each year in laboratories in the United States range from 17 million to 100 million: 200,000 dogs, 50,000 cats, 60,000 primates, 1.5 million guinea pigs, hamsters, and rabbits, 200,000 wild animals, thousands of farm animals and birds, and millions of rats and mice. The conditions in general—lack of exercise, isolation from other animals, lengthy confinement in tiny cages—are stressful. Many experiments are painful or produce fear, anxiety, or depression. For instance, in 1987 researchers at the Armed Forces Radiobiology Research Institute reported that nine monkeys were subjected to whole-body irradiation; as a result, within two hours six of the monkeys were vomiting and hypersalivating. In a proposed experiment at the University of Washington pregnant monkeys, kept in isolation, will be infected with the simian AIDS virus; their offspring, infected or not, will be separated from the mothers at birth.

Not all animals in laboratories, of course, are subjects of medical research. In the United States each year some 10 million animals are used in testing products and for other commercial purposes. For instance, the United States Surgical Corporation, in Norwalk, Connecticut, uses hundreds of dogs each year to train salesmen in the use of the company's surgical staple gun. In 1981 and 1982 a group called Friends of Animals brought two lawsuits against United States Surgical to halt these practices. The company successfully argued in court that Friends of Animals lacked "standing" to sue, since no member of the organization had been injured by the practice; after some further legal maneuvering by Friends of Animals both suits were dropped. Last November [1988] a New York City animal-rights advocate was arrested as she planted a bomb outside United States Surgical's headquarters.

In 1987, according to the USDA, 130,373 animals were subjected to pain or distress unrelieved by drugs for "the purpose of research or testing." This figure, which represents nearly seven percent of the 1,969,123 animals reported to the USDA that year as having been "used in experimentation," ignores members of species not protected by the AWA (cold-blooded animals, mice, rats, birds, and farm animals). Moreover, there is reason to believe that the USDA's figures are low. For example, according to the USDA, no primates were subjected to distress in the state of Maryland, the home of Sema, in any year from 1980 to 1987, the last year for which data are available.

Steps seemingly favorable to animals have been taken in recent years. In addition to the passage of the 1985 amendments to the AWA, the Public Health Service [PHS], which includes the NIH, has revised its "Policy on Humane Care and Use of Laboratory Animals," and new legislation has given legal force to much of this policy. Under the revised policy, institutions receiving NIH or other PHS funds for animal research must have an "institutional animal care and use committee" consisting of at least five members, including one nonscientist and one person not affiliated with the institution.

Many activists are pessimistic about these changes, however. They argue that the NIH has suspended funds at noncompliant research institutions only in response to political pressure, and assert that the suspensions are intended as a token gesture, to help the NIH regain lost credibility. They note that Sema, which continues to keep primates in isolation cages (as regulations permit), is an NIH contractor whose principal investigators are NIH employees. As to the makeup of the animal-care committees, animal-rights advocates say that researchers control who is appointed to them. In the words of one activist, "The brethren get to choose."

However one interprets these changes, much remains the same. For example, the AWA authorizes the USDA to confiscate animals from laboratories not in compliance with regulations, but only if the animal "is no longer required . . . to carry out the research, test or experiment"; the PHS policy mandates pain relief "unless the procedure is justified for scientific reasons." Fundamentally, the underlying attitude that animals may appropriately be used and discarded persists.   *don't agree*

If the law is ever to reflect the idea that animals have rights, more drastic steps—such as extending the protection of the Constitution to animals—must be taken. Constitutional protection for animals is not an outlandish proposition. The late U.S. Supreme Court Justice William O. Douglas wrote once, in a dissenting opinion, that the day should come when "all of the forms of life . . . will stand before the court—the pileated woodpecker as well as the coyote and bear, the lemmings as well as the trout in the streams."

Suppose, just suppose, that the AWA were replaced by an animal-rights act, which would prohibit the use by human beings of any animals to their detriment. What would be the effect on medical research, education, and product *agree ?* testing? Microorganisms; tissue, organ, and cell cultures; physical and chemical systems that mimic biological functions; computer programs and mathematical models that simulate biological interactions; epidemiologic data bases; and clinical studies have all been used to reduce the number of animals used in experiments, demonstrations, and tests. A 1988 study by the National Research Council, while finding that researchers lack the means to replace all animals in labs, did conclude that current and prospective alternative techniques could reduce the number of animals—particularly mammals—used in research.

Perhaps the report would have been more optimistic if scientists were as zealous about conducting research to find alternatives as they are about animal research. But we should not be misled by discussions of alternatives into thinking that the issue is merely empirical. It is broader than just whether subject A and procedure X can be replaced by surrogates B and Y. We could undergo a shift in world view: instead of imagining that we have a divine mandate to dominate and make use of everything else in the universe, we could have a sense of *I agree* belonging to the world and of kinship with the other creatures in it. The us-versus-them thinking that weighs animal suffering against human gain could *don't agree* give way to an appreciation that "us" includes "them." That's an alternative too.

Some researchers may insist that scientists should not be constrained in their quest for knowledge, but this is a romantic notion of scientific freedom that never was and should not be. Science is always constrained, by economic and social priorities and by ethics. Sometimes, paradoxically, it is also freed by these constraints, because a barrier in one direction forces it to cut another path, in an area that might have remained unexplored.

Barriers against the exploitation of animals ought to be erected in the law, because law not only enforces morality but defines it. Until the law protects the interests of animals, the animal-rights movement will by definition be radical. And whether or not one approves of breaking the law to remedy its shortcomings, one can expect such activities to continue. "I believe that you should do for others as you would have done for you," one member of the ALF says. "If you were being used in painful experiments, you'd want someone to come to your rescue."

POSTSCRIPT

Is the Use of Animals in Research Justified?

$\mathbf{M}$uch debate about the lethal experiments that were conducted on nonconsenting human subjects by the Nazis during World War II, as well as the ensuing trials of the Nazi physicians in Nuremburg, Germany, has established a consensus that no scientist can treat people the way the Nazis did. Informed consent is essential, and research on humans must aim to benefit those same humans.

As these ideas have gained currency, some people have tried to extend them to say that, just as scientists cannot do whatever they wish to humans, they cannot do whatever they wish to animals. Harriet Ritvo, in "Toward a More Peaceable Kingdom," *Technology Review* (April 1992), says that the animal rights movement "challenges the ideology of science itself . . . forcing experimenters to recognize that they are not necessarily carrying out an independent exercise in the pursuit of truth—that their enterprise, in its intellectual as well as its social and financial dimensions, is circumscribed and defined by the culture of which it is an integral part." The result is a continuing debate, driven by the periodic discovery of researchers who seem quite callous (at least to the layperson's eye) in their treatment of animals (see Kathy Snow Guillermo, *Monkey Business: The Disturbing Case That Launched the Animal Rights Movement* [National Press, 1993]) and by the charge that animal rights advocates are misanthropes who just do not understand nature. See Richard Conniff, "Fuzzy-Wuzzy Thinking About Animal Rights," *Audubon* (November 1990).

In the February 1997 issue of *Scientific American,* Andrew N. Rowan presents a debate entitled "The Benefits and Ethics of Animal Research." The opposing articles are Neal D. Barnard and Stephen R. Kaufman, "Animal Research Is Wasteful and Misleading" and Jack H. Botting and Adrian R. Morrison, "Animal Research Is Vital to Medicine." In addition, staff writer Madhusree Mukerjee contributed "Trends in Animal Research." Among books that are pertinent to this issue are F. Barbara Orlans, *In the Name of Science: Issues in Responsible Animal Experimentation* (Oxford University Press, 1993); Rod Strand and Patti Strand, *The Hijacking of the Humane Movement* (Doral, 1993); and Deborah Blum, *The Monkey Wars* (Oxford University Press, 1994).

It must be noted, however, that the animal rights movement sometimes goes to extremes that do not help its case, such as when activists destroy laboratories and issue death threats to researchers and their families. See Robert Koenig, "European Researchers Grapple With Animal Rights," *Science* (June 4, 1999).

ISSUE 16

Should Genetic Engineering Be Banned?

YES: Andrew Kimbrell, from *The Human Body Shop: The Engineering and Marketing of Life* (HarperSanFrancisco, 1993)

NO: James Hughes, from "Embracing Change With All Four Arms: A Post-Humanist Defense of Genetic Engineering," *Paper Presented at the University of Chicago Health and Society Workshop* (May 6, 1994)

ISSUE SUMMARY

YES: Andrew Kimbrell, policy director of the Foundation on Economic Trends in Washington, D.C., argues that the development of genetic engineering is so marked by scandal, ambition, and moral blindness that society should be deeply suspicious of its purported benefits.

NO: James Hughes, assistant director of research at the MacLean Center for Clinical Medical Ethics in the Department of Medicine at the University of Chicago, contends that the potential benefits of genetic engineering greatly outweigh the potential risks.

In the early 1970s scientists first discovered that it was technically possible to move genes–biological material that determines a living organism's physical makeup–from one organism to another and thus (in principle) to give bacteria, plants, and animals new features and to correct genetic defects of the sort that cause many diseases, such as cystic fibrosis. Most researchers in molecular genetics were excited by the potentialities that suddenly seemed within their grasp. However, a few researchers–as well as many people outside the field– were disturbed by the idea; they thought that genetic mix-and-match games might spawn new diseases, weeds, and pests. Some people even argued that genetic engineering should be banned at the outset, before unforeseeable horrors were unleashed.

Researchers in support of genetic experimentation responded by declaring a moratorium on their own work until suitable safeguards could be devised. Once those safeguards were in place in the form of government regulations, work resumed. James D. Watson and John Tooze document the early years of this research in *The DNA Story: A Documentary History of Gene Cloning* (W. H. Freeman, 1981). For a shorter, more recent review of the story, see Bernard D. Davis,

"Genetic Engineering: The Making of Monsters?" *The Public Interest* (Winter 1993).

By 1989 the technology had developed tremendously: researchers could obtain patents for mice with artificially added genes ("transgenic" mice); firefly genes had been added to tobacco plants to make them glow (faintly) in the dark; and growth hormone produced by genetically engineered bacteria was being used to grow low-fat pork and increase milk production by cows. Critics argued that genetic engineering was unnatural and violated the rights of both plants and animals to their "species integrity"; that expensive, high-tech, tinkered animals gave the competitive advantage to big agricultural corporations and drove small farmers out of business; and that putting human genes into animals, plants, or bacteria was downright offensive. See Betsy Hanson and Dorothy Nelkin, "Public Responses to Genetic Engineering," *Society* (November/December 1989).

The skepticism about the benefits remains, but agricultural genetic engineering has proceeded at a breakneck pace, largely because, as Robert Shapiro, CEO of Monsanto Corporation, said in June 1998, it "represents a potentially sustainable solution to the issue of feeding people." Between 1996 and 1998, the area planted with genetically engineered crops jumped from 1.7 million hectares to 27.8 million hectares. Sales of genetically engineered crop products are expected to reach $25 billion by 2010. See Brian Halweil, "The Emperor's New Crops," *WorldWatch* (July/August 1999).

By 1990 the first proposals to add genes to *human* cells in order to restore normal function were being made (Inder M. Verma, "Gene Therapy," *Scientific American* [November 1990]). Not long after that, the first gene therapy attempts were approved by the National Institutes of Health (NIH), despite objections that altering a human being's genes meant violating that person's nature and identity at the deepest possible level. To avoid producing genetic changes that would be passed on to future generations, which cannot consent to the changes, researchers have been restricted to modifying only somatic (body) cells, not germ cells (sperm and eggs). Still, in 1994 Mark A. Findeis, a group leader at OsteoArthritis Sciences in Cambridge, Massachusetts, described numerous genetic therapies under development in "Genes to the Rescue," *Technology Review* (April 1994).

Anti-genetic-engineering activist Jeremy Rifkin, president of the Foundation on Economic Trends in Washington, D.C., has stressed that because we do not know the future undesirable side effects of genetic engineering, and because those side effects may be horrible, we should reject the technology. In the following selection, Andrew Kimbrell echoes this view of genetic engineering and argues that its history is so marked by scandal, ambition, and moral blindness that it poses an exceedingly disturbing precedent for the future.

James Hughes, representing the voice of optimism, argues in the second selection that genetic engineering offers "such good that the risks are dwarfed" and finds "faith in the potential unlimited improvability of human nature and expansion of human powers far more satisfying than a resignation to our current limits."

need to accept
death + limit technology

This is mainly "germ line"; nearly all therapy is somatic

Andrew Kimbrell

Engineering Ourselves

In an age of protests, this was the first of its kind. It was early March 1977, and hundreds of demonstrators had flocked to the futuristic, domed auditorium of the National Academy of Sciences (NAS). The protesters chanted slogans such as "We will not be cloned," and they carried signs bearing warnings, including "Don't Tread on My Genes."

The object of the protest was a three-day symposium being held under the auspices of the NAS. The forum was intended to bring together scientists, government officials, and business leaders to discuss the future prospects of genetically altering life-forms, including humans. The chairman of the meeting, Dr. David Hamburg, president of the NAS Institute for Medicine, undoubtedly had anticipated that this would be the usual scientific conference, a collegial discussion of current scientific and legislative issues that had been cropping up as a result of advances in genetic manipulation. It was not to be.

The demonstrators, led by activist Jeremy Rifkin, crowded the auditorium with their signs and dominated the session with their chants and shouted questions to the symposium's panels. They relentlessly prodded the scientists and bureaucrats, urging them to confront the moral and ethical implications of engineering the genetic code of life. They also repeatedly demanded that speakers disclose who was financing their research. (The forum was supported in part by funds from a variety of drug manufacturers.) Finally, under a barrage of questions about the eugenic [breed- or race-improving] and discriminatory potential of biotechnology, the chairman had no choice but to offer the podium to Rifkin and others to air their concerns.

Speaking up with the protesters were many prominent scientists. At a press conference prior to the demonstration, Nobel Prize winner George Wald called the use of genetic engineering "the biggest break in nature that has occurred in human history." Renowned biochemist Dr. Erwin Chargoff warned against the use of genetic research to attempt to control the evolution of humans and other life-forms.

The activists and scientists who voiced their concerns that day were part of a growing chorus of those who feared the engineering of life. As early as 1967, Marshall Nirenberg, the Nobelist who first described the "language" of the

From Andrew Kimbrell, *The Human Body Shop: The Engineering and Marketing of Life* (HarperSanFrancisco, 1993). Copyright © 1993 by Andrew Kimbrell, 1997 by Regnery Publishing. Reprinted by permission of Regnery Publishing, Inc., Washington, DC. Notes omitted.

genetic code, had delivered a stern lecture about engineering human beings, along with a remarkably prescient prophecy:

> My guess is that cells will be programmed with synthetic messages within 25 years.... The point that deserves special emphasis is that man may be able to program his own cells long before he will be able to assess adequately the long-term consequences of such alterations, long before he will be able to formulate goals, and long before he can resolve the ethical and moral problems which will be raised.

The fears of the early gene engineering critics focused on proposals to engineer the human germline—to permanently alter the genetic makeup of an individual that is passed on to succeeding generations. Many scientists were predicting that, by manipulating the genes in sperm, eggs, or embryos, future physicians would be able to excise "bad" genes from the human gene pool. Critics envisioned a future human body shop industry in eliminating the genes responsible for sickle-cell anemia or cystic fibrosis by mass engineering of these "problem" genes from the sex cells (the sperm and ova) of individuals. Future genetic engineers could also add foreign genes to a patient's genome, genes from other humans or even different species. These genes might protect an individual from various diseases, or confer desired qualities like better looks or brains. Ultimately, they believed that as scientists learned more about the relationship of genes to disease and other human traits, there would be an inevitable push to treat life-forms as so many machines whose working parts, genes, could be engineered or replaced if they were "defective."

Moreover, it was clear that if the genetic engineering of human beings should come, and most believed it would, there would be a quantum leap in both negative and positive eugenics. No longer would it be necessary to attempt to carefully control generations of breeding to create "good" characteristics, or to resort to sterilization, abortion, or genocide in order to remove abnormal or undesirable traits. Individuals could be altered through genetic surgery that would repair or replace bad genes and add good ones. Nobel Prize winner Jean Rostand's early visions of the eugenic potential of gene engineering went even further: "It would be no more than a game for the 'man farming biologist' to change the subject's sex, the colour of his eyes, the general proportions of body and limbs and perhaps the facial features." Many agreed with scientists such as Wald and Chargoff that the genetic alteration of people could eventually change the course of evolution. In 1972, ethicist Dr. Leon Kass wrote, "The new technologies for human engineering may well be 'the transition to a wholly new path of evolution.' They may therefore mark the end of *human* life as we and all other humans know it."

For over two decades, scientists, activists, ethicists, and the media have engaged in the debate over the medical and moral questions surrounding the germline genetic engineering of human beings. Editorials have appeared with headlines questioning "Whether to Make Perfect Humans" and how to arrive at "The Rules for Reshaping Life." Many critics have continued to argue against the entire enterprise of "the remaking of man." They question the wisdom of having scientists decide which part of the human genome should be eliminated

silly, I mouthing

and which enhanced. And if not scientists, who, they ask, will determine which human genes are bad and which good? They warn that even supposedly "bad" genes may bring extraordinary benefits to humanity. Recently, it was discovered that cystic fibrosis genes appear to provide individuals with protection from melanoma, an increasingly common form of skin cancer. Research conducted in the 1980s determined that sickle-cell anemia genes appear to help provide individuals with immunity to malaria. Excising such genes from the human gene pool in the effort to eliminate human disease could backfire with potentially catastrophic results.

There is also the question of how and when society will ensure that the powerful technology of germline gene engineering will be limited to the treatment of serious human diseases.... [G]enetic screening of embryos is already being used for eugenic purposes, including sex selection; and genetically engineered drugs are being used for cosmetic purposes in a way that helps foster certain forms of discrimination. Who will ensure that germline therapy is not abused in the same discriminatory and eugenic way? Will those with under normal height or I.Q. become key targets of the future entrepreneurs of germline therapy? Other novel legal questions arise from the prospect of germline therapy, issues similar to those being asked in reference to advances in prenatal genetic screening. Do children have the right to an unmanipulated germline? Or, conversely, do they have a right to the best germline that genetic surgery can offer and money can buy?

As the debate around germline gene therapy continues, another form of human genetic engineering has already begun. This form of genetic manipulation does not involve sex cells, but rather those cells that do not partake in reproduction. These cells are called *somatic cells*. Engineering these cells is both easier and far less controversial than attempting to manipulate germ cells. Altering somatic cells triggers far less concern about eugenics, in that the cells being repaired or added affect only the single individual being engineered. They do not affect the inheritance of genetic traits. Early uses of somatic cell engineering include providing individuals with healthy or repaired genes that might replace those that are faulty and causing disease.

Though somatic cell gene therapy does not affect the genetic inheritance of future generations, there are still fears. Will individuals with "poor" genetic readouts—those predisposed to a variety of disorders or abnormal traits—be under pressure by parents, education providers, insurance companies, and employers to undergo gene therapy to remove their "bad" genes? Will the therapy be used "cosmetically" to add or eliminate nondisease traits, such as growth, skin color, or intelligence? Will victims of discrimination be pressured by societal prejudice to alter in themselves those traits society views as negative?

The early concerns about germline and somatic cell genetic engineering relied primarily on future projections of the potential abuse of the technology. However, two early cases involving misuse of gene therapy contributed significantly to the controversy that marked the early years of experimentation on the genetic manipulation of humans. The first scandal involving the nascent technology happened over two decades ago.

[In the next section of the original source, which is not reprinted here, Kimbrell discusses two instances of early gene therapy experimentation, one in 1970 and one in 1980, that were considered unethical because of the scientists' seeming lack of regard for the treated patients. The first case, which involved Dr. Stanfield Rogers, led to the first proposed legislation on genetic engineering and eventually provoked the National Institutes of Health (NIH) to produce guidelines regulating the use of human gene engineering. The later case, which involved Dr. Martin Cline of the University of California, also contributed to a promulgation of legislative and regulatory action on human gene engineering, including the establishment of a White House commission led by ethicist Alexander Morgan Capron and of the Biomedical Ethics Review Board to explore the ethical implications of human gene technology.—Ed.]

Throughout the 1980s, the criticisms of gene therapy continued. In 1983, Jeremy Rifkin organized a religious and scientific coalition against the use of genetic engineering on humans. The coalition and its signed statement opposing germline engineering were front-page stories around the United States. Unlike Capron's commission, the coalition's resolution on germline therapy was unambiguous: "Resolved, the efforts to engineer specific genetic traits into the germline of the human species should not be attempted." Its logic on prohibiting heritable gene alterations was also straightforward: "No individual, group of individuals, or institutions can legitimately claim the right or authority to make such decision on behalf of the rest of the species alive today or for future generations." The resolution, which was presented to Congress, was signed by a remarkable variety of religious leaders, including mainstream Jewish, Catholic, and Protestant religious organizations, as well as by many prominent scientists.

Six years later, an important and detailed religious statement on biotechnology was issued by the World Council of Churches (WCC). It contained a strong policy statement calling on all churches to support a "ban on experiments involving the genetic engineering of the human germline." The WCC was also deeply concerned about somatic cell gene experiments. The report called upon member churches to urge "strict control on experiments involving genetically engineered somatic cells, drawing attention to the potential misuse of . . . [this technique] against those held to be 'defective.' " The timing of the WCC statement could not have been more pertinent, for 1989 was to be the year that the age of human genetic engineering officially began.

Playing God?

On January 30, 1989, almost twelve years after the first demonstration on human genetic engineering, another such protest took place. The protesters came to a meeting of the National Institutes of Health Recombinant DNA Advisory Committee (RAC). Since publishing its guidelines in 1976, RAC had met dozens of times to discuss and approve experiments in genetic engineering. The advisory committee, composed mainly of scientists, held meetings that were usually staid affairs replete with lengthy discussion of arcane data and procedures.

This RAC meeting was like no other. There, demanding to be heard by the NIH scientists and genetic engineers, were fifteen of the nation's most prominent leaders in disability rights, many themselves suffering from disabilities. Additionally, several biotechnology activists were present to demand accountability of the scientists on the RAC. Many of the scientists appeared visibly uncomfortable at the prospect of discussing human gene engineering with people concerned about a new age of eugenics—and all under the unaccustomed glare of TV cameras. Those present knew that they were at a historic moment in the genetic engineering revolution, for this RAC meeting had as an agenda item discussion of approval for the world's first legally sanctioned genetic engineering experiment on humans.

The experiment involved genetic engineering but was not intended to be a cure. Researchers wished to insert novel genetic "markers" into certain immune cells taken from the bodies of terminally ill cancer patients, and then transfuse those cells back into the patients. With the help of the markers, they hoped to track which cells were working effectively and which were not. The procedure was to be carried out by the NIH's prime genetic engineering team of Drs. French Anderson, Steven A. Rosenberg, and Michael Blaese.

Minutes after RAC chairman Dr. Gerard J. McGarrity called the meeting to order, critics began to express deep concern that the NIH had begun the historic process of approving human gene engineering protocols while still doing nothing to put in place a review process on the ethical and legal implications of human genetic alteration. Jeremy Rifkin announced that his Foundation on Economic Trends had filed suit that morning, calling on a federal court to halt the experiment until the NIH committed itself to allowing the public a greater voice in decisions on gene therapy. Rifkin also noted that the lawsuit was based on the fact that the historic experiment was approved by a secret mail ballot, the first in RAC's history. He repeated the concerns he and other demonstrators had expressed over a decade before: "Genetic engineering raises unparalleled ethical and social questions for the human race. They cannot be ignored by the NIH. If we are not careful we will find ourselves in a world where the disabled, minorities, and workers will be genetically engineered." Another protesting voice at the meeting was Evan Kemp, then Commissioner of the Equal Opportunity Commission (EEOC), and himself disabled:

> The terror and risk that genetic engineering holds for those of us with disabilities are well grounded in recent events.... Our society seems to have an aversion to those who are physically and mentally different. Genetic engineering could lead to the elimination of the rich diversity in our peoples. It is a real and frightening threat.

Those present asked the RAC to set up an outside review board for human genetic engineering experiments that would include experts in the rights of minorities, workers, and the disabled. They insisted that the RAC scientists, though astute on advances in genetics, were no experts in the public policy implications of their work. "This group cannot play God when it comes to deciding what genes should be engineered in and out of individual patients," Rifkin said during heated arguments with members of the committee. "What will be the criteria for good or bad genes? Who will decide what genes, and which people, will be engineered?" he continued. "The people in this room are just not qualified to raise these monumental social issues. You're just not going to be able to maintain that control of power within a small group. We need to broaden this group." A few members of the RAC board became belligerent, denying, sometimes angrily, the suggestion that they lacked the expertise to oversee the larger social and political implications of their work. Others simply ignored the proposal. When the vote came, the RAC board unanimously (twenty in favor, three abstentions) turned down the proposal to set up a public policy review committee.

The RAC critics lost the NIH vote, but they won the battle in court. On May 6, the NIH settled the law case filed against the NIH, agreeing to immediately make changes in the RAC guidelines that would forbid mail or secret ballots and would also provide more review for gene therapy experiments. The legal settlement cleared the way for the first legally sanctioned gene engineering experiment on humans. The gene "marker" experiment took place a few days later, on May 22, 1989.

Claiming Immunity

The second gene experiment on humans was performed just over a year after the first. It was the first official attempt to use somatic cell human gene engineering as a therapy for disease. On September 14, 1990, a four-year-old girl from Cleveland with the immune disorder popularly known as the "bubble boy syndrome" was injected with a billion cells into which a new gene had been inserted. The girl was born without the gene that controls successful functioning of certain immune cells called T lymphocytes. The rare condition (it affects only about twenty children worldwide), known as adenosine deaminase (ADA) deficiency, leaves victims helpless in the face of disease and infection. Many children suffering from ADA deficiency have been kept alive by isolating them in a germ-free capsule, as was "David," the famous "Boy in the Bubble" at Baylor College of Medicine in Houston, Texas.

Dr. French Anderson and a team at NIH intravenously infused the child with blood cells containing the missing ADA gene in hope that it would help her recover normal functioning of her immune system. On the surface the medical procedure looked little different from a normal blood transfusion. The procedure, which took place in the Pediatric Intensive Care Unit of the Clinical Center of NIH, in Bethesda, Maryland, lasted twenty-eight minutes. One hour later the young patient was wandering around the hospital playroom, eating M&Ms.

The young girl who had become the first human gene therapy patient to be legally engineered with human genes became something of a celebrity, as did Dr. Anderson. The media reported the historic occasion in glowing terms. Soon reporters were writing about "Dr. Anderson's Gene Machine." After some initial reports of success, it was not uncommon to hear that genetic engineering had cured the "bubble boy syndrome." A second patient began gene treatment in January 1991. It was hard to imagine a more altruistic beginning for a technological development that so many had feared as the beginning of a new eugenic movement.

The experiment had its dark side, however, including some unfortunate parallels with Rogers's scandalous experiments on children in the early 1970s. A careful examination revealed that Anderson's procedure may have been more hype than cure. The "bubble boy syndrome" cases were now a misnomer: None of the handful of existent cases required the bubble to protect the immunologically impaired children from disease. Since the mid-1980s, these children were being adequately treated with a new drug therapy. Anderson, however, had started his research into ADA before the drug therapy was available. Many felt that he continued on with his protocol more out of stubbornness and ambition than medical necessity. Months before the experiment took place, members of the Human Genome Subcommittee had openly questioned Anderson on the rationale for subjecting children to the risks of gene therapy when they were already being treated successfully. So concerned were the RAC members about the effectiveness of Anderson's therapy that they restricted Anderson and his team to working only with patients who were already receiving the drug therapy. This in turn led to the question of how Anderson could accurately assess the results of his experiment. One scientist noted that it would be a little like attempting to assess the results of aspirin on a patient who was being treated with antibiotics.

Whether or not Anderson is using his patients as gene therapy guinea pigs, his experiments appear to violate the general bioethical rule that the expected benefits to an individual from an experimental therapy should equal or exceed the potential harm. The experiment's protocol was clear. The procedure did not offer children suffering from the genetic disorder a cure, but merely a supplemental therapy. The beneficial results of the experiment are at best marginal. A cure awaits improvements in bone marrow transplantation.

By contrast, the dangers to children from Anderson's experiment could be quite real. Anderson and others involved in inserting genes into patients use animal retroviruses to carry those genes. The retrovirus used in all early gene therapy experiments, including the ADA experiment, is one called murine leukemia virus (MuLV). It is a retrovirus obtained from mice. Anderson engineers the ADA gene into the retrovirus and then injects the gene package into a patient. Once inside the patient, the retrovirus invades cells and drops off the genes. Genetic engineers like Anderson attempt to render these carrier retroviruses harmless, but there are still concerns that these viruses could cause cancer or other serious disease in patients. Except in the case of Anderson's ADA experiments, MuLV had only been approved for use in terminally ill patients in whom the retrovirus could do little additional harm. Yet Anderson used this suspect retrovirus on children who were living relatively normal lives with potentially long life spans ahead of them.

In December 1991, less than a year after Anderson began genetically engineering his second patient, an unsettling report was made public. A researcher, Arthur Nienhaus, described his discovery that the MuLV virus had caused cancer in primates. The researcher suspects that the cancer may have been caused by a contaminant that leaked into the virus during production. Anderson and others were quick to note that they used a different system to produce their MuLV, one less prone to contamination. However, the discovery bolsters the view that much more needs to be learned before MuLV is widely used as a gene therapy tool.

In a rare demonstration of scientific breaking of ranks, several fellow genetic engineers openly expressed their displeasure with the Anderson experiment. One gene therapy expert called the Anderson procedures "absolutely crazy." Dr. Arthur Bank, professor of medicine and human genetics at Columbia University, charged that gene therapy researchers at NIH were driven by ambition and not by good science. "The main impetus [for the ADA experiment] is the need for French Anderson to be the first to do gene therapy in man.... This may turn out to be bad news for all of us," Bank told a genetics conference within a week after the experiment had started. Dr. Stuart Orkin, professor of pediatric medicine at Harvard Medical School, noted, "A large number of scientists believe the experiment is not well founded scientifically.... I'm quite surprised that there hasn't been more of an outcry against the experiment by scientists who are completely objective." Dr. Richard Mulligan, a pioneer in gene therapy work and a member of the RAC board—the only one who voted against the experiment—was more direct. "If I had a daughter, no way I'd let her get near these guys if she had that defect."

Anderson has more than his experiments to defend. Critics of the approvals of the first gene therapy experiments also point out that over a five-year period, Anderson has almost singlehandedly pioneered delivering federally funded human gene engineering research to a private company with which he is a collaborator. In 1987, Anderson did what many viewed as "scientifically unthinkable" when he joined forces with venture capitalist Wallace Steinberg to help build a human gene engineering company, Genetics Therapy, Inc. (GTI), a company one observer has called the "ultimate body shop."

Steinberg had long headed the venture capital arm of Johnson & Johnson and was looking for a new market challenge in what promised to be the cutting-edge industry of the future—human genetic engineering. Traditionally, government scientists have regarded joining forces with private investors as unseemly if not unethical. Anderson's relationship to human gene engineering entrepreneurs has cast a shadow over both the science and the procedures that led to the approval of the first of several human gene therapy experiments. Concerns about conflict of interest were heightened in late 1990 when GTI hired former NIH/RAC chairman Gerard McGarrity. McGarrity had been a leading supporter of GTI's and Anderson's gene therapy experiments, and as chairman of RAC had helped shepherd the therapy proposals through the NIH approval process. In 1991, GTI's numerous maneuvers paid off: Sandoz Pharma, Ltd., one of the world's major multinational companies, bought $10 million of GTI stock and agreed to provide $13.5 million over the subsequent three years in project funding. GTI ended 1991 with cash and marketable securities of $20.8 million.

Human gene engineering is progressing quickly. Currently, over a dozen somatic cell gene engineering experiments are ongoing on three continents. Numerous other gene engineering protocols are being developed for approval in the near future. Large-scale use of gene engineering to cure disease or cosmetically change individuals is still several years away; nevertheless, the scandal, ambition, and moral blindness that have characterized the early history of human genetic engineering set a profoundly disturbing precedent for the future.

Moreover, many of the protections against abuses in the use of gene technology put in place in the 1980s are fast disappearing. The Congressional Biomedical Ethics Board, established in 1985, was disbanded in 1990. Additionally, in 1991 Dr. Anderson and others successfully urged the disbanding of the RAC Human Gene Therapy Subcommittee. Finally, in the face of a massive influx of profit-seeking and potential conflicts of interest, the viability of RAC as a responsible regulatory agency of human gene engineering is in considerable doubt.

In the future we will be genetically engineering ourselves in numerous ways—applications of biotechnology with which our society is ill prepared to deal. As researchers successfully locate genes responsible for height, weight, and I.Q., there are still no restrictions that would prevent an industry from altering these traits through somatic gene therapy. Further, researchers are now more determined than ever to begin the first germline gene engineering experiments on humans. There is general consensus that such research will become a reality over the next decade. We have no national or international mechanisms that will prevent germline engineering from permanently altering our human genome, no restrictions on the unlimited genetic alteration of sperm and eggs, or the engineering of embryos. Despite continuing controversy, publicity, and massive public funding of gene technology research, the questions demonstrators shouted at scientists over fifteen years ago have still not been answered.

NO

Embracing Change With All Four Arms: A Post-Humanist Defense of Genetic Engineering

Introduction

Nine years ago, while I rode a bus through the small, crooked, immaculate and beautiful streets of Kyoto, Jeremy Rifkin convinced me that genetic technology would determine the shape of the future. I was reading his *Algeny,* an alarmist attack on the coming of the gene age, alongside *What Sort of People Should There Be?,* a moderate defense of genetic engineering by Jonathan Glover. In a sense, in the nine years since, I have recoiled from the radical Rifkin to embrace the reformist Glover.

While extreme, Rifkin is a bellwether of Luddite tendencies in bioethics and the political Left, two of the movements within which I construct my worldview. Among bioethicists the anti-technological agenda has focused on abuses and social dangers in medical research and practice, and our alleged need to accept death and technological limits. The post-60s, environmentalist Left focuses on the ways that technology serves patriarchy, racism, imperialism, corporate profits, structural unemployment, the authoritarian state, and domination by scientific discourse. The response of bioethicists and the Left to genetic engineering has been particularly fevered, driven by accusations of eugenics and the defilement of sacred boundaries.

Since that bus ride in Kyoto my initial horrified agreement with Rifkin has shifted to determined agreement with Glover, that we can control genetic technology and make it a boon rather than a bane. Instead of a *Brave New World,* I see genetic engineering offering a grand, albeit somewhat unpredictable, future. While many of the concerns of ethicists and the Left about this technology are well-founded, I now believe they are answerable. While I still acknowledge the need for democratic control and social limits, I am now convinced that banning genetic engineering would be a profound mistake.

Those who set aside angst about changing human nature, and embrace the possibility of rapid diversification of types of life, are establishing a new moral and political philosophy for the 21st century, a system some refer to as

From James Hughes, "Embracing Change With All Four Arms: A Post-Humanist Defense of Genetic Engineering," *Eubios Journal of Asian and International Bioethics,* vol. 6, no. 4 (July 1996). Copyright © 1996 by James Hughes. Reprinted by permission.

"post-humanism." Like all philosophical systems, post-humanism incorporates prior philosophic and political systems but recasts them around new definitions of personhood, citizenship, and the limits of social solidarity and human knowledge. Like Glover, post-humanists view the coming of genetic technology the way most Americans now view organ transplants or chemotherapy; there are many practical questions about how the technologies get developed and tested, who needs them, and how we pay for them, but there is no question that they should be available. In this essay I will be trying to imagine what liberal democracies could be like if we allow a post-humanist flowering of genetic technology.

Distinctions Without a Difference

Many writers on these technologies draw distinctions between "negative" and "positive" genetic modification, and the modification of the somatic versus germ-line cells. Negative genetic modification has been defined as the correction of a genetic disease, while positive modification has been defined as the attempt to enhance human ability beyond its normal limits. The somatic/germ-line distinction has been made to address the alleged ethical difference in modifying only one's own body, versus modifying one's progeny as well.

Both distinctions have been made by those who wanted to draw a line to demarcate the ethical boundaries of genetic research. The distinctions are quite fuzzy, however. Take for instance Culver and Gert's effort to define "malady" to distinguish when a genetic therapy is or isn't "enhancement":

> A person has a malady if and only if he has a condition, other than his rational beliefs and desires, such that he is suffering, or at increased risk of suffering, an evil (death, pain, disability, loss of freedom or opportunity or loss of pleasure) in the absence of distinct sustaining cause.

Doesn't any cause of illness, suffering and death, or inadequacy in the face of one's goals, fit this criterion? Take for instance a potential future genetic therapy that turned off a hypothetical aging switch, doubling the human life span; is this therapy for the diseases which result from the activation of the aging switch, such as Alzheimers or cancer, or an unconscionable intervention into the natural span of life?

As to the modification of one's own genes versus future progeny, the argument is made that current generations would be violating the self-determination of future generations by doing so. The first response is that our choice of breeding partners already "determines" the biology of future generations. Take the case of a couple who both carry a gene for latent inheritable mental illness. The only difference between their choosing not to breed with one another, and choosing to have germ-line therapy on themselves or their child to correct the illness, is that the latter choice is a far happier one.

The second response to the somatic/germ-line distinction is that advancing genetic technology will make it possible for future generations to change their genes back if they don't like them. Only modifications which remove decision-making autonomy from future generations altogether would truly

we do it anyway, a form of eugenics

raise issues of "self-determination," and I will discuss such fascist scenarios below.

These distinctions are extremely fuzzy, and do not represent important ethical boundaries. In this essay I want to defend genetic therapy and enhancement, as well as self-modification by competent adults and modification of one's progeny. Even the most liberal, and most recent, of international bioethics consensus documents, the 1995 draft UNESCO Declaration on the Protection of the Human Genome, draws the line at germ-line enhancement.

Therefore ground-zero of the terrain that I want to defend is germ-line enhancement, the modification of the genetic code such that the parent passes on the enhancements to their progeny. The defense of this practice necessarily addresses the concerns about many other technologies, such as:

- In-vitro Fertilization
- Surrogate Mothering
- Extra-uterine Gestation
- Genetic Screening and Diagnosis
- Genetic Selection, including Sex Selection
- Cloning of Embryos

In a more fundamental sense I am writing in defense of our control of our bodies, individually and collectively. I want to build a broad enough defense to cover any technology offering modification of human abilities, whether a specific genetic application has been imagined for that purpose or not.

Ethical Starting Points for a Defense

Rule Utilitarianism

In general I assume the ethical stance of Millsian rule utilitarianism: acts are ethical which lead to the greatest good or happiness for the greatest number. Rule utilitarianism means that, when confronted with a distasteful case, such as throwing a Christian to a lion for the amusement of thousands of Romans, I fall back on general rules of thumb: "In general, societies that respect individual rights and liberties will lead to greater happiness for all."

In the case of genetic engineering my broad assertion is that gene-technologies can, and probably will, give people longer, healthier lives, with more choices and greater happiness. In fact, these technologies offer the possibility that we will be able to experience utilities greater and more intense than those on our current mental pallet. Genetic technology will bring advances in pharmaceuticals and the therapeutic treatment of disease, ameliorating many illnesses and forms of suffering. Somewhat further in the future, our sense organs themselves may be re-engineered to allow us to perceive greater ranges of light and sound, our bodies re-engineered to permit us to engage in more strenuous activities, and our minds re-engineered to permit us to think more profound and intense thoughts. If utility is an ethical goal, direct control of our body and mind suggests the possibility of unlimited utility, and thus an immeasurable good.

Privacy, Self-Determination and Bodily Autonomy *ask - entire section!*

But there are other rules to consider, rules which are the basis of other ethical systems. Most utilitarians, and many others, accept the general rule that liberal societies, which allow maximum self-determination, will maximize social utility. The rule of, or right to, self-determination also argues that society should have very good reasons before interfering with competent adults applying genetic technology to themselves and their property. Self-determining people should be allowed the privacy to do what they want to with their bodies, except when they are not competent, or their actions will cause great harm to others.

Acknowledging self-determination as an ethical starting point addresses half of the revulsion to genetic engineering: the concern that people will be forced to conform to eugenic policies. I will discuss this fear of racist and authoritarian regimes at greater length, but suffice it to say here that individuals should not be forced to have or abort children, or to modify their own or their children's genetic code. I am addressing the desirable genetics policies of liberal societies, not of authoritarian regimes.

Within liberal societies, competent adults should generally be allowed to do as they like with their bodies, including genetically modify them. The potential risks to others from such modifications, which I will try to discuss below, are all soluble, and not sufficient to warrant contravening the right of bodily autonomy.

I also view the embryo and fetus as the biological property of the parents, and exclusively of the mother when in utero. Again, the rights of the future child and of society may restrict what we allow parents to do to their prenatal property. But I would again argue that the risks to society and to the children themselves of prenatal genetic manipulation are negligible for the near future, and regulable as they become apparent.

Freedom from Biological Necessity *Do we want this freedom?*

Genetic technology promises freedom and self-determination at an even more basic level: freedom from biological necessity. Social domination pales before our domination by the inevitability of birth, illness, aging and death, burdens that genetic technology offers to ameliorate. As for Marx, the goal of this revolution is to move from the realm of necessity to the realm of freedom.

Social domination also builds on a biological foundation. Patriarchy is, in part, based on women's physical vulnerability, and their special role in reproduction. While industrialization, contraception and the liberal democratic state may have removed the bulk of patriarchy's weight, genetic technology offers to remove the rest. Similarly, while racism, ageism, heterosexism, and so on may be only 10% biological and 90% social construction, at least the biological factors can be made a matter of choice by genetic and biological technology.

Justice and a Better Society

While the biological factors in most forms of inequality are probably slight, genetic technology does promise to create a more equal society in a very basic way: by eliminating congenital sources of illness and disability that create the most intractable forms of inequality in society. We can go to great lengths to give the ill and disabled full access to society, but their disabilities place basic limits on how equal their social participation and power can be. Our ability to ameliorate these sources of congenital inequality may even impose obligations on us to do so, at least for those who are cognitively impaired and incompetent. Admittedly, we will probably have surmounted most disabilities through non-genetic technological fixes long before we do so through genetic therapy. But the general principle is that genetic technology promises to make it possible to give all citizens the physical and cognitive abilities for equal participation, and perhaps even to bring about a general enhancement of the abilities essential to empowered citizenship.

A Critical Defense

Unlike those libertarians who hold self-determination as a cardinal principle, I adopt more of a social democratic stance, and foresee legitimate limits that we can and should place on these technologies. For instance, some characteristics of society, such as social solidarity and general equality, are so important that they warrant the regulation of these technologies in the furtherance of these goals. Collective interests should also be pursued through active means, such as government subsidies for the research, development and application of genetic technologies.

Nor am I an unquestioning advocate of technological progress. Some technologies are so inscribed with harmful ends that no amount of regulation and social direction can make them worth the risk. If I were convinced that genetic technology, like nuclear weapons technology, had no redeeming qualities and only great risks then I would embrace a complete ban.

But the potential benefits of genetic technology far outweigh the potential risks. In short, I advocate a position of critical support, a position which reflects the suspicious optimism that most Americans have toward genetic technology.

Arguments Against Genetic Technology

There are at least two kinds of criticisms of genetic technology, fundamentalist and non-fundamentalist. The fundamentalist or "bio-Luddite" concerns, such as those of Jeremy Rifkin, I reject fundamentally. On the other hand, I accept the validity of many of the non-fundamental concerns, but see the problems they suggest as soluble. Few of these concerns about genetic technology raise new questions for medical ethics. The same questions have been raised by previous medical research and therapy, and those challenges have been met without bans on those technologies.

Some non-fundamentalist critics believe that, cumulatively, the risks posed by new genetic technologies are great enough to warrant postponing genetic research for some indefinite period of study and preparation. With these concerns I will argue that, with adequate technology assessment and anticipatory regulation, there will be adequate time to regulate genetic technology as we proceed; none of the risks are sufficiently weighty, individually or cumulatively, to outweigh the potential benefits.

The fundamentalist or bio-Luddite concerns I will address are:

- Bio-Luddism 1: Medicine Makes People Sick
- Bio-Luddism 2: Sacred Limits of the Natural Order
- Bio-Luddism 3: Technologies Serve Ruling Interests
- Bio-Luddism 4: The Genome Is Too Complicated to Engineer

The non-fundamentalist or pragmatic concerns I will discuss are:

- Gene Angst 1: Fascist Applications
- Gene Angst 2: The Value of Genetic Diversity
- Gene Angst 3: Genetic Discrimination and Confidentiality
- Gene Angst 4: Discrimination Against the Disabled
- Gene Angst 5: Unequal Access, Priority Setting and the Market
- Gene Angst 6: The Decline of Social Solidarity

Bio-Luddism 1: Medicine Makes People Sick

One extreme bio-Luddite position was elaborated by Ivan Illich: medicine itself makes us sick and should be done away with. A variant on this argument is that genetic screening will eventually determine that all of us are "at risk," making everyone see themselves as sick. More troubling, genetic diagnosis might create a two-tier social system, divided between those with relatively clean genes and those with genetic disease. In other words, genetic diagnosis will make us all genetically diseased. This would be even more problematic if the genetic diagnosis was for a disease which was not yet curable.

Some medicine makes some people sicker, but I hold fast to the modernist promise that scientific progress generally improves our lives and that knowledge is better than ignorance. It is unlikely that we will ever force people to know their likelihood of developing disease, though perhaps we should educate parents and physicians to be cautious about informing children of their risks. In any case, we all know that we are at risk of dying, and with or without genetic diagnosis people view the medical history of their parents and relatives as harbingers of things to come. Both knowing and refusing to know one's genetic makeup are empowering choices for competent adults; denying people the option of making this choice does not improve their lives.

This argument also presumes just the first, screening phase of the new eugenics, and not the latter correction phase. Far from making everyone sick, the advance of genetic therapy promises to make everyone well.

don't agree

Bio-Luddism 2: Sacred Limits of the Natural Order

Rifkin has joined forces with religious leaders to assert another fundamentalist tenet, that genetic engineering transgresses sacred limits beyond which we should not "play God." I don't believe that divine limits are discernible, and I don't believe in any "natural order" except the one we've got. As Love and Rockets point out: "you can't go against nature, 'cause when you go against nature, it's part of nature too." There are no "natural limits" in our taking control of our biology or ecology. There is no "natural" way to have a baby or die. Even if there was a natural way to birth or die I don't believe we are morally compelled to adopt it.

Bio-Luddism 3: Technologies Serve Ruling Interests

Some hesitate to argue that medical technology is bad in and of itself, but argue instead that the powerful always shape and apply technologies to further their domination of the less powerful. While this is probably true, the conclusion is that all technology should be abandoned. The wealthy and powerful have more access to telephones than the poor and powerless, and telephones are used by the wealthy and powerful to collect more wealth and power. But I see the answer to be subsidized phone service and social reform, not banning the telephone.

Bio-Luddism 4: The Genome Is Too Complicated to Engineer

A fourth fundamentalist conviction is that the genome is too complicated to engineer, and therefore there are certain to be unpleasant, unintended consequences. This argument is directly parallel to the deep ecologists' conclusion that human management of the complex global eco-system is impossible, and that our only hope is to leave the planet alone to its own self-organization.

The genome and eco-system are both very complicated, and the ability to do more than correct local defects in either may be many decades away. But eventually we will have the capacity to write genetic code and re-engineer eco-systems, and to computer-model the structural consequences of our interventions on future bodies and planets. Of course, it will be difficult to decide when the consequences of a genetic blueprint are sufficiently well-understood that it is safe for use, and our current regulatory scheme is probably not yet adequate to the task.

Our understanding of the genome and ability to predict consequences must be very robust before we allow human applications or the release of animal applications. While Elias and Annas object to "positive" germ-line therapy, which I would defend, they propose three sensible preconditions on the application of gene-engineering:

1. that there should be considerable prior experience with human somatic cell gene therapy, which has clearly established its safety and efficacy; and
2. that there should be reasonable scientific evidence using appropriate animal models that germ-line gene therapy will cure or prevent the disease in question and not cause any harm; and

3. all applications should be approved by the NIH's [National Institutes of Health] Working Group on Gene Therapy and local Institutional Review Boards, with prior public discussion.

Those of us who believe in the possibility of effective public regulation may differ widely as to the appropriate standards the public and these regulatory bodies may use. But liberals and conservatives differ fundamentally from those bio-Luddites who believe that the natural world is so complicated, and governments so unwise, that all intervention must be forbidden.

Gene Angst 1: Fascist Applications

Another concern expressed by many critics of genetic technology is the dire consequences of the re-emergence of fascist, racist and authoritarian regimes, and their use of engineering to produce compliant, genetically uniform subjects. The first point to make about fascist uses of eugenic ideology or technology is that nothing a democratic society does to forbid itself genetic technology will have any impact on future or contemporary fascist regimes. Indeed, if there is any "national security" to be gained from genetic technology then it would behoove liberal democracies to gain them as well. For instance, public health campaigns to detect and correct the genetic predisposition to alcoholism, or to enhance the intelligence of children, could make nations much more powerful and productive than their more conservative neighbors; would it not be in the interest of democracy itself for democracies to pursue these measures?

Yet, what if the fascist regimes found strength in breeding different castes à la *Brave New World,* and democracies could only meet the challenge by becoming equally repugnant? This is a possibility, and it raises the important point: the way to stop fascist uses of genetics is to prevent the rise of fascism, not to restrict the emergence of genetic technology. As we see today with Iraq and North Korea, firm agreements by right-thinking nations that only the United States is sufficiently moral to be allowed the ownership of nuclear and chemical weapons has little impact on recalcitrant regimes. If we cannot effectively prevent the proliferation of nuclear technology, with its large radioactive facilities visible to satellites, we will have even less success with genetic laboratories. I support the strengthening of the legal, judicial and military might of the U.N. so that it might begin to enforce global law, but I think the proper task for such a New World Order is the suppression of fascist regimes likely to use genetics for nefarious ends, not the policing and suppression of outlawed genetic technologies.

Genetic science does not itself encourage racism or authoritarianism. In fact, the advance of scientific knowledge may even erode the pseudo-scientific basis on which most eugenics has rested. Presumably the advance of genetic science will tell us whether there is a genetic basis for gender and racial differences in abilities, or not, and how important these are. If there are genetic factors in gender or racial difference, they will most likely be revealed as minor beside the social factors, and the genetic factors will become ameliorable through a technical fix. Some insist that knowledge itself, or knowledge about forbidden topics, will lead to fascism; I prefer the modernist optimism that knowledge is at least neutral towards, and sometimes a scourge of, obscurantism.

Gene Angst 2: The Value of Genetic Diversity *too casual*

Another concern that is often expressed vis-à-vis genetic engineering is the alleged aesthetic or biological virtues of genetic diversity. Many refer to the evidence from ecology that ecosystems are more stable when they contain a greater diversity of gene-lines. Some suggest, for instance, that our very survival as a species might hinge on genetic diversity if we faced some blight that only a few were resistant to.

The first objection to this argument is that diversity is not a sufficiently compelling ethical or aesthetic virtue that it can trump the prevention of disease, or the improvement of the quality of our lives. We "reduced diversity" when we eradicated smallpox and polio, with no regrets. We "reduce diversity" when we insist on compulsory education because we don't value the diversity of extreme class inequality.

The second objection to the diversity argument is that any loss of adaptiveness through biological diversity will be compensated for by an increase in biological knowledge and control. It is unlikely that a future society would have the ability to create "superior genes" and yet be unable to meet the challenge of infectious disease.

Third, the regime of genetics I have outlined is a liberal one, which should produce as much diversity as it reduces. While I support public provision of genetic screening for disease, I oppose any eugenic coercion. People desire different attributes and abilities, for themselves and their children; for every Aryan parent that chooses a blond, blue-eyed Barbie phenotype, I expect there would be a Chinese parent choosing a classic Chinese ideal of beauty. True, this might lead to the convergence toward a few physical and mental ideals, though I suspect that phenotypic fashions will change quickly. But I see no ethical difference between permitting people to change their genes in conformity with social fashions, and permitting them to change their clothes, makeup and beliefs to do so.

Yet, perhaps there is some aesthetic and or even civic virtue in diversity. If it is valued by the public, let us establish incentives for diversity. If the number of parents choosing to raise blond boys is offensive to public opinion, we can give tax incentives for parents who bear dark-haired girls. In any case, we will quickly know if there are broad trends that we find offensive, and I trust our ability to craft non-coercive policy responses to re-establish any valued diversity we feel may be eroding.

Gene Angst 3: Genetic Discrimination and Confidentiality

Many opponents of genetic investigation are concerned that growing genetic knowledge will lead to discrimination against the "genetically diseased and disabled." Some assert that genetic therapy itself will increase this discrimination by bringing intense pressure to bear on those with genetic diseases to have the disease corrected, and not burden society and future generations with their diseases.

It is certainly true that employers are already attempting to discover the genetic risks of their employees, and deny employment or health insurance on the basis of this risk profile. A bill guaranteeing the confidentiality of genetic information has been introduced in Congress, and while it has not yet passed, some form of confidentiality is certain to be guaranteed by the turn of the millennium. In addition, the Americans with Disabilities Act and similar legislation will clearly be mustered to defend workers from genetic discrimination.

Keeping genetic information confidential from health insurers is trickier, since they would be reimbursing for any special screening or treatment that genetic risks called for. Unregulated, the use of genetic risk information could greatly strengthen the ability of insurers to exclude the illness-prone from their risk pools, or charge them premiums equivalent to the costs of their potential treatments. Again, however, popular insurance reform legislation before Congress will ban "risk-rating" and excluding clients with "pre-existing conditions." These two reforms will likely reduce the number of insurance companies in the country by half or more, and make genetic discrimination in health insurance a more or less moot point. Some have suggested further that the pervasiveness of genetic information will make private health insurance impossible; to which I say, good riddance. *is socialized medicine inevitable?*

There are undoubtedly many other nefarious uses to which knowledge of someone's genetic make-up can be put. But genetic information is only one small category of the information about our lives which is potentially in the public domain, and potentially injurious. The regulation of genetic technology really has very little to do with whether we establish data privacy in the 21st century.

Gene Angst 4: Discrimination Against the Disabled

Opponents of sex selection and of eugenic efforts against genetic disease argue that these decisions are acts of prejudice against women and the disabled, and perpetuate the second-class status of women and the disabled by focusing on genetic rather than social amelioration. In the first place, embryos and fetuses are not persons, and therefore their rights cannot be violated as persons or as members of oppressed social groups. While parents may make reproductive decisions for many reasons we disapprove of, such as aborting a fetus because the father was accidentally of the "wrong" race, this is not a reason to intervene.

The alleged link between choosing to abort a disabled child, or correcting their disability through genetic therapy, and the perpetuation of oppression of the disabled seems tenuous at best. Perhaps by reducing the population of disabled we reduce their power at the ballot box. But a parent's moral obligation to give their children the greatest quality of life, and the fullest range of abilities, includes not only the obligation to treat a disabled child with respect and love, but also the obligation to keep them from having disabilities in the first place. It also seems likely that a society with fewer disabled would increase rather than decrease their per capita expenditures on the disabled.

Gene Angst 5: Unequal Access, Priority Setting and the Market

My worry

As a social democrat, one of my gravest concerns is how social inequality will constrain access to genetic technology, and how genetic technology may reinforce social inequality. Establishing the appropriate balance of state and market in genetics starts with the creation of a national health budget, most likely through the creation of a national health system, such as the [President Bill] Clinton plan or some other form of national health insurance. Such a system allows the ethical determination of utility trade-offs, from what the level of health care expenditures should be, to what should be included in the basic package of guaranteed medical services and what should be consigned to the private medical market.

If we had such a system, I don't think most fertility treatments would make the cut, nor would future positive genetic "enhancements." On the other hand, genetic screening and corrective genetic therapy would clearly be socially acceptable, cost-effective, and therefore a plausible positive right. This leaves me in a quandary; I want fertility treatments and positive genetic enhancement to be legal and available, but I'm not prepared to argue that they are a positive right worthy of public subsidy. Yet, if gene products are left in the market, only the wealthy will have access to them, with the upper-classes having more life opportunities and potentially becoming genetically healthier and more intelligent than the poor, which is unethical in an equal opportunity society.

These problems are really a sub-category of the larger task of determining which medical tests and procedures should be:

- required by law, e.g. vaccinations
- publicly funded, but not obligatory, e.g. abortion in progressive states
- encouraged, but unsubsidized, e.g. exercise
- discouraged, but not banned, e.g. smoking
- banned., e.g. heroin

Any assignment of genetic technologies to the categories between obligatory and forbidden allows for potential inequality. Most opponents of genetic technology, when pressed, would stop short of banning these technologies outright, and thus leave them to be inequitably distributed by the market. At the other extreme, there are no audible voices calling for a program of mandatory, universal genetic redesign. This leaves me with Glover in the usual social democratic, mixed-market middle: try a little public, and a little private, and we will tinker with it as we proceed.

Gene Angst 6: The Decline of Social Solidarity

Finally some critics suggest that parents would become alienated from their genetically engineered children. Dator and other post-humanists suggest that genetic engineering and other technologies may create conflict between humans and post-humans, and threaten social solidarity. I think this is a serious concern, and one goal of the social regulation of genetic technology would be to moderate the rapidity with which society genetically advances and diversifies. The gaps between the bodies and abilities of parents and children should not be so great as to make parenting impossible. Also the unenhanced public's concerns will inevitably be a factor in regulating the enhancement of the modified minorities. While some of these conservative concerns may be warranted, if the enhanced feel they have no responsibility to the unenhanced and seek to dominate or exploit them, we must also avoid allowing simple chauvinism and fear of the unknown to stop genetic enhancement.

While tremendous social conflicts can be imagined, they are not that different from the conflicts between ethnic minorities and majorities, or between the First World and the Third, or between social classes. Like other sources of social division, the relations between new genetic communities will hopefully be mediated by the same institutions, courts and legislatures, minority rights and majority rule. The real challenge faced by a post-human ethic is to define new parameters for which forms of life should be considered property, social wards (neither property nor competent persons, such as children), and persons with full citizenship.

Conclusion

While humanists and economists urge us to embrace financial and existential limits, and give up the quixotic quest for immortality, the post-humanists say "Some alive today may never die." The potential problems created by new medical technology are numerous, and we must work hard to ensure that our societies are free and equal enough that these tools create more good than harm. But I believe this to be an achievable goal, and that genetic technology offers, if not immortality, such good that the risks are dwarfed. Like all speculation (and all utilitarian judgments are based on social speculation) this optimism is founded on numerous points of faith. But I find faith in the potential unlimited improvability of human nature and expansion of human powers far more satisfying than a resignation to our current limits.

POSTSCRIPT

Should Genetic Engineering Be Banned?

Genetic engineering has had and will have applications in agriculture (improved crop plants and animals) and in the pharmaceutical industry (drug production). In the last few years, much of the excitement and the alarm have centered on its use to treat diseases by modifying human genes. Gene therapy has not yet become a multimillion-dollar industry, but there have been some successes. In October 1993 researchers reported that giving hemophiliac dogs —dogs with a hereditary defect that delays blood clotting—a copy of the gene for the blood-clotting agent they lacked improved the ability of their blood to clot. In March 1994 a similar approach repaired mice that had an autoimmune condition similar to the human disease lupus erythematosus. In April 1994 researchers announced that giving a woman with familial hypercholesterolemia —a rare genetic disorder that is marked by very high levels of blood cholesterol and early death from heart attack—the proper version of her defective gene reduced her cholesterol levels by 20 percent. Clinical trials of gene therapy against cystic fibrosis were under way in 1999. The same year saw reports of viruses being used to replace cancer-causing genes in cancer patients, with promising results; see N. Seppa, "Therapy Pits Gene Against Tumor," *Science News* (May 15, 1999).

A great many genetic therapies have been devised and tested in humans. However, technical difficulties remain and the successes have not been decisive. For a discussion of how researchers are transferring genes into human cells, and of their prospects for success in treating disease, see Eric B. Kmiec, "Gene Therapy," *American Scientist* (May–June 1999).

The technology is still young, its growth is still largely ahead, and its promise is yet to be fulfilled. *Will* that promise be fulfilled? Many people remain worried about the negative possibilities: In Germany tough regulations have made genetic engineering research of any kind almost impossible to carry out. In England a cancer research project was shut down in February 1994 because of fears that common cold viruses engineered to carry cancer genes might escape and cause a cancer plague (the actual risk was almost zero because the virus had been made unable to reproduce in cells, but government regulators judged the lab's containment measures to be inadequate). The availability of genetic information has raised fears of discrimination by insurers and employers. See Kathy L. Hudson et al., "Genetic Discrimination and Health Insurance: An Urgent Need for Reform," *Science* (October 20, 1995). And religious groups have objected to the patenting of genes. See Ronald Cole-Turner, "Religion and Gene Patenting," *Science* (October 6, 1995).

ISSUE 17

Is It Ethical to Sell Human Tissue?

YES: David B. Resnik, from "The Commodification of Human Reproductive Materials," *Journal of Medical Ethics* (December 1, 1998)

NO: Dorothy Nelkin and Lori Andrews, from "Homo Economicus: Commercialization of Body Tissue in the Age of Biotechnology," *Hastings Center Report* (September 1998)

ISSUE SUMMARY

YES: Professor David B. Resnik argues that it is morally acceptable to sell body parts that do not have the potential to become human beings.

NO: Dorothy Nelkin and Lori Andrews contend that treating body parts as salable property endangers individual and cultural values, encourages exploitation, and threatens to turn people into marketable products.

T he April 1999 issue of *Scientific American* offers readers a special section on "The Promise of Tissue Engineering." David J. Mooney and Antonios G. Mikos discuss "Growing New Organs." Roger A. Pedersen writes about "Embryonic Stem Cells for Medicine." Michael J. Lysaght and Patrick Aebischer cover "Encapsulated Cells as Therapy." Nancy Parenteau discusses "Skin: The First Tissue-Engineered Products: The Organogenesis Story," and in that word *products* lies the crux of a vigorous debate.

Researchers have found a great many ways to use human genes, organs, and cells, and the substances they produce, to save lives. They have obtained patents on their discoveries and have founded businesses to meet health care needs. And—not at all coincidentally—they have made money. See Karen Wright, "The Body Bazaar," *Discover* (October 1998).

To some, such practices seem reminiscent of slavery and the sale of men, women, and children as if they were things instead of people. Others think of grave robbers who would sell corpses to medical schools for dissection by anatomy students. Reports that the Chinese use the organs of executed criminals for the organ-transplant market have not helped. Neither have proposals to use cells taken from aborted fetuses to treat patients such as the 500,000

Americans with Parkinson's disease, a progressive deterioration of the brain marked by progressively worsening tremors and other movement difficulties. Drugs are of limited value for this disorder and have serious side effects. However, researchers have theorized that if the damaged portion of the brain could somehow be replaced or if the brain's production of the chemical dopamine (one of many chemicals that carry signals from cell to cell within the brain) could be supplemented by living, growing fetal tissue, patients could at least be helped. See the Council on Scientific Affairs and Council on Ethical and Judicial Affairs, "Medical Applications of Fetal Tissue Transplantation," *Journal of the American Medical Association* (January 26, 1990).

In the mid-1970s, soon after abortion was legalized in the United States, the National Institutes of Health (NIH) established a moratorium on (a suspension of) federal funding of research using human fetuses, either alive or dead. Legislation soon changed the moratorium to a ban, with the only exception being research intended to aid the fetus. In 1988, an NIH panel declared that the government should fund research on fetal tissue transplantation, and in 1992, Congress voted to end the ban. However, then-president George Bush vetoed the legislation because he felt that it might encourage abortion. The ban on federal funding for fetal tissue research remained in place until 1993, when President Bill Clinton ended it. However, in 1994, a presidential directive barred government-funded researchers from making human embryos for research purposes. The debate continued; see Jon Cohen, "New Fight over Fetal Tissue Grafts," *Science* (February 4, 1994).

Among the most recent results of fetal tissue research has been the isolation of embryonic stem cells, which are capable of differentiating to become all or most of the cell types in the body. In 1998, researchers announced that they had been able to induce these cells to multiply in the lab and that there was immense potential for repairing and replacing damaged organs and tissues. See Gregg Easterbrook, "Medical Evolution," *New Republic* (March 1999).

Some ethicists insist that because the stem cells come from embryos, they and their use should fall under the fetal research ban. But they promise to be much more versatile and useful than fetal tissue, and they can be obtained from "extra" embryos, left over from in vitro fertilization work, instead of from aborted fetuses.

If the work succeeds, embryonic stem cells will become a major component of an industry that now sells engineered skin and other organs, blood and blood products, sperm and eggs, antibodies, cytokines, and other components of the human body for medical purposes. In the selection that follows, David B. Resnik argues that it is morally acceptable to sell such things as long as they do not have the potential to become human beings.

Dorothy Nelkin and Lori Andrews are less accepting. They studied several body-as-property disputes that "reflect a conviction that turning tissue, cell lines, and DNA into commodities violates body integrity, exploits powerless people, intrudes on community values, distorts research agendas, and weakens public trust in scientists and clinicians."

David B. Resnik

 **YES**

The Commodification of Human Reproductive Materials

$\mathbf{T}$he burgeoning reproductive assistance industry has created an uneasy tension between individual economic interests and human dignity. On the one hand, people who donate sperm or eggs claim to have a right to remuneration for goods and services. If a person has a right to sell blood or hair, then that person should have a right to sell gametes. On the other hand, the commodification of tissues which have the potential to become adult human beings threatens human dignity and other moral values. Matters become even more complicated when we consider ownership of human genomes, since genomes are not simply pieces of tissue, but are blueprints for making and regulating organisms.

This essay develops a framework for thinking about the moral basis for a market in human reproductive materials. It argues that the commodification of gametes and genes is morally acceptable although there should not be a market for zygotes, embryos, or genomes. This position may be at odds with current property laws of many countries, which forbid the buying and selling of bodies and body parts, but the paper is concerned with moral, not legal issues. However, this essay may have some bearing on the morality of current or pending statutes, regulations, or court decisions.

The Moral Basis for Commodifying Body Parts

Before turning to this paper's main topic, it will be useful to discuss the moral basis for the commodification of body parts in general. Commodification is a social practice for treating things as commodities, i.e., as properties that can be bought, sold, or rented. Since commodities are alienable—they can be sold—it is possible to regard something as a form of property but not as a commodity. For example, we might view voting rights as a type of property but not as a type of commodity, since voting rights may be acquired, lost, or owned, but not sold.

Even if we treat a thing as a commodity, we may impose restrictions on its commerce for moral, social, economic, or political reasons. For example, condominiums are commodities that are bought, sold, and rented with various restrictions pertaining to redecorating, pets, sub-leasing, pricing, etc. Thus, one may distinguish between two forms of commodification: complete commodification (commodification with no restrictions) and incomplete commodification (commodification with restrictions). This distinction allows us to focus more clearly on this paper's main question: should human reproductive materials be treated as complete commodities, incomplete commodities, or not as commodities at all?

The moral basis for treating these body parts or products as commodities stems from the body-as-property view found in libertarian political thought, which holds that the body and its parts may be bought, sold, and rented. This philosophy traces its conceptual ancestry to the seventeenth century philosopher John Locke, who argued that each individual's body belongs to that individual, and that individuals can acquire other properties by appropriating them from nature and mixing their labour with those things. This position implies that individuals also own their body parts and products. Locke's views on property still play an important role in contemporary debates, and modern libertarians have refined his position.

In the bioethics literature, several writers have defended the body-as-property view. According to Andrews, the principle of autonomy provides a basis for treating the body as property. Most of our autonomous choices presuppose some control over our own bodies. If we think of ownership of an object as a collection of rights to control the use of that object, then autonomous individuals own their bodies, body parts, and body products. Many of the most important standards in medical ethics also reflect this viewpoint. For example, invasive medical procedures require ethical justification. The very notion of an invasion of the body draws on the body-as-property image, since an invasion is an intrusion into a territory. The doctrine of informed consent also draws on the body-as-property view. Informed consent holds that competent individuals have a right to exclusive control over their bodies, and exclusive control over an object is a characteristic of ownership.

For the purposes of this essay, I will accept the body-as-property view. I realise that this is a controversial position, but I will not defend it fully here. (I refer the reader to other authors for further discussion.) Instead of defending this view, I will consider some arguments against commodification and use them to argue for incomplete commodification of the living body (I include the word "living" here to indicate that this discussion does not apply to cadavers, unless indicated otherwise.)

Why might one regard the body as commodity but resist its complete commodification? To answer this question it will be useful to address two important moral arguments against commodification. The first argument appeals to Kantian concerns about human dignity and personhood; the second examines the social consequences of ownership practices, attitudes, and policies. I will discuss these arguments in different contexts throughout this essay.

Unconditional Value

According to the Kantian argument, commodification of the human body treats people as things that can be bought and sold. If human beings can be bought and sold, then they have a market value and can be treated as mere objects by themselves or other people. According to Kant, it is always wrong to treat people as mere objects, since human beings have inherent moral worth and dignity. Although objects can be treated as commodities and can be assigned a market value, human beings should not be treated as commodities and should not be assigned a market value. Human beings have an unconditional or absolute value. Thus, commodification of human beings is inherently wrong because it violates human dignity and worth.

I accept this Kantian position. However, I think it is possible to treat human bodies as commodities without violating human dignity and worth. Although Kant uses the term "humanity" in describing our moral obligations, it is clear from reading his work that this term refers to the rational nature in human beings, i.e., "persons" or "rational agents". Kant recognised that the body houses many elements, such as emotions, physical desires, and so on, that are distinct from the body's rational nature. If we accept this separation of person and body, then one might commodify the body without treating a person as a commodity. Thus, bodies that do not contain persons, such as anencephalic newborns, bodies in a persistent vegetative state (PVS), or cadavers, could be commodified without violating the dignity or worth of persons.

Unrealistic Portrait

However, this argument paints an unrealistic portrait of the connection between persons and bodies. The body is not like a coat that we can wear or a tool that we can use. Although it is possible to distinguish between the person and the body, these two entities are intimately connected in human beings. Selling a living human body is virtually the same thing as selling a person, and having exclusive control over someone else's body is tantamount to slavery. Only those who maintain a rigid mind/body dualism will not concede that there is an intimate relationship between the mind and body.

Yet this close connection only holds between the whole body and the person; it does not hold between parts (or products) of the body and the person. Although we think of persons as being connected to whole bodies, we do not think of persons as being tied to particular body parts or products. One does not lose a part of one's self by cutting one's hair, urinating, or donating blood. Thus, it is important to distinguish between a whole human body and its parts or products. Doing something to a part of the body does not imply doing something to the whole body, and selling a part (or product) of the body need not imply selling a whole body. Hence, one may commodify a part or product of the body without commodifying the whole body. (Some people view their personal identity as being closely connected to certain parts, such as the brain or heart, but this observation does not undermine my general point.)

With this distinction in mind, one might hold that parts of the body may be commodified even if the whole body should not be. Since the whole body is intimately connected to the person, it should not be viewed as alienable property. Hence, the whole body should not be treated as a complete commodity. But we can treat parts of the body as alienable even if the whole body should not be treated this way. Thus, one may hold that selling a whole body is immoral but regard commerce in human tissue as morally acceptable. However, there still may be some good reasons for regulating the sale of body parts. For instance, one might hold that it is immoral to sell body parts that are essential to the body's proper functioning because this form of commerce would imply murder, suicide, or other forms of killing. People may sell one kidney but not two kidneys, since human bodies cannot function without two kidneys. (A person might still give away his or her second kidney, but I will not address that question here.) Some organs, such as the heart and brain, may not be sold, given our current medical limitations and philosophical views about the connection between the person and the brain.

The second argument against treating bodies as commodities addresses slippery slope concerns: although it is not inherently wrong to sell body parts or products, the acceptance of this practice will lead to adverse social consequences as we move toward complete commodification of the body. According to Kass, if we allow body parts or products to be sold, then we will start to view the whole body as an object or commodity. This attitude will lead to the dehumanisation and objectification of people. Our downward slide might start with the selling of body parts, but it will lead to trade in children, anencephalic babies, cadavers, and PVS patients. Eventually we will sell adults into slavery. To preserve our belief in the inherent worth of human life and dignity, we must not view any part of the body as having commercial value.

While I appreciate the force of this argument, I think that we can avoid these adverse social consequences by regulating the market in body parts or products. We could forbid the sale of things whose commercialisation would have an adverse impact on our respect for human life and dignity, such as human cadavers, PVS bodies, anencephalic newborns, and so on. Informed consent would also seem to be a wise restriction on any commerce in body parts or products. By requiring that sellers and buyers give informed consent before a transaction takes place, we may be able to avoid many pitfalls. One of the biggest threats from a market in body parts comes when other people are allowed to treat a person's body as a commodity without that person's consent.

Other writers object to commodification on the grounds that it undermines the gift relationship that currently exists between donors and recipients of human organs. A market in body parts and products will eventually destroy this relationship by transforming it into an economic transaction. I do not find this argument very convincing since many commodities that are routinely bought and sold are also given as gifts, such as clothing, land, cars, and labour. People will always have reasons and motives for giving gifts, even when those gifts have commercial value. The mere fact that an object can be bought or sold need not destroy our ability to transfer that object as a gift.

Some writers have pointed out that commodifying parts of the body might lead to a practice where people are required to sell body parts or products to pay outstanding debts or to meet the demands of retributive justice. Thus the phrase "it cost me an arm and a leg" would be too real to invoke laughter. However, I think we can avoid these disturbing consequences if we enact some restrictions on the transference of body parts or products. For instance, we could make it illegal to take body parts or products to pay debts or administer punishments.

Finally, one might argue that the selling of body products could lead to the exploitation of the economically worse-off members of our society. People might sell their kidneys out of economic hardship. But why would we think it is wrong to sell body parts out of economic need? After all, people take on many dangerous and degrading occupations for economic reasons. If it is wrong to sell kidneys out of economic need, then it is also wrong to work in a coal mine or deliver pizzas in dangerous neighbourhoods. The problem with working under these conditions is not the economic transaction itself; it is the fairness of the transaction. We have laws that protect people from exploitation and regulate working conditions. Similar laws could also apply to a market in body parts and products.

The preceding arguments against commodification all suggest a common response: body parts and products, but not the whole body, should be regarded as incomplete commodities. In order to answer Kantians' concerns about the objectification of people, we should not permit a market in whole, living, human bodies; in order to address the slippery slope argument, we should regulate the market in body parts and products. I will now apply this analysis to the commodification of human reproductive materials, paying special attention to the two main arguments against commodification.

The Commodification of Reproductive Materials

Is it immoral to buy and sell sperm, eggs, zygotes, embryos, or genomes? . . .

Commodification of Gametes

If it is morally acceptable to commodify body parts or products, then gametes may be bought and sold, since gametes are body products. If individuals can buy and sell blood, hair, or tissue, then they should also be allowed buy and sell gametes. However, the two arguments against commodification pertain to the sale of gametes. First, one might object to the commodification of gametes on the grounds that gametes are unlike other cells and tissues. Sperm and eggs contain half a human genome and can unite to form a zygote. A zygote can become a child if it implants in a uterus and develops normally. Thus, selling gametes is dangerously close to selling persons, since gametes can become persons. Although I agree that gametes (germ cells) are unlike other body cells (somatic cells), I do not find this argument very persuasive. Selling gametes is

YES / David B. Resnik

not the same thing as selling persons or zygotes, since gametes are not even potential persons. A gamete is more like half of a blueprint for making a house (person) than a whole blueprint (zygote) or house that is under construction (fetus or child).

Second, one might argue that the commodification of gametes will have adverse effects on other social values, such as our respect for human life and dignity. The commodification of gametes could create a market in children or adults, or it could lead to the exploitation of poor women for their eggs. For example, suppose that sperm are sold in fertility clinics and are advertised in magazines and newspapers. The market could set a price for gametes and those people with the "best" qualities could demand the highest prices for their reproductive materials. I think this type of development could threaten our notions of human dignity and worth; hence, we may need to regulate the market in gametes. Since the selling of gametes has not yet invaded our popular culture, this situation bears watching. In any case, this argument only shows that gametes should be treated as incomplete commodities.

The Commodification of Zygotes and Embryos

One might also argue that zygotes and embryos (henceforth just zygotes) can be commodified on the grounds that they are simply body products. If gametes can be bought and sold, then zygotes can also be bought and sold. To make full sense of the objections to this argument, we must say something about when a human organism becomes a person, since the Kantian view forbids a market in persons but not a market in bodies, as such. If we follow the Kantian account of personhood, then a human being does not become a person until he or she can understand and follow moral imperatives. Thus, zygotes and other later stages of development are not persons. Kantian concerns about the objectification of persons therefore have little bearing on the selling of zygotes.

However, zygotes are potential persons. Zygotes, unlike gametes, have a complete set of genetic instructions and normally also have their own genetic identity. Although human development depends on many different environmental factors and gene-environment interactions, zygotes are much more like adult human beings than gametes. As potential persons, zygotes merit special moral concern. Potential persons merit special moral concern because the way we treat these beings can have a profound effect on the way we treat actual persons. A society that allows babies to be bought and sold is more likely to allow adults to be bought and sold than one that does not. Likewise, a society that allows zygotes to be bought and sold is more likely to accept a market for children and adults than one that does not. Moreover, this is not a problem that can be handled simply through regulation, since a market in zygotes would imply a profound change in our understanding of human beings and could lead to the commodification and objectification of children and adults. Since even a limited market for zygotes can create this dangerous slippery slope, zygotes should not be commodified. . . .

The Commodification of Genomes

The last issue I would like to consider is the ownership of human genomes. To understand issues pertaining to the commodification of genomes and their parts (i.e., genes or gene fragments), it is important to realise that there is a fundamental difference between genomes, gametes, and zygotes. Gametes and zygotes are physical entities that can be produced, destroyed, corrupted, stored, or harvested; genomes and genes, on the other hand, are not mere physical entities. Gametes and zygotes have spatial-temporal boundaries; genomes and genes cannot be located in any particular time or place. Genomes and genes are essentially information for making and regulating organisms. As information, they constitute abstract objects that can be realised in biochemical structures or represented by linguistic symbols. They are more like software than hardware. In legalistic terms, genomes (and genes) are best viewed as intellectual property.

Viewing the genome as intellectual property has important implications for moral arguments for and against its commodification. Western intellectual property laws distinguish between items that can belong to individuals and items that cannot be owned. For example, people cannot own scientific laws or concepts, though they may have copyrights over works that express those laws or concepts. People also cannot own natural phenomena, such as benzene, but they may patent processes for making benzene. The general thrust of these laws is to distinguish between ideas (or abstract objects) and tangible expressions or applications of those ideas. Ideas are common resources and cannot be owned by individuals, although particular expressions or applications of ideas can become personal property. Thus, these laws assume that only tangible expressions of ideas can be commodified.

There are two moral arguments for distinguishing between ideas and their expressions or applications. If we think of ideas as natural resources, then Locke's views on property imply that ideas can be treated as common resources. People may own things that result from adding labour to those ideas, for example, inventions or original works, but they may not own the ideas themselves. According to the utilitarian approach to intellectual property, intellectual property laws should promote social utility through encouraging scientific and technological progress. The most effective way to promote this kind of progress is to encourage the sharing of ideas, data, and theories while allowing scientists and inventors to profit from and receive credit for their works. Thus, there is a solid moral basis for laws that treat ideas as common resources but allow the ownership of particular expressions or applications of ideas.

I believe that the preceding discussion of intellectual property can provide us with some insights into the commodification of human genomes. If we treat genomes as intellectual property, then genomes are natural phenomena. As such, they are common resources that may not be owned, although individuals may own particular expressions or applications of genomes. If I invent a technique for analysing, sequencing, or cloning a genome (or one of its parts), then I may patent that invention; if I create an original work describing a genome (or one of its parts), then I may have copyrights that govern the reproduction of that work. Hence, people may buy and sell inventions and original works pertaining to the genome or genes, but they may not buy or sell naturally occurring genomes or genes.

Having said this much in favour of some form of ownership of the genome, I would like to address the two objections to commodification discussed previously. We can imagine some objectionable forms of ownership pertaining to the genome. For example, biotechnology companies have patented genetically engineered mice. What if a company attempted to patent a genetically engineered human being? Since patents govern the buying, selling, and production of inventions, this form of ownership would entail the ownership of persons, since the patent would allow the company to control the production and marketing of whole human bodies. Copyrights on the whole genome could result in similar problems. A person who copyrighted an entire genome would be able to sell these copyrights to interested buyers. Although this form of commerce would not constitute commodification of a whole human body, it could threaten our respect for human life and human dignity: a society that allows copies of genomes to be bought and sold is more likely to allow human beings to be bought and sold than one that does not. Selling copyrights to an entire genome is very much like selling a zygote, since genomes can be used to make zygotes.

On the other hand, patents and copyrights on parts of the genome would not entail the commodification of whole human bodies and probably would not threaten our respect for human life and human dignity. Patents or copyrights on individual genes would be no more pernicious than patents or copyrights on artificial body parts, such as artificial skin, blood, or heart valves. Thus, copyrights and patents can be extended to parts of the genome, but they should not be applied to the whole genome. However, there may be some good reasons to regulate the market in gene patents and copyrights in order to prevent slippery slope effects. For instance, we might choose to restrict the marketing of human genes used for the sole purpose of genetic engineering; we might forbid people or companies from acquiring a whole genome; we might take steps to prevent companies from obtaining monopolies on human genes, and so on. Hence, the entire human genome should not be regarded as a commodity, although parts of the genome may be regarded as incomplete commodities.

Dorothy Nelkin and Lori Andrews

Homo Economicus

In recent years, biotechnology techniques have transformed a variety of human body tissue into valuable and marketable research materials and clinical products. Blood can serve as the basis for immortalized cell lines for biological studies and the development of pharmaceutical products; the catalogue from the American Tissue Culture Catalogue lists thousands of people's cell lines that are available for sale. Snippets of foreskin are used for the development of artificial skin. Biopsied tissue is used to manufacture therapeutic quantities of genetic material.

Body tissue also has commercial value beyond the medical and research contexts. Placenta is used to enrich shampoos, cosmetics, and skin care products. Kary Mullis, a Nobel Prize-winning geneticist, founded a company called Star Gene that uses gene amplification techniques to make and market jewelry, containing DNA cloned from famous rock stars and athletes. The idea, says Mullis, is that "teenagers might pay a little money to get a piece of jewelry containing the actual piece of amplified DNA of somebody like a rock star."

There is also a market for services to collect and store one's tissue outside the body. People can pay to store blood prior to surgery or embryos in the course of in vitro fertilization. A Massachusetts company, BioBank, stores excess tissue removed during cosmetic or other surgical procedures for the patient's future use. New companies such as Safe-T-Child and Child Trail have formed to collect and store tissue samples to identify children who have been kidnapped. And a company called Identigene advertises on taxicabs and billboards (call 1-800-DNA-TYPE) for a service to collect tissue for DNA identification that would establish paternity in child support disputes. There are about fifty private DNA testing centers in the United States, hundreds of university laboratories undertaking DNA research, and over 1,000 biotechnology companies developing commercial products from bodily materials.

These expanding markets have increased the value of human tissue, and institutions with ready access to tissue find they possess a capital resource. Access to stored tissue samples is sometimes included in collaborative agreements between hospitals and biotechnology firms. In a joint venture agreement, Sequana Therapeutics, Inc., a California biotechnology firm, credited the New York City cancer hospital, Memorial-Sloan Kettering, with $5 million in order

From Dorothy Nelkin and Lori Andrews, "Homo Economicus: Commercialization of Body Tissue in the Age of Biotechnology," *Hastings Center Report*, vol. 28, no. 5 (September/October 1998). Copyright © 1998 by The Hastings Center. Reprinted by permission. References omitted.

to obtain access to its bank of cancer tissue biopsies that could be useful as a source of genetic information.

Physicians who treat families with genetic disease are approaching geneticists and offering to "sell you my families"—meaning that they will, for a fee, give the researcher their patients' blood samples. Scientists who isolate certain genes are then patenting them and profiting from their use in genetic tests. Hospitals in Great Britain and Russia sell tissue in order to augment their limited budgets. Between 1976 and 1993 Merieux UK collected 360 tons of placental tissue each year from 282 British hospitals and sent them to France for use in manufacturing drugs. Human tissue has become so valuable that it is sometimes a target for corporate espionage and theft.

In the United States the potential for commercial gain from the body grew as a consequence of legislative measures that were enacted in the 1980s to encourage the commercial development of government-funded research. Legislation allowed universities and nonprofit institutions to apply for patents on federally funded projects and also provided tax incentives to companies investing in academic research. At the same time, changes in patent law turned commercial attention toward research in genetics. A landmark U.S. Supreme Court case in 1980 granted a patent on a life form—a bacterium—setting the stage for the patenting of human genes. In the mid-1980s the U.S. Patent Office began granting patent rights for human genes. It has since received over 5,000 patent applications and has granted more than 1,500, including patents for bone and brain tissue and DNA coding for human proteins.

Today, joint ventures between industry and universities are thriving, and research scientists are increasingly tied to commercial goals. Industry has become a significant source of funding for genetics research. As Francis Collins observed, companies have resources for gene hunting that the academies cannot match: "It's important not to ignore the way things have changed in the last 3 years in human genetics [because of industry]. Gene hunting used to be a purely academic exercise." Nearly every major geneticist is associated with a biotechnology firm; some as directors, others as consultants. And scientists, hospitals, and universities are patenting genes.

The body, of course, has long been exploited as a commercial and marketable entity, as athletes, models, prostitutes, surrogate mothers, and beauty queens are well aware. Yet there is something strange and troubling about the traffic in body tissue, the banking of human cells, the patenting of genes. In the 1984 public hearings concerning anatomical gifts, Albert Gore, then a U.S. Congressman, was troubled by a growing tendency to treat the body as a commodity in a market economy: "It is against our system of values to buy and sell parts of human beings.... The notion has perhaps superficial attraction to some because we have learned that the market system will solve lots of problems if we just stand out of the way and let it work. It is very true. This ought to be an exception because you don't want to invest property rights in human beings.... It is wrong."

But what *is* troubling about the commodification of the body? What is the problem with the growing interest in human tissue for the manufacturing of pharmaceutical or bioengineered products? Clearly the interest in the body is driven by instrumental and commercial values; but so too, as Gore suggested, are most technological endeavors. Moreover, much of the body tissue useful for biotechnology innovation—hair, blood, sperm—is replenishable. And we normally regard body materials such as umbilical cord blood, foreskin, the tissue discarded after surgery—and, in some cases, even the excess embryos created for in vitro fertilization—as simply refuse, like bloodied bandages and other medical wastes. Why not, then, view the body as a useful and exploitable resource if this can advance scientific research, contribute to progress, or provide lifesaving benefits to others? Why are there demonstrations against the privatization of cordblood, lawsuits against the commercialization of cell lines, protests against the patenting of genes? Why are commercial developments in the removal, storage, and transformation of human tissue controversial?

To answer these questions, we undertook a study of several prominent disputes over the ownership of the body, the collection of human tissue, and its distribution as a resource. These disputes reflect the collision between commercial claims for body tissue and individual interests or cultural values. They reflect a conviction that turning tissue, cell lines, and DNA into commodities violates body integrity, exploits powerless people, intrudes on community values, distorts research agendas, and weakens public trust in scientists and clinicians.

Historical Controversies

Research and clinical uses of body parts have been controversial since the early days of anatomical dissection. The process of cutting and fragmenting the body once evoked images of evil, and Dante-esque visions of Hell. As the Renaissance brought growing interest in anatomy, the use of bodies in medical schools was gradually accepted. . . .

Today, old tensions have taken on new dimensions as the commercial potential of human tissue has caught the entrepreneurial imagination. Few laws are in place to address the proper uses of cells, tissues, and genes. Instead, disputes over the ownership, collection, and distribution of human tissue have ended up in the media and in the courts.

The Ownership of Body Tissue

John Moore, a patient with hairy cell leukemia, had his spleen removed at the University of California, Los Angeles, School of Medicine in 1976. His physician, Dr. David W. Golde, patented certain chemicals in Moore's blood purportedly without his knowledge or consent and set up contracts with a Boston company, negotiating shares worth $3 million. Sandoz, the Swiss pharmaceutical company, paid a reported $15 million for the right to develop the Mo cell line.

Moore began to suspect that his tissue was being used for purposes beyond his personal care when UCLA cancer specialists kept taking samples of blood, bone marrow, skin, and sperm for seven years. When Moore discovered in 1984 that he had become patent number 4,438,032, he sued the doctors for malpractice and property theft. His physicians claimed that Moore had waived his interest in his body parts when he signed a general consent form giving the UCLA pathology department the right to dispose of his removed tissue. But Moore felt that his integrity was violated, his body exploited, and his tissue turned into a product: "My doctors are claiming that my humanity, my genetic essence, is their invention and their property. They view me as a mine from which to extract biological material. I was harvested."

The court held that clinicians must inform patients in advance of surgical procedures that their tissue could be used for research, but it denied Moore's claim that he owned his tissue. Who then should reap the *profits* from parts taken from an individual's body? The court decided that the doctor and biotechnology company rather than the patient should profit. The decision rested on the promise of biotechnology innovation. The court did not want to slow down research by "threaten[ing] with disabling civil liability innocent parties who are engaged in socially useful activities, such as researchers who have no reason to believe that their use of a particular cell sample is against a donor's wishes." The court was concerned that giving Moore a property right to his tissue would "destroy the economic incentive to conduct important medical research."

Justice Stanley Mosk, dissenting, objected to the notion that the body— "the physical and temporal expression of the unique human persona"—could be regarded as a product for commercial exploitation. For, he argued, the spectre of direct abuse, of torture, of involuntary servitude haunts the laboratories and boardrooms of today's biotechnological research industrial complex (p. 515).

The privileging of biotechnology companies encouraged a genetics gold rush. In 1992 Craig Venter, a molecular biologist, left the National Institutes of Health to form The Institute for Genomic Research (TIGR), where he compiled the world's largest human gene data bank containing at least 150,000 fragments of DNA sequences. The Institute for Genomic Research was initially funded by a $70 million grant from a firm, Human Genome Services (HGS). Two months after the agreement, HGS contracted with SmithKline Beecham, which gained an exclusive stake in the database with first rights on patentable discoveries. Geneticist David King described the situation: "You have a corporation trying to monopolize control of a large part of the whole human genome, literally the human heritage. Should this become private property?"

The concerns about commercial exploitation of the body expressed in *Moore* have assumed more complex dimensions in disputes over the collection of human tissue in a global context. Scientists and biotechnology companies are searching the world for disease genes. But critics have viewed the collection of tissue from indigenous populations as a violation of cultural values, and associate these efforts with past forms of exploitation.

Collecting Tissue from Indigenous Populations

Because people from isolated populations may have unique body tissue, western geneticists, biotechnology companies, and researchers from the Human Genome Diversity Project (HGDP) are seeking blood and hair samples from indigenous groups throughout the world. Their goals are to find disease genes by identifying families with a high rate of genetically linked conditions; to develop genetic tests and therapeutic products; and to "immortalize" the DNA from "vanishing populations."

In March 1995 researchers from the National Institutes of Health [NIH] obtained a virus-infected cell line from a man from the Hagahai tribe in Papua, New Guinea. The cell line, which could be used to develop a diagnostic test, became patent number 5,397,696. Accused of exploitation, the NIH withdrew the patent claim in December 1996. Meanwhile, Sequana Therapeutics, collaborating with the University of Toronto, collected DNA samples from the island of Tristan de Cunha for research on asthma and then sold the rights to develop therapeutic technologies for $70 million to a German company, Boehringer Ingelheim. Western scientists are also negotiating contracts to collect DNA samples from Chinese families with genetic diseases. But China's eugenics policies include efforts to identify families with genetic abnormalities so as to prevent them from reproducing. Thus the DNA samples may also be a valuable resource for Chinese authorities seeking to implement oppressive eugenics laws.

The HGDP has confronted angry opposition. Indigenous groups view the taking of their tissue as exploitation. They have accused the program of violating community values, "biopiracy" or "biocolonialism," one more effort to divide their social world. A representative of an indigenous group opined, "You've taken our land, our language, our culture, and even our children. Are you now saying you want to take part of our bodies as well?" Some objections reflect beliefs, expressed in collective rituals involving blood or body parts, about the social meaning of body tissue—its role in maintaining the integrity of the community and the relationship of the individual to the collective. Others believe that their future might be compromised by the collection of their DNA. Once scientists have what they need from them, there would be no reason to help them stay alive. This pessimistic view was fueled by researchers who promoted the project as a way to "immortalize" the cell lines of groups that will become extinct.

Indigenous groups also question the relevance of the scientific work to their own health needs, which have less to do with genetic disease than with common disorders such as diarrhea. They argue that DNA is collected, often without adequate knowledge or consent, and then used for products relevant only in wealthy nations. . . .

In response to concerns about exploitation of indigenous resources, the United Nations Convention on Biodiversity (1992) had sought to assure that national governments receive just compensation for commercial use of both human and agricultural resources. But the interest in genetic resources suggests that this approach may lead to further exploitation of indigenous groups as they become profit centers for their governments. Moreover, some groups do not want compensation—the very idea of commercializing the body offends them and contradicts their world view. For them, the body has a social meaning tied to colonial history, traditional communal rituals, and concerns about continued exploitation. . . .

Theft—The Ultimate Symbol of Commodification

Products that attain commercial value are inevitably subject to theft, a not uncommon form of redistribution. The traffic in body parts has persisted, spurred as in the nineteenth century, by a shortage of organs and tissue. Body parts have been bought from coroners, stolen from the site of accidents, and sold to meet the demands of industry and medicine. Today, cell lines are a target for international espionage. In a sting operation, agents of the Food and Drug Administration posed as representatives of a tissue bank and ordered tissue from a California dentist who tried to sell them body parts at a discount. In France, a government investigation exposed an embezzlement scheme in which private companies billed local hospitals for synthetic ligament tissue that, it turned out, came from human tissue, which in France cannot legally be bought and sold.

Funeral home personnel and coroners have also engaged in tissue theft. In one case, a morgue employee allegedly stole body parts and sold them nationally—a situation uncovered unexpectedly when the body of a twenty-one-day-old infant was exhumed for other purposes and found to be missing his heart, lungs, eyes, pituitary gland, aorta, kidneys, spleen, and key brain parts. In Britain seventeen people who contracted Creutzfeld Jacob disease from human growth hormone accused the Medical Research Council and the Department of Health of unlawfully buying, from mortuaries, the pituitary glands from 900,000 bodies to extract the growth hormone. The tissue was taken without the consent of the individuals before death or their families, in violation of British law.

Demands for spare embryos have also led to undercover redistribution in the in vitro fertilization business. At the University of California at Irvine, over 75 couples were affected by theft of eggs and embryos at the university clinic where Dr. Ricardo Asch had apparently been secretly selling some of the eggs extracted from his infertility patients to other patients who were duped into thinking they were from legitimate donors. More than forty civil lawsuits were filed. In July 1997 the university agreed to pay $14 million to seventy-five couples; two dozen lawsuits still remain. Embryo theft was "predictable, almost inevitable," says Boston University health law professor George Annas. "The field [of in vitro fertilization] is so lucrative and so unregulated that someone was just bound to do it."

Problems With the Business of Bodies

References to body parts in the medical and scientific literature increasingly employ a language of commerce—of banking, investment, insurance, compensation, and patenting. Gene sequences are patented; cord blood is a "hot property," the body is a "medical factory." Companies "target" appropriate markets for their products. Pathology organizations lobby the government to allow them to use stored tissue samples without consent, for they view such samples as "treasure troves" or "national resources" for research. Geneticists talk of "prospecting" for genes. The body is a "project"—a system that can be divided and dissected down to the molecular level. In a striking statement in the *Moore* case, the defendant, UCLA, claimed that even if Moore's cells were his property, as a state university it had a right to take the cells under "eminent domain."

The body tissue disputes we have described—over the ownership, collection, and distribution of body tissue—raise questions about the assumptions underlying this language of commerce. Who will profit? Who will lose? How will exploitation be avoided? They reflect conflicting beliefs about the body. Is body tissue to be defined as waste, like the material in a hospital bed pan? Is it refuse that is freely available as raw material for commercial products? Or does body tissue have inherent value as part of a person? Are genes the essence of an individual and a sacred part of the human inheritance? Or are they, as a director of SmithKline Beecham purportedly claimed, "the currency of the future."

Disputes suggest that commodifying human tissue, usually without the person's knowledge or consent, is troubling because it threatens the well-being of individuals and violates social assumptions about the body. And they suggest that commercialization can also have serious implications for science and medical practice.

Individual Concerns. Commercial interests continue to evoke fears of patient exploitation. John Moore's experience suggested that the commercial interests of doctors can encourage them to take more tissue than is needed for the benefit of their patients. Physicians or institutions with economic interests can also easily influence the decisions of individuals in vulnerable situations. Patients who are hospitalized may be reluctant to withhold consent. New parents, at an uncertain time in their lives, are vulnerable to the pitch of cord blood company salesmen.

The market incentives to treat body tissue as a valuable and collectible commodity may also have troubling psychological effects. Psychologists have found that a sense of coherence and body integrity is essential to individual development and a person's sense of self, and that control over what is done to the body or its parts is important to psychological well-being. Some people try to place limits on how their body is used. In light of past research exploitation, some African-American women refuse to allow amniotic tissue to be collected for prenatal diagnosis out of concern about the uses that could be made of this tissue. And some families with genetic diseases who provided tissue to trusted researchers for investigations related to their disease object when they learn their tissue was to be sold to commercial enterprises for unrelated research. Using individuals' tissue in ways that violate their beliefs can disturb their sense of self-agency.

The potential for commercialization creates incentives for researchers and physicians to ignore patients' wishes and their beliefs about the body. Jewish tradition maintains that as man was created in the image of God, in death the body should retain the unity of that image. Consequently, in the Orthodox Jewish community, the body must be buried whole. Unauthorized taking of tissue for commercial use would violate these religious beliefs about the body. . . .

Social Concerns. The body is not just a neutral object. We have, says historian Anthony Synnott, "imposed layers of ideas, images, meanings and associations on these biological systems which together operate and maintain our physical bodies. Our bodies and body parts are loaded with cultural symbolism." The norms that guide the disposition of body tissue reflect community ideals and social priorities. The history of blood donation, for example, suggests the importance of beliefs about the relationship of blood to communal values. Giving blood and body tissue is a way to affirm social connectedness by linking donors to strangers and donations to the public good. "Donations" based on economic self-interest rather than altruism tend to be devalued.

... [C]ritics [have] viewed commercialization as violating the social values involved in free and anonymous donation. They questioned the legitimacy of treating human tissue as private property and worried about fairness and equity in its distribution. So too in the patent disputes....

Commercial interests in the body also evoke more general moral and religious reservations. The Boston-based Council for Responsible Genetics declared that "[t]he commercialization and expropriation of these life materials is a violation of the sanctity of human, animal, and plant life." If secular groups are vaguely uncomfortable about patenting the body, religious groups are more explicit: they believe that patenting turns the body into a product, violating the sovereignty of God and the "inherent sanctity of life." The issue, said a representative from the Southern Baptist Convention, "is going to dwarf the pro-life debate within a few years."

Implications for Science and Medicine

The business of bodies affects the fiduciary relationship between doctors and patients. Medical research and clinical practice are ideally considered distinct from the motives of the market. We are leery of scientists who have profit motives in the outcomes of their research or clinicians who have economic interests in particular procedures. Yet a 1996 study of 789 biomedical papers published by academic scientists in Massachusetts found that in 34 percent, one or more authors stood to make money from the results they were reporting. This was because they either held a patent or were an officer or advisor of a biotech firm exploiting the research. In *none* of the articles was this financial interest disclosed.

Patenting in biomedicine hardly enhances trust. Nor does it necessarily encourage the best research. Though considered essential to protect discoveries and provide incentives for investment in research, patenting may actually impede research. Surveys find that patenting has led to reductions in openness and data sharing, delays in publication, and tendencies to select research projects of short-term commercial interest. In several cases, corporations with vested interests have tried to suppress the publication of research findings that were not in their interests. Strains over conflicting commitments have caused some researchers to sever their commercial ties....

... [C]ommercialization of body parts may prevent patients from obtaining appropriate health care services by obstructing the distribution of research benefits. Patent rights allow the researcher who identifies a gene to earn royalties on any test or therapy created with that gene. A British hospital that tested a patient for cystic fibrosis was asked to pay royalties because a private company held the patent on the gene. Some laboratories are giving up a useful hormone test to determine whether a fetus has Down syndrome because the royalty fees exceed Medicaid reimbursement. A patent monopoly on cord blood storage would hamper the development of community cord blood banks, leaving patients who do not have the money to store their infant's blood without a remedy if their child develops a disorder requiring a cord blood transplantation. The real costs in such cases are borne by patients denied appropriate treatment.

There is growing concern that market principles have been improperly applied. People have obtained commercial rights without making an inventive contribution or without determining the purpose of their discovery. Dr. Mark Bogart merely noted the correspondence between a particular hormone level and the chance that a fetus has Down syndrome, yet he was granted a patent and is trying to collect a fee for each diagnostic test relying on measurement of that hormone. Protesting health care providers have filed suit to challenge the patent.

Similarly, numerous patents have been issued on partial gene sequences, even though the patent seekers did not know what the sequences did. In July 1991 Human Genome Sciences received a patent on the DNA sequence for the CCR5 receptor on immune system cells. Now it has been found the receptor opens cells to HIV infection, providing a basis for the development of treatments for HIV infection. But every researcher developing such a treatment will have to pay a licensing fee to Human Genome Sciences.

Incidents like these trouble even venture capitalists. Michael Heller and Rebecca Eisenberg of the University of Michigan School of Law point out a paradoxical consequence of the grant of biotechnology patents: "A proliferation of intellectual property rights upstream may be stifling life-saving innovations further downstream in the course of research and development."

The Policy Response

The law has not yet settled with respect to controlling commercial interests in body tissue and resolving questions of consent and compensation for the use of cells and genes. However, we are beginning to see some efforts to extend to this area the principles of consent and noncommodification that were developed to regulate organ donation. Certain professional organizations are emphasizing the need to obtain patient consent even if the tissue used has already been removed from the patient's body. When researchers sought to analyze previously collected tissue samples at the Centers for Disease Control, an advisory group pointed out that "retaining tissue samples or immortalizing cell lines may violate cultural or religious beliefs." Guidelines issued by the American College of Medical Genetics require that patients be asked for consent before research is done on their tissue samples and that patients have an option to have their samples withdrawn or destroyed at any time.

But the policy world is going further, questioning whether commercialization of the body should be allowed even with patient consent. Some scientists as well as activists have challenged the patenting of human genes. And at least one government has stepped in to challenge the transformation of a research tissue bank into a private company resource: when a French foundation holding the DNA fragments of 5,000 diabetics tried to sell this database to an American biotechnology company, the French government intervened; the ownership of this resource remains in dispute.

Robert Bellah has observed that "[a]ll the primary relationships in our society, those between employers and employees, between lawyers and clients, between doctors and patients... are being stripped of any moral understanding other than that of market exchange." In this climate, developments in biotechnology are increasingly linking the biomedical sciences with the aggressive commercialization that is invading nearly every sector of human life. But as biomedical research becomes more closely tied to commercial goals, the encroachment of the market is triggering a growing sense of disillusionment and mistrust. For the encroachment of commercial practices on the human body is increasingly challenging individual and cultural values, encouraging exploitation through the collection and use of tissue, and turning tissue (and potentially people) into marketable products.

POSTSCRIPT

Is It Ethical to Sell Human Tissue?

As noted in the Introduction to this issue, the ethics of selling human organs, tissues, cells, and products is hardly a new issue. But it has been given a new urgency by the recent discovery of embryonic stem cells. Ethicists Karen Lebacqz, Micheal M. Mendiola, Ted Peters, Ernie W. D. Young, and Laurie Zoloth-Dorfman reviewed the situation at some length in "Research with Human Embryonic Stem Cells: Ethical Considerations," *Hastings Center Report* (March 1999), concluding that such research can be performed even though there are a number of unanswered questions, including those of control of fetal tissue, global justice, and consensus in a pluralistic society.

American society as a whole seems to agree that it is appropriate to forge ahead, albeit with some caution. For the moment, only two companies, Advanced Cell Technology (ACT) of Worcester, Massachusetts, and Geron Corporation of California, are progressing with plans to develop embryonic stem cells as a medical resource, using only private funds. On April 21, 1999, the NIH posted on its Web site a "Fact Sheet on Stem Cell Research" (http://www.nih.gov/news/pr/apr99/od-21.htm) saying, "After a thorough analysis of the law, DHHS [Department of Health and Human Services] concluded that the congressional prohibition on the use of DHHS funds for certain types of human embryo research does not apply to research utilizing human pluripotent stem cells because such cells are not embryos.... [C]urrent law permits federal funds to be used for research utilizing human pluripotent stem cells. The National Institutes of Health (NIH) plans to move forward in a careful and deliberate fashion to develop rigorous guidelines that address the special ethical, legal, and social issues relevant to this research. The NIH will not fund research using human pluripotent stem cells until guidelines are developed and widely disseminated to the research community and an oversight process is in place." Proposed guidelines were scheduled to be published in the *Federal Register* during the summer of 1999.

Caution is necessary because the issue—particularly its link to embryos and abortion—has aroused opposition from conservative legislators and pro-life activists. There is even considerable disagreement on whether or not federal law permits NIH to fund the research, despite its claims. In May 1999, Senate Majority Leader Trent Lott (R-Mississippi) said that the ban on federal funding of human embryo research was not about to be lifted despite a draft recommendation of the National Bioethics Advisory Commission (NBAC). See Joyce Howard Price, "Pro-Lifers Gear up to Guard Ban on Stem Cell Research," *Washington Times* (May 30, 1999). At its 32nd meeting in June 1999, the NBAC affirmed that "federally financed scientists be allowed to derive embryonic stem cells from human embryos and conduct research on stem cells derived by others" ("Ethics Panel Recommends Stem Cell Use," *The New York Times* [June 30, 1999]).

For other views of this issue, see Emanuel D. Thorne, "Tissue Transplants: The Dilemma of the Body's Growing Value," *The Public Interest* (Winter 1990); Andrew Simons, "Brave New Harvest," *Christianity Today* (November 19, 1990); Stephen G. Post, "Fetal Tissue Transplant: The Right to Question Progress," *America* (January 12, 1991); and John Fletcher, "Human Fetal and Embryo Research: Lysenkoism in Reverse—How and Why?" in Robert H. Blank and Andrea L. Bonnicksen, eds., *Emerging Issues in Biomedical Policy, vol. 2* (Columbia University Press, 1993).

ISSUE 18

Is It Ethically Permissible to Clone Human Beings?

YES: Steven Vere, from "The Case for Cloning Humans," March 1997, <http://www.best.com/~vere/cloning.htm> (October 26, 1999)

NO: Leon R. Kass, from "The Wisdom of Repugnance," *The New Republic* (June 2, 1997)

ISSUE SUMMARY

YES: Computer scientist Steven Vere states that "human cloning has enormous potential benefits and few real negative consequences." He maintains that human cloning should be reasonably regulated but not banned.

NO: Biochemist Leon R. Kass argues that human cloning is "so repulsive to contemplate" that it should be prohibited entirely.

In February 1997 Ian Wilmut and Keith H. S. Campbell of the Roslin Institute in Edinburgh, Scotland, announced that they had cloned a sheep by transferring the gene-containing nucleus from a single cell of an adult sheep's mammary gland into an egg cell whose own nucleus had been removed and discarded. The resulting combination cell then developed into an embryo and eventually a lamb in the same way a normal egg cell does after being fertilized with a sperm cell. That lamb, named Dolly, was a genetic duplicate of the ewe from which the udder cell's nucleus was taken. Similar feats had been accomplished years before with fish and frogs, and mammal embryos had previously been split to produce artificial twins. And in March researchers at the Oregon Regional Primate Research Center announced that they had cloned monkeys by using cells from monkey embryos (not adults). In July the Roslin researchers announced the cloning of lambs from fetal cells—this time cells including human genes. But the reactions of the media, politicians, ethicists, and laypeople have been largely negative. Dr. Donald Bruce, director of the Church of Scotland's Society, Religion and Technology Project, for example, has argued at some length about how "nature is not ours to do exactly what we like with."

Many people seem to agree. In 1994 the U.S. National Advisory Board on Ethics in Reproduction called the whole idea of cloning oneself "bizarre... narcissistic and ethically impoverished." Arthur Caplan, director of the Center for Bioethics at the University of Pennsylvania, wonders, "What is the ethical purpose of even trying?" Conservative columnist George Will asks whether humans are now uniquely endangered since "the great given—a human being is the product of the union of a man and a woman—is no longer a given" and "humanity is supposed to be an endless chain, not a series of mirrors."

Others go further. President Bill Clinton asked the National Bioethics Advisory Commission (see its home page at http://bioethics.gov/), chaired by Harold T. Shapiro, president of Princeton University, to investigate the implications of this "stunning" research and to issue a final report by the end of May 1997. He also barred the use of U.S. funds to support work on cloning humans. The Commission's report called for extending the ban and called any attempt to clone a human "morally unacceptable" for now. Many countries besides the U.S. agreed, and bans on cloning research were widely imposed.

Yet, says J. Madeleine Nash in "The Case for Cloning," *Time* (February 9, 1998), "hasty legislation could easily be too restrictive." Cloning could serve a great many useful purposes, and further development of the technology could lead to much less alarming procedures, such as growing replacement organs within a patient's body. See Arlene Judith Klotzko, "We Can Rebuild...," *New Scientist* (February 27, 1999). Some of these benefits were considered when George Washington University researchers, using nonviable embryos, demonstrated that single cells could be removed from human embryos and induced to grow into new embryos. If permitted to develop normally, the cells would grow into genetically identical adults. The resulting adults would be duplicates, but only of each other (like identical twins), not of some preexisting adult.

Did Dolly represent something entirely new? For the very first time, it seemed more than science fiction to say it might soon be possible to duplicate an adult human, not just an embryo. But when Robertson spoke at the National Bioethics Advisory Commission conference held in Washington, D.C., March 13–14, 1997, he repeated his position, saying, "At this early stage in the development of mammalian cloning a ban on all human cloning is both imprudent and unjustified. Enough good uses can be imagined that it would be unwise to ban all cloning and cloning research because of vague and highly speculative fears."

In the following selection, Steven Vere is less reserved. He argues that "much of the negativity about human cloning is based simply on the breathtaking novelty of the concept rather than on any real undesirable consequences. On balance, human cloning would have overwhelming advantages if regulated in a reasonable way."

In the second selection, Leon R. Kass contends that people should trust their initial repugnance about human cloning because it threatens important human values, such as the profundity of sex, the sacredness of the human body, and the value of individuality. Human reproduction must not be debased by turning it into mere willful manufacturing. Kass concludes that human cloning is "so repulsive to contemplate" that it should be prohibited entirely.

I guess i agree, but he is rather flippant!

,ask

Steven Vere

The Case for Cloning Humans

The cloning of humans is now very close to reality, thanks to the historic scientific breakthrough of Dr. Ian Wilmut and his colleagues in the UK. This possibility is one of incredible potential benefit for all of us. Unfortunately the initial debate on this issue has been dominated by misleading, sensationalized accounts in the news media and negative emotional reactions derived from inaccurate science fiction. Much of the negativity about human cloning is based simply on the breathtaking novelty of the concept rather than on any real undesirable consequences. On balance, human cloning would have overwhelming advantages if regulated in a reasonable way. A comprehensive ban on human cloning by a misinformed public would be a sorry episode in human history. This essay will discuss both the advantages and the alleged negative consequences of human cloning. *agree*

What is a Human Clone?

A human clone is really just a time-delayed identical twin of another person. Science fiction novels and movies have given people the impression that human clones would be mindless zombies, Frankenstein monsters, or "doubles." This is all complete nonsense. Human clones would be human beings just like you and me, not zombies. They would be carried and delivered after nine months by a human mother and raised in a family just like everyone else. They would require 18 years to reach adulthood just like everyone else. Consequently, a clone-twin will be decades younger than the original person. There is no danger of people confusing a clone-twin with the original person. As with identical twins, the clone and DNA donor would have different fingerprints. A clone will not inherit any of the memories of the original person. Because of these differences, a clone is not a xerox copy or "double" of a person, just a much younger identical twin. Human clones would have the same legal rights and responsibilities as any other human being. Human clones will be human beings in every sense. You could not keep a clone as a slave. Human slavery was abolished in the United States in 1865.

It should be emphasized that all human cloning must be done on an individual voluntary basis. The living person who is to be cloned would have to *ask: good reasons?*

give their consent, and the woman who gives birth to the clone-twin and raises the child must also be acting voluntarily. No other scenario is conceivable in a free democratic country. Because cloning requires a woman to gestate the baby, there is no danger of evil scientists creating thousands of clones in secret laboratories. Cloning will be done only at the request and with the participation of ordinary people, as an additional reproduction option.

Many people have asked, "Why would anyone want to clone a human being?" There are at least two good reasons: to allow families to conceive twins of exceptional individuals, and to allow childless couples to reproduce. In a free society we must also ask, "Are the negative consequences sufficiently compelling that we must prohibit consenting adults from doing this?" We will see that in general they are not. Where specific abuses are anticipated, these can be avoided by targeted laws and regulations, which I will suggest below.

Cloning Exceptional People

Exceptional people are valuable in many ways, both culturally and economically. For example, US movie stars and sports stars are often worth hundreds of millions of dollars. Let's consider the specific example of Clint Eastwood. His films have grossed several billion dollars over thirty years. Today he is 67 years old and nearing the end of his acting and directing career. He is one of the most popular living movie stars. As Richard Schickel says in an essay on Eastwood, "For actors, more than for most people, genetics is destiny." The cultural and economic value of cloning Clint Eastwood would be enormous. Tens of millions of fans would be delighted. Furthermore, this could be done very conveniently. He certainly has the financial resources to pay for the procedure. His new wife is of child-bearing age, and could easily carry and deliver the child, which would be brought up in the family. If the Eastwood family decided they wanted to do this, why should government prohibit it? Why should this be a crime?

The same argument applies to distinguished intellectuals, and scientists, such as science fiction visionary Arthur C. Clarke, Dr. Jonas Salk, inventor of the polio vaccine, and even Dr. Ian Wilmut himself. Wilmut is certain to win the Nobel prize in medicine/physiology. In fact any Nobel prize winner would be worth cloning for the potential future contribution which their twin might make. Again we are talking about the decision being made by the individuals directly involved: the DNA donor, the woman who will bear the child, and her husband who would help in raising the child.

Cloning is also reasonable in the case of even ordinary individuals. The concept of "exceptional people" is not limited to movie stars and Nobel prize winners. All of us know people we admire and respect. We sometimes think to ourselves, "Wouldn't it be nice if there were more people in the world like that?" Human cloning allows us to go beyond wistful thoughts of this kind. Suppose old Uncle Max is a great guy, regarded with affection and respect in the community and by his family. His niece and her husband decide they would like to have a child just like Uncle Max. He is flattered and agrees to allow himself to be cloned. Why should the US Congress, in its infinite wisdom, intervene and declare that Uncle Max and his niece are criminals who should be jailed by the reproduction police? Where is the evil consequence for them and for society? Why should this be a crime?

What might we expect from human clones? The answers come from studies of natural identical twins. Human clones will look just like the original person and have essentially the same height and build. For famous super-models and movie stars, these may be the most important characteristics. Identical twins have a 70% correlation of intelligence and a 50% correlation of personality traits. This means that if someone clones a distinguished scientist, the clone-twin might actually be more intelligent than the original scientist! If a clone of Elizabeth Taylor has a somewhat different personality, who cares? At the present time we cannot be sure what percentage of twins of distinguished people will make equally valuable contributions, but if we ban cloning we will never know. Drive and determination are certainly important characteristics of many distinguished people. Perhaps drive and determination are genetically influenced characteristics. If we find that clones of distinguished people are not living up to the reputations of their predecessors, then the incentive for human cloning will be diminished. We would then see human cloning done less frequently based on informed individual choice.

Alleged Objections to Human Cloning

Some politicians in the United States are now proposing to save us from the horrors of human cloning by a comprehensive prohibition. The interesting thing is that under close analysis there really aren't any serious problems. In the few cases where abuses are likely to occur, these can be avoided by targeted legislation. There is nothing about human cloning *per se* that justifies its criminalization. The only objection that stands up under analysis is that the technology has not been perfected. This is a justification for further research, not for a prohibition.

The number of fantastic and absurd objections to human cloning is absolutely astonishing, and indicate a fundamental lack of understanding of the concept by the general public. Instead of pandering to uninstructed fears, politicians would do better to undertake a program to educate the public to a realistic understanding of cloning. If lawmakers are foolish enough to criminalize human cloning in the US, there are good prospects that the Supreme Court will declare this to be unconstitutional. Failing that, Americans will still have the option of flying to a free country to obtain the procedure.

Let us now consider in detail some of the major objections to human cloning which people have put forth:

The very thought is repugnant and disgusting. Creating another person with the same genetic code would violate human dignity and uniqueness   These arguments are invalidated by the existence of over 150 million people in the world today whose genetic codes are not unique. I am speaking of natural identical twins, which occur on average once in every 67 births. Natural twins are much more alike than clone-twins, because natural twins are exactly the same age, whereas a clone-twin and the DNA donor will usually be decades apart in age. Are twins or triplets repugnant and disgusting? Do twins violate human dignity? Of course not!

This reaction in many cases is simply a response to misinformation and confusion about the concept of a human clone. But if you find cloning offensive, by all means don't do it. Even if many people still consider the thought of human clones disgusting, this is not sufficient grounds for a prohibition. For the sake of individual freedom, many activities are allowed in this world which people find disgusting. For example many people find nose rings and sex change operations disgusting, but these are not outlawed because we value freedom of choice. There is a notion that truly "victimless crimes" should not be crimes. In the case of human cloning, who would be the victim? It is difficult to believe that the human clones would consider themselves victims simply because they share the same genetic code as someone else. The millions of identical twins do not think of themselves as victims. It is also difficult to see how society as a whole would be victimized by allowing human cloning. Human clones are likely to think of themselves as special, particularly when they are the twins of distinguished individuals. They will also have the advantage of knowing early in life what they are good at. Where is the problem? *That is the problem*

It would diminish genetic diversity, leaving us more vulnerable to disease epidemics, etc.   This objection is based on an extreme, unjustified extrapolation. There are over five billion people on this planet. Certainly human cloning will be done on a very modest scale, because of the costs involved and because most women will not want to be the mother of a clone-twin. It will be many decades before the total number of human clones approaches even one million people in the entire world. On a percentage basis they would constitute a microscopic fraction of the total population, and would not have any effect on human genetic diversity. I will also argue later that human cloning may actually allow us to recover lost genetic diversity. If at some remote future date human cloning became widespread, then some limitation of this activity would be warranted. However, bear in mind that even if one clone of every person on the planet were created, genetic diversity would be undiminished because we would still have five billion genetically different individuals.

It could lead to the creation of human monsters or freaks   Human cloning is not the same as human genetic engineering. In human cloning, the DNA is copied to create someone who is an exact twin of an existing person, and consequently not a monster or a freak. Human genetic engineering would involve the modification of human DNA to create a person who may be unlike any person who previously existed. This could conceivably lead to the creation of very unusual individuals, even monsters. Human genetic engineering, while having vast positive potential, is indeed a very risky undertaking and should be conducted only with the greatest circumspection and oversight. Cloning is tame in comparison with genetic engineering. If you are afraid of human cloning, you are going to be petrified by human genetic engineering.

note – below

Evil dictators might abuse human cloning   There is the possibility that unscrupulous dictators such as Fidel Castro or Saddam Hussein might try to perpetuate their power by creating a clone of themselves and transferring power to the clone when they die. There is also the possibility that such people might try to create a super army of thousands of clones of Arnold Schwarzenegger, and so on. These possibilities cannot be dismissed. However, it is important to keep in mind that passing laws in the US or other democratic countries cannot control the behavior of rogue dictators in totalitarian countries. The prohibition of human cloning in the US or Europe is not going to stop cloning in Iraq. If Saddam Hussein wants to clone himself, nothing short of a major military invasion can stop him. The evil in these scenarios derives not from cloning but from dictatorships. The proper solution would be a world-wide ban on dictators, which of course is not likely to happen.

agree

The technology has not been perfected. It could lead to the death of the fetus   No area of human activity is free of accidental death. Human cloning is no exception. Some of the other cloned lambs at Roslin [Institute] were stillborn. At the moment the technology for cloning mammals is experimental and the success rate is still low. By additional experimentation on higher mammals, we may anticipate that cloning procedures will be perfected to the point where the risk of miscarriage or death of the baby is the same as for any other birth.

Millionaires might clone themselves just to obtain organs for transplant   This is one of the most preposterous of all claims about cloning. A human clone is a human being. In a free society you cannot force another human being to give you one of their internal organs. You certainly cannot kill another human being to obtain one of their organs. Existing laws already prevent such abuse. Note also that if your clone-twin is injured in an accident, you might be asked to give up one of your kidneys to save the clone! If the organ donor is still a child, society may want to intervene and declare that this is prohibited. In fact the removal of an organ from any child, clone or not, for transplant into another person is a very questionable practice which must be stringently regulated.

agree

Many legitimate future applications of cloning technology have been envisioned in the areas of organ replacement, skin grafts for burn victims, etc. These would not involve cloning an entire person, but only application of the same nucleus transfer technology to grow new tissue or organs for medical purposes.

note

Do we really want 200 clones of Sophia Loren or Cindy Crawford?   Perhaps not, and it is unlikely to happen. If we are talking about the cloning of a living person, and their consent is required, as it should be by law, they are extremely unlikely to agree to the creation of 200 clones. A person is likely to approve the creation of at most one or two clones of themselves. Also, remember that human clones cannot be mass produced in the laboratory. Each one must be gestated and carried to term by a woman, just like any other baby. How do the cloning critics imagine that 200 women are going to be persuaded to carry

agree

these 200 identical babies? If we are really worried about this possibility, society could simply prohibit the creation of more than two clones of the same person, rather than prohibit all cloning.

If we are talking about cloning someone who is now dead, a more distant possibility, then the question of limiting the number of clone-twins becomes a reasonable subject for thought and debate. We will have plenty of time for this debate. Certainly the mere existence of multiple individuals with identical appearances, as with triplets and quintuplets, is not inherently degrading to the humanity of those individuals.

It amounts to playing God   The Bible and the holy texts of other major religions do not explicitly prohibit human cloning. Consequently, religious opposition to human cloning is not firmly based. There will nevertheless be many who think that cloning humans is "wrong" for religious reasons. These people should of course not participate in cloning. Religious leaders who believe human cloning is wrong are entitled to preach their beliefs and persuade whom they can. They discredit themselves when they propose to jail people that they cannot persuade. Jesus never advocated force to compel people to live according to Christian beliefs. Legal enforcement of religious beliefs is a very poor idea and also a violation of the US Constitution.

In contrast with abortion, which involves the termination of the life of a fetus, cloning involves the creation of new life. Consequently, opposition to human cloning is not based on established moral principles. It is also possible to argue that if God had not wanted us to clone mammals or people, he would not have created Dr. Wilmut. By all means remain true to your own beliefs, but don't tell me what to do with my DNA. I personally wouldn't want to clone myself, but free people should be free to make that choice without compulsion from society.

The accusation of "playing God" is a vague but recurring criticism. We hear it every time there is a major advance in medicine. At one time birth control pills, in vitro fertilization, and heart transplants were criticized on the same grounds. God often performs good deeds which we should try to imitate. If playing God by cloning humans can have bad consequences, the critics are obliged to specify precisely what those bad consequences might be. So far they have not done so.

Desirable Governmental Regulations

Human cloning is a new and unexplored legal arena and will definitely require some legal regulation to prevent abuse. Here are some suggestions for moderate legislation which seems desirable:

1. Human clones should be declared to have the same legal rights and responsibilities as any other human being. People will not be able to keep a human clone in the wine cellar for spare body parts any more than they can an identical twin. The abuse of any human being is a crime, regardless of whether or not their genetic code is unique.

2. A living person should not be cloned without their written consent. A person is entitled to an automatic copyright for their genetic code, and this should remain under their control. A person should be allowed to specify in their will whether they wish to allow themselves to be cloned after their death, and under what circumstances. We may want to prohibit the cloning of someone who has not reached adulthood, because they may not have the maturity to make this kind of decision.

3. Human clones should only be gestated and delivered by a voluntary adult woman. The growth of a human fetus outside of a woman's body, for example in a laboratory apparatus, should be prohibited. At present the technology does not exist for an artificial uterus, but Japanese researchers are working on it.

4. The cloning of convicted murderers and other violent criminals should be prohibited. There is reason to believe that a predisposition to violence and murder are genetically determined. It should be illegal to clone Charles Manson. The world has an ample supply of criminals without artificially creating more of them. This should definitely include notorious mass-murderers of the past, such as Hitler, Lenin, and Stalin, in anticipation of the day when this will become possible.

Cloning the Dead

An interesting but little-known fact about the Wilmut cloning procedure is that it was performed with frozen cells, not fresh cells. (This information was obtained directly from Ian Wilmut by Dr. Patrick Dixon.) This means that the DNA donor, whether animal or human, need not even be alive when the cloning occurs. If a tissue sample of a person is properly frozen, the person could be cloned long after their death. In the case of people who have already died and whose tissue has not been frozen, cloning becomes much more difficult, and present procedures are inadequate. However, any biologist would be brave indeed to now declare that this is impossible. Let us now look ahead to the near future and speculate on the possibilities which will open up if research can develop a method for creating a clone from non-living DNA. There are grounds for believing that this is feasible in principle, although it is clearly beyond the capabilities of present cloning technology.

The prospect of cloning outstanding people of the past is an extremely exciting possibility, and justifies the most intensive research efforts. Isaac Newton and Albert Einstein are two of the greatest scientists of all time. Imagine the potential for scientific advancement if these two scientists could be cloned and educated in the 21st century. Having due regard for cultural sensitivities, Newton's clone would be raised in England, and Einstein's clone would no doubt be raised in a Jewish family, perhaps by the actual descendants of Einstein. As with clones of movie stars and sports figures, there is no guarantee that their twins would necessarily want to study physics. They might instead find some other field of science more interesting in their new existence, such as artificial intelligence or genetic engineering. Assuming they were born at about the same time, it would even be possible for the clone-twins of Newton and Einstein to collaborate scientifically! What scientific marvels might these two great minds discover working together?

It is also possible to imagine that the great political leaders of the past might be cloned from hair or bone samples. Names that come to mind include Winston Churchill, Abraham Lincoln, Theodore and Franklin Roosevelt, and John F. Kennedy. There is some evidence that leadership traits are genetically determined. Of course a person's life experience has a major impact on their personality, interests, and ambitions. Yet it does not seem unlikely that some of the twins of these great men might also want to enter politics and even aspire to high office, just as the son's of politicians sometimes follow the same career. How incredibly exciting it would be to witness a presidential race in the next century between the twin of Abraham Lincoln and the twin of Franklin Roosevelt, unstricken by polio. Who would win in a contest between clone-twins of John F. Kennedy and Ronald Reagan? Would the twin of Winston Churchill once again be chosen prime minister of Great Britain, or would he be out of place in the presumed peace of the 21st century? He might instead become a distinguished television commentator and author.

There would also be tremendous interest and advantage in cloning great sports figures of the past, such as Jim Thorpe, Ty Cobb, Babe Ruth, and Jesse Owens. The Olympic games of the year 2032 would be a sensation if the clone-twins of Jim Thorpe and Jesse Owens were to compete against each other.

Another potential for human cloning may be in the partial restitution of great iniquities of the past. It is possible that many of the millions of victims of the Nazi concentration camps could be cloned to recover lost genetic strains. The same technology that could clone Adolf Hitler could also be used to clone Anne Frank! Human cloning would for the first time offer the world's Jewish community a constructive response to the Holocaust. In Russia there remains a serious concern about the diminution of the gene pool caused by Stalin's mass executions of their society's best and brightest. In a limited sense, cloning could give a chance for new life to individuals of the past whose lives were unjustly and prematurely ended.

And what about DNA from the Egyptian mummies? Perhaps the ancient Egyptians were wiser than we thought to preserve the body after death. The complete mummy of Ramses II reposes in excellent condition in the Egyptian museum in Cairo. This is the Pharaoh of the Old Testament. An advanced technology for human cloning would allow a modern Egyptian woman to give birth to the twin of this great historical figure. Who would not want to see the living image of Ramses II and hear the same voice that spoke to Moses over three thousand years ago?

Case Closed

It is clear that human cloning has enormous potential benefits and few real negative consequences. As with many scientific advances of the past, such as airplanes and computers, the only real threat is to our own narrow mental complacency. In the areas of scientific advancement and cultural achievement, human clones can make major contributions. In specific cases where abuse of cloning is anticipated, these abuses can be prohibited by targeted legislation. With a little common sense and reasonable regulation, human cloning is not something to be feared. We should look forward to it with excited anticipation, and support research which will hasten its realization. Exceptional people are among the world's greatest treasures. Human cloning will allow us to preserve and eventually even recover these treasures.

NO

Leon R. Kass

The Wisdom of Repugnance

Our habit of delighting in news of scientific and technological break-throughs has been sorely challenged by the birth announcement of a sheep named Dolly. Though Dolly shares with previous sheep the "softest clothing, woolly, bright," William Blake's question, "Little Lamb, who made thee?" has for her a radically different answer: Dolly was, quite literally, made. She is the work not of nature or nature's God but of man, an Englishman, Ian Wilmut, and his fellow scientists. What's more, Dolly came into being not only asexually—ironically, just like "He [who] calls Himself a Lamb"—but also as the genetically identical copy (and the perfect incarnation of the form or blueprint) of a mature ewe, of whom she is a clone. This long-awaited yet not quite expected success in cloning a mammal raised immediately the prospect—and the specter—of cloning human beings: "I a child and Thou a lamb," despite our differences, have always been equal candidates for creative making, only now, by means of cloning, we may both spring from the hand of man playing at being God.

After an initial flurry of expert comment and public consternation, with opinion polls showing overwhelming opposition to cloning human beings, President Clinton ordered a ban on all federal support for human cloning research (even though none was being supported) and charged the National Bioethics Advisory Commission to report in ninety days on the ethics of human cloning research. The commission (an eighteen-member panel, evenly balanced between scientists and non-scientists, appointed by the president and reporting to the National Science and Technology Council) invited testimony from scientists, religious thinkers and bioethicists, as well as from the general public. It is now deliberating about what it should recommend, both as a matter of ethics and as a matter of public policy.

Congress is awaiting the commission's report, and is poised to act. Bills to prohibit the use of federal funds for human cloning research have been introduced in the House of Representatives and the Senate; and another bill, in the House, would make it illegal "for any person to use a human somatic cell for the process of producing a human clone." A fateful decision is at hand. To clone or not to clone a human being is no longer an academic question.

to frame the discussion

358   ISSUE 18 / Is It Ethically Permissible to Clone Human Beings?

... [S]ome cautions are in order and some possible misconceptions need correcting. For a start, cloning is not Xeroxing. As has been reassuringly reiterated, the clone of Mel Gibson, though his genetic double, would enter the world hairless, toothless and peeing in his diapers, just like any other human infant. Moreover, the success rate, at least at first, will probably not be very high: the British transferred 277 adult nuclei into enucleated sheep eggs, and implanted twenty-nine clonal embryos, but they achieved the birth of only one live lamb clone. For this reason, among others, it is unlikely that, at least for now, the practice would be very popular, and there is no immediate worry of mass-scale production of multicopies. The need of repeated surgery to obtain eggs and, more crucially, of numerous borrowed wombs for implantation will surely limit use, as will the expense; besides, almost everyone who is able will doubtless prefer nature's sexier way of conceiving.

Still, for the tens of thousands of people already sustaining over 200 assisted-reproduction clinics in the United States and already availing themselves of in vitro fertilization, intracytoplasmic sperm injection and other techniques of assisted reproduction, cloning would be an option with virtually no added fuss (especially when the success rate improves)....

In anticipation of human cloning, apologists and proponents have already made clear possible uses of the perfected technology, ranging from the sentimental and compassionate to the grandiose. They include: providing a child for an infertile couple; "replacing" a beloved spouse or child who is dying or has died; avoiding the risk of genetic disease; permitting reproduction for homosexual men and lesbians who want nothing sexual to do with the opposite sex; securing a genetically identical source of organs or tissues perfectly suitable for transplantation; getting a child with a genotype of one's own choosing, not excluding oneself; replicating individuals of great genius, talent or beauty—having a child who really could "be like Mike"; and creating large sets of genetically identical humans suitable for research on, for instance, the question of nature versus nurture, or for special missions in peace and war (not excluding espionage), in which using identical humans would be an advantage. Most people who envision the cloning of human beings, of course, want none of these scenarios. That they cannot say why is not surprising. What is surprising, and welcome, is that, in our cynical age, they are saying anything at all.

The Wisdom of Repugnance

"Offensive." "Grotesque." "Revolting." "Repugnant." "Repulsive." These are the words most commonly heard regarding the prospect of human cloning. Such reactions come both from the man or woman in the street and from the intellectuals, from believers and atheists, from humanists and scientists. Even Dolly's creator has said he "would find it offensive" to clone a human being.

People are repelled by many aspects of human cloning. They recoil from the prospect of mass production of human beings, with large clones of lookalikes, compromised in their individuality; the idea of father-son or mother-daughter twins; the bizarre prospects of a woman giving birth to and rearing a genetic copy of herself, her spouse or even her deceased father or mother; the grotesqueness of conceiving a child as an exact replacement for another who has died; the utilitarian creation of embryonic genetic duplicates of oneself, to be frozen away or created when necessary, in case of need for homologous tissues or organs for transplantation; the narcissism of those who would clone themselves and the arrogance of others who think they know who deserves to be cloned or which genotype any child-to-be should be thrilled to receive; the Frankensteinian hubris to create human life and increasingly to control its destiny; man playing God. Almost no one finds any of the suggested reasons for human cloning compelling; almost everyone anticipates its possible misuses and abuses. Moreover, many people feel oppressed by the sense that there is probably nothing we can do to prevent it from happening. This makes the prospect all the more revolting.

⊷⦿⊶

Revulsion is not an argument; and some of yesterday's repugnances are today calmly accepted—though, one must add, not always for the better. In crucial cases, however, repugnance is the emotional expression of deep wisdom, beyond reason's power fully to articulate it. Can anyone really give an argument fully adequate to the horror which is father-daughter incest (even with consent), or having sex with animals, or mutilating a corpse, or eating human flesh, or even just (just!) raping or murdering another human being? Would anybody's failure to give full rational justification for his or her revulsion at these practices make that revulsion ethically suspect? Not at all. On the contrary, we are suspicious of those who think that they can rationalize away our horror, say, by trying to explain the enormity of incest with arguments only about the genetic risks of inbreeding.

The repugnance at human cloning belongs in this category. We are repelled by the prospect of cloning human beings not because of the strangeness or novelty of the undertaking, but because we intuit and feel, immediately and without argument, the violation of things that we rightfully hold dear. Repugnance, here as elsewhere, revolts against the excesses of human willfulness, warning us not to transgress what is unspeakably profound. . . .

⊷⦿⊶

Typically, cloning is discussed in one or more of three familiar contexts, which one might call the technological, the liberal and the meliorist. Under the first, cloning will be seen as an extension of existing techniques for assisting reproduction and determining the genetic makeup of children. Like them, cloning is to be regarded as a neutral technique, with no inherent meaning or goodness, but subject to multiple uses, some good, some bad. The morality of cloning thus depends absolutely on the goodness or badness of the motives and intentions of the cloners. . . .

The liberal (or libertarian or liberationist) perspective sets cloning in the context of rights, freedoms and personal empowerment. Cloning is just a new option for exercising an individual's right to reproduce or to have the kind of child that he or she wants. Alternatively, cloning enhances our liberation (especially women's liberation) from the confines of nature, the vagaries of change, or the necessity for sexual mating. Indeed, it liberates women from the need for men altogether....

The meliorist perspective embraces valetudinarians and also eugenicists.... These people see in cloning a new prospect for improving human beings—minimally, by ensuring the perpetuation of healthy individuals by avoiding the risks of genetic disease inherent in the lottery of sex, and maximally, by producing "optimum babies," preserving outstanding genetic material, and (with the help of soon-to-come techniques for precise genetic engineering) enhancing inborn human capacities on many fronts. Here the morality of cloning as a means is justified solely by the excellence of the end....

very subjective

These three approaches, all quintessentially American and all perfectly fine in their places, are sorely wanting as approaches to human procreation. It is, to say the least, grossly distorting to view the wondrous mysteries of birth, renewal and individuality, and the deep meaning of parent-child relations, largely through the lens of our reductive science and its potent technologies. Similarly, considering reproduction (and the intimate relations of family life!) primarily under the political-legal, adversarial and individualistic notion of rights can only undermine the private yet fundamentally social, cooperative and duty-laden character of child-bearing, child-rearing and their bond to the covenant of marriage....

The technical, liberal and meliorist approaches all ignore the deeper anthropological, social and, indeed, ontological meanings of bringing forth new life. To this more fitting and profound point of view, cloning shows itself to be a major alteration, indeed, a major violation, of our given nature as embodied, gendered and engendering beings—and of the social relations built on this natural ground. Once this perspective is recognized, the ethical judgment on cloning can no longer be reduced to a matter of motives and intentions, rights and freedoms, benefits and harms, or even means and ends. It must be regarded primarily as a matter of meaning: Is cloning a fulfillment of human begetting and belonging? Or is cloning rather, as I contend, their pollution and perversion? To pollution and perversion, the fitting response can only be horror and revulsion; and conversely, generalized horror and revulsion are prima facie evidence of foulness and violation. The burden of moral argument must fall entirely on those who want to declare the widespread repugnances of humankind to be mere timidity or superstition.

Yet repugnance need not stand naked before the bar of reason. The wisdom of our horror at human cloning can be partially articulated, even if this is finally one of those instances about which the heart has its reasons that reason cannot entirely know....

The Perversities of Cloning

First, an important if formal objection: any attempt to clone a human being would constitute an unethical experiment upon the resulting child-to-be. As ... animal experiments ... indicate, there are grave risks of mishaps and deformities. Moreover, because of what cloning means, one cannot presume a future cloned child's consent to be a clone, even a healthy one. Thus, ethically speaking, we cannot even get to know whether or not human cloning is feasible.

I understand, of course, the philosophical difficulty of trying to compare a life with defects against nonexistence. Several bioethicists, proud of their philosophical cleverness, use this conundrum to embarrass claims that one can injure a child in its conception, precisely because it is only thanks to that complained-of conception that the child is alive to complain. But common sense tells us that we have no reason to fear such philosophisms. For we surely know that people can harm and even maim children in the very act of conceiving them, say, by paternal transmission of the AIDS virus, maternal transmission of heroin dependence or, arguably, even by bringing them into being as bastards or with no capacity or willingness to look after them properly. And we believe that to do this intentionally, or even negligently, is inexcusable and clearly unethical....

꩜

Cloning creates serious issues of identity and individuality. The cloned person may experience concerns about his distinctive identity not only because he will be in genotype and appearance identical to another human being, but, in this case, because he may also be twin to the person who is his "father" or "mother" —if one can still call them that. What would be the psychic burdens of being the "child" or "parent" of your twin? The cloned individual, moreover, will be saddled with a genotype that has already lived. He will not be fully a surprise to the world. People are likely always to compare his performances in life with that of his alter ego. True, his nurture and his circumstance in life will be different; genotype is not exactly destiny. Still, one must also expect parental and other efforts to shape this new life after the original—or at least to view the child with the original version always firmly in mind....

Since the birth of Dolly, there has been a fair amount of doublespeak on this matter of genetic identity. Experts have rushed in to reassure the public that the clone would in no way be the same person, or have any confusions about his or her identity: as previously noted, they are pleased to point out that the clone of Mel Gibson would not be Mel Gibson. Fair enough. But one is shortchanging the truth by emphasizing the additional importance of the intrauterine environment, rearing and social setting: genotype obviously matters plenty. That, after all, is the only reason to clone, whether human beings or sheep. The odds that clones of Wilt Chamberlain will play in the NBA are, I submit, infinitely greater than they are for clones of Robert Reich....

Genetic distinctiveness not only symbolizes the uniqueness of each human life and the independence of its parents that each human child rightfully attains. It can also be an important support for living a worthy and dignified life. Such arguments apply with great force to any large-scale replication of human individuals. But they are sufficient, in my view, to rebut even the first attempts to clone a human being. One must never forget that these are human beings upon whom our eugenic or merely playful fantasies are to be enacted.

Troubled psychic identity (distinctiveness), based on all-too-evident genetic identity (sameness), will be made much worse by the utter confusion of social identity and kinship ties. . . .

Social identity and social ties of relationship and responsibility are widely connected to, and supported by, biological kinship. Social taboos on incest (and adultery) everywhere serve to keep clear who is related to whom (and especially which child belongs to which parents), as well as to avoid confounding the social identity of parent-and-child (or brother-and-sister) with the social identity of lovers, spouses and co-parents. True, social identity is altered by adoption (but as a matter of the best interest of already living children: we do not deliberately produce children for adoption). True, artificial insemination and in vitro fertilization with donor sperm, or whole embryo donation, are in some way forms of "prenatal adoption"—a not altogether unproblematic practice. Even here, though, there is in each case (as in all sexual reproduction) a known male source of sperm and a known single female source of egg—a genetic father and a genetic mother—should anyone care to know (as adopted children often do) who is genetically related to whom.

In the case of cloning, however, there is but one "parent." The usually sad situation of the "single-parent child" is here deliberately planned, and with a vengeance. In the case of self-cloning, the "offspring" is, in addition, one's twin; and so the dreaded result of incest—to be parent to one's sibling—is here brought about deliberately, albeit without any act of coitus. Moreover, all other relationships will be confounded. . . .

Human cloning would also represent a giant step toward turning begetting into making, procreation into manufacture (literally, something "handmade"), a process already begun with in vitro fertilization and genetic testing of embryos. With cloning, not only is the process in hand, but the total genetic blueprint of the cloned individual is selected and determined by the human artisans. . . . In clonal reproduction, . . . and in the more advanced forms of manufacture to which it leads, we give existence to a being not by what we are but by what we intend and design. As with any product of our making, no matter how excellent, the artificer stands above it, not as an equal but as a superior, transcending it by his will and creative prowess. Scientists who clone animals make it perfectly clear that they are engaged in instrumental making; the animals are, from the start, designed as means to serve rational human purposes. In human cloning, scientists and prospective "parents" would be adopting the same technocratic mentality to human children: human children would be their artifacts.

Such an arrangement is profoundly dehumanizing, no matter how good the product. Mass-scale cloning of the same individual makes the point vividly; but the violation of human equality, freedom and dignity are present even in a single planned clone. . . .

Finally, and perhaps most important, the practice of human cloning by nuclear transfer—like other anticipated forms of genetic engineering of the next generation—would enshrine and aggravate a profound and mischievous misunderstanding of the meaning of having children and of the parent-child relationship. When a couple now chooses to procreate, the partners are saying yes to the emergence of new life in its novelty, saying yes not only to having a child but also, tacitly, to having whatever child this child turns out to be. In accepting our finitude and opening ourselves to our replacement, we are tacitly confessing the limits of our control. In this ubiquitous way of nature, embracing the future by procreating means precisely that we are relinquishing our grip, in the very activity of taking up our own share in what we hope will be the immortality of human life and the human species. This means that our children are not *our* children: they are not our property, not our possessions. Neither are they supposed to live our lives for us, or anyone else's life but their own. To be sure, we seek to guide them on their way, imparting to them not just life but nurturing, love, and a way of life; to be sure, they bear our hopes that they will live fine and flourishing lives, enabling us in small measure to transcend our own limitations. Still, their genetic distinctiveness and independence are the natural foreshadowing of the deep truth that they have their own and never-before-enacted life to live. They are sprung from a past, but they take an uncharted course into the future. . . .

Meeting Some Objections

The defenders of cloning, of course, are not wittingly friends of despotism. Indeed, they regard themselves mainly as friends of freedom: the freedom of individuals to reproduce, the freedom of scientists and inventors to discover and devise and to foster "progress" in genetic knowledge and technique. They want large-scale cloning only for animals, but they wish to preserve cloning as a human option for exercising our "right to reproduction"—our right to have children, and children with "desirable genes." As law professor John Robertson points out, under our "right to reproduce" we already practice early forms of unnatural, artificial and extramarital reproduction, and we already practice early forms of eugenic choice. For this reason, he argues, cloning is no big deal.

We have here a perfect example of the logic of the slippery slope, and the slippery way in which it already works in this area. Only a few years ago, slippery slope arguments were used to oppose artificial insemination and in vitro fertilization using unrelated sperm donors. Principles used to justify these practices, it was said, will be used to justify more artificial and more eugenic practices, including cloning. Not so, the defenders retorted, since we can make the necessary distinctions. And now, without even a gesture at making the necessary distinctions, the continuity of practice is held by itself to be justificatory.

The principle of reproductive freedom as currently enunciated by the proponents of cloning logically embraces the ethical acceptability of sliding down the entire rest of the slope—to producing children ectogenetically from sperm to term (should it become feasible) and to producing children whose entire genetic makeup will be the product of parental eugenic planning and choice. If reproductive freedom means the right to have a child of one's own choosing, by whatever means, it knows and accepts no limits.

But, far from being legitimated by a "right to reproduce," the emergence of techniques of assisted reproduction and genetic engineering should compel us to reconsider the meaning and limits of such a putative right. In truth, a "right to reproduce" has always been a peculiar and problematic notion. Rights generally belong to individuals, but this is a right which (before cloning) no one can exercise alone. Does the right then inhere only in couples? Only in married couples? Is it a (woman's) right to carry or deliver or a right (of one or more parents) to nurture and rear? Is it a right to have your own biological child? Is it a right only to attempt reproduction, or a right also to succeed? Is it a right to acquire the baby of one's choice? . . .

Ban the Cloning of Humans

What, then, should we do? We should declare that human cloning is unethical in itself and dangerous in its likely consequences. In so doing, we shall have the backing of the overwhelming majority of our fellow Americans, and of the human race, and (I believe) of most practicing scientists. Next, we should do all that we can to prevent the cloning of human beings. We should do this by means of an international legal ban if possible, and by a unilateral national ban, at a minimum. Scientists may secretly undertake to violate such a law, but they will be deterred by not being able to stand up proudly to claim the credit for their technological bravado and success. Such a ban on clonal baby-making, moreover, will not harm the progress of basic genetic science and technology. On the contrary, it will reassure the public that scientists are happy to proceed without violating the deep ethical norms and intuitions of the human community. . . .

I appreciate the potentially great gains in scientific knowledge and medical treatment available from embryo research, especially with cloned embryos. At the same time, I have serious reservations about creating human embryos for the sole purpose of experimentation. There is something deeply repugnant and fundamentally transgressive about such a utilitarian treatment of prospective human life. This total, shameless exploitation is worse, in my opinion, than the "mere" destruction of nascent life. But I see no added objections, as a matter of principle, to creating and using *cloned* early embryos for research purposes, beyond the objections that I might raise to doing so with embryos produced sexually.

And yet, as a matter of policy and prudence, any opponent of the manufacture of cloned humans must, I think, in the end oppose also the creating of

cloned human embryos.... We should allow all cloning research on animals to go forward, but the only safe trench that we can dig across the slippery slope, I suspect, is to insist on the inviolable distinction between animal and human cloning.

Some readers, and certainly most scientists, will not accept such prudent restraints, since they desire the benefits of research. They will prefer, even in fear and trembling, to allow human embryo cloning research to go forward.

Very well. Let us test them. If the scientists want to be taken seriously on ethical grounds, they must at the very least agree that embryonic research may proceed if and only if it is preceded by an absolute and effective ban on all attempts to implant into a uterus a cloned human embryo (cloned from an adult) to produce a living child. Absolutely no permission for the former without the latter.

The National Bioethics Advisory Commission's recommendations regarding this matter should be watched with the greatest care. Yielding to the wishes of the scientists, the commission will almost surely recommend that cloning human embryos for research be permitted. To allay public concern, it will likely also call for a temporary moratorium—not a legislative ban—on implanting cloned embryos to make a child, at least until such time as cloning techniques will have been perfected and rendered "safe" (precisely through the permitted research with cloned embryos). But the call for a moratorium rather than a legal ban would be a moral and a practical failure. Morally, this ethics commission would (at best) be waffling on the main ethical question, by refusing to declare the production of human clones unethical (or ethical). Practically, a moratorium on implantation cannot provide even the minimum protection needed to prevent the production of cloned humans.

Opponents of cloning need therefore to be vigilant. Indeed, no one should be willing even to consider a recommendation to allow the embryo research to proceed unless it is accompanied by a call for *prohibiting* implantation and until steps are taken to make such a prohibition effective.

Technically, the National Bioethics Advisory Commission can advise the president only on federal policy, especially federal funding policy. But given the seriousness of the matter at hand, and the grave public concern that goes beyond federal funding, the commission should take a broader view. (If it doesn't, Congress surely will.)...

The proposal for such a legislative ban is without American precedent, at least in technological matters, though the British and others have banned cloning of human beings, and we ourselves ban incest, polygamy and other forms of "reproductive freedom." Needless to say, working out the details of such a ban, especially a global one, would be tricky, what with the need to develop appropriate sanctions for violators. Perhaps such a ban will prove ineffective; perhaps it will eventually be shown to have been a mistake. But it would at least place the burden of practical proof where it belongs: on the proponents of this horror, requiring them to show very clearly what great social or medical good can be had only by the cloning of human beings....

The president's call for a moratorium on human cloning has given us an important opportunity. In a truly unprecedented way, we can strike a blow for the human control of the technological project, for wisdom, prudence and human dignity. The prospect of human cloning, so repulsive to contemplate, is the occasion for deciding whether we shall be slaves of unregulated progress, and ultimately its artifacts, or whether we shall remain free human beings who guide our technique toward the enhancement of human dignity.

POSTSCRIPT

Is It Ethically Permissible to Clone Human Beings?

Have humans already been cloned? In 1978 writer David Rorvik claimed to document the deed in *In His Image: The Cloning of a Man* (Lippincott), in which he describes "Max," a millionaire, who had hired a scientist to set up a lab somewhere in Asia, tap local women for eggs, refine the necessary techniques, and produce Max, Jr. Rorvik's claims provoked controversy reminiscent of that surrounding the current issue, but in the end no one believed him.

Now, however, the technique has been shown to work in sheep, cattle, monkeys, and other animals. Useful applications are already being developed, as described by Ian Wilmut in "Cloning for Medicine," *Scientific American* (December 1998). It seems very much on the verge of possibility for humans, and the debate over whether or not that possibility is desirable is vigorous. For the moment, the debate has been settled by the report of the National Bioethics Advisory Commission, which commission chair Harold T. Shapiro summarized in the July 11, 1997, issue of *Science*. He said, "[The commission] made every effort to consult widely with ethicists, theologians, scientists, scientific societies, physicians, and others in initiating an analysis of the many scientific, legal, religious, ethical, and moral dimensions of the issue [including] potential risks and benefits of using this technique to create children and a review of the potential constitutional challenges that might be raised if new legislation were to restrict [its use]."

Speaking to the commission, Ruth Macklin, of the Albert Einstein College of Medicine, said, "It is absurd to maintain that the proposition 'cloning is morally wrong' is self-evident.... If I cannot point to any great benefits likely to result from cloning, neither do I foresee any probable great harms, provided that a structure of regulation and oversight is in place. If objectors to cloning can identify no greater harm than a supposed affront to the dignity of the human species, that is a flimsy basis on which to erect barriers to scientific research and its applications."

Nathan Myhrvold, chief technology officer at Microsoft, takes a different tack in opposing bans on cloning in "Human Clones: Why Not? Opposition to Cloning Isn't Just Luddism—It's Racism," *Slate* (March 13, 1997). In it, he argues, "Calls for a ban on cloning amount to discrimination against people based on another genetic trait—the fact that somebody already has an identical DNA sequence."

Contributors to This Volume

EDITOR

THOMAS A. EASTON is a professor of life sciences at Thomas College in Waterville, Maine, where he has been teaching since 1983. He received a B.A. in biology from Colby College in 1966 and a Ph.D. in theoretical biology from the University of Chicago in 1971. He has also taught at Unity College, Husson College, and the University of Maine. He is a prolific writer, and his articles on scientific and futuristic issues have appeared in the scholarly journals *Experimental Neurology* and *American Scientist,* as well as in such popular magazines as *Astronomy, Consumer Reports,* and *Robotics Age.* He is also the science columnist for the online magazine *Tomorrowsf* (http://www.tomorrowsf.com/). His publications include *Focus on Human Biology,* 2d ed. (HarperCollins, 1995), coauthored with Carl E. Rischer, and *Careers in Science,* 3rd ed. (National Textbook, 1996). Dr. Easton is also a well-known writer and critic of science fiction.

STAFF

Theodore Knight   List Manager
David Brackley   Senior Developmental Editor
Juliana Poggio   Developmental Editor
Rose Gleich   Administrative Assistant
Brenda S. Filley   Production Manager
Juliana Arbo   Typesetting Supervisor
Diane Barker   Proofreader
Lara Johnson   Design/Advertising Coordinator
Richard Tietjen   Publishing Systems Manager
Larry Killian   Copier Coordinator

AUTHORS

LORI ANDREWS is a professor of law in the Chicago-Kent College of Law and director of the Institute for Science, Law, and Technology at the Illinois Institute of Technology. She teaches courses on health law, reproductive technology law, and genetics law.

ELIZABETH BALDWIN is a research ethics officer for the American Psychological Association's Science Directorate. Her work involves a broad range of research ethics issues, including those relating to the use of animals in research. Prior to her position at the American Psychological Association, she worked at the Congressional Research Service in the Division of Science Policy. She holds a B.A. in biology, an M.S. in entomology, and an M.A. in science, technology, and public policy.

ROBERT BERGER is president of Internet Bandwidth Development and has been working with the Internet and UNIX since 1981.

SVEN BIRKERTS is the author of three books of criticism, including *American Energies: Essays on Fiction* (William Morrow, 1992). He has won the National Book Critics Circle Citation of Excellence in Reviewing, a P.E.N. Speilvogel/Diamondstein Special Citation for *The Electric Life: Essays on Modern Poetry* (William Morrow, 1989), and Lila Wallace–Reader's Digest Foundation and Guggenheim fellowships. His essays and reviews have appeared in the *New York Times Book Review, The Atlantic Monthly, Harper's Magazine,* and *The New Republic.*

PAUL BRODEUR is an author and a staff writer for the *New Yorker* magazine. He has published books on asbestos, ozone depletion, and the electromagnetic field–cancer link, including *Currents of Death: Power Lines, Computer Terminals, and the Attempt to Cover Up Their Threat to Your Health* (Simon & Schuster, 1989). He has won the National Magazine Award, the Sidney Hillman Foundation Award, and the American Association for the Advancement of Science Award, and the United Nations Environment Program has named him to its Global 500 Roll of Honor.

LESTER R. BROWN is president of the Worldwatch Institute. He is the author or coauthor of dozens of books, including *Tough Choices: Facing the Challenge of Food Scarcity* (W. W. Norton, 1996) and *Full House: Reassessing the Earth's Population Carrying Capacity,* with Hal Kane (W. W. Norton, 1994).

DANIEL CALLAHAN, a philosopher, is cofounder and president of the Hastings Center in Briarcliff Manor, New York, where he is also director of International Programs. He is the author or editor of over 31 publications, including *Ethics in Hard Times* (Plenum Press, 1981), coauthored with Arthur L. Caplan; *Setting Limits: Medical Goals in an Aging Society* (Simon & Schuster, 1987); and *The Troubled Dream of Life: In Search of Peaceful Death* (Simon & Schuster, 1993). He received a Ph.D. in philosophy from Harvard University.

EDWARD W. CAMPION is deputy editor of *The New England Journal of Medicine* and an assistant professor of medicine at Harvard Medical School and Massachusetts General Hospital.

JOHN CARR is an Internet consultant to NCH Action for Children, a major British child-care charity.

EDWARD B. DAVIS is a professor of the history of science at Messiah College in Grantham, Pennsylvania.

RICHARD DAWKINS is the Charles Simonyi Professor of the Public Understanding of Science at Oxford University and the recipient of the American Humanist Association's 1996 Humanist of the Year Award.

NEIL de GRASSE TYSON, an astrophysicist, is the Frederick P. Rose Director of New York City's Hayden Planetarium.

MICHAEL DERTOUZOS is director of the Massachusetts Institute of Technology's Computer Science Lab. He is the author of *What Will Be: How the New World of Information Will Change Our Lives* (Harper, 1997).

DANIEL C. DENNETT is the Distinguished Arts and Sciences Professor at Tufts University, where he is also director of the Center for Cognitive Studies. He is the author of *Brainstorms: Philosophical Essays on Mind and Psychology* (MIT Press, 1980), *Elbow Room: The Varieties of Will Worth Wanting* (MIT Press, 1984), and *Consciousness Explained* (Little, Brown, 1991).

A. K. DEWDNEY is a computer scientist at the University of Western Ontario in London, Ontario, Canada. For several years, he wrote *Scientific American's* "Computer Recreations" and "Mathematical Recreations" columns.

FRANK DRAKE is a professor of astronomy and astrophysics at the University of California, Santa Cruz, where he has also served as dean of natural sciences. He is president of the SETI Institute and former president of the Astronomical Society of the Pacific, which is one of the world's leading astronomical organizations.

ANNE H. EHRLICH is a senior research associate in biological sciences at Stanford University in Stanford, California. She is coauthor, with Paul R. Ehrlich, of *Betrayal of Science and Reason: How Anti-Environmental Rhetoric Threatens Our Future* (Island Press, 1996) and coeditor, with John Birks, of *Hidden Dangers: Environmental Consequences of Preparing for War* (Sierra Club Books, 1991).

PAUL R. EHRLICH is the Bing Professor of Population Studies and a professor of biological sciences at Stanford University in Stanford, California. His many publications include *The Population Bomb* (Ballantine Books, 1971) and *Healing the Planet: Strategies for Resolving the Environmental Crisis,* coauthored with Anne H. Ehrlich (Addison-Wesley, 1991).

BILL GATES is founder, chairman, and chief executive officer of the Microsoft Corporation, the world's leading provider of software for personal computers.

DAVID H. GUSTON is an assistant professor of public policy at the Eagleton Institute of Policies at Rutgers–The State University of New Jersey. In 1990–1991 he served on the staff of the Panel on Scientific Responsibility and the Conduct of Research at the National Academy of Sciences. He is coeditor, with Kenneth Keniston, of *The Fragile Contract: University Science and the Federal Government* (MIT Press, 1994).

HANK HOFFMAN, a Beat scholar, is a staff writer for the *New Haven Advocate.*

PETER W. HUBER is a senior fellow at the Manhattan Institute. He has authored or edited a number of books, including *Galileo's Revenge: Junk Science in the Courtroom* (Basic Books, 1993) and *Law and Disorder in Cyberspace: Abolish the FCC and Let Common Law Rule the Telecosm* (Oxford University Press, 1997).

JAMES HUGHES, a sociologist, is assistant director of research in the MacLean Center for Clinical Medical Ethics, Department of Medicine, at the University of Chicago and the editor of *Doctor-Patient Studies.* His special interests include health care reform and the social construction of personhood at the intersection of medical and environmental ethics. He received his doctorate in sociology from the University of Chicago in 1994.

D. GALE JOHNSON is the Eliakim Hastings Moore Distinguished Service Professor of Economics Emeritus at the University of Chicago.

LEON R. KASS is the Addie Clark Harding Professor in the College and the Committee on Social Thought at the University of Chicago and an adjunct scholar at the American Enterprise Institute. A trained physician and biochemist, he is the author of *Toward a More Natural Science: Biology and Human Affairs* (Free Press, 1985).

KENNETH KENISTON is the Andrew W. Mellon Professor of Human Development in the Program in Science, Technology, and Society at the Massachusetts Institute of Technology. He is coeditor, with David H. Guston, of *The Fragile Contract: University Science and the Federal Government* (MIT Press, 1994).

ANDREW KIMBRELL is policy director of the Foundation on Economic Trends in Washington, D.C., which was founded in 1977 to disseminate information through lectures and the distribution of educational materials on issues such as the environment, religion, genetics, and engineering in order to effect social change.

ROBERT KUNZIG is the European editor of *Discover* magazine.

HANS MORAVEC is a principal research scientist in the Robotics Institute at Carnegie Mellon University in Pittsburgh, Pennsylvania, and director of the university's Mobile Robot Laboratory. He received a Ph.D. from Stanford University in 1980 for his design of a TV-equipped, computer-controlled robot that could negotiate cluttered obstacle courses. His publications include *Mind Children: The Future of Robot and Human Intelligence* (Harvard University Press, 1988).

DOROTHY NELKIN teaches at New York University in the Department of Sociology and the School of Law. She writes on the relationship of science to the public, with particular focus on genetics and biotechnology. She is a member of the National Academy of Sciences Institute of Medicine and a fellow of the American Association for the Advancement of Science.

DAVID B. RESNIK is an associate professor in the Department of Medical Humanities, East Carolina University School of Medicine, in Greenville, North Carolina.

JOHN SEARLE is the Mills Professor of the Philosophy of Mind at the University of California, Berkeley.

P. J. SKERRETT is a contributing writer for *Technology Review*.

RAYMOND W. SMITH is chairman of the Bell Atlantic Corporation.

DAVA SOBEL is a science and medicine writer for several newspapers and magazines, including *Harvard Magazine, Omni, Good Housekeeping,* and the *New York Times Book Review.* She is a former science reporter for the *New York Times,* and she is the author of *The Incredible Planets: New Views of the Solar Family* (Reader's Digest Association, 1992) and *Longitude* (Walker, 1995).

WEN STEPHENSON is editor of the *Atlantic Monthly*'s online edition.

JOHN TIERNEY is a columnist for the *New York Times.*

STEVEN VERE has worked in artificial intelligence for over 20 years and has published research in the areas of machine learning, planning, and autonomous agents. He has held academic and research positions at the University of Illinois, Chicago, and at the NASA Jet Propulsion Laboratory. He earned his Ph.D. in computer science from the Univeristy of California at Los Angeles.

MALCOLM WALLOP is founder and chairman of the Frontiers of Freedom Institute (FFI), which is dedicated to a federal government that is clearly limited and focuses on defending American sovereignty, protecting every citizen's property, and sustaining liberty through the rule of law. A third-generation rancher from Big Horn, Wyoming, he was elected to the Wyoming legislature in 1969 and then to the U.S. Senate in 1976, where he served for 18 years, retiring in 1994. During his tenure, he served as the ranking Republican member of the Energy and Natural Resources Committee.

STEVEN ZAK is an attorney in Los Angeles, California. He received a B.A. in psychology from Michigan State University in 1971, an M.S. from the Wayne State University School of Medicine in 1975, and a J.D. from the University of Southern California Law School in 1984. He has written about animals with regard to ethics and the law for numerous publications, including the *Los Angeles Times,* the *New York Times,* and the *Chicago Tribune.*

CARL ZIMMER is a senior editor at *Discover* magazine, where he has been reporting on the fields of evolution, paleontology, ecology, and earth sciences, among others, for eight years. He is the author of *At the Water's Edge: Macroevolution and the Transformation of Life* (Touchstone, 1999), which takes a look at major evolutionary transitions. His work has earned him a number of awards, including the American Institute of Biological Sciences Media Award and the Evert Clark Award for science journalism.

Index